Judeophobia

Judeophobia

Attitudes toward the Jews
in the Ancient World

Peter Schäfer

Harvard University Press
CAMBRIDGE, MASSACHUSETTS
LONDON, ENGLAND
1997

Library of Congress Cataloging-in-Publication Data
Schäfer, Peter, 1943–
Judeophobia : attitudes towards the Jews in the ancient world /
Peter Schäfer.

p.   cm.

Includes bibliographical references and index.

ISBN 0–674–48777–X (alk. paper)

1. Antisemitism—Greece—History.   2. Antisemitism—
Rome—History.   3. Judaism—Controversial literature—
History and criticism.   4. Classical literature—History and
criticism.   5. Civilization, Greco–Roman.   I. Title.

DS146.G8S33   1997

305.892′4038—dc20

96–27431

For Barbara

Acknowledgments

The first stages of this study go back to a seminar which I conducted at the Institute of Jewish Studies of the Freie Universität Berlin. It is with pleasure and gratitude that I thank my students for their criticism and stimulating contributions.

I began writing the book in the fall of 1992 during my tenure as the Horace W. Goldsmith Visiting Professor at Yale University. A preliminary version of Chapter 1 was published as "The Exodus Tradition in Pagan Greco-Roman Literature" in *The Jews in the Hellenistic-Roman World: Studies in Memory of Menahem Stern,* edited by Isaiah M. Gafni, Aharon Oppenheimer, and Daniel R. Schwartz (Jerusalem: Zalman Shazar Center for Jewish History, 1996). The great bulk of the book was written during my tenure in 1993 as a visiting member and from 1994 to 1996 as the Visiting Mellon Professor at the Institute for Advanced Study in Princeton. I am most grateful to the faculty of the School of Historical Studies and the Mellon Foundation for giving me the opportunity to participate in the invigorating and challenging scholarly life at the Institute.

This is the first book I have ever dared to write completely in English, no doubt provoked and encouraged by my surroundings in Princeton. I found immense pleasure in writing in English and experiencing how much we are influenced in our thinking by the language in which we write. Had I written in German, a different book would surely have emerged. However, there would hardly have been any book at all without the generous support of my secretaries at the Institute, Suki Lewin, Dorothy David, and, above all, Terrie Bramley. They not only typed the various versions of the manuscript but also provided invaluable help in correcting and improving my English.

At Harvard University Press I had the good fortune to work with Margaretta Fulton, who polished the English and helped with her rigorous criticism to transform the manuscript into a book, and Camille Smith, who copyedited the manuscript. I owe them special thanks for their professional care.

I benefited greatly from the criticism and stimulus of a number of friends and colleagues, who discussed with me certain problems or read all or parts of the manuscript. They include Elaine Pagels, Glen Bowersock, Pieter van der Horst, and Hans-Jürgen Becker. Above all, Tony Spawforth selflessly offered me his time and knowledge, and saved me from falling into some traps in the field of classical ancient history. I recall with admiration the patience with which he introduced me to what must have seemed to him the basics of his field.

The book is dedicated to my wife, Barbara, as a small and insufficient token of my gratitude. I owe her much more than just writing a book.

Contents

Judeophobia

Introduction

"*A*NTI-SEMITISM" HAS A LONG and endless history. A recent, quite telling offshoot of it appeared in the German spell-check on my computer (an American product). The spell-check stumbled over the word "judenfreundlich" (friendly toward the Jews), which I had used in an article written in German, and suggested replacing it with "judenfeindlich" (hostile toward the Jews). At first I was convinced I had spotted a little anti-Semite inside my computer who had ventured a nasty joke, but, of course, the reality is less dramatic and yet highly significant for our subject. The German dictionary implanted into the computer simply doesn't include the word "judenfreundlich" and therefore suggests a substitute which in the arrangement of its characters comes closest to it: "judenfeindlich." Hence it turns out that the composer of the spell-check had ventured, not a bad joke, but a sophisticated judgment about the German language and the attitude toward the Jews expressed by it: the word "judenfreundlich" does not exist because Germans never have been, and never are, friendly toward the Jews. Nothing could illuminate better the terrain on which a German author writing on anti-Semitism, even if only on the "remote" history of ancient anti-Semitism, must tread.

"Hatred of Jews and Jew-baiting (*Judenhetzen*) are as old as the Diaspora itself"—with this sentence in volume 5 of his *Römische Geschichte* Theodor Mommsen inaugurated the modern study of what is usually termed "ancient anti-Semitism." Mommsen began the chapter "Judea and the Jews" early in 1884,[1] only a few years after his public argument with Heinrich von Treitschke, a colleague at the University of Berlin, in the so-called Berlin Anti-Semitism Dispute (*Berliner Antisemitismusstreit*). This connection is no mere accident. Research on ancient anti-Semitism had begun in the late

1870s and early 1880s, concurrent with the rise of anti-Semitic sentiment which had shortly followed the successful founding of the new German Reich; that is, it was contemporaneous with the emergence of modern anti-Semitism. As Christhard Hoffmann has shown in an excellent study, much can be said for the idea that "the similarity between ancient and modern forms of anti-Jewish hostility (in contrast, e.g., to the phenomenon in medieval times) was the main reason for the increase in scientific interest in ancient 'anti-Semites', e.g. Apion, and that the new term [anti-Semitism] was soon applied to the situation in antiquity."[2]

Mommsen's rather casual statement was certainly not intended to provide a theory of anti-Semitism, nor was it in any way aimed at justifying its contemporary variety; on the contrary, in the Anti-Semitism Dispute he had spoken out as a committed opponent of the new form of anti-Semitism. Most German historians, however, reacted quite differently. For the most part, they were openly preoccupied with extracting from antiquity not only information about, but vindication of current sentiment. Thus, for example, Arthur G. Sperling wanted "to retrieve the honor" of the Alexandrian Apion, the "greatest agitator against the Jews in antiquity" and champion of a movement "in which the classical education of Hellenism, in union with the passion of Orientals, wages war once more upon the wild growth of Judaism," and who for this very reason, according to Sperling, was entitled to demand attention in the present day.[3] Similarly, Konrad Zacher found in ancient anti-Semitism "the most interesting parallels to manifestations of our own time."[4] Like the "Historians' Debate" *(Historikerstreit)* of the late 1980s, this more ideological than scientific controversy was characteristically conducted not only in professional journals but frequently, and quite deliberately, in public. A striking example is Hugo Willrich, who had his "Die Entstehung des Antisemitismus" published in the anti-Semitic monthly *Deutschlands Erneuerung*.[5]

The majority of studies of ancient anti-Semitism, from the nineteenth century to the present, start with the methodological premise that the unique religious, cultural, and social characteristics of Judaism itself are the causes of what later becomes known as "anti-Semitism." Hoffmann has aptly named this approach "substantialist" or "essentialist." It is a model of interpretation which presupposes that anti-Semitism is, so to speak, a "natural" phenomenon within every society, needing no further explanation, a model that operates with categories such as "the essence of Judaism" or "the antagonism between Judaism and Hellenism," which can, of course, be interpreted in a number of ways.[6] This methodical approach is by no means limited to outspokenly anti-Semitic authors, but also applies to a wide variety of ideological viewpoints—including determinedly Christian as well as Jewish positions. Under this category we find both Mommsen and Zacher, who, without even mentioning Mommsen, lent his dictum a significant turn: "anti-Semitism . . . is as old *as Judaism itself* and the Jewish Diaspora," and argued as follows: "As one can see, it [anti-Semitism] is the simple result of the barrier which Jewry itself increasingly erected against the world in whose midst it lived."[7] In the end no less a figure than the great historian Eduard Meyer omitted the "Diaspora" completely by simply declaring: "It [hatred of the Jews] is thus just as old as Judaism itself." For him the reason lies in Judaism's "numerous bizarre attitudes and superstitious rites and customs," its "arrogant presumptuousness and . . . spiteful aloofness toward all those of other creeds," its "energetic bustling in commercial life, which viewed the ruthless exploitation of the infidels as the good, God-given right of the Jews"—all of these being peculiarities which had "by necessity to provoke" hatred of the Jews.[8] In the same year (1921) Hugo Willrich[9] voiced similar sentiments with clearly anti-Semitic overtones, and both Meyer and Willrich had been preceded earlier in the century by Fritz Staehelin with his gross statement: "The essence of Judaism which now prevailed—rigid, exclusive, and malevolent toward all those of other creeds—could only have met with repulsion by the naturally tolerant Greeks."[10]

The distinctiveness of the Jews, which is the result of the special nature of their religion, and in particular their separation from other social groups, has become the standard reasoning offered by the "substantialist" interpretation of anti-Semitism. The opening sentence of Benno Jacob's entry "Anti-Semitism: I. In Antiquity" in the *Encyclopaedia Judaica,* an obvious allusion to the later variations of Mommsen's dictum, reads as follows: "If one understands anti-Semitism to be the hostile attitude toward Judaism, then it is as old as the Jewish people, for every nation *(Volk)* with particular characteristics, which might be unpleasant to others, and every community which claims to represent distinctive values, is treated with hostility, and Judaism entered history with this claim from the very beginning."[11] In his famous study *Verus Israel* Marcel Simon formulated the almost classic statement: "The basic cause of Greco-Roman anti-Semitism lay in Jewish separatism. This means, in the last analysis, that it lay in their religion, since the religion produced the separatism."[12] Victor Tcherikover, who expressly acknowledged himself to be an advocate of the "substantialist" school of interpretation, argued in a similar vein, albeit with unmistakably Zionist overtones:

The main danger that lies in wait for him [the historian] is a confusion between the inner quality of anti-Semitism, which is always and everywhere the same, and its various manifestations, which alter according to place and circumstance. The inner quality of anti-Semitism arises from the very existence of the Jewish people as an alien body among the nations. The alien character of the Jews is the central cause of the origin of anti-Semitism, and this alien character has two aspects: The Jews are alien to other peoples because they are foreigners derived from another land, and they are alien because of their foreign customs which are strange and outlandish in the eyes of the local inhabitants.[13]

The same is true of the most comprehensive monograph to date on "pagan Anti-Semitism" by J. N. Sevenster, who emphasizes the distinctiveness of the pagan type of anti-Semitism as compared with the later Christian one. According to Sevenster, "pagan anti-Semitism in the ancient world is fundamentally of a religious character" and its "most fundamental reason . . . almost always proves to lie in the strangeness of the Jews midst ancient society . . . The Jews were never quite like the others; they were always inclined to isolate themselves . . . There was always something exceptional about the religion of the Jews, and this made them difficult in social intercourse, ill-adapted to the pattern of ancient society."[14]

The counterthesis to the "substantialist" interpretive school, aptly termed the "functionalist" model by Hoffmann,[15] was developed by Isaak Heinemann in his essay "Ursprung und Wesen des Antisemitismus im Altertum"[16] and in his entry on "Antisemitismus" in *Paulys Realencyclopädie der Classischen Altertumswissenschaft*,[17] which was much more extensive and exerted greater influence than the earlier article. According to Heinemann, ancient anti-Semitism was not based on the "essence" of Judaism, however defined, but rather on very concrete *political* conflicts. He elaborated three such "foci of conflict" (*Konfliktsherde*, as he called them), namely, the Syrian-Palestinian, the Egyptian, and the Roman. In all of these foci, ideological hostility toward the Jews was not the cause but the consequence of the political power struggle:

Nowhere is ideological hatred of the Jews *(der geistige Judenhaß)* a sufficient reason for political entanglements. However, power struggles which are for the most part motivated by purely political or national interests have provided the breeding ground for unfavorable judgments on the essence of the Jewish religion. Thus the ideological struggle *(der geistige Kampf)* should be viewed here also primarily as a reflex of the political one, in the same sense—and with the same reservations—as in the present.[18]

Insofar as Heinemann accorded a preeminent role to the Syrian-Palestinian focus of conflict, both chronologically as well as in its significance for later developments,[19] his functionalist model also has wide-reaching implications for the question of the origin of ancient anti-Semitism. According to Heinemann, anti-Semitism arose out of a concrete historical situation in Syria-Palestine, not in the Diaspora (he thus expressly rejected Mommsen's dictum): it is "not the root, but rather the necessary fruit of the Hellenization policies of Epiphanes and those who pursued his principles."[20] Heinemann's approach was developed further by the other great historian of ancient Judaism, Elias Bickerman, and in more recent literature also by Martin Hengel, Christian Habicht, and Klaus Bringmann, among others.[21] All of these authors follow the "functionalist" model of interpretation (though admittedly with "substantialist" elements) and agree that the decisive role in promoting the rise of ancient anti-Semitism was played by the Maccabean revolt and the successful expansionist policies of the Hasmoneans in the second century B.C.E. which followed the violent Hellenization instigated by Antiochus IV Epiphanes.

The most recent version of the functionalist model stems from the work of Adalberto Giovannini.[22] He, too, views ancient "anti-Semitism" solely as an outcome of the political conflicts of the second century B.C.E., but one resulting not so much from the Hasmonean conquests as from the emergence of Rome on the political stage of the Near East. Linked to this, he argues, was not only an improvement in the situation of the Jews in the Diaspora but also a "reversal of the hierarchy" between Jews and Greeks in favor of the Jews: "From the moment when the Jews chose to place themselves under the protection of Rome, the hostile reaction of the Greeks became inevitable."[23] Although this may be an appropriate description of the political state of affairs at the time, it fails to explain the connection to "anti-Judaism" (Giovannini's preferred term). By simply claiming that this, and this alone, was the cause of Greek "anti-Judaism," he is dodging the question at hand.[24]

In opposition to the "substantialist" interpretative model and receptive to Heinemann's functionalist model, a further approach developed following World War II. Its proponents see a fundamental difference between pagan hostility toward Jews and Christian anti-Semitism; that is, they want to restrict the term "anti-Semitism," in its original, narrower meaning, to the Christian variant of this phenomenon. Accordingly, Christian anti-Semitism is something new and unique, and in no way comparable to the occasional outbursts of pagan antipathy toward the Jews. Advocates of this view include Jules Isaac,[25] Marcel Simon,[26] Léon Poliakov,[27] and most particularly Rosemary Ruether.[28] John Gager can also be considered one of its proponents. Although he admits that "there is evidence to suggest" that the political conflicts of the second century B.C.E. in Syria-Palestine "mark the beginnings of pagan anti-Semitism,"[29] he nevertheless dates the heyday of ancient anti-Semitism clearly in the first century C.E., especially in Alexandria. (His treatment of the Greco-Roman Exodus tradition serves, incidentally, as a good example of those studies aiming to attribute a later date to all the available evidence and thus to exonerate, if possible, pre-Alexandrian Hellenism of anti-Semitic tendencies.) Altogether, he cautions against overvaluing pagan anti-Semitism and against underestimating the sympathies that Greeks and Romans felt toward Jews.[30] The emphasis upon both sympathy for Jews and their achievements in the Greco-Roman world is also the declared purpose of *Jew and Gentile in the Ancient World* by Louis Feldman, which being overly apologetic, however, grossly overshoots its mark. Only once is the term "anti-Semitism" mentioned, and then—as the index expressly points out—only to document its "inappropriateness."[31] No further examination of the phenomenon, regardless of what one might call it, is offered.

The present book is an attempt to look at an old subject not with new evidence, as there is none, but with a fresh approach to all the available sources illuminating the history of hostility toward the Jews in the Greco-Roman world, so-called pagan or ancient anti-Semitism. It starts from the presupposition that there did exist in antiquity a phenomenon which may be called "hatred of Jews," "hostility toward Jews," "anti-Semitism," "anti-Judaism," or whatever label one chooses to describe it. Although it is true, as Gager, Feldman, and others maintain, that we also encounter a remarkable degree of sympathy for Judaism in the ancient world, the patterns of animosity are undeniable. What precisely it means, however, to talk about "hostility," "hatred," and "anti-Semitism" in antiquity will be shown in the course of the book through detailed analyses of the sources.

Even though I employ several terms to describe the phenomenon we are in search of, I have no reservations about using the term "anti-

Semitism," despite its obvious anachronism (the more reluctant reader may add imaginary quotation marks). The term is used throughout the book in the broader sense of hostility toward the Jews on the part of Greeks and Romans. Whether or not we may use it in the particular sense of describing a unique kind of hatred and hostility reserved solely for the Jews is discussed in the final chapter. The only term I avoid is "anti-Judaism," thus following those scholars who restrict it to early Christian expressions of hostility toward the Jews.[32]

I have no ambition to invent a new term, unless the word "Judeophobia" is regarded as an invention for which, however, I cannot claim the credit. When writing this book I used it in the belief that I had created it—only to be disappointed to find, when Zvi Yavetz published his article, that my creation was not as original as I had thought.[33]

I have no reservations either about employing the term "pagan," although I have kept its use to a minimum, preferring the adjective "Greco-Roman." When used, "pagan" is meant to designate Greek and Roman as opposed to Jewish (and Christian) customs and beliefs, with no ideological background whatsoever.

The scope of my study is confined to the pagan Greco-Roman world and does not include Christianity. I do not deal with the phenomenon of early Christian anti-Judaism, important as it is for the later development of anti-Semitism, nor do I discuss how Christian hostility toward the Jews was molded by pagan anti-Semitism.[34] My study is, moreover, primarily concerned with *hostile* attitudes toward the Jews, and I do not pretend to have dealt with, let alone to have done justice to, all aspects and facets of the encounter between Jews and Gentiles in the ancient world.[35]

Finally, with regard to the methodological implications, I maintain that neither the substantialist model of interpretation nor its functionalist counterpart is adequate to explain Greco-Roman anti-Semitism (as a matter of fact, they hardly exist in their pure form, as in most cases scholars adopt a blend of both, with different emphases on either side). An exclusively functionalist approach runs the risk of dissolving the phenomenon it describes, anti-Semitism, into ever-changing political and social relations with nothing concrete behind these functions—and in the end of explaining it away. (It is no accident that the proponents of the functionalist approach talk so much about politics and so little about religion.) On the other hand, an exclusively substantialist approach, based on the idea of a monolithic, always self-identical anti-Semitism arising out of the very essence of Judaism itself, runs the certainly more dangerous risk of confusing cause with pretext and in the end finding the Jews themselves guilty of what happened to them.[36] Since "function" never exists without, and therefore can never be isolated from, "essence," I would opt for a harnessing of both approaches—substantialist and functionalist—in research on ancient anti-Semitism. As I argue in more detail in the final chapter, one always needs both components to "create" anti-Semitism: the anti-Semite and the Jew or Judaism, concrete Jewish peculiarities and the intention of the anti-Semite to distort and to pervert these peculiarities. Anti-Semitism always happens in the mind of the anti-Semite, but it needs its object, the Jew or Judaism. The fact that anti-Semitism is sometimes found even in the absence of Jews, as modern history has taught us, is no argument against this, precisely because it is the distorted imagination of the anti-Semite, nourished by real Jews as well as by his fantasies about Jews, which creates anti-Semitism.

The book is composed of three parts. Part I analyzes the major topics and motifs referring to Jews and Judaism in the Greco-Roman literature, Part II surveys the historical evidence, Part III binds the two together, and the final chapter examines the specific meaning of "anti-Semitism" in antiquity.

Ancient Greek and Roman literature is full of references to and remarks on the Jews, some longer and some shorter, some friendly and many hostile. The Jews were a people with a well-recognized, distinctive, and ancient past. Their history and their way of life aroused curiosity. The picture of the Jews as mirrored in Greek and Roman literature is sometimes informed by an intimate knowledge of their customs; sometimes—and more often—it is the product of the transmission and continuous reshaping of ethnographic traditions, echoing a remote past as well as age-old prejudices.

Any attempt to reconstruct this picture requires scrutinizing an enormous amount of literature, a project made much easier since the publication of Menachem Stern's monumental three-volume *Greek and Latin Authors on Jews and Judaism.*[37] As useful as this collection of all the bits and pieces of information on the Jews arranged according to authors is, it cannot replace a survey of the topics and motifs which were of concern to the Greeks and Romans, and which reveal their assessment of the Jews and their customs. I agree with Amos Funkenstein and Zvi Yavetz that "anti-Jewish propaganda or hatred of the Jews or antisemitism . . . should not be studied as a literary genre. This would be *Ideengeschichte* at its worst."[38] Indeed, to reduce "anti-Semitism," even in antiquity, to a literary genre reveals a minimalist approach which disregards its historical force. However, this insight and Stern's volumes do not excuse us from reviewing the literary traditions in order to determine their importance within the respective historical constellations. Yavetz is certainly correct in arguing that it is not enough to ask "why" or "how" a given phenomenon started, that one also has to explain "how, and especially by whom, a latent animosity was triggered off by special developments, . . . how words were sometimes converted into deeds";[39] but these historical questions cannot be answered without taking the literary evidence into consideration. The literary topics did not evolve in a vacuum, and what is even more important, they were exploited by those "whodunnit." It is therefore not at all negligible, for example, whether Manetho, early in the third century B.C.E. and relying on older material, expresses his own anti-Jewish feelings, or whether these feelings are expressed by a much later anonymous Pseudo-Manetho who is part of the well-known anti-Semitic climate of Greek Alexandria.

The Greeks and Romans were mostly preoccupied with the monotheism of the Jews, their customs and rituals such as abstinence from pork, Sabbath, and circumcision, and their success: proselytism. These topics are analyzed in Part I, each in its own right and not only with regard to its contribution to the subject of anti-Semitism. In addition, the legendary tradition of the expulsion of the Jews from Egypt because of a fatal disease plays an important role in the discussions of the Greek and Roman authors; since it differs from the other topics in that it is not, at least originally, connected with the "real" Exodus and since it is the starting point for many of the Greco-Roman deliberations on the Jews, it opens this first part of the book. With the exception of Chapters 3, 4, and 5, each chapter follows a chronological sequence in order to present the historical development of the given topic.

Part II examines historical events associated with fierce outbursts of hostility toward the Jews. Here I attempt to determine precisely what characterizes these events, what motivated them, how the interaction between politics and the different cultural-religious features of the various ethnic groups worked, what fueled the hostility, and whether there is anything conspicuous about it that allows us to label it anti-Semitic.

The two events examined are the disturbances of the year 410 B.C.E. in the Egyptian military settlement on the island of Elephantine, which led to the destruction of the Jewish Temple there, and the riots of the year 38 C.E. in the Greek city of Alexandria, which for many historians serve as the prime example of ancient anti-Semitism. These two events—relatively minor from the point of view of received Jewish or classical history—are paradigmatic, in demonstrating key causes and patterns of anti-Semitism in the decisive Egyptian and Greco-Egyptian contexts respectively. The Roman variety of anti-Semitism, crucial for later history as it was, never stirred up the hatred of the masses against the Jews in the same way, and never prompted riots on the scale and with the complexity of motivation found at Alexandria. The two Jewish wars against Rome, the first during the years 66–73 C.E. under Vespasian and Titus and the second during the years 132–135 C.E. under Hadrian (with its so-called Hadrianic persecution), were devastating events which determined the course of Jewish history more fatefully than did the riots in Elephantine and Alexandria; and both were no doubt loaded with hostility and hatred. But to view them as the result of anti-Jewish resentments accumulated over a long period of time within Roman society would be to put the cart before the horse. Thus, they cannot help us illuminate the origins and nature of ancient anti-Semitism.

The same is true for the persecution under Antiochus IV Epiphanes and the Maccabean revolt (167 B.C.E.). Hardly anyone would seriously argue any longer that the Antiochan persecution was triggered by anti-Semitic feelings on the part of the king or was anti-Semitic in character. Antiochus was idealized by his own and, even more so, by his successors' propaganda as the vanguard of Greek culture who "endeavoured to abolish Jewish superstition and to introduce Greek civilization,"[40] and accordingly was demonized by contemporary Jewish literature as the personification of evil and religious hubris,[41] but one has to distinguish carefully between his attitude and later interpretation. Moreover, it has become more or less *communis opinio* since Bickerman's and Hengel's pioneering research[42] that the king, in what is called his "religious persecution," relied at least as much on the inspiration and encouragement of the Hellenized Jewish establishment in Jerusalem as on his own misguided instinct. What has been argued, however, is that the particular political circumstances following the successful expansionist policy of the Maccabean/Hasmonean leaders created an atmosphere of propaganda and counter-propaganda which was also the hotbed of anti-Semitism. I deal with this in detail in Chapters 2, 3, and 10, and argue that many of the motifs connected with these stories point back to a much earlier origin in ancient Egypt.

Part III, building on the ground laid in Parts I and II and taking up those elements which have proved crucial for the historical reconstruction, reopens the question of the origin and historical development of anti-Semitism. It follows Heinemann's division of three geographically and chronologically different "foci of conflict," namely Syria-Palestine, Egypt, and Rome, but it disagrees fundamentally with the order of importance attached by Heinemann (and his successors) to these foci. Whereas Heinemann and others emphasize the importance of second century B.C.E. Syria-Palestine for the origin of anti-Semitism, Hellenistic Egypt around 300 B.C.E. is here reinstated as the "mother" of anti-Semitism—with roots reaching back into Egypt's pre-Hellenistic history.[43] Egypt is where it all started, where the major tensions and vectors which produced anti-Semitism were laid out. Hellenistic Syria-Palestine takes up the most efficacious anti-Jewish motif provided by Egypt, the charge of misanthropy and xenophobia, and transforms it into a powerful weapon which, together with its later Egyptian ramifications, finds its way into Western "civilization."

Anti-Semitism assumes a very peculiar shape in the historical context of the third focus of conflict, imperial Rome. Rome is influenced by its Egyptian and Greek precursors and yet adds to their hatred and contempt a new element, fear, born out of the ambivalence between fascination and rejection. This distinctive contribution to the history of anti-Semitism seems to me best conveyed by the term "Judeophobia" in its double meaning of hatred and fear.

In the concluding chapter I ask in what sense, if any, the specific term "anti-Semitism" can be applied to the ancient world. In order to elucidate this problem I test the most elaborate modern theory of anti-Semitism, developed by Gavin I. Langmuir, against the evidence for classical antiquity. This latest attempt to shift the origin of anti-Semitism to an even later date—and to reserve the emergence of "true" anti-Semitism (as opposed to the more "moderate" anti-Judaism of the Greeks and Romans and the early Christians) to the twelfth and thirteenth centuries with their new accusations of ritual murder, host desecration, and well poisoning—is rejected as yet another oversimplification. Langmuir's theory does not do justice to the complexity of the evidence of the Greco-Roman period (nor, I suspect, to that of early Christianity).

I realize that I am thus also making a statement about the later development of anti-Semitism.[44] No one of our generation, and certainly no German born not long before the end of World War II who has made the history of Judaism his profession, can ignore the effect anti-Semitism has had, and still has, on our history. It is my conviction, indeed, that we are the heirs of antiquity, for better and for worse.

PART I

Who Are the Jews?

CHAPTER ONE

Expulsion from Egypt

THE EXODUS FROM EGYPT under the leadership of Moses is one of the decisive events of Jewish history. According to the biblical story, the people of Israel left Egypt voluntarily and against the will of the Pharaoh and his fellow Egyptians—it was only after the last of the ten plagues, the smiting of the firstborn, that the Pharaoh could be convinced to let the people of Israel go (Ex. 12:28ff). Quite different is the Egyptian and Greco-Roman tradition of the Exodus: the Jews were driven out of Egypt by force in a kind of "ethnic cleansing" because they were polluted lepers and/or unwelcome foreigners; it was after this expulsion that they founded Jerusalem and became Jews in the full sense of the word.[1]

This early example of counter-history proved to be one of the most powerful anti-Jewish statements, not only in ancient history but until modern times. The legend can be traced back to the early third century B.C.E. and reached its literary climax in the "grand synthesis" of anti-Jewish traditions written by Tacitus. It is the aim of this opening chapter to focus on the literary development of the tradition as it unfolds in the various discussions of the origins of the Jews.

HECATAEUS OF ABDERA

The earliest account of the Exodus in pagan literature is to be found in Hecataeus of Abdera's lost *Aegyptiaca,* which has come down to us as an excerpt from Diodorus Siculus' *Bibliotheca Historica* in the *Bibliotheca* of Photius. Hecataeus visited Egypt during the reign of Ptolemy I; his *Aegyptiaca* was written therefore around 300 B.C.E.[2] He opens his statement on the origins of the Jews as follows:[3]

> When in ancient times a pestilence arose in Egypt, the common people ascribed their troubles to the workings of a divine agency; for

indeed with many strangers of all sorts *(pollōn . . . xenōn)* dwelling in their midst and practising different rites of religion and sacrifice, their own traditional observances in honour of the gods *(tas patrious tōn theōn timas)* had fallen into disuse. Hence the natives of the land surmised that unless they removed the foreigners *(tous allophylous),* their troubles would never be resolved. At once, therefore, the aliens were driven from the country *(xenēlatoumenōn tōn alloethnōn),* and the most outstanding and active among them banded together and, as some say, were cast ashore in Greece and certain other regions; their leaders were notable men, chief among them being Danaus and Cadmus. But the greater number were driven into what is now called Judea, which is not far distant from Egypt and was at that time utterly uninhabited. The colony was headed by a man called Moses, outstanding both for his wisdom and for his courage.

Scholars unanimously agree that Hecataeus' account, especially in what follows on Moses and his newly founded theocratical state, is, "if anything, sympathetic," "devoid of anti-Semitic feelings,"[4] and a "typical example of early Hellenistic ethnography" with "its idealizing tendencies."[5] It is true that the story in its present form "is directed at all foreigners in Egypt, not just the Jews"[6] and by this is remarkably different from later versions "whose explicit purpose is to denigrate Moses and the Jews."[7] There is, however, a conspicuous divergence in Hecataeus' dealing with the Greek and the Jewish foreigners: the former are "the most outstanding and active among them," the latter are "the greater number," that is, the less noble crowd.[8] Gager minimizes this difference by arguing that "this distinction is only natural in the present form of the account which is written from a Greek point of view."[9] This may be the case, but still it is only the Jews and not the Greeks who, as a result of their expulsion as foreigners, decide to introduce customs which distinguish them from all other nations: "The sacrifices that he [Moses] established differ from those of other nations, as does their way of living, for as a result of their own expulsion *(tēn idian xenēlasian)* from Egypt he introduced a way of life which was somewhat unsocial and hostile to foreigners *(apanthrōpon tina kai misoxenon bion).*"[10]

This *misoxenos bios* of the Jews as a result of their own *xenēlasia* (expulsion because they were foreigners) obviously is not only a strange conclusion which the Greeks did not reach (although Hecataeus does not say so explicitly); it also stands in sharp contrast to Hecataeus' otherwise very positive description of the Jewish state, which was directed by a priest "regarded as superior to his colleagues in wisdom and virtue," and of the Jewish customs and manners. Moreover, it should be noticed that Hecataeus mentions the sacrifices established by Moses and the different way of living of the Jews immediately after having explained that Moses did not fabricate any images of the gods, "being of the opinion that God is not in human form" *(dia to mē nomizein anthrōpomorphon einai ton theon)*. Thus the Jews' unsocial and hostile way of life seems to be connected with their belief in a God who does not take human form.

I am therefore not convinced that there is an overall pro-Jewish attitude in Hecataeus' version of the Exodus tradition. It implies that the Jews are distinct not only from the Egyptians but also from the Greeks, and that this distinction is derived from their belief in a God who does not take human form. Even though all foreigners, including the Greeks, were expelled from Egypt because of their "different rites of religion and sacrifice," only the Jews adhered to this strange belief in a non-anthropomorphic God and to sacrifices and customs that "differ from those of other nations." If, as most scholars assume, the historical introduction as quoted[11] derives from Egyptian sources,[12] this slightly anti-Jewish bias already belongs to Hecataeus' Egyptian antecedent, but it is reinforced and strengthened by the emphasis put on the *apanthrōpos* and *misoxenos bios* of the Jews as a result of their *xenēlasia*. Whether this explanation also stems from Hecataeus' Egyptian sources or is to be regarded as his own addition cannot be decided with certainty, but I am inclined to believe the latter.[13] There is a strong tension between his generally sympathetic attitude toward the Jews, and in particular toward Moses, and the anti-Jewish bias with regard to the expulsion of the Jews and to their customs being different from those of all other nations. It is therefore Hecataeus who combines for the first time in history the *misoxenia* motif with the Exodus tradition, and thus creates, or transmits (and by doing so strengthens), a powerful argument against the Jews.

MANETHO

Manetho, the Egyptian priest at Heliopolis (third century B.C.E.), wrote his version of the Exodus story shortly after Hecataeus of Abdera. Strictly speaking, we have two versions of it, both preserved from his lost *Aegyptiaca* in Josephus' *Contra Apionem*.[14] The first relates the history of the Hyksos in Egypt: the rule of their Shepherd-kings over Egypt, the revolt of the kings of the Thebaïd and the rest of Egypt against the Shepherds, and the defeat of the Shepherds and their expulsion from Egypt. Having left Egypt, the Shepherds first journeyed into Syria, which, however, they left, dreading the power of Assyria, in order to build, "in the land now called Judea, a city" they called Jerusalem. This version no doubt reflects the foreign rule of the Hyksos in Egypt—particularly noteworthy is their cruelty: "they burned our cities ruthlessly, razed to the ground the temples of the gods, and treated all the natives with a cruel hostility, massacring some and leading into slavery the wives and children of others."[15] The Jews are not mentioned at all. Only by implication may one assume that the expelled Hyksos became the ancestors of the Jewish nation and may thus be identified with the Jews.

The second version is more complicated and more important for this discussion. Josephus, by the way, compares the two versions, exercising in doing so an interesting example of his *Quellenkritik*. According to this second version the Egyptian king Amenophis "conceived a desire to behold the gods" and was instructed by his namesake Amenophis that his wish could be fulfilled only "if he cleansed the whole land of lepers and other polluted persons." The king then collected 80,000 of them (among them "some learned priests, who had been attacked by leprosy") and sent them to the stone quarries. Subsequently he assigned to them the former capital of the Hyksos, Auaris, which the exiled used as a base for their revolt under the leadership of one of the priests of Heliopolis called Osarseph. This Osarseph "made it a law that they should neither worship the gods (*mēte proskynein theous*) nor refrain from any of the animals prescribed as especially sacred in Egypt, but should sacrifice and consume all alike, and that they should have intercourse with none save those of their own confederacy (*synaptesthai de mēdeni plēn tōn synomōmosmenōn*). After framing a great number of laws like these, completely opposed to Egyptian custom,"[16] he convinced the inhabitants of Jerusalem, the former "Shepherds" who had been expelled from Egypt, to combine efforts in an attack upon Egypt. King Amenophis fled into Ethiopia, and the polluted Egyptians together with the Solymites

> treated the people so impiously and savagely that the domination of the Shepherds seemed like a golden age . . . For not only did they set towns and villages on fire, pillaging the temples and mutilating images of the gods without restraint, but they also made a practice of using the sanctuaries as kitchens to roast the sacred animals which the people worshipped; and they would compel the priests and

prophets to sacrifice and butcher the beasts, afterwards casting the men forth naked.[17]

It is only here that we learn—introduced by the phrase "it is said" (*legetai*)—that the Egyptian priest Osarseph, the leader of this outrageous terror, is to be identified with Moses.

It has long been observed that this story is an amalgam of different traditions—most prominent among them the impiety and the refusal of intercourse with other people (*misanthrōpia*)—and that Manetho cannot be held responsible for all of them. Most scholars agree that the core of the story (the suppression of the Egyptians and their religion by "foreigners" and the foreigners' subsequent expulsion) is of Egyptian origin, and that the application to the Jews (and especially the equation Osarseph = Moses) is to be viewed as secondary;[18] thus, that one has to distinguish between Manetho and Pseudo-Manetho.[19] No one would seriously question the premise: it is most likely that there was an Egyptian expulsion story as an antecedent of the Exodus tradition. The basic elements of which this expulsion story apparently was composed are an invasion of Egypt by foreigners, their temporary success and brutal regime, and their final expulsion by a savior king.[20] Since the regime of the foreigners was directed mainly against the indigenous Egyptian *religion,* we may further assume that the motif of impiety was already an important element in the early Egyptian version of the expulsion story.[21]

This does not seem to be the case with the *misanthrōpia* motif. In contrast to the impiety motif, there is no indication that it already belonged to the (pre-Greek) Egyptian version of the expulsion story, as Gager wants us to believe.[22] The "hostility toward the indigenous population and religion [which] served as the focal point in the Egyptian expulsion stories long before they were transferred to the Jews"[23] does not lead to Manetho's refusal of intercourse with other people "save those of their own confederacy." That foreign invaders exercise a brutal regime against the native population and their religion is a common theme in Egyptian literature among others, but the idea that these foreigners, once driven out of the occupied country, resort to *misoxenia* and *misanthrōpia* seems to be reserved for the Jews.[24]

From this distinction, however, between an early Egyptian expulsion story and its (later) impregnation with the Jewish *misanthrōpia*, the conclusion does not necessarily follow that the latter has to be relegated to a mysterious and late Pseudo-Manetho. The most outspoken opponent of this prevalent tendency to absolve Manetho from any anti-Jewish inclination has been Stern, who does not see any valid reason "for denying to Manetho either the whole story, or even the crucial paragraph" (that is, the identification of Osarseph with Moses).[25] His main arguments are, first, that "an anti-Jewish atmosphere in Egypt should not be considered typical of only the later Ptolemaic or early Roman age," and second, that it was not Manetho but Hecataeus who "combined the story of the defiled people with that of Moses and the Jews."[26]

When looking at Manetho's account again it seems to be quite obvious that the identification of Osarseph with Moses in the final paragraph is indeed a later addition. This follows not only from the suspicious introduction of this identification by *legetai*[27] but also from the fact that in the body of the story, when mentioning the leader of the lepers, Josephus, or Manetho (Josephus claims to quote Manetho here *verbatim*), does not hint at any connection of this Osarseph with Moses: Osarseph is an Egyptian, "one of the priests of Heliopolis," and in correspondence with this, the "lepers and other polluted persons" are Egyptians, not foreigners (as in Hecataeus) and certainly not Jews.[28] Thus we do have to distinguish between an "Egyptian" layer of the story—impure Egyptians with their leader Osarseph were cast into the stone-quarries and took revenge by revolting against their "pure" fellow countrymen—and a "Jewish" layer which still has to be determined more precisely.

It is true that the most forceful association with the Jews is being made by the equation Osarseph = Moses, but it is equally true, and Stern is right in pointing to this, that the insertion of the Jews by no means rests solely on this equation. It is the polluted Egyptians' allies, the Shepherds, who come from Jerusalem in order to help them, who strongly suggest this association with the Jews. Although Osarseph had already decreed that his followers should not worship the Egyptian gods and even should sacrifice and consume their sacred animals, it is the Solymites who treated the Egyptian people impiously and roasted the sacred animals; it is their brutal domination which makes the rule of their ancestors, the Shepherd-Hyksos, appear a golden age. The subject in this vivid description of the thirteen years of foreign rule over Egypt is the Solymites, the lepers being mentioned only incidentally ("Meanwhile, the Solymites made a descent along with the polluted Egyptians . . .").

Thus, we clearly have here a blend of "Egyptian" and "Jewish" motifs, but this very fusion cannot be relegated to a later Pseudo-Manethian, Alexandrian, "anti-Jewish" stage of development; it belongs to the core of the story itself.[29] The Egyptian version as presented by Manetho has an invasion of Egypt by outsiders at its center, but these outsiders are not foreigners in general but precisely the Solymites, the people of Jerusalem. Moreover, even though Osarseph is not identified with Moses in the body of the story, he nevertheless is modeled very much after the image of Moses the lawgiver: he made a law *(nomon etheto),* and what was the nature of this law peculiar only to him and his followers? First, that they should not worship the gods (the impiety motif), and second, "that they should have no connection with any save members of their own confederacy"[30] (the *misoxenia/misanthrōpia* motif). Both motifs are immediately reminiscent of Hecataeus, namely his allusion to Moses' belief in a (one) God not in human form and, even more important, to the Jews' *misoxenos bios,* their hostility to foreigners. Hence the *misoxenia/misanthrōpia* motif and its combination with the impiety motif belong to the very core of both Hecataeus' and Manetho's versions of the Exodus story[31] and cannot be shifted, by distinguishing between Manetho and Pseudo-Manetho, to the later Alexandrian milieu of the early first century C.E. with its well-known anti-Jewish outbursts.[32]

APOLLONIUS MOLON

The next author to refer to Jewish impiety and misanthropy is the famous rhetor Apollonius Molon (first century B.C.E.), who is regarded as the first Greek writer after Hecataeus to have written a book about the Jews. According to Josephus, however, he "has not grouped his accusations together, but scattered them here and there over his work."[33] The only evidence preserved is several quotations and references in Josephus' *Contra Apionem,* and one fragment in Eusebius' *Praeparatio Evangelica.*[34] The Exodus is not mentioned here, unless one wishes to see a vague allusion to it in the remark that Noah was "expelled from his native place by the inhabitants of the land."[35]

That Apollonius Molon did refer to the Exodus tradition we learn from a remark by Josephus when he discusses the date of the departure of the Jews from Egypt, but the text itself unfortunately is not quoted.[36] In addition, Josephus mentions as one of the most striking features of Apollonius' characterization of the Jews that he reviles them as atheists and misanthropes *(hōs atheous kai misanthrōpous).*[37] Although we do not know anything about the context of this remark (nothing tells us that it belongs to the Exodus motif but nothing excludes this possibility either), it is important to notice that Apollonius' assessment of the Jews comes very close to Hecataeus and Manetho: they have contempt for the proper religion and dislike not only foreigners but all human beings.[38]

DIODORUS SICULUS

The Egyptian origin of the Jews is mentioned in several passages in the *Bibliotheca Historica* of Diodorus Siculus (first century B.C.E.). He knows that the Jews belonged to the emigrants who left Egypt in order to found a new "colony,"[39] presenting as a "proof" of the Egyptian origin of the Jews the custom of circumcision common among the Egyptians as well as among the Jews.[40] It seems very probable, as Stern argues, that these two passages derive from Hecataeus,[41] since Hecataeus is the only source which includes the Jews among the colonists and, even more important, since Diodorus explicitly quotes Hecataeus' account of the Exodus tradition.[42]

Yet there is another version of the Exodus tradition in Diodorus, the source of which is less certain. The passage refers to Antiochus VII Sidetes' siege of Jerusalem in about 135/34 B.C.E. The king is advised by his counselors

> to take the city by storm and to wipe out completely the nation of the Jews, since they alone of all nations avoided dealings with any other people *(akoinōnētous einai, tēs pros allo ethnos epimixias)* and looked upon all men as their enemies *(polemious hypolambanein pantas)*. They pointed out, too, that the ancestors of the Jews had been driven out of all Egypt as men who were impious and detested by the gods *(hōs asebeis kai misoumenous hypo tōn theōn)*. For by way of purging the country all persons who had white and leprous marks on their bodies had been assembled and driven across the border, as being under a curse; the refugees had occupied the territory round about Jerusalem, and having organized the nation of the Jews had made their hatred of mankind into a tradition *(paradosimon poiēsai to misos to pros tous anthrōpous),* and on this account had introduced utterly outlandish laws *(nomima pantelōs exēllagmena):* not to break bread with any other people, nor to show them any good will at all.[43]

Most scholars believe that the source for this and especially for the following story about the statue in the Jewish Temple of a bearded man seated on an ass, supposed to be an image of Moses, is the famous philosopher Posidonius of Apamea (135–51 B.C.E.).[44] Whether or not this is the case, it does not help us in evaluating the Exodus story proper because we do not have Posidonius' version.[45]

If one looks closely at Diodorus' account there can be no doubt that there are striking similarities to Lysimachus, who is considered to be one of the arch-antisemites, in the ranks of Chaeremon and Apion.[46] The key question, however, is whether these similarities are restricted to Lysimachus or whether there are resemblances to earlier authors as well. In my opinion, the latter is true because we already find all the important elements of Diodorus' account in Hecataeus, Manetho, and Apollonius Molon. First, the most striking feature in Diodorus' characterization of the Jews is that they avoid dealings with other people, regard others as their enemies, and have adopted this hatred of humankind *(misos to pros tous anthrōpous)* as a permanent tradition. This is exactly the *misoxenos bios* of Hecataeus, Osarseph/Moses' decree to "have no connection with any save members of their own confederacy" in Manetho, and Apollonius Molon's *misanthrōpia*. Second, the motif of impiety is also present in all three authors: in Hecataeus the Jews do not worship images of God (as the Egyptians do) but believe "that God is not in human form"; in Manetho they are ordered not to worship the gods of the Egyptians but to sacrifice and consume them; and in Apollonius Molon they are called atheists. And third, Diodorus' "outlandish laws" of the Jews appear in Hecataeus as sacrifices and a way of living that "differ from those of other nations," and in Manetho as "laws completely opposed to Egyptian custom." In addition, the "specific mention of leprosy and the need to purify the country by expelling the lepers" which Gager regards as characteristic of both Diodorus and Lysimachus is to be found explicitly in Manetho at least—if one wishes to distinguish the leprosy from Hecataeus' pestilence (a distinction which seems to me rather artificial).[47]

In conclusion, Diodorus, with his charge of Jewish impiety and misanthropy, is a true heir of the chain of tradition going back to Hecataeus and Manetho. The attempt to connect him with later authors like Lysimachus seems to be guided by the desire to postpone the anti-Jewish impact of the Exodus story rather than by a close analysis of the sources.

The distinguished historian and geographer Strabo of Amaseia (about 64 B.C.E. to 20 C.E.) transmits in his *Geographia* one of the most substantial essays on Jewish history and religion. He knows of the Egyptian origin of the Jews but refers to it in a way completely different from all the accounts quoted so far. According to him, the Jews were not driven out of Egypt but left it voluntarily because they were dissatisfied with the Egyptian religion:

> Moses, namely, was one of the Egyptian priests, and held a part of Lower Egypt, as it is called, but he went away from there to Judea, since he was displeased with the state of affairs there, and was accompanied by many people who worshipped the Divine Being *(timōntes to theion).* For he said, and taught, that the Egyptians were mistaken in representing the Divine Being by the images of beasts and cattle, as were also the Libyans; and that the Greeks were also wrong in modelling gods in human form *(anthrōpomorphous typountes);* for, according to him, God is one thing alone *(hen touto monon theos)* that encompasses us all and encompasses land and sea—the thing which we call heaven, or universe, or the nature of all that exists *(ho kaloumen ouranon kai kosmon kai tēn tōn ontōn physin)* . . . Now Moses, saying things of this kind, persuaded not a few thoughtful men *(eugnōmonas andras)* and led them away to this place where the settlement of Jerusalem now is.[48]

This is, as Gager has fittingly labeled it, "a remarkable piece of idealizing ethnography."[49] The Jews left Egypt because of their belief in a God who encompasses all, being one thing only *(hen monon),* and who is thus completely different not only from the zoomorphic gods of the Egyptians (and Libyans) but also from the anthropomorphic gods of the Greeks. That this one God of the Jews is also superior to the gods of the Egyptians and the Greeks one may gather from Strabo's very sympathetic portrayal as well as from the fact that Moses, as the continuation of the story tells us, set up an excellent government upon the basis of this belief, "as a result of which the surrounding people were won over on account of their association with him and the advantages which were offered."[50]

In order to evaluate fully this unique version of the Exodus tradition it is important to compare it with its predecessors (the common view that Posidonius was Strabo's source here[51] is not much help because we do not have Posidonius' version of the story). First of all it is most obvious that Strabo shares a good deal with Hecataeus: in both accounts Moses argues against the belief in anthropomorphic deities, and in both heaven, which encompasses land (Hecataeus)[52] and sea (Strabo), is to be identified with God (Hecataeus: *ouranon monon einai theon;*[53] Strabo: *hen touto monon theos . . . ho kaloumenon ouranon*). Stern concludes from this: "Thus, we may assume that the concept of the Jewish God as it emerges in Strabo is an elaboration of that represented by Hecataeus."[54] In addition, both Hecataeus and Strabo point to the fact that Judea was "utterly uninhabited" (Hecataeus; Strabo: "He took it easily since the region was not desirable or such that anyone would be eager to fight for it").[55] And finally, although only Strabo elaborates with great detail on the decline of the Jewish state in the course of history because of their *deisidaimonia*,[56] Hecataeus at least hints at it when he concludes his account of the Jews by saying: "But later, when they became subject to foreign rule, as a result of their mingling with men of other nations . . . , many of their traditional practices were disturbed."[57]

Here the "idealizing ethnographer" Strabo becomes a bit less fond of the Jews. If Hecataeus' account was his source, he has considerably changed it, because according to Hecataeus the decline of the Jewish customs was due to the Jews' mingling with other nations whereas Strabo sees Jewish superstition as the reason for their strange customs like abstinence from flesh, circumcision, and even excision (for females). Thus, Gager's certainty in arguing that "the element of anti-Semitic propaganda" is "completely absent" in Strabo's account seems to be exaggerated.[58] When he comes to the Jews of his own time, Strabo does use a quite common anti-Jewish cliché.

With regard to the Exodus motif, it is indeed very likely that Strabo was influenced by Hecataeus. Nevertheless, as idealizing and free of any anti-Jewish bias as Strabo's account of the Exodus itself clearly is (but not all of Strabo, as we have just seen), I do not see why "it demonstrates beyond any doubt that the story of Egyptian origins [of the Jews] was not in itself anti-Semitic in character."[59] Gager presupposes here, without any evidence, not only that there existed an (the) "original" version of the story but also that it has been preserved precisely by Strabo (who shares some common features with Hecataeus and Diodorus), or that Strabo at least comes very close to it. Gager's argument becomes even less convincing when he hints at the possibility that the pro-Jewish tendency of Strabo's account may be part of Strabo's own contribution.

Strabo's version is an example of one possible direction the Exodus tradition could take, admittedly the most positive and friendly toward the Jews that we know. But whether it is the result of Strabo's deliberate revision of an antecedent or whether he just quotes a source we do not have (if the former proves true we must assume that Strabo liked the Jews of the remote past and their "pure" belief in one God much more than the "superstition" of their concrete observances of his day), it does not lead us back to the "true" story of the Exodus tradition.

POMPEIUS TROGUS

The *Historiae Philippicae* of the Roman historian of the Augustan age, Pompeius Trogus (end first century B.C.E./beginning first century C.E.), have been preserved only in the *Prologues* and *Epitome* of Justin. In book 36 he also deals with the origin of the Jews and combines two versions.[60]

According to the first, the Jews stem from Damascus, which they governed as powerful kings, in succession to Azelus and Adores (= Hazael and Hadad). King Israhel divided his kingdom among his ten sons, the youngest of them being Joseph, whom his brothers sold to some foreign merchants who brought him into Egypt. Here Joseph was immediately recognized by his shrewd nature *(ingenium)* and knowledge of magic as an outstanding personality who was "eminently skilled *(sagacissimus)* in prodigies," "such being the proofs of his knowledge that his admonitions seemed to proceed, not from a mortal, but a god."[61] He also had a son by the name of Moses who inherited his father's knowledge *(scientia)* and beauty *(formae pulchritudo)*.

After this we would expect anything but the sudden reference that the Egyptians, "being troubled with scabies and leprosy," expelled this model of knowledge and beauty in order to prevent the distemper from spreading all over Egypt: Pompeius Trogus obviously uses here, as a second source, the Egyptian Exodus tradition, which does not fit at all with the Damascene version. In his account he is almost devoid of any anti-Jewish bias—if one does not want to see an unfriendly overtone in his remark, which is not exactly concordant with the biblical story (Ex. 12:35f.), that the Jews upon their Exodus had stolen the sacred utensils of the Egyptians. He even mentions the *misoxenia* motif, but quite differently from the way we encountered it in Hecataeus and Diodorus: "And as they remembered that they had been driven from Egypt for fear of spreading infection, they took care, in order that they might not become odious, from the same cause, to their neighbours *(ne eadem causa invisi apud incolas forent),* to have no communication with strangers *(ne cum peregrinis conviverent).*"[62]

According to both Hecataeus and Pompeius the trauma of the expulsion causes the strange behavior of the Jews, but the exact motives for the behavior itself are different. Whereas in Hecataeus it is misanthropy and hostility toward foreigners (Diodorus mentions only misanthropy), in Pompeius the Jews just avoid contact with foreigners. Thus, the powerful *misanthrōpia* and *misoxenia* motif, which no doubt was in Pompeius' *Vorlage*, has been "toned down" and converted into timidity toward foreigners. The essential point is not that "the separateness of Jewish culture is here explained as a natural response to the expulsion from Egypt"[63] (we have this in Hecataeus, too) but the nature of separateness itself: in Hecataeus as well as in Manetho and Diodorus (and in Apollonius Molon) it is active, expressing itself in hostility; in Pompeius Trogus it is passive. I therefore would argue that Pompeius has to be regarded as an important exception and cannot be put in the same category with Hecataeus, Manetho, Diodorus, and even Strabo.[64]

LYSIMACHUS

With the Greco-Egyptian writer Lysimachus, whose date is unknown (he lived sometime between the second century B.C.E. and the first century C.E.),[65] we enter the chorus of authors with remarkably undisguised anti-Jewish tendencies. Whether or not he is to be identified with the Greek grammarian and mythographer Lysimachus of Alexandria, he comes very close to the outspoken anti-Jewish propaganda of his Alexandrian colleagues Apion and Chaeremon. His lost *Aegyptiaca* is quoted by Josephus in *Contra Apionem*.[66]

According to Lysimachus' version of the Exodus tradition, it is the Egyptian king Bocchoris who ordered that the land be purged of lepers as well as of impure and impious people: the former should be drowned; the latter should be driven into the wilderness. His order being executed, the unclean persons were exposed in the desert and gathered around "a certain Moses" who advised them to head for another inhabited country, "instructing them to show goodwill to no man *(mēte anthrōpōn tini eunoēsein)*, to offer not the best but the worst advice *(mēte arista symbouleusein alla ta cheirona)*, and to overthrow any temples and altars of the gods which they found *(theōn te naous kai bōmous . . . anatrepein)*."[67] Following this advice, the impure and impious people "maltreated the population, and plundered and set fire to the temples" wherever they went, until they reached "the country now called Judea." In this country they settled and built a city which originally was called Hierosyla ("because of their sacrilegious propensities") and was later renamed Hierosolyma ("to avoid the disgraceful imputation").

Apart from some minor differences from the other versions of the story[68] it is most revealing that Lysimachus is unambiguous as to who the impure people are. We learn that they are Jews not only at the end of the story when they reach Judea; rather, we are told from the very outset that "the Jewish people *(ton laon tōn Ioudaiōn)* were afflicted with leprosy, scurvy, and other maladies."[69] In accordance with this he does not need the Hyksos and can also forgo the Egyptian origin of Moses. He knows that it was the Jews who were driven out of Egypt because of their impurity and impiety.

Against this background it comes as no surprise that Lysimachus remodels the motifs which we know from most of his predecessors, both of the belief in a different (non-anthropomorphic or non-zoomorphic) God and of *misoxenia* or *misanthrōpia* (let alone Pompeius' *xenophobia*) in an extremely negative fashion: the Jews deliberately destroy all the temples of the gods of other peoples, and they are hostile to all humankind, purposely offering the worst advice.

We do not know anything about Lysimachus' sources, but the differences between him and Manetho (and also Hecataeus and Diodorus) do not necessarily prove "that the historical construction of Lysimachus is founded on a different version of the rise of the Jewish nation than that of Manetho."[70] It may well be that Lysimachus "is not merely derivative"[71] but has used the sources we know (mainly Hecataeus and Manetho) and deliberately changed them in order to intensify the anti-Jewish bias.

APION

Apion, the grammarian of Egyptian origin (first half of the first century C.E.), who probably held office as the head of the Museum in Alexandria, is Josephus' arch-antisemite. He belonged to the delegation of the Greeks of Alexandria who traveled to Rome in order to convince the Emperor Gaius of their charges against the Alexandrian Jews. His *Aegyptiaca* is lost and known mainly through quotations in Josephus' *Contra Apionem*.

Apion's version of the Exodus, as far as we can reconstruct it from Josephus, is unfortunately not very informative; it must originally have been more detailed than what has been preserved by Josephus. We learn only that Moses was a native of Heliopolis who, when he arrived in

Jerusalem, "being pledged to the customs of his country, erected prayer-houses, open to the air, in the various precincts of the city, all facing eastwards."[72] As far as the Exodus itself is concerned (which is, to be sure, an "exodus of the lepers, the blind and the lame under Moses' leadership"),[73] Josephus is mainly interested in mocking Apion's dating (namely the first year of the seventh Olympiad)[74] and the number of the fugitives he states (namely 110,000).[75] In connection with this he adds, however, one important detail from Apion's account which is without precedent in any of the known Exodus stories: "After a six days' march . . . they developed tumours in the groin, and that was why, after safely reaching the country now called Judea, they rested on the seventh day, and called that day *sabbaton,* preserving the Egyptian terminology; for disease of the groin in Egypt is called sabbatosis."[76]

This interpretation of the Sabbath is extremely hostile and fits in well with Apion's overall anti-Jewish polemic, which "manifests the implacable hostility that filled the air in the late 30s and early 40s of the first century C.E."[77] Yet the other new detail mentioned above, namely that Moses, "pledged to the customs of his country, erected prayer-houses," is not hostile at all. On the contrary, since we have to assume that "the customs of his country" refers to Moses' Egyptian customs, and that the prayer-houses he erected are the prayer-houses in Jerusalem, we have to conclude that Moses transferred the religious customs of his native country (Egypt) to his new country (Judea). This is a remarkable difference from his predecessors in that Apion in the context of the expulsion story[78] makes use of neither the motif of impiety (that the Jews had to leave Egypt because of their different belief in one God and their different customs) nor the motif of *misoxenia/misanthrōpia,* but rather wants us to believe that the religion Moses introduced in Jerusalem actually was Egyptian.

We do not know whether this version goes back to an unknown source or whether it is Apion's own creation. It is, however, important to notice that one of the most powerful anti-Jewish arguments, which not only is part and parcel of the Alexandrian Exodus tradition but also belongs to the earliest evidence we possess, has not been used by one of the most influential anti-Jewish authors. How to explain this is another question. It may well be, as Gager has argued, that Apion wanted "to malign the Jews by portraying the Mosaic cult as an offshoot of Egyptian religion,"[79] but it may just as well be that the motifs of the Jews' disbelief in the Egyptian gods— and of their *misanthrōpia*—are not as "Alexandrian" and late as Gager suggests.

Like Apion, the Stoic philosopher and Egyptian priest Chaeremon (first century C.E.) was a representative of both Egyptian and Greek culture. He probably succeeded Apion in his office as head of the Museum in Alexandria, and he is referred to as the teacher of Nero.[80] If he is to be identified with Chaeremon, the son of Leonidas, he was one of the Alexandrian Greeks sent to congratulate the Emperor Claudius on his assumption of power in 41 C.E.[81] There is only one fragment of his *Aegyptiaca Historia* preserved in Josephus' *Contra Apionem*. According to Chaeremon's account of the Exodus tradition,

> Isis appeared to Amenophis in his sleep, and reproached him for the destruction of the temple in war-time. The sacred scribe Phritibautes told him that, if he purged Egypt of its contaminated population, he might cease to be alarmed. The king, thereupon, collected 250,000 afflicted persons and banished them from the country. Their leaders were scribes, Moses and another sacred scribe—Joseph. Their Egyptian names were Tisithen (for Moses) and Peteseph (Joseph).[82]

When the exiled reached the city Pelusium they joined forces with some 380,000 persons who had been refused permission by Amenophis to cross the Egyptian frontier, and marched upon Egypt. King Amenophis fled to Ethiopia, leaving behind his pregnant wife, who gave birth to a son named Ramesses, who subsequently became Egypt's savior and drove the Jews into Syria.[83]

Scholars have long observed that Chaeremon's account bears close resemblance to Manetho.[84] Despite the differences (mainly Isis' anger[85] vs. the king's desire to behold the gods; the scribe Phritibautes vs. the diviner Amenophis; the addition of Joseph; and the different Egyptian name of Moses), both stories follow the same pattern. The complaint of Isis that her temple had been destroyed seems to be a weak echo of the impiety motif (although no connection is being made between the destruction of the temple and the Jews), and the 380,000 people with whom the expelled joined forces obviously are Manetho's Shepherd-Hyksos.

Most striking, however, is again the almost complete absence of any open hostility toward the Jews, quite in contrast to Manetho. The impiety is not connected with the Jews and moreover there is no indication at all of the *misoxenia/misanthrōpia* motif. Gager has argued that "various forms of similar Egyptian expulsion stories" have been adapted "for similar ends and in a common milieu," the "similar ends" being anti-Jewish polemic, and the "common milieu" being Alexandria.[86] He is certainly right with regard to the first part of his proposition (the similar ends) but as far as the second part (the common milieu) is concerned, we have encountered much stronger anti-Jewish polemics than in the Exodus story of Chaeremon and Apion, the two most outstanding representatives of the "Alexandrian milieu."

TACITUS

The illustrious Roman historian Tacitus (about 56–120 C.E.) has left us in the fifth book of his *Historiae* "the most detailed account of the history and religion of the Jewish people extant in classical Latin literature," which "reflects the feeling of influential circles of Roman society in the age following the destruction of the Temple."[87] Concordant with the pattern of ancient historiography, it takes the form of an ethnographic excursus which starts with the origin of the people described.

As to the origin of the Jews, Tacitus mentions six different explanations without indicating his own preference. Since the last one, however, not only is by far the most detailed but also is introduced by the remark "most authors agree," it is more than likely that Tacitus expresses here his own personal view. From the very outset it can be easily identified as a version of the Egyptian-Greek Exodus tradition we are reviewing.[88]

During a plague in Egypt king Bocchoris was told by the oracle of Ammon to purge his country "and to transport this nation into other lands, since it was hateful to the gods *(id genus hominum ut invisum deis alias in terras avehere)*." The leader of the exiles, Moses, guided them safely through the desert until they reached a country in which, after expelling the former inhabitants, they founded a city. In their new country "Moses introduced the religious practices, quite opposed to those of all other human beings *(novos ritus contrariosque ceteris mortalibus)*."[89] Thus, they dedicated in their sanctuary a statue of that animal (a wild ass) which had guided them in the desert to a stream of water, "sacrificing a ram, apparently in derision of Ammon." They also sacrificed oxen in their temple, "because the Egyptians worship Apis."

Tacitus goes on to describe some other Jewish customs, giving hostile explanations for most of them (abstinence from pork, fasts, unleavened bread, Sabbath). However much these last-mentioned customs are supported by their antiquity, all their other institutions are "base and abominable, and owe their persistence to their depravity *(sinistra foeda, pravitate valuere)."*

There is no doubt that we have here the essence and climax of all the motifs which in antiquity are connected with the Jews in general and with the Exodus tradition in particular—summarized and interpreted by a distinguished representative of the Roman elite at the beginning of the second century C.E. who is deeply concerned with the decline of ancient Roman customs and virtues. Whatever his sources may be, it is obvious that he presents a compendium, albeit with some new elements, of the traditions connected with the Exodus, which probably comes closest to Lysimachus' account.[90] What characterizes his excursus most, however, is an overall hostile tone, from the beginning to the end. He knows, like Lysimachus,[91] from the very outset that the plague was caused by the Jews—who else could have been meant by *id genus hominum ut invisum deis?* Also, with regard to the occupation of Judea, he chooses the most negative possibility, namely that Moses and his followers expelled the former inhabitants. This is in contrast to both Hecataeus and Strabo, who stress that the country was uninhabited, and comes closest again to Lysimachus, who explicitly mentions that they "maltreated the population" when they reached inhabited country.[92]

When describing the customs introduced by Moses, Tacitus refers to the well-known motif of Jewish impiety. However, this impiety is not only related to the Egyptian religion, as in the other Greco-Egyptian accounts of the Exodus tradition (and as such is pushed to the extreme, for the Jews sacrifice a ram "apparently in derision of Ammon," and they offer the ox "because the Egyptians worship Apis"); in addition, it is viewed as a perversion of the religious practices common to all other human beings. The impiety motif returns even more forcefully when Tacitus deplores the conduct of the proselytes who renounce their ancestral religions, despise the gods, and disown their country. Here speaks the Roman senator who adopts an ancient anti-Jewish motif in order to express his disgust for those who leave the religion of their forefathers and follow the *absurdus sordidusque mos.* There is no doubt that this vituperation chimes with other (elite) Roman ideas of what constituted "proper" religiosity and at the same time has a very concrete political background in the growing Jewish proselytism in the first and early second centuries.[93]

And finally, like most of his predecessors, Tacitus connects with the motif of impiety that of *misanthrōpia:* the Jews are loyal only to their fellow countrymen but express *hostile odium* toward all other people *(adversus omnes)*. This is reminiscent of Hecataeus, Manetho, Apollonius Molon, Diodorus Siculus, Pompeius Trogus, and above all Lysimachus, according to whom the Jews should not show good will to any man and should always offer the worst possible advice. Tacitus makes this clear by pointing out that "they sit apart at meals and sleep apart"—which in itself could be taken as a correct description of Jewish customs but again takes on a hostile tone when he adds: "and although as a people, they are prone to lust, they abstain from intercourse with foreign women; yet among themselves nothing is unlawful."[94]

Altogether, Tacitus' account of the Exodus, in adopting both the impiety and the *misanthrōpia* motifs and in accommodating them to his own time and experience after 70 C.E., is a summary not just of the Alexandrian version[95] but of the mainstream Greco-Egyptian tradition starting with Hecataeus. Through him it became common property of the Western "civilization."

CHAPTER TWO

The Jewish God

ONE GOD

The Jewish notion of a God who is unique and by definition excludes the possibility of other gods besides him[1] is mirrored in most of the pagan discussions about Judaism and its customs and beliefs, mediated to us by a wide range of reactions: from admiration through curiosity and amazement to disapproval and satirical contempt.

What clearly most strikes the Greek and Roman authors is the aniconism of the Jewish God, the evident fact, contrary to all the customs of the Greco-Roman world, that he is invisible and wants to remain invisible, that is, that he does not allow any image to be made of him.[2] One possible and common response to this, which can take a positive as well as a negative connotation, is to identify him with heaven, more specifically with the remote and invisible "heights of heaven" (together with this sometimes goes the notion that he is incorporeal). Related to the "heights of heaven" is the epithet "highest god" *(summus deus),* or "most high," which acknowledges the Jewish God as the highest of many other gods and therefore identifies him with Jupiter or Zeus. Another, and clearly negative, conclusion to be drawn is that he does not exist at all, that the Jews do not recognize any God and therefore are to be regarded as godless or atheists.

Between these two extremes we find the idea that the Jews do worship a God who, or whose name, is unknown *(ignotus* or, according to the later Neoplatonic terminology, *agnōstos)* to the Gentiles. This concept of the unknown Jewish God often implies not only the admission of ignorance on the part of the Gentiles but also, and primarily, the charge of unwillingness on the part of the Jews to share their God with the Gentiles: the Jews separate themselves from the common set of cultural-religious customs and beliefs; they radiate the aura of exclusiveness and arrogance. This charge can easily be combined with the powerful argument of Jewish xenophobia and misanthropy which plays such an important role in the Exodus tradition.

The earliest attempt to comprehend the strangeness of the idea of a God who is not only unique but also aniconic seems to be the equation of the Jewish God with the heights of heaven, which are assumed to be the object of Jewish worship. It may be attested to as early as Theophrastus (372–288/87 B.C.E.),[3] the eminent disciple of Aristotle, who describes in his work *De Pietate* the Jewish custom of sacrifice: "During this whole time [of sacrificing animals and burning them at night], being philosophers by origin, they converse with each other about the deity *(to theion)*, and at nighttime they make observations of the stars, gazing at them and calling on God by prayer."[4] Although Theophrastus does not mention here the Jewish belief in one God, let alone the equation of God with heaven, most scholars agree that at least the former can be presupposed (because of his use of the term *to theion,* "the Divine," which may refer to the concept of the "One Highest Being" according to the pre-Socratic systems).[5] One even may argue that because of the emphasis he puts on the observation of the stars, which obviously evokes prayer as the appropriate response, Theophrastus actually does see in the celestial bodies an expression of God's absoluteness.[6]

The first undeniable evidence of the conclusion that the Jews, because they refuse any images, worship heaven, is Hecataeus.[7] He says of Moses: "He had no images whatsoever of the gods made for them, being of the opinion that God is not in human form *(mē . . . anthrōpomorphon einai ton theon);* rather the Heaven that surrounds the earth is alone divine *(ton . . . ouranon monon einai theon),* and rules the universe *(kai tōn holōn kyrion).*"[8] The description of a Jewish belief in the divinity of heaven, in itself, sounds sympathetic;[9] one should not overlook, however, the context of this remark. Immediately following it, Hecataeus refers to the sacrifices Moses established and to the Jews' "way of life which was somewhat unsocial and hostile to foreigners."[10] Thus, one may well conclude that the Jews differ from all other nations not only in their sacrifices and their way of living but also in their belief in the divinity of heaven, and that as a result of this, the *misoxenos bios* does not apply to the Jewish sacrifices and way of life only, but also to their rejection of images and their worship of heaven. This would, as I have already argued,[11] make the Jewish belief in a God who does not take human form, Jewish monotheism and aniconism, responsible for their *misoxenos bios.*

The very idea that the Jews worship heaven instead of different gods in different images was not invented, as has been long observed, by Hecataeus or any other pagan writer. It obviously goes back to the Jews' own designation of their God as "God of Heaven" (Hebrew: *elohe ha-shamayim,* Aramaic: *elah shemayya*), which was in common use during the Persian period (by the Persians[12] as well as by the Jews)[13] and well into Hellenistic times.[14] This "God of Heaven" could easily be identified with the Persian Ahura Mazda,[15] the Semitic Ba'al Shamem,[16] and the Greek Zeus Olympios.[17] Thus it seems only natural that the Greek philosophers and historians adopted this name in order to describe the Jewish belief in one God exclusively.

The fact that the Jews did not produce images of their God led some to another, more radical conclusion: that the Jews simply were to be regarded as godless. This is exactly the way the Egyptian priest Manetho describes the principles of the Jewish religion as defined by Osarseph/Moses.[18] It is true that Manetho's main concerns are the Egyptian gods and the Jewish disdain for the sacred Egyptian animals, but there can be no doubt that his anger at this blasphemy, and his lack of understanding of this refusal to "worship the gods," reflects the general Greek attitude.[19] Most important (as I have already pointed out), like Hecataeus he combines this with Jewish misanthropy: the Jews are different from all other people in that they do not worship the gods (all other people worship) and in that they refuse to have contact with any other people. Exactly the same link was made about two hundred years later by Apollonius Molon who, according to Josephus, condemned the Jews as atheists and misanthropes.[20] In the eyes of the Greeks there could hardly be a verdict more devastating than this one.

Terentius Varro, the famous scholar of republican Rome, also focuses on the lack of images in the Jewish religion; his approach, however, contrasts sharply with those of Manetho and Hecataeus. In his *Antiquitates Rerum Humanarum et Divinarum,* written between 63 and 47 B.C.E. and transmitted by Augustine, he compares the Jewish with the Roman religion:

> He [Varro] also says that for more than one hundred and seventy years the ancient Romans worshiped the gods without an image *(antiquos Romanos . . . deos sine simulacro coluisse).* "If this usage had continued to our own day," he says, "our worship of the gods would be more devout." And in support of his opinion he adduces, among other things, the testimony of the Jewish people *(testem adhibet . . . gentem Judaeam).* And he ends with the forthright statement that

those who first set up images of the gods for the people diminished reverence in their cities as they added to error, for he wisely judged that gods in the shape of senseless images might easily inspire contempt *(deos facile posse in simulacrorum stoliditate contemni).*[21]

This is one of the most sympathetic statements from a pagan author on the Jewish religion and its custom of worshipping a God with no image, a custom Varro claims also for the ancient Romans. Thus by implication he regards the Jews as more "religious" in the traditional sense than the Romans because they have not betrayed their *patria nomima.* Setting up images of the gods is a deterioration of religion which in the end leads to hatred and even contempt of the gods.

Another possible way to understand the peculiarity of the Jewish concept of God, and integrate it into the Greek or Roman pantheon, was to declare the Jewish God the highest of all gods and thus to identify him with Jupiter or Zeus. This is also suggested, probably for the first time, by Varro, as attested again by Augustine:

> Yet Varro, one of themselves—to a more learned man they cannot point—thought the God of the Jews to be the same as Jupiter *(deum Iudaeorum Iovem putavit),* thinking that it makes no difference by which name he is called, so long as the same thing is understood. I believe that he did it being terrified by his sublimity *(illius summitate deterritus).* Since the Romans habitually worship nothing superior to Jupiter, a fact attested well and openly by their Capitol, and they consider him the king of all the gods *(regem omnium deorum),* and as he perceived that the Jews worship the highest God *(Iudaeos summum deum colere),* he could not but identify him with Jupiter.[22]

Here Varro proposes a very simple equation: Jupiter is the highest god, and the Jews worship the highest god, thus the God of the Jews must be Jupiter.[23] Again, like the related term "God of heaven," the notion of the "highest god" *(summum deum)* is well known among the Jews. The Hebrew or Aramaic equivalent *(el ʿelyon/elaha ʿila'ah)* is verified in the Bible (mainly in the Psalms) and in Jewish literature of the Hellenistic period; as a matter of fact the references occur most frequently from about 200 B.C.E. to the first century B.C.E.[24] It seems to have expressed very well the way the Hellenized Jews of this period saw themselves in a Greek and Roman environment.[25] It comes as no surprise, therefore, that it has been adopted by pagan writers well disposed toward the Jews like Varro. That Varro could distinguish, however, between the idea of *summum deum* (among others) and that of *unum deum* (with no other) is illustrated by another remark quoted by Augustine: "Varro believes that he [Jupiter] is worshipped even by those who worship one God only *(unum Deum solum)*, without an image, though he is called by another name."[26]

A very similar concept to the one presented by Hecataeus, in fact according to most scholars an elaboration of it,[27] can be found in Strabo of Amaseia.[28] Here again, as in Hecataeus and in Varro, the starting point is the peculiarity of the Jewish God *(to theion)*, who cannot be adequately portrayed by either animal or human images. The most appropriate expression for this aniconic being that "encompasses us all and encompasses land and sea" is heaven, or the universe, or (and here he expands Hecataeus, obviously under the influence of the Stoa) "the nature of all that exists." However pantheistic this equation of the Jewish God with the all-embracing heaven and nature may sound, it is certainly an oversimplification to call it just an "error."[29] As we have seen, the Jews did the same, and apart from this, one should not overlook the fact that both Hecataeus and Strabo emphasize the uniqueness of this Heaven-God (Hecataeus: *ton ouranon monon einai theon;* Strabo: *hen touto monon theos*), thereby coming as close as one probably might expect to the Jewish concept of God.

The lack of images as the most distinctive feature of the Jewish religion was also noticed by Livy, the great Roman historian (59 B.C.E.–17 C.E.). In the *Scholia in Lucanum* Livy is quoted as saying: "They [the Jews] do not state *(non nominant)* to which deity pertains the Temple at Jerusalem, nor is any image found there *(neque ullum ibi simulacrum est)*, since they do not think the God partakes of any figure."[30] According to Stern, this remark is taken from the lost 102nd book of Livy's History.[31] It refers to the absence of any statue of the Jewish God in the Temple of Jerusalem, which is, as usual, ascribed to the Jews' rejection of images. By maintaining, however, that they do not *communicate* the name of the God they worship, Livy adds another facet to the possible pagan responses to the strangeness of the Jewish God: secretiveness on the part of the Jews and ignorance on the part of the Gentiles. This comes very close to the concept of the *ignotus* or *incertus deus* which, according to Johannes Lydus, the late antiquarian author of the middle of the sixth century C.E., has been used by Livy himself: "Livy in his general Roman History says that the God worshipped there is unknown *(agnōston)*."[32] It is not clear whether this term *(agnōstos = ignotus* or *incognitus)* goes back to Livy, or whether Lydus attributes here to Livy a Neoplatonic concept.[33] Yet it may well be that Livy used the similar term *incertus* ("uncertain") in connection with the Jewish God,[34] as first attested by Lucan (39–65 C.E.),[35] who in turn, in his historical material, is believed to depend on Livy.[36]

Apion does not mention the nature of the Jewish God (according to what we know about his arguments from Josephus) but complains, within the context of the discussion about Alexandrian citizenship, that the Jews "do not worship the same gods as the Alexandrians" (*eosdem deos quos Alexandrini non colunt*).[37] From Josephus' response it becomes clear that he refers to the native Egyptian gods against whom Josephus argues so fervently ("you worship and breed with so much care animals that are hostile to humanity").[38] Interestingly enough, the next charge which Josephus has Apion raising against the Jews is their inclination to foment sedition (*seditio*) and their notorious concord (*concordia*) among themselves.[39] Thus again, as in Hecataeus, Manetho, and Apollonius Molon, the peculiar Jewish solidarity and dislike of those who do not belong to them are linked with their worshipping a God who is different from all other gods.

Most remarkable is the way in which Tacitus, in his famous digression about the Jews, describes the Jewish belief in one God:

> The Egyptians worship many animals and monstrous images; the Jews conceive of one god only, and that with the mind only (*mente sola unumque numen intellegunt*); they regard as impious those who make from perishable materials representations of gods in man's image; that supreme and eternal being (*summum illud et aeternum*) is to them incapable of representation and without end (*neque imitabile neque interiturum*). Therefore they set up no statues in their cities, still less in their temples; this flattery is not paid their kings, nor this honour given to the Caesars.[40]

As with many of his predecessors, Tacitus' starting point is the refusal of the Jews to set up images or even to conceive of their God in a concrete fashion; it is "with the mind only," not with images, that they "imagine" their God (already here Tacitus adopts a "philosophical" tone which characterizes the whole paragraph). Contrasting this sharply with the religion of the Egyptians, who worship "monstrous images" (*effigies compositas*),[41] he seems much more sympathetic to the Jews than to the Egyptians.

Most scholars dealing with this paragraph have found it useful to compare it with what Tacitus has to say about the religion of the Germans in his *Germania:*[42]

Apart from this they [the Germans] deem it incompatible with the majesty of the heavenly host *(ex magnitudine caelestium)* to confine the gods within walls *(nec cohibere parietibus deos),* or to mould them into any likeness of the human face *(neque in ullam humani oris speciem adsimulare):* they consecrate groves and coppices, and they give the divine names to that mysterious something *(deorumque nominibus appellant secretum illud)* which is visible only in the eyes of faith *(quod sola reverentia vident).*[43]

It is obvious that Tacitus views the aniconic character of both the German and the Jewish religions with respect, having in mind probably the aniconism of the ancient Roman religion, which was evoked so vividly by Varro, but perhaps also referring to a continuous pattern of Roman religion.[44] The fact that the expression *ex magnitudine caelestium* is missing in the description of the Jewish religion has been taken by some scholars[45] as a slightly more negative approach toward the Jews and as a sign of greater sympathy with the Germans. This seems to me a somewhat arbitrary overinterpretation of the text which does not do full justice to the core of both paragraphs.

To begin with, whereas Tacitus is rather vague with regard to the German gods (they are the "heavenly host" and the "gods" but also "something mysterious"), his description of the Jewish God is very clear. As a matter of fact, Tacitus is among the few authors in antiquity[46] who declare explicitly that the Jews worship one God only *(unum numen* which is, apart from not being *imitabile* and *interiturum,* also *summum* and *aeternum).* In describing the "one God" of the Jews as *summum,* he comes very close again to Varro and to the Jewish notion of *el ʿelyon,* and in defining it as "eternal" and "endless," that is, without beginning and end, he develops a highly philosophical and rather abstract concept of the Jewish religion *(sola mente)* which could hardly seem more empathic. Even the offensive habit of not setting up statues for the Caesars finds a sympathetic, though slightly ironical, explanation.

This positive explanation of the aniconism of the Jewish religion and its consequences for an abstract comprehension of God stand in conspicuous contrast to the overall tone of the digression. As we have noticed already,[47] the digression distinguishes between two categories of Jewish customs, those which are "maintained by their antiquity," and those which are "base and abominable." The idea of the "one god only" actually belongs to the second category; it is meant to illustrate that, in contrast to the "belief about the world below" which is very similar to the one of the Egyptians, the Jewish ideas of "heavenly things are quite the opposite." Thus, the belief in *unum numen* forms the end of the "base and abominable" customs; it is followed only by Tacitus' fierce rejection of the suggestion that the Jewish worship could be identified with the cult of Dionysus, which ends with the most contemptuous verdict: *Iudaeorum mos absurdus sordidusque*. If we also consider that the paragraph on the Jewish customs begins with the devastating statement that the "new religious practices" introduced by Moses were "opposed to those of all other human beings" because they "regard as profane all that we hold sacred" *(profana . . . omnia quae apud nos sacra)* and "permit all that we abhor" *(concessa . . . quae nobis incesta)*, then it becomes very clear that the positive assessment of the Jewish God is embedded in an overwhelmingly anti-Jewish context, or to put it differently, that even the profound anti-Jewish bias of the digression as a whole could not prevent Tacitus from, consciously or unconsciously, describing the Jewish God in a surprisingly favorable way.[48]

Tacitus' contemporary Juvenal takes up in his satires the identification of the Jewish God with the highest heaven, which he calls *summum caelum* and *caeli numen*. In *Satura* VI he ridicules the Jewish beggars of Rome, satirizing an interpreter of dreams as "interpreter of the laws of Jerusalem" *(interpres legum Solymarum)*, "high priestess of the tree" *(magna sacerdos arboris)*, and "trusty go-between of highest heaven" *(summi fida internuntia caeli)*.[49]

The *caeli numen* ("divinity of heaven") is mentioned in *Satura* XIV, which will be analyzed below.[50] In this context it is important to notice that Juvenal qualifies the worship of *caeli numen* by adding "nothing but the clouds" *(nil praeter nubes)*,[51] thus giving it a decidedly absurd ring: the worship of highest heaven is not a serious and solemn cult in the open air (or at least under trees) but the adoration of something which is of a very volatile and changeable nature—clouds, that is, almost nothing.[52] By this Juvenal has given the old motif of the worship of heaven a deliberately negative tint.

Of the Greek authors of the second century C.E., the Alexandrian astronomer Ptolemy (Claudius Ptolemaeus) comes back to the accusation of godlessness introduced by his Egyptian predecessor Manetho and repeated by the Greek rhetor Apollonius Molon. According to his astrological work *Apotelesmatica*, the Jews are "bold" *(thraseis)*, "godless" *(atheoi)* and "scheming" *(epibouleutikoi)* because they are "more closely familiar to Aries and Mars."[53] Whereas the boldness may refer to the revolts under Trajan and Hadrian,[54] there is no further indication which explains the godlessness; it presumably goes back to the ancient Egyptian strand of anti-Jewish tradition which finds its most graphic expression in the Egyptian version of the Exodus.

The first author who explicitly connects the aniconism of the Jewish God and his identification with heaven to the idea that he also must be incorporeal is Numenius of Apamea (second half of the second century C.E.), the admirer of oriental cults and precursor of Neoplatonism. This is mentioned by Origen in his *Contra Celsum* where he regards Numenius "the Pythagorean" to be "much better than Celsus": "In the first book on 'The God' where he [Numenius] speaks of the nations that believe God to be incorporeal *(asōmatos),* he also included the Jews among them, and did not hesitate to quote the sayings of the prophets in his book and to give them an allegorical interpretation."[55]

According to Lydus, Numenius was also of the opinion "that the power of this [the Jewish] god is not to be shared by any other *(akoinōnēton),* and that he is the father of all the gods *(patera pantōn tōn theōn),* and that he deems any other god unworthy of having a share in his cult."[56] It is not "the power" of the Jewish God which is not to be shared by any other god, but the Jewish God himself is *akoinōnētos,* that is, "unsociable" in the sense of "exclusive";[57] he does not allow any other god besides himself. The phrase "father of all gods" rather stands in contrast to this, but it seems to be merely a reverence toward the pagan pantheon, and is at any rate almost revoked by the further explanation "that he deems any other god unworthy of having a share in his cult." We do not know exactly how Numenius wanted the *akoinōnētos (theos)* to be understood because we do not have the context of his dictum, but it seems most likely that it is his exclusiveness and his intolerance of other gods. This can be used in a negative, anti-Jewish way[58] as well as in a positive way, and we do not have clear proof here for either of these possibilities; however, the impression of an overall sympathetic attitude to be gathered from Numenius' scattered quotations[59] speaks in favor of the latter.

The work of Numenius' contemporary Celsus, of Egyptian or Syrian origin, the "eclectic philosopher, whose views were tinged mainly by Middle Platonism . . . and who also made free use of the arsenal of Stoic argumentation,"[60] has been lost but can be reconstructed to a considerable degree by the detailed quotations in Origen's *Contra Celsum.* Celsus' *Alēthēs Logos*[61] is mainly a refutation of the false and dangerous doctrines of Christianity, thus also dealing quite extensively with Judaism. The most striking characteristic of the Jewish religion as defined by their leader Moses (who was of Egyptian origin)[62] is the belief in one God:

The goatherds and shepherds thought that there was one God *(hena theon)* called the Most High *(hypsiston)*, or Adonai, or the Heavenly One *(ouranion)*, or Sabaoth, or however they like to call this world *(tonde ton kosmon)*; and they acknowledged nothing more . . . It makes no difference whether one calls the supreme God *(ton epi pasi theon)* by the name Zeus used among the Greeks, or by that, for example, used among the Indians, or by that among the Egyptians.[63]

Celsus combines here the most common designations of the Jewish God which were in circulation so far ("one god," "Most High" = *el ʿelyon*, "Heaven"), adding only the Hebrew names "Adonai" and "Sabaoth," which he obviously has taken from the Bible.[64] In saying that this divine being may also be called Zeus or any other name different peoples chose to give him, he is stressing that the "one God" of the Jews is none other than the supreme god worshipped under different names by different peoples. His focus is not to describe the peculiarities of the Jewish belief in one God but to make it clear that the Jews cannot take pride in being different from other peoples.

This is the issue of paramount importance in his second, much larger, statement about the Jewish religion and its customs:

If indeed in accordance with these principles the Jews maintained their own law *(ton idion nomon)*, we should not find fault with them but rather with those who have abandoned their own traditions and professed those of the Jews. If, as though they had some deeper wisdom, they are proud and turn away from the society of others *(semnynontai te kai tēn allōn koinōnian . . . apostrephontai)* on the ground that they are not on the same level of piety, they have already heard that not even their doctrine of heaven *(to peri ouranou dogma)* is their own but . . . was also held long ago by the Persians, as Herodotus shows in one place. "For their [the Persians'] custom," he says, "is to go up to the highest peaks of the mountains to offer sacrifice to Zeus, and to call the whole circle of heaven *(ton kyklon panta tou ouranou)* Zeus." I think, therefore, that it makes no difference whether we call Zeus the Most High *(hypsiston)*, or Zen, or Adonai, or Sabaoth, or Ammon like the Egyptians, or Papaeus like the Scythians.[65]

The polemical tone of this whole passage is set at the very beginning. The targets are not only the Jews as such but also the proselytes who have "abandoned their own [that is, of course, 'pagan'] traditions"; the Jews actually are to be praised for holding to their *nomoi* because keeping the ancient customs and *patria nomima* despite many obstacles is in itself commendable.

Whether the continuation that "they are proud and turn away from the society of others" refers to the proselytes only, or to all Jews, is not entirely clear, but the reason for their pride—their conviction that they have obtained an exceptional "level of piety"—obviously applies to all Jews. Celsus thus, like many of his predecessors, combines Jewish exclusiveness with the essence of their religion; furthermore, he gives it a tint of arrogance which we have not observed so far.

That Celsus' main subject is the alleged Jewish conviction of being different from and superior to other people becomes even more apparent in the continuation, which deals also with circumcision and abstinence from pork:

> Moreover, they would certainly not be holier than other people *(oude kata tauta hagiōteroi tōn allōn an eien)* because they are circumcised; for the Egyptians and Colchians did this before they did. Nor because they abstain from pigs; for the Egyptians also do this, and in addition abstain also from goats, sheep, oxen and fish. And Pythagoras and his disciples abstain from beans and from all living things. Nor is it at all likely that they are in favour with God and are loved any more than other folk *(oud' eudokimein para tō theō kai stergesthai diaphorōs ti tōn allōn toutous eikos)* . . . Let this chorus depart, then, after suffering the penalty of their arrogance *(alazoneias)*. For they do not know the great God *(ton megan theon),* but have been led on and deceived by Moses' sorcery and have learnt about that for no good purpose.[66]

Here the same argument is made: the Jews cannot claim to have invented these customs and concepts or to be the only ones adhering to them. Therefore, they cannot argue that they have a special relation to God, that they are a chosen people—all this is an expression of their arrogance, for which they have already received the proper punishment (by being driven out of their land). The devastating conclusion, that "they do not know the great God" because they have been "deceived by Moses' sorcery," stands to some extent in contrast to his former argument that the Jewish God is identical with the "Most High" of any other people, but it is no doubt meant to be the climax of the whole paragraph: despite their claim of superiority the Jews are in reality misled by sorcery and do not know the true god. Celsus does not reveal who this "great god" is but we can be sure that he is not the God of the Jews. Celsus' later identification of the Jewish God with the god of the Christians[67] only adds to his contempt for the arrogance in believing the Jews are chosen and different from other peoples.

Quite another tone is set in the *Historia Romana* of Cassius Dio (ca. 160 C.E.–230 C.E.), the famous Greek historian and Roman official of high rank from Asia Minor. When relating the capture of Jerusalem by Pompey in 63 B.C.E. he digresses on the country and the customs of the Jews:

> They have also another name that they have acquired: the country has been named Judea, and the people themselves Jews. I do not know how this title came to be given them, but it applies also to the rest of mankind, although of alien nation *(alloethneis ontes)*, who affect their customs *(ta nomima autōn . . . zēlousi)*. This class exists even among the Romans, and though often repressed has increased to a very great extent and has won its way to the right of freedom in its observances.
>
> They are distinguished from the rest of mankind *(kechōridatai de apo tōn loipōn anthrōpōn)* in practically every detail of life, and especially by the fact that they do not honour any of the usual gods *(hoti tōn men allōn theōn oudena timōsin)*, but show extreme reverence for one particular divinity *(hena de tina ischyrōs sebousin)*. They never had any statue of him in Jerusalem itself, but believing him to be unnamable and invisible *(arrēton de dē kai aeidē)*, they worship him in the most extravagant fashion on earth.[68]

Like his colleagues in the first century C.E., Cassius Dio seems to be concerned mainly with Jewish proselytism, confirming the view that proselytism was a "continuing power . . . in the time of the Severi."[69] He knows very well that anyone from a different *ethnos* can become a Jew by accepting the Jewish *nomima,* and that many "even among the Romans" have been attracted by these customs. He does not describe the Jewish customs in detail, except for the belief in one God, but emphasizes that the Jews, in following their *nomima,* separate themselves from all other human beings. It is most remarkable, however, that this notion of Jewish separateness lacks any negative tinge (quite in contrast to his predecessors, especially to Celsus), let alone any accusation of *misanthrōpia.*

The details he gives about the most peculiar feature of the Jewish religion, the belief in one God, are well known: starting from the observation that there is *one* God only, he immediately proceeds to that God's aniconic (cf. Tacitus) and nameless character. It has been suggested that in this combination of "unnamable" and "invisible" Dio may depend on Livy, his "presumed source for the history of the late Roman republic";[70] however, in using the particular word *arrētos,* which can mean "unnamable" as well as "unutterable" (the latter in the sense of "ineffable"),[71] Dio goes beyond Livy; he may have been aware that the Jewish God does have a (secret) name which cannot be pronounced. Whether or not this is the case, the respectful tone of this whole passage cannot be overlooked (he goes on to mention the beauty of the Jerusalem Temple). Unfortunately, he refuses to answer the questions of "who" the Jewish God "is" and "why he has been so honored," because there are so many explanations and because "these matters have naught to do with this history."[72]

In the third century we can observe another aspect in descriptions of the Jewish God, obviously under the influence of Gnosticism and Neoplatonism, namely the notion of the Jewish God as the demiurge. The first author who explicitly identifies the God of the Jews with the demiurge is Porphyry (232/33 to the beginning of the fourth century C.E.), as quoted by Lydus: "But Porphyry in his Commentary on the Oracles says that the god worshipped by the Jews is the second god *(dis epekeina),* i.e. the creator of all things *(ton tōn holōn dēmiourgon)* whom the Chaldaean in his discourse on the gods counts to be the second from the first god *(deuteron apo tou hapax epekeina),* i.e. the Good."[73]

The distinction between the *hapax epekeina,* in Lewy's translation the "uniquely"[74] or "singly transcendent,"[75] and the *dis epekeina,* the "doubly transcendent" or the one "to whom duality is attached,"[76] is of paramount importance for the philosophical system of the Chaldean Oracles; it depends, as Lewy has convincingly argued, on the Neoplatonic pattern of a first = highest and a second principle, the former being pure thinking and producing the noetic form of the sensible world, the latter being the demiurgic intellect and fashioning the world according to the primordial archetypes.[77] By identifying the Jewish God with the demiurge, the second principle, Porphyry integrates him into the Neoplatonic system and subordinates him to the first principle, the pure intellect.[78] Moreover, in following the Chaldean designation of the first god as the "Good," he clearly gives the second = Jewish God a negative connotation.[79]

The notion of the Jewish God as the demiurge is also ascribed by Lydus to Porphyry's student Iamblichus (third/fourth century C.E.), as well as to the much later Neoplatonic philosophers Syrianus (fifth century C.E.)

and Proclus (second half of the fifth century C.E.).[80] It appears again in the fourth century in the letters of Julian, the "apostate" emperor, although embedded there in a much broader context; as a matter of fact, Julian (331–363 C.E.) appears to be a truly syncretistic writer who amalgamates some of the most important pagan ideas about the nature of the Jewish God (nourished by his profound knowledge of the Septuagint).

In his famous treatise against the Christians, *Contra Galilaeos*, he is torn between his contempt for the Christians, who betrayed the gods of the pagans and the God of the Jews alike, and his sympathy for the Jews and their customs; accordingly, his remarks are ambiguous and even contradictory, depending on which attitude prevails. Thus, when at the very outset he accuses the Jews of atheism *(tēn atheotēta)*, he indeed follows an old argument already set up by Manetho and Apollonius Molon;[81] but it is probably more important to take into account that it is the Christians who are his main target here, who "from both religions . . . have gathered what has been engrafted like powers of evil, as it were, on these nations—atheism from the Jewish levity, and a sordid and slovenly way of living from our indolence and vulgarity."[82]

A recurrent motif in the treatise, which obviously is not directed against the Christians but exercises a kind of rationalistic Bible criticism, is the jealousy of the Jewish God. A god who does not want man to share his wisdom (Gen. 3:22) must be called envious *(baskanos)*.[83] God even boasts of being jealous (Ex. 20:5)—but what kind of quality is that, because "if a man is jealous and envious you think him blameworthy, whereas if God is called jealous you think it a divine quality?"[84] Moreover, if he is so jealous that he does not tolerate any other god except himself, "how is it that he did not himself restrain them . . .? Can it be that he was not able to do so, or did he not wish even from the beginning to prevent the other gods also from being worshipped?"[85]

With regard to the demiurge, Julian seems to follow the Neoplatonic distinction between the supreme being and the demiurge;[86] his main concern, however, is not this distinction, but to make clear that the Jewish concept of the "immediate creator of this universe" *(ton prosechē tou kosmou toutou dēmiourgon)* is inferior to Plato; because, according to it, "God is the creator of nothing that is incorporeal *(asōmatōn)*, but is only the disposer of matter that already existed *(hylēs de hypokeimenēs kosmētora)*."[87] The inferiority of the Jewish demiurge becomes even more apparent when one considers Israel's claim to be the chosen people. This claim, in fact, also limits the power of its God, for if he is the God of all of us alike, and the creator of all why did he neglect us? Wherefore it is natural to think that the God of the Hebrews was not the begetter of the whole universe with lordship over the whole, but rather . . . that he is confined within limits, and that since his empire has bounds we must conceive of him as only one of the crowd of other gods. Then are we to pay further heed to you because you or one of your stock imagined the God of the universe, though in any case you attained only to a bare conception of Him?[88]

Thus the Jewish God preferred to limit himself and not to be the god of the pagans, who therefore do not owe him a debt of gratitude.[89]

Julian's ambivalent attitude toward the Jewish God reveals itself most clearly when he deals with the Christian proselytes. On the one hand, "they have abandoned the everliving gods and have gone over to the corpse of the Jew,"[90] because "the Hebrews . . . have persuaded you to desert to them";[91] on the other hand, it would have been much better if they had stayed with the Jews instead of becoming Christians: "For you would be worshiping one god instead of many *(hena gar anti pollōn theōn)* . . . And though you would be following a law that is harsh and stern and contains much that is savage and barbarous, instead of our mild and humane laws, . . . yet you would be more holy and purer than now in your forms of worship."[92]

It is precisely in this context of the comparison between Christians and Jews that he arrives at his most sympathetic judgments on the Jews. The Jewish customs may be "savage and barbarous," but at the same time the Hebrews at least have "precise laws concerning religious worship and countless sacred things and observances which demand a priestly life and profession."[93] Thus he even can come to the conclusion that "the Jews agree with the Gentiles, except that they believe in only one God *(hena theon monon).* That is indeed peculiar to them and strange to us *(autōn men idion, hēmōn de allotrion),* since all the rest we have in a manner in common with them."[94] In the end, the Jewish monotheism, which he emphasizes time and again,[95] remains the only true distinction between Jews and Gentiles. And yet, even this distinction in a way can be overcome, and Julian forces himself to the confession: "but nevertheless, I revere always the God of Abraham, Isaac, and Jacob, . . . who was ever gracious to me and to those who worshiped him as Abraham did, for he is a very great and powerful God *(megas te ōn pany kai dynatos)*—but he has nothing to do with you [the Christians]."[96] Jews and Gentiles come very close, indeed, in paradoxical contrast with the Christians, who so stubbornly claim to be the heirs of Judaism.

The tone is slightly different in his letter to Theodorus. Julian expresses again his sympathy for the Jews who are "in part god-fearing" *(en merei theosebeis)*, and for their God who is "truly most powerful *(dynatōtatos)* and most good *(agathōtatos)* and governs this world of sense *(ton aisthēton kosmon)*, and, as I well know, is worshipped by us also under other names."[97] However, and here he becomes more explicit than in his letter to the Christians, the latter is exactly the problem with the Jews: we acknowledge their God but they refuse to "conciliate the other gods also" who "they think have been allotted to us Gentiles only."[98] Thus we are confronted again with the old motif of Jewish separateness and exclusiveness, which is connected with their belief in one God who arrogantly does not allow for other gods in the double sense that the Jews are forbidden to worship any of them, and that the Gentiles are forbidden to identify their gods with the Jewish God. The very special relationship with their God the Jews claim for themselves is the true offense and the result of their "barbaric conceit" *(alazoneia:* Julian uses here the same word as Celsus does in a similar context), which in the end prevents them from becoming fully integrated into the civilized world.

It is only natural that also in his famous letter "To the Community of the Jews"[99] he refers sympathetically to the Jewish God. He promises, no doubt shortly before his departure for the Persian campaign,[100] to abolish unjust taxes and levies imposed on the Jews in order to enable them to "offer more fervid prayers for my reign to the Most High God, the Creator" *(tō pantōn kreittoni kai dēmiourgō theō)* or, as he also calls him, the "Mighty God" *(tō meizoni);* and he even hints at the possibility that he may, after the war with Persia, rebuild the "sacred city of Jerusalem" and may personally "glorify the Most High God *(tō kreittoni)* therein."[101]

The term *to kreitton* or *ho kreittōn* Julian uses here for the designation of the "Most High God" seems to be rather late and distinctively pagan and Christian,[102] in contrast to the very early and Biblical *hypsistos theos.*[103] As in his treatise against the Christians he identifies, in the typical Neoplatonic manner, the "Most High God" of the Jews with the demiurge,[104] but here he refrains from any allusion to the inferiority or inadequacy of this demiurge-God. His main concern in this letter obviously is not theological subtlety but to urge the Jews to pray for him and for the success of his campaign—which was, to be sure, also meant to prove the superiority of the pagan gods (and of the Jewish God!) against the Christian perversion of religion.

Probably at the end of the fourth century C.E., the unknown author of the biography of Claudius within the *Historia Augusta* again refers to the concept of the unknown god, familiar, though under different terms, from Livy (*non nominant* and *agnōstos theos*), Lucan (*incertus deus = adēlos theos*), and Cassius Dio *(arrētos theos)*. Discussing the life span of human beings, he mentions that Moses, when complaining that he had to die at the age of one hundred and twenty-five years, received the reply "from an unknown god" *(incertum numen)* that no one should ever live longer.[105] The author comes closest, then, to Livy's (according to Lydus) and Lucan's terminology; by adding *ferunt* ("so they say") to *incertum numen,* he insinuates a well-established tradition which he probably, but not necessarily, wants to derive from the Jews themselves.

With this the range of pagan responses to the unique and aniconic Jewish God has been covered. The notion of the Jewish God to be identified with the "highest god," however, needs some further consideration. It presupposes that any "foreign" god, even the "unknown" Jewish God, might be integrated into the pagan pantheon, and might be identified with different Greek or Roman gods.

THEOCRASY

The concept of theocrasy, the "blending" of various gods in one "highest" god, evolved from the idea that the different gods and the different religions represented by them were in fact the manifestation of one universal divinity—despite the differences which have developed in the course of history, and no matter by which name one prefers to call it. We have observed this already with Varro, who identifies the Jewish God with Jupiter and states explicitly: "it makes no difference by which name he is called, so long as the same thing is understood."[106] Augustine, summarizing the idea that Jupiter is "the soul of this material world *(corporei huius mundi animus),* filling and moving this entire mass which is composed and compacted of the four elements," probably refers to Varro when he angrily and ironically concludes:

> If they are not ashamed, let the one god Jupiter be all this that I have said and more that I haven't said . . . Let him be all these gods and goddesses *(hi omnes dii deaeque sit unus Jupiter);* or, as some will have it, let all these be parts of him, or powers of his *(sive sint . . . omnia ista partes eius sive virtutes eius).* This is the view of those who hold that he is the world soul *(mundi animum),* a view which is that of the supposedly great and learned.[107]

The notion of *mundi animus* and the four elements points to stoicism as the philosophical concept behind Varro[108] and the idea of theocrasy, and M. Hengel has argued convincingly that in fact it goes back to Zeno himself, the "Greco-Phoenician founder of the Stoa,"[109] to whom Diogenes Laertius attributes the dictum: "God is one and the same *(hen t'einai theon)* with Reason *(nous)*, Fate *(heimarmenē)* and Zeus; he is also called by many other names *(pollas t'heteras onomasias prosonomazestai)*."[110]

It has been suggested that the first reference to the Jews in Italy, the expulsion of Jewish missionaries from Rome in 139 B.C.E., may be taken as proof that some syncretistic Jews from Asia Minor responded positively to the pagan concept of theocrasy and propagated in Rome a syncretistic cult of Jupiter Sabazius.[111] However, the evidence for this is anything but unequivocal. The only witness is Valerius Maximus (beginning of the first century C.E.), whose full text is not preserved but has come down to us only in two epitomes, one by Iulius Paris (fourth century C.E.?) and one by Ianuarius Nepotianus (fourth-fifth century C.E.?).[112] According to Paris' epitome, "Cn. Cornelius Hispalus, *praetor peregrinus* in the year of the consulate of P. Popilius Laenas and L. Calpurnius,[113] . . . compelled the Jews, who attempted to infect the Roman customs with the cult of Jupiter Sabazius *(qui Sabazi Iovis cultu Romanos inficere mores conati erant)*, to return to their homes."[114]

Sabazius was a Phrygian god whose orgiastic cult came to Athens as early as the fifth century B.C.E. and who is very well attested in the imperial period. He was identified with Dionysus and, in Asia Minor, with Zeus-Jupiter.[115] The equation of the Jewish God with Jupiter Sabazius no doubt was facilitated by the similarity of "Sabazius" with either "Sabaoth"[116] or "Sabbath,"[117] and those who are in favor of a Jewish syncretistic cult point to Asia Minor as the fertile soil of Jewish-pagan blends and to the possibility that the expulsion of the "heterodox Jews" from Rome was arranged by Simeon the Maccabee's delegation to Rome, which allegedly visited Rome in 139 B.C.E.[118] This is, however, mere conjecture, and especially the latter argument is invalidated for chronological reasons.[119] It seems most likely, then, that the "Jupiter Sabazius" is either a corruption of "Iao Sabaoth" by Valerius Maximus' source[120] (or by the epitomist Iulius Paris or his medieval copyists respectively)[121] or another piece of evidence for the *pagan* attempt to identify the Jewish God with Jupiter, the highest God of the Roman pantheon.[122] From a historical point of view it is more probable that the Jews tried to introduce their "original" Jewish cult[123] in Rome and that later on, either by Valerius Maximus or by his source, this cult was identified with the one of Jupiter Sabazius.

The most far-reaching and prominent evidence for the concept of theocrasy in pagan antiquity is the famous saying of the Oracle of Clarus, preserved in a quotation by Macrobius from Cornelius Labeo (third century C.E.);[124] the date of the Oracle itself, of course, is uncertain, although the oracular cult of Clarus is well known from, for example, Tacitus and Iamblichus and seems to have been very popular in the second and third century C.E.[125] After quoting the famous Orphic verse "One is Zeus, one Hades, one Sun, one Dionysus" *(heis Zeus, heis Aidēs, heis Helios, heis Dionysos)*, Macrobius goes on to bolster this equation by means of the Oracle of Clarus:

> The authority of this last line is supported by an oracle of Apollo of Clarus, in which yet another name is attached to the sun, which is called in the same sacred verses, among other names, by the name of Iao *(Iaō)*. For when Apollo of Clarus was asked who among the gods should be identified with him that is called Iao he declared as follows:
> > "But if the understanding is little and the mind feeble,
> > Then ponder that Iao is the supreme god among all *(ton pantōn hypaton theon emmen Iaō)*,
> > In winter he is Hades, at the beginning of the spring he is Zeus,
> > In summer he is Helios, while in autumn he is the graceful Dionysus."[126]
>
> The meaning of this oracle, and the explanation of the deity and the name by which Iao is denoted Liber pater and the sun, are expounded by Cornelius Labeo in a book entitled "On The Oracle of Apollo of Clarus."[127]

According to Macrobius and Cornelius Labeo respectively, the Orphic equation of Zeus, Hades, Sun, and Dionysus is confirmed by the Oracle of Clarus, which moreover identifies these four gods, who represent the four seasons, with Iao.[128] This Iao is "the supreme god" in the sense that he incorporates the four mentioned gods = seasons, the emphasis being put, however (at least according to Macrobius/Cornelius Labeo), on the equation of Iao with Helios ("yet another name is attached to the *sun,* which is called . . . Iao") and Pater Liber = Dionysus. Both equations are well attested, and whereas there is no further evidence for the equation Iao = Hades, the identification of Iao with Zeus obviously depends on the idea of the "supreme God."

Neither the Oracle nor Macrobius/Cornelius Labeo says explicitly that Iao, the embodiment of Hades, Zeus, Helios, and Dionysus, is the *Jewish* God. There can be little doubt, however, that the Oracle and Macrobius/Cornelius Labeo knew very well that Iao is the name of the God of the Jews. This is evident from the pagan authors who mention the name Iao as well as from the use of Iao in the magical papyri, and from the identification of Iao with Helios and with Dionysus; one therefore need not refer to the many Jews living in Asia Minor in particular in order to explain the Oracle.[129] Nevertheless, it is clear that it is not the Jewishness of the "supreme god" Iao which is emphasized; "Iao," rather, seems to be a kind of code, probably evoked by his magical potency (cf. the mention of the *Orgia* which should kept in secrecy), for the unifying tendency of neo-Pythagorean and neo-Platonic philosophy in late antiquity.[130]

The "theoretician" of the identification of the Jewish God with Dionysus is, as in the case of the Jewish abhorrence of eating pork, Plutarch (ca. 46–120 C.E.). One section of his *Quaestiones Convivales* is devoted to the question "Who the God of the Jews is." After Plutarch's brother Lamprias has hinted at the possible identity of Dionysus with Adonis and connected the Jews' dislike of the pig with the fact that "Adonis is said to have been slain by the boar,"[131] the Athenian Moeragenes embarks upon a long digression in which he identifies the Jewish worship with the cult of Dionysus.[132] His first argument refers to the resemblance of the Dionysian rites with what seems to be a mixture of different Jewish autumn feasts:

> First, he said, the time and character of the greatest, most sacred holiday of the Jews clearly befit Dionysus. When they celebrate their so-called Fast, at the height of the vintage, they set out tables of all sorts of fruit under tents and huts plaited for the most part of vines and ivy. They call the first of the days of the feast Tabernacles (*skēnē*). A few days later they celebrate another festival, this time identified with Bacchus not through obscure hints but plainly called by his name, a festival that is a sort of "Procession of Branches" or "Thyrsus Procession," in which they enter the temple each carrying a thyrsus. What they do after entering we do not know, but it is probable that the rite is a Bacchic revelry, for in fact they use little trumpets to invoke their god as do the Argives at their Dionysia.[133]

This description for the most part goes very well with the Feast of Tabernacles (*Sukkot*), which Plutarch himself calls by the name *skēnē* ("tent").[134]

What he considers to be a different feast, identified with Bacchus, is probably *Shemini Azeret,* the feast that immediately follows *Sukkot* and marks the end of the seven days period.[135] In any case, the thyrsus procession (the *thyrsos* is the *lulav,* "palm branch") which according to him characterizes this particular feast, is part of the celebration of all seven days of *Sukkot* (but not of *Shemini Azeret*). The use of the "little trumpet" *(salpinx)* also belongs to *Sukkot* (but to other rituals in the Temple as well). The only feature which does not fit with *Sukkot* (nor with the joyous character of both the Dionysian rites and his description of the Feast of Tabernacles) is the "Fast" *(nēsteia).* It may well be that it is a confusion with the Day of Atonement *(Yom Kippur)* which precedes the Feast of Tabernacles.[136]

Moeragenes' next argument relates the Sabbath to Dionysus (the Bacchants are called *Sabi,* and the Jews "keep the Sabbath by inviting each other to drink and to enjoy wine"),[137] and finally he points to the outfit of the High Priest ("a mitre and clad in a gold-embroidered fawnskin," "bells attached to his clothes and ringing below him as he walks"), which resembles the one of Dionysus and his entourage, and to the "noise as an element in their nocturnal festivals": "all this surely befits (they might say)"—and Plutarch leaves no doubt that he agrees with this assertion—"no divinity but Dionysus."[138]

Plutarch's positive and sympathetic approach (as is also the case with his reaction to the abstinence from pork)[139] becomes even more remarkable if we finally compare it with his contemporary Tacitus. Immediately after his implicitly but reluctantly positive description of the *unum numen* of the Jews, Tacitus mentions the suggested identification with "Father Liber," that is, Dionysus:

> But since their priests used to chant to the accompaniment of pipes and drums and to wear garlands of ivy, and because a golden vine was found in their temple, some have thought that they were devotees of Father Liber *(Liberum patrem coli),* the conqueror of the East, in spite of the incongruity of their customs. For Liber established festive rites of a joyous nature, while the ways of the Jews are preposterous and mean *(Iudaeorum mos absurdus sordidusque).*[140]

Tacitus thus fiercely rejects any possible similarity between the cult of Dionysus and Jewish rites (let alone between the two gods). He is definitely not in favor of admitting the Jewish God to the Roman pantheon.

If the Jewish God is invisible and aniconic but nevertheless does exist, one wonders what kind of worship would be appropriate for him. Of course, the Temple in Jerusalem was well known to most of the Greek and Roman authors dealing with the origin and the customs of the Jews,[141] but Gentiles were not allowed to enter it, and its services and sacrifices were surrounded with an aura of mystery and secrecy.

One particularly malevolent way to "reveal" the alleged mystery of the Jewish God to a curious and hostile audience is the famous fable of the ass-worship *(onolatreia)* of the Jews, which was later also associated with the Christians.[142] It can be traced back to the writer Mnaseas of Patara in Lycia (about 200 B.C.E.), a student of Eratosthenes, the philologian, librarian, and educator of the royal princes in Alexandria. His books (mythological tales and *thaumasia*) are lost, but he is quoted several times by Josephus in his *Contra Apionem*.

Among these quotations is the story about the statue of an ass in the Jewish Temple in Jerusalem:

> This model of piety [Apion] derides us again in a story which he at-
> tributes to Mnaseas. The latter, according to Apion, relates that in
> the course of a long war between the Jews and the Idumeans, an in-
> habitant of an Idumean city, called Dorii, who worshipped Apollo
> and bore (so we are told) the name of Zabidus, came out to the Jews
> and promised to deliver into their hands Apollo, the god of his city,
> who would visit our temple if they all took their departure. The Jews
> all believed him; whereupon Zabidus constructed an apparatus of
> wood, inserted in it three rows of lamps, and put it over his person.
> Thus arrayed he walked about, presenting the appearance to distant
> onlookers of stars perambulating the earth. Astounded at this amaz-
> ing spectacle, the Jews kept their distance, in perfect silence. Mean-
> while, Zabidus stealthily passed into the sanctuary, snatched up the
> golden head of the pack-ass *(tēn chrysēn aposyrai tou kanthōnos
> kephalēn)* (as he facetiously calls it), and made off post-haste to
> Dora.[143]

The setting of this story is very clear: it is the hostile relationship between the Jews and the Idumeans, which has become manifest in a war between both nations (the city Dor, of course, is not Dora south of Mt. Carmel but

Adora, together with Marisa the center of Idumea)[144] and which is mirrored in the rivalry of their respective gods (the pack-ass and Apollo = Cos, the national god of the Idumeans). Thus, the story may fittingly be called a *Kriegslistgeschichte,* as Bickerman has labeled it.[145] Its core is not the alleged ass-worship of the Jews (he does not speak about worship at all) but the war between the Jews and the Idumeans, the outcome of which depends on which god in the end proves to be more powerful. In successfully stealing the Jewish idol (actually only the most valuable part of it, the golden head), the Idumean Zabidus no doubt provides for the final victory of the Idumeans. A pejorative tone is heard only in the Greek word for the Jewish idol, which is not the common *onos* but *kanthōn,* "pack-ass," and probably also in the comment "as he facetiously *(asteïzomenos)* calls it" (yet this may well be not Mnaseas'/Apion's but Josephus' comment). That the Jews have the statue of a pack-ass in their Temple is taken as a fact and only slightly mocked.

The crucial question, of course, is the *historical* setting of the story. One immediately thinks of the war between the Jews and the Idumeans in the time of John Hyrcanus, which finally led to the conquest of Adora and Marisa in the twenties of the second century B.C.E. and the forced circumcision of the Idumeans.[146] But this is much too late if the attribution of the story to Mnaseas is reliable (and there is no reason to question it). Since the ass-worship is not the focal point of this Idumean version of the story, it is futile to look for strained relations between the Jews and the Idumeans as its background either in the Maccabean period[147] or in the period preceding the Hasmonean revolt or even from the time of the Babylonian Exile.[148] Most scholars agree, therefore, that the original historical setting belongs to the "remote past" and "was born in Hellenistic Egypt in an atmosphere hostile to the Jews."[149] The most vehement dissent from this hypothesis comes from E. Bickerman in his famous article "Ritualmord und Eselskult,"[150] in which he, rather ambiguously, argues that the story is "doubtlessly Idumean, although it was probably not invented by the Idumeans either but adopted by them, and was originally native to another people." Nonetheless Bickerman does not find any connection with Egypt nor, especially, any proof of the alleged identification of the God of the Jews with Seth-Typhon, which he regards to be essential for an Egyptian origin of the story.[151]

Here two things have to be distinguished clearly, namely a possible Egyptian setting for the story and the identification of Seth-Typhon with the Jewish God. For the latter there is indeed, no unequivocal evidence, but it is very questionable whether it is needed to prove the hypothesis of an Egyptian origin of the story. With regard to the former, there can be no doubt, to begin with, that the Greek god Typhon was identified very early with the Egyptian god Seth and that Seth was associated with the ass or, more precisely, with the wild ass.[152] Seth, the god of the desert and the incarnation of "all that is dry, fiery, and arid,"[153] the "power of drought, which gains control and dissipates the moisture which is the source of the Nile and of its rising,"[154] is the antagonist and enemy of Osiris, the god of the water of the Nile, the incarnation of moisture and fertility.[155] Being identified with the animal that kills Osiris, Seth finally represents the power of evil and is outlawed, up to the systematic scraping out of his image.[156] During the late empire in which foreigners ruled Egypt, Seth is the embodiment of these foreign rulers who have to be expelled from Egypt.[157]

Second, and decisive for our context, there is clear evidence that the Jewish *origin* was connected with Typhon-Seth. It is again Plutarch who reports: "But those who relate that Typhon's flight from the battle [with the gods] was made on the back of an ass and lasted for seven days, and that after he had made his escape, he became the father of sons, Hierosolymus and Iudaeus, are manifestly, as the very names show, attempting to drag Jewish traditions into the legend."[158] What Plutarch indignantly denounces here as "Jewish traditions" no doubt is an early Egyptian source which tries to connect the origin of the Jews with Typon-Seth, feared and despised in both Greek and Egyptian mythology.[159] Bickerman rightly points to the erudite etiological character of this legend[160] but overlooks the hostile implications of suggesting that the Jews are the offspring of Typhon. Hence his assertion that this story belongs to the category of learned etiology, which only tries to explain the ass-worship in a scholarly manner, and that it has nothing to do with "anti-Semitism,"[161] seems more than questionable; it is on the contrary, for the erudite Greek reader, quite a powerful anti-Jewish legend.[162]

The alleged relationship between the Jews and Typhon has been established in still another, and much older, source which scholars have largely failed to notice in this context. It is Manetho's second account of the lepers' expulsion to the stone-quarries and subsequently to the deserted city of Auaris, the city of the Shepherds, who in the meantime had founded Jerusalem and who later joined forces with the lepers under their leader Osarseph and established a reign of terror in Egypt.[163] About Auaris Manetho says in passing: "According to religious tradition this city was from earliest times dedicated to Typhon."[164] Thus the Shepherd-Hyksos, the notorious foreign rulers over Egypt, are associated with Typhon-Seth.[165] Since they are to be identified with the Jews in the double sense that they themselves had founded Jerusalem and that they united with Osarseph = Moses' lepers, it is not far-fetched to connect the Jews with this god (who by the time of Manetho, and probably much earlier, had become the embodiment of evil). It may well be, therefore, that Manetho's remark points not only to the connection of the Jewish *origin* with Typhon-Seth but also to the early Jewish *worship* of this god, and that we do have the link missed by Bickerman.[166] In any case, any kind of association of the Jews with Typhon-Seth was likely to depreciate them in the eyes of their Egyptian and Greek countrymen alike, and clearly was an expression of hostility toward the Jews; and there can be no doubt that it originated in Egypt, most probably long before Mnaseas[167] and Manetho. It must be regarded as another piece of evidence[168] of anti-Jewish sentiment rooted in early Egypt which was adopted by Greek writers and became efficacious in the course of history.

The further development of the legend depends on rather complicated chronological and literary questions. Josephus, in his *Contra Apionem,* leads up to Apion's shocking two stories about the alleged ass-worship and cannibalism of the Jews with the remark: "I am no less amazed at the proceedings of the authors who supplied him [Apion] with his materials, I mean Posidonius and Apollonius Molon. On the one hand they charge us with not worshipping the same gods as other people; on the other, they tell lies and invent absurd calumnies about our temple, without showing any consciousness of impiety . . ."[169]

He goes on to give an account of Apion's version of the ass-worship legend, hence clearly implying that Apion's sources were Posidonius and Apollonius Molon. This suggestion, however, meets with severe difficulties. We have neither Posidonius' nor Apollonius' adaptation of the story because the works of both are lost, but we do possess the version related by Diodorus Siculus (first century B.C.E.), which is commonly held to derive from Posidonius.[170] In his account of Antiochus VII Sidetes' fiercely anti-Jewish counselors, which refers to the expulsion story, to the "outlandish" Jewish laws as an expression of their *misanthrōpia,* and to Antiochus IV's sacrifice of a pig in the Jewish Temple, he also mentions the ass:

> His friends reminded Antiochus [VII Sidetes] also of the enmity that in times past his ancestors had felt for this people. Antiochus [IV], called Epiphanes, on defeating the Jews had entered the innermost sanctuary of the god's temple [in Jerusalem], where it was lawful for

the priests alone to enter. Finding there a marble statue of a heavily bearded man seated on an ass *(lithinon agalma andros bathypōgōnos kathēmenon ep'onou)*, with a book in his hands, he supposed it to be an image of Moses, the founder of Jerusalem and organizer of the nation, the man, moreover, who had ordained for the Jews their misanthropic and lawless customs *(nomothetēsantos ta misanthrōpa kai paranoma ethē)*. And since Epiphanes was shocked by such hatred directed against all mankind *(tēn misanthrōpian pantōn ethnōn)*, he had set himself to break down their traditional practices *(katalysai ta nomima)*.[171]

Although set in a context highly hostile to the Jews (Antiochus IV as the prime example of someone who successfully attempted to uproot the misanthropic and xenophobic laws of the Jews, and the advice of Antiochus VII's counselors to follow his pattern), the story of the ass in the Jerusalem Temple does not have any particularly malevolent tendency: its target is not ass-worship at all, and it is not concerned so much with the statue of an ass but rather with Moses who is responsible for the strange Jewish laws and who is depicted in the Temple sitting on an ass. It does not seem to be important that he sits on an ass; what is crucial for the argument of Antiochus VII's advisors is that he had ordained "the misanthropic and lawless customs." If there is any hint at all of the marble statue as the object of worship,[172] it certainly is Moses who is being worshipped and not the ass. Hence we have here a story which obviously is not related to Mnaseas' account and which hardly can be regarded as a version of the ass-worship legend.

This conclusion makes it very difficult to consider the same Posidonius who is supposed to be Diodorus' *Vorlage* as the source of Apion's crude story about the ass-worship: if Apion depends on Posidonius, we do not have his original story because the version in Diodorus does not fit in with Apion's general tendency. The attempts by scholars to reconcile these obvious discrepancies are not very satisfactory. Stern, for example, considers the possibility that the different statements in Diodorus and in Josephus' *Contra Apionem* derive from different passages of Posidonius or that Posidonius collected different versions of the story, but he admits that these explanations are "no more than pure conjecture" and pronounces a *"non liquet* on the question of Posidonius' real views on the Jews and their religion"[173] (and thereby also on the question of Diodorus' dependence on Posidonius).[174]

Bickerman "solves" the problem with a breathtaking literary and historical reconstruction. Maintaining the assumption that Posidonius is Diodorus' source and being aware, nevertheless, that in his version nothing malicious ("Hetzerisches") against the Jews can be found, Bickerman concludes that Posidonius must have changed his gross and silly *Vorlage* about Jewish ass-worship (or more precisely: worship of the head of an ass).[175] This conjecture is necessary for Bickerman in order to come chronologically close to the time of the Maccabean battles[176] and to declare the fable of ass-worship or the worship of an ass's head respectively an invention by Antiochus IV Epiphanes' apologists in the second half of the second century B.C.E. when they were attempting to ridicule the Jews and their protests against the king.[177]

Since there is nothing to sustain Bickerman's reconstruction (except for the attractiveness of the idea of locating the fable of ass-worship in the context of Seleucid propaganda), and since all the earlier versions are not particularly interested in ass-*worship*, we are left with Apion's story, which reads as follows:

> Within this sanctuary Apion has the effrontery to assert that the Jews kept an ass's head *(asini caput collocasse Iudaeos)*, worshipping that animal and deeming it worthy of the deepest reverence *(et eum colere ac dignum facere tanta religione)*; the fact was disclosed, he maintains, on the occasion of the spoliation of the temple by Antiochus Epiphanes, when the head, made of gold and worth a high price, was discovered.[178]

This is the most blatant version so far of the alleged ass-worship: the Jews worship in their Temple in Jerusalem an ass or, what is even more ridiculous, an asinine head, and this allegation obviously is meant to "solve" the enigma of the mysterious cult in the Jerusalem Temple to which no foreigner had access. No doubt this is a crude anti-Jewish statement, the danger of which can fully be realized from Josephus' lengthy refutation.[179] In the light of what has been said above on the difficulties of relating Apion to Posidonius (let alone Apollonius Molon), it is only natural to conclude that it was Apion himself who, in order to "lend more authority to his calumnies, traced them to the works of such illustrious predecessors as Posidonius and Apollonius";[180] and one may even go a step further and argue that it also was none other than Apion himself who gave the story its peculiar tone and thereby invented the fable of Jewish ass-worship. He may have had an Egyptian source[181] on some connection of the Jews with Typhon-

Seth and the ass,[182] but the sharp anti-Jewish bias with its emphasis on the absurdity of actually *worshipping* an ass may well have been his invention and therefore belong to the milieu of the Alexandrian anti-Semites.

In fact, Apion's version of the story not only seems to have originated in Alexandrian circles, it apparently is also confined mainly to this particular setting. The only other evidence we have is the historian Damocritus, whose exact date is uncertain but who probably wrote after 70 C.E.[183] and thus after Apion. He is mentioned in the *Suda* as the author of a book about tactics and of a work *Peri Ioudaiōn:* "In the latter he states that they [the Jews] used to worship an asinine golden head and that every seventh year they caught a foreigner and sacrificed him. They used to kill him by carving his flesh into small pieces."[184] As far as the ass-worship is concerned he does not add anything to Apion and may well depend on Apion's version.

Finally, another and very different account of Jewish ass-worship is given by Tacitus in his famous digression on the Jews. It is part of his version of the Exodus tradition, which concludes with the journey of the impure Jews through the desert after their expulsion:

> Nothing caused them so much distress as scarcity of water, and in fact they had already fallen exhausted over the plain nigh unto death, when a herd of wild asses *(grex asinorum agrestium)* moved from their pasturage to a rock that was shaded by a grove of trees. Moses followed them, and, conjecturing the truth from the grassy ground, discovered abundant streams of water. This relieved them, and they then marched six days continuously, and on the seventh seized a country, expelling the former inhabitants; there they founded a city and dedicated a Temple.[185]

This is, as Bickerman has already pointed out, a fine example of an etiology of the type "Rechtleitung durch Tiere" ("guidance and rescue by animals") which is a popular motif in ancient etiological science;[186] it is known also by Plutarch and mentioned in his *Quaestiones Convivales.*[187] It has nothing anti-Jewish in it but is a "learned etiological hypothesis which aims at explaining the ass-worship in a scholarly way."[188]

However, strictly speaking, the ass-*worship* is not mentioned in the etiology itself but in the following paragraph, where it does take on a clearly negative connotation. What follows is the introduction by Moses of the peculiar Jewish customs which are described as "opposed to those of all other human beings," and the very first of those is the ass-worship: "They dedicated, in a shrine, a statue of that creature *(effigiem animalis)* whose guidance enabled them to put an end to their wandering and thirst, sacrificing a ram, apparently in derision of Ammon."[189] Thus, in dedicating a statue of the ass, they not only honored the animal which saved them in the wilderness but also derided the Egyptian Ammon by sacrificing a ram (the sacrifice of the ram is connected directly to the dedication of the statue).[190] It is the mocking of the Egyptian cult which is the focal point of this passage, the statue of the ass and the sacrifice of the ram providing an excellent example of what Tacitus means by a religious practice opposed to another religion.[191] Needless to say, Tacitus' "predilection" for the Egyptian cult is hardly altruistic; he expresses it only for the sake of belittling the Jewish religion.

HUMAN SACRIFICE

The main herald of another "malicious slander"[192] against the Jews, namely their alleged slaughter, sacrifice, and subsequent consumption of a human being *(anthrōpophagia)*, is again Apion of Alexandria.[193] According to Josephus, his version of the story reads as follows:

> Antiochus [IV Epiphanes] found in the temple a couch, on which a man was reclining, with a table before him laden with a banquet of fish of the sea, beasts of the earth, and birds of the air, at which the poor fellow was gazing in stupefaction. The king's entry was instantly hailed by him with adoration, as about to procure him profound relief; falling at the king's knees, he stretched out his right hand and implored him to set him free. The king reassured him and bade him tell him who he was, why he was living there, what was the meaning of his abundant fare.
>
> Thereupon, with sighs and tears, the man, in a pitiful tone, told the tale of his distress. He said, Apion continues, that he was a Greek and that, while travelling about the province for his livelihood, he was suddenly kidnapped by men of foreign origin *(ab alienigenis hominibus)* and conveyed to the temple; there he was shut up and seen by nobody, but was fattened on feasts of the most lavish description. At first these unlooked for attentions deceived him and caused him pleasure; suspicion followed, then consternation. Finally, on consulting the attendants who waited upon him, he heard of the unutterable law of the Jews *(legem ineffabilem Iudaeorum),* for the sake of which he was being fed.

The practice was repeated annually at a fixed season. They would kidnap a Greek foreigner *(Graecum peregrinum)*, fatten him up for a year, and then convey him to a wood, where they slew him *(occidere quidem eum hominem)*, sacrificed his body with their customary ritual *(eiusque corpus sacrifare secundum suas sollemnitates)*, partook of his flesh *(et gustare ex eius visceribus)*, and, while immolating the Greek, swore an oath of hostility to the Greeks *(iusiurandum facere in immolatione Graeci, ut inimicitias contra Graecos haberent)*. The remains of their victim were then thrown into a pit.

The man (Apion continues) stated that he had now but a few days left to live, and implored the king, out of respect for the gods of Greece *(erubescens Graecorum deos)*, to defeat this Jewish plot upon his life-blood and to deliver him from his miserable predicament.[194]

This is a most artistically and dramatically structured story which only gradually reveals its dreadful secret, the "unutterable law of the Jews" to sacrifice annually a Greek foreigner in their Temple. Bickerman has provided a thorough and learned analysis of the story, adducing a wide range of evidence from classical literature as well as from ethnographic sources.[195] He mainly argues that it is composed of two very different components, namely the tradition of the "King of the Saturnalia" and the motif of the *coniuratio*. The former is a ritual according to which a foreigner, often a prisoner of war, is fattened for a certain period (most often a year), and then sacrificed; the subsequent consumption of the sacrifice is never part of this tradition.[196] The latter is a kind of cannibalic conspiracy *(coniuratio)* which is well attested in classical literature. It consists of an oath combined with a human sacrifice and either the touching or the consumption of the remains (very often the entrails but also the flesh and the blood). Bickerman sees the origin of this custom in an archaic magical ritual which has been replaced, in the Greek and Roman literature, by a "bourgeois" criminal plot in order to bind the conspirators together. The specific version of the *coniuratio* presented by our story is an oath of hostility toward foreigners, also well known among the Greeks.

The two components of the story do not belong together originally. Bickerman even wants to find a trace of this later fusion of separate strands in the sentence "and then (they would) convey him to a wood, where they slew him and sacrificed his body with their customary ritual," because "it is a little too late to sacrifice someone who is already dead."[197] Although this seems to be an overinterpretation of the wording of the story—any sacrifice has to be "killed" in order to be "sacrificed"—there can be no doubt that Apion's story contained elements of the motifs both of the sacrifice of a prisoner and of the *coniuratio*.[198]

Obviously the main point of the story lies in the oath of hostility to the Greeks, as has been already observed by Bickerman.[199] Much later in his discussion of Apion's calumnies, after having quoted Mnaseas' version of the fable of ass-worship (which is also reported by Apion), Josephus comes back to the oath:[200] "Then he attributes to us an imaginary oath, and would have it appear that we swear by the God who made heaven and earth and sea to show no goodwill to a single alien, above all to Greeks *(mēdeni eunoēsein allophylō, malista de Hellēsin)*."[201]

Here we have, most probably in his original words (in contrast to the above-quoted text, which is preserved in Latin only), the core of Apion's attack on the Jews: they show no goodwill to any alien, and especially to the Greeks. It is certainly no coincidence that the very phrasing *(mēdeni eunoēsein allophylō)* is almost identical with the allegation of Lysimachus (probably the Greco-Egyptian writer also from Alexandria) that Moses advised the Jews "to show goodwill to no man" *(mēte anthrōpon tini eunoēsein)*,[202] the only difference being that Lysimachus speaks of no goodwill to any "man" in general instead of Apion's "alien" (or "foreigner"). Thus, whereas Lysimachus is concerned with misanthropy *(misanthrōpia)*, Apion focuses his accusations more specifically on hostility to foreigners *(misoxenia)*. Both motifs are combined almost indistinguishably, as we have seen, in the Exodus tradition but are conspicuously missing in Apion's (and also his successor Chaeremon's) version of the expulsion story. It may well be that Apion did not use the *misoxenia* motif in his version of the Exodus tradition because he had a most powerful variant of it in the story of the human sacrifice in the Jewish Temple.[203] In any case, it has become clear that the motif itself is present in Apion.

In connecting the motif of hostility to foreigners with the Temple, Apion turns it into a forceful argument against the Jewish religion. What he in fact conveys to his readers is that he has revealed the secret of the Jewish God and the essence of his worship: a continually renewed ritual of hostility toward foreigners. The Jews are a secret confederacy which conspires against foreigners and whose worship consists of a ritual which enforces this conspiracy; their mysterious God is a cruel God who demands human sacrifices. In stressing that the hostility is directed toward Greeks in particular, Apion makes it entirely clear that the Jewish worship in its very essence stands against the accepted values of the civilized, that is Greek, world. This also becomes evident from the concluding remark of the poor foreigner when he asks the king to rescue him "out of respect for the gods of Greece": the gods of Greece are contrasted with the Jewish God; what is at stake is the common civilized religion of all Greeks versus the barbaric religion of the Jews.

This finally leads to the crucial question of who invented the story of human sacrifice—whether it was Apion himself or whether it derives from other, earlier sources. That the story connects itself with Antiochus IV is no proof that it belongs to this period; but Josephus also associates it with Antiochus and gives a reason for its origin: "In their anxiety to defend Antiochus and to cover up the perfidy and sacrilege practised upon our nation under pressure of an empty exchequer, they [some authors] have further invented, to discredit us, the fictitious story which follows. Apion, who is here the spokesman of others, asserts that . . ."[204] This remark has been taken literally by Bickerman, according to whom the story of human sacrifice was invented by Seleucid propagandists in order to defend Antiochus against the accusation of desecrating the Jewish Temple because of his desperate need for money, an accusation which was, as Bickerman argues and amply documents, a popular weapon of "international propaganda." From this it follows that the "others" of whom Josephus makes Apion the "spokesman" are the sources which refer back to the Seleucid "propaganda office."[205]

This is again an ingenious reconstruction, but there is actually no evidence that our story derives from Seleucid propaganda of the second century B.C.E. The parallels accumulated by Bickerman only prove that the allegation of human sacrifice was indeed used for propagandistic purposes, but there is no direct historical link between our story and Seleucid propaganda—except for Josephus' remark.[206] Josephus, however, can be read differently. He explicitly speaks of some people *(isti)* who are concerned with the king's reputation, by whom he no doubt refers to "authors" like Apion himself or like the previously mentioned Posidonius and Apollonius Molon. Of these Apion is the spokesman, and it does not seem very likely to conceive these authors as the representatives or supporters of any official Seleucid propaganda—if there ever was such a thing. It is much more probable that the story derives from those circles which were obsessed with Jewish *misoxenia/misanthrōpia,* circles which originated and were concentrated, as we have seen, in Greek Egypt long before the second century B.C.E. Apion is a worthy descendant of this tradition, and it may even be that he himself made up this particular story out of all the components demonstrated so convincingly by Bickerman. He is the spokesman and in a way the climax of an ancient Egyptian anti-Jewish tradition.[207]

CHAPTER THREE

Abstinence from Pork

THE PROHIBITION AGAINST eating pork is one of the most prominent Jewish dietary laws: according to Lev. 11:2ff. and Dtn. 14:3ff. only those animals may be eaten that both have "true hoofs, with clefts through the hoofs" and "chew the cud." The pig has true hoofs but is forbidden because it does not chew the cud.[1] This prescription is unequivocal and leaves no room for interpretation. Isaiah, therefore, when he enumerates abhorrent (pagan?) practices, mentions also those who "eat the flesh of swine, with broth of unclean things in their bowls."[2] He obviously refers here to the custom of sacrificing pigs, which seems to have been practiced very rarely by Semitic peoples[3] but is well attested in Greece and in Ptolemaic Egypt.[4]

PIG SACRIFICE IN THE JEWISH TEMPLE

The taboo against eating and sacrificing unclean meat, exemplified by pork, no doubt very early was among the most prominent practices of the observant Jew: it is the law that Antiochus IV abolished when he issued his famous decrees against the Jewish religion in 167 B.C.E.—along with requiring that the Sabbath be violated and circumcision be forbidden. This is mentioned by the first book of the Maccabees[5] as well as by Josephus.[6] According to Josephus, the order to sacrifice the swine "daily" was preceded by a sacrifice of the pig by Antiochus himself who, "when he captured the city, sacrificed swine upon the altars and bespattered the temple with their grease, thus perverting the rites of the Jews and the piety of their fathers."[7] This abominable perversion of the Jewish law drove the Jews, according to Josephus, to war against Antiochus.

Josephus' source for Antiochus IV Epiphanes' sacrifice of a pig in the Jewish Temple was most probably Diodorus, or Posidonius if one favors, as most scholars do, the dependence of Diodorus on Posidonius for this episode:[8]

> And since Epiphanes was shocked by such hatred directed against all mankind *(tēn misanthrōpian pantōn ethnōn)*, he had set himself to break down their traditional practices *(katalysai ta nomima)*. Accordingly, he sacrificed before the image of the founder[9] and the open-air altar of the god a great sow *(megalēn hyn)*, and poured its blood over them. Then, having prepared its flesh, he ordered that their holy books, containing the xenophobic laws *(ta misoxena nomima)*, should be sprinkled with the broth of the meat; that the lamp, which they call undying and which burns continually in the temple, should be extinguished; and that the high priest and the rest of the Jews should be compelled to partake of the meat.[10]

The governing themes which determine not only this account but also the preceding ones (the Exodus tradition and Moses seated on the ass) are the Jewish *misanthrōpia* and *misoxena nomima* which embody this "hatred of mankind." The most radical way to annihilate these *nomima* would be to do exactly what the Jews most abhor: to sacrifice sows and to eat their flesh. The sacrifice of a pig in the Temple and the eating of pork are seen here as the most extreme perversion of the Jewish religion in order to exterminate once and for all their *misanthrōpia*. The prohibition against eating pork is the embodiment of *misanthrōpia*; once the Jews eat pork, they have given up their *misoxena nomima* and will become like any other nation.

We have no evidence whether this unprecedented outburst of hatred of the Jews, symbolized in the sacrifice of a pig, took place during the course of Antiochus IV's capture of Jerusalem in 169 B.C.E., but it is most unlikely. What we know from both 1 and 2 Maccabees is that the king did enter the Temple, "guided by Menelaus,"[11] the High Priest, "and carried off the gold altar, the lampstand with all its fittings . . . He stripped the gold plating from the front of the temple, seized the silver and gold, the precious vessels, and whatever secret treasures he found, and carried them all away when he left for his own country."[12] Thus, his only interest was to plunder the Temple in order to increase the public finances, a custom which was not unfamiliar to him (his father, Antiochus III, was killed when he tried to plunder the temple of Bel in the Elymaïs). The decrees against the Jewish religion were issued two years later (167 B.C.E.), following Antiochus' humiliating expulsion from Egypt by the Romans and a revolt in Jerusalem, and apparently were not accompanied by a visit of the king himself to Jerusalem, let alone by his entering the Temple and sacrificing a pig. It is only Seleucid historiography which combines the Jewish revolt and the subsequent religious persecution of 167 with the plundering of the Temple of 169, according to Bickerman "in order to explain, and thus excuse, the measures taken by Antiochus against the Jews."[13] In the wake of this combination of the two events a second wicked entering of the Temple by the king must have emerged, culminating this time not in pillaging the Temple's treasury but in sacrificing a pig.[14]

If the detail of the king himself sacrificing a pig in the Jewish Temple and sprinkling the holy books of the Jews with the broth of its meat does not seem to have a historical basis in the events connected with Antiochus IV, when did it then originate? One might speculate that it is another version of the attempt of Seleucid propaganda to explain the profanation of the Jewish Temple by Antiochus: that is, the king did not plunder the Temple; on the contrary, in his zeal for the peaceful social life of humankind, he unfortunately had to resort to brutal but effective means— sacrifice of a pig—to break down Jewish antisocial customs (incidentally, it seems to fit this purpose that the "lamp, which they call undying" is not carried off, as 1 Maccabees has it, but "should be extinguished").[15] Another possibility may be that the detail of the king's sacrifice of the pig with its fierce anti-Jewish bias is an embellishment introduced into the story at a later stage, namely by Antiochus VII's counselors, who so strongly advised the king "to wipe out completely the nation of the Jews, since they alone of all nations avoided dealings with any other people and looked upon all men as their enemies."[16] In this case it would have originated at the beginning of the reign of John Hyrcanus I, and its message would be: follow the example of your predecessor and try "to make an end of the Jewish people completely,"[17] before it is too late; if you do not stop them now, they may become too powerful and in the end overcome us. (Obviously Antiochus VII did not follow the advice of his counselors and was satisfied with exacting tribute and dismantling the walls of Jerusalem; immediately after his death Hyrcanus started his successful campaigns of conquest.)

Of these two hypotheses the latter seems likelier: the "anti-Jewish version" depicts the political climate during the transition of power from the first to the second generation of the Maccabees. Jonathan and Simon had conquered many "pagan" cities and extended the Jewish territory considerably, and there was no reason to expect a different attitude from John Hyrcanus. Thus, the motif of the sacrifice of the pig by the king himself as the ultimate perversion of the Jewish religion, and the almost desperate attempt to uproot the Jewish nation, may well have originated at exactly this time (around 134 B.C.E.), when the Maccabees had gained sufficient strength and incited considerable hatred in the Gentile population of Palestine, but still were weak enough to be defeated.[18]

CASUAL REFERENCE AND ETHNOGRAPHIC EXPLANATION

After this aggressive start, if we trace the further development of the pagan attitude toward the Jewish aversion to pork, it is conspicuous how many authors mention it only incidentally, without any further comment, or try to explain it in an ethnographic way. To the category of passing reference belong such culturally diverse authors as Apion, Epictetus, Sextus Empiricus, Julian, and Damascius; in the category of ethnographic explanation may be included Plutarch, Tacitus, and Porphyry.

The prohibition against eating pork is one of Apion's many indictments against the Jews, which Josephus discusses in his *Contra Apionem*: "He [Apion] denounces us for sacrificing domestic animals and for not eating pork, and he derides the practice of circumcision."[19] Since we do not know the original context of Apion's "denunciation" (even the combination of "not eating pork" with "sacrificing domestic animals" and "circumcision" may have originated with Josephus and not Apion), we cannot interpret it. We cannot be sure whether Apion has mentioned the prohibition of eating pork in passing only or whether he has combined it with some nasty remarks which Josephus did not bother to hand down (although the latter seems to be less likely: Josephus' main concern was to refute and to ridicule the anti-Semitic monstrosities).

A clearly neutral attitude, which only reveals that the Jewish abhorrence of pork was "a matter of common knowledge,"[20] can be found in a remark by Erotianus (second half of the first century C.E.), the glossator of Hippocrates, about the "sacred disease," epilepsy: "Some say that the 'Sacred Disease' is of divine origin, because this disease is god-sent, and being of divine origin it is said to be sacred. Others suppose that superstition is implied. They say that one should inquire to which type the sick man belongs, in order that if he is a Jew we should refrain from giving him pig's flesh, and if he is an Egyptian we should refrain from giving him the flesh of sheep or goats."[21]

The Stoic philosopher Epictetus (ca. 50–130 C.E.) twice compares the customs of the Jews, the Syrians, the Egyptians, and the Romans. In the first case he discusses the question of how to determine about "right" and "wrong," and illustrates it by the different opinions on dietary laws: "It is absolutely necessary, if the views of the Egyptians are right, that those of the others are not right; if those of the Jews are well founded, than those of the others are not."[22] In the second instance he is concerned with holiness: "This is the conflict between Jews and Syrians and Egyptians and Romans, not over the question whether holiness should be put before everything else and should be pursued in all circumstances, but whether the particular act of eating swine's flesh is holy or unholy."[23] Epictetus' allusion to dissimilar attitudes toward eating pork cannot be regarded as purely neutral. He disapproves of those who link the question of whether or not one should eat pork with the perception of holiness, apparently striving for a more "abstract" idea of holiness dissociated from any dietary laws. Whether he criticizes only the Jews for their deficient understanding of holiness cannot be decided with certainty; we know that at least the Egyptian priests[24] and probably also the Syrians[25] abstained from pork.

The Jews and the Egyptian priests are coupled in Sextus Empiricus' (second century C.E.) statement that "a Jew or an Egyptian priest would prefer to die instantly rather than eat pork, while to taste mutton is reckoned an abomination in the eyes of a Libyan, and Syrians think the same about pigeons, and others about cattle."[26] In contrast to Epictetus, this statement is markedly neutral: different people behave differently "in respect of food in people's worship of their gods,"[27] and there is nothing surprising about it. Dietary laws, like the prohibition of eating pork, belong to the worship of gods, and they are as diverse as the belief in different gods. In the same way as a sacrifice is not holy or unholy by nature *(physei)*, are there no rules of ritual and of unlawful foods that exist by nature *(physei)* because, if this were the case, "they would have been observed by all men alike."[28]

About two hundred years later the emperor Julian, who laments the decline of Greek and Roman religious practices and praises the Jews for their belief in a "most powerful and most good god,"[29] also mentions the Jewish prohibition of eating pork:

"For I saw that those whose minds were turned to the doctrines of the Jewish religion are so ardent in their belief that they would choose to die for it, and to endure utter want and starvation rather than taste pork or any animal that has not the life [i.e. the blood] squeezed out of it immediately;[30] whereas we are in such a state of apathy about religious matters that we have forgotten the customs of our forefathers *(tōn patriōn),* and therefore we actually do not know whether any such rule has ever been prescribed.[31]

Julian juxtaposes here the Jews' consistency and rigor in following their religious convictions with the indifference and apathy of his countrymen, whose "reverence for the heavenly powers has been driven out by impure and vulgar luxury."[32] He leaves no doubt that he is in favor of the Jews' obeying their laws,[33] and one may even argue that he at least implicitly approves of the particular custom of not eating pork. This may be inferred from his "Hymn to the Mother of the Gods" (that is, the Phrygian Cybele) in which he maintains that the pig "is banned as food during the sacred rites" of the *Magna Mater.*[34]

The last pagan writer who in passing mentions the Jewish abstinence of pork as a well-known fact is Damascius, the Neoplatonic philosopher (first half of the sixth century C.E.) who went to Persia after Justinian had closed the Academy at Athens. He relates the following story about the philosopher Plutarch of Athens and the "rather superficial" philosopher of Syrian origin, Domninus:

Asclepius at Athens enjoined by means of incubation the same cure to Plutarch the Athenian and the Syrian Domninus. Domninus frequently used to spit out blood and bore this name of the disease [blood-spitter], while Plutarch had a disease the nature of which I do not know: the remedy prescribed consisted of being filled with pork. Plutarch, though it was not unlawful for him according to his ancestral customs *(ta patria),* could not bear such a cure, but stood up, and leaning his elbow on his hammock and gazing at the statue of Asclepius, for he happened to be sleeping in the *prodomos* of the sanctuary, exclaimed: "Lord, what would you have ordered a Jew if he had got this disease? Surely you would not have urged him to be filled with pork?" That is what he said, and Asclepius, immediately sending forth from the statue some harmonious sound, suggested another cure for the illness. On the other hand, Domninus, contrary to what had been traditionally allowed to the Syrians, was persuaded by the dream and did not take Plutarch for an example but partook of it then and always ate this meat. It is said that if he left an interval of even one day without taking this food, the malady would undoubtedly attack him until he was filled up with pork.[35]

The subject of this story is not the Jews and not the Jewish aversion to pork, but whether or not one adheres to one's ancestral customs. In this respect it concurs, as Stern has already observed,[36] with the views held especially by Julian. The Syrian Domninus is not only a "rather superficial" philosopher (except in mathematics), he also ate pork, "contrary to what had been traditionally allowed to the Syrians"; Plutarch the Athenian could not eat pork, "though it was not unlawful for him according to his ancestral customs" (one may infer by analogy that he also was a better philosopher). Damascius' sympathy obviously is with Plutarch, and probably, again by analogy, also with the Jews who are so rigorous in following their "ancestral customs" and for whom Asclepius certainly would have prescribed a different cure.

The (mainly Greek) authors reviewed so far represent a group which looks at the Jewish abstinence from pork in a rather neutral way. They compare it with the dietary customs of other people and find it quite natural that different people follow different traditions (most noteworthy in this regard is Sextus Empiricus). Some tint this remark with more or less explicit criticism (Epictetus, Celsus), and others are concerned with medicine and recommend that Jews should not be given pork as a remedy for epilepsy (Erotianus) or any other disease (Damascius). It is striking, moreover, that the so-called Alexandrian anti-Semites apparently do not make use of this motif. The only witness we have, Apion, seems to have mentioned the custom of not eating pork only incidentally.

Turning now to the category of ethnographic explanations, the longest discussion about the question of *why* the Jews abstain from pork is to be found in the *Quaestiones Convivales* of Plutarch, probably written at the end of the first decade of the second century.[37] The fifth question asks "whether the Jews abstain from pork because of reverence or aversion for the pig," and according to the phrasing of the question both possibilities are being discussed, with no definite answer at the end. The advocate of the first is the sophist Callistratus, the spokesman for the second is Lamprias, Plutarch's brother.

Callistratus develops a lengthy argument that the pig indeed

> enjoys a certain respect *(tina timēn to zōon echein)* among that folk [the Jews]; granted that he is ugly and dirty, still he is no more absurd in appearance or crude in disposition than dung-beetle, crocodile, or cat, each of which is treated as sacred by a different group of Egyptian priests. They say, however, that the pig is honoured for a

good reason: according to the story, it was the first to cut the soil with its projecting snout, thus producing a furrow and teaching man the function of a ploughshare. Incidentally, this is the origin, they say, of the word *hynis* (from *hys*, "swine") for that implement.

The Egyptians who cultivate the soft soil of their low-lying areas have no use for ploughing at all. After the Nile overflows and soaks their acres, they follow the receding water and unload the pigs, which by trampling and rooting quickly turn over the deep soil and cover the seed. We need not be surprised if some people do not eat pork for this reason. Other animals receive even greater honours among the barbarians for slight and in some cases utterly ridiculous reasons . . .

Or when we remember that the Magi, followers of Zoroaster, especially esteem the hedgehog and abominate water mice, regarding the person who kills the greatest number of the latter as blest and dear to the gods? So I think the Jews would kill pigs if they hated them, as the Magi kill water mice; but in fact it is just as unlawful for Jews to destroy pigs as to eat them. Perhaps it is consistent that they should revere the pig *(houtōs kai tēn hyn sebesthai)* who taught them sowing and plowing, inasmuch as they honour the ass who first led them to a spring of water.[38]

What Callistratus offers here is a typical etiology: the pig is a highly respected animal among the Jews because it taught them how to cultivate the soil. In this regard the Jews are similar to the Egyptians, who revere many different animals (some of them even uglier and dirtier than the pig), and who use the pig for covering the seed.[39] Taking into consideration the predilection of ancient authors for age-old customs and inventions which foster civilization, this is definitely a positive statement. That the Jews do not eat pork for that reason distinguishes them from other barbarians who honor or even worship animals for irrational or ridiculous reasons (like the Egyptians who deified the field-mouse because of its blindness, "since they regarded darkness as superior to light," the Pythagoreans who respect a white cock and abstain from the red mullet and the sea anemone, or the Persian Magi).[40] Thus, it would be only consistent *(isōs echei logon)*, if they revered the pig—as they actually do with the ass who helped them in a similar way.

Callistratus does not insinuate that the Jews worship the pig, but it is clear that he has nothing against this idea and could well understand if they came to such a conclusion. His mention of the alleged ass-worship without any critical hint speaks for itself.

Lamprias' counterargument invokes some popular prejudices against the pig:

> The Jews apparently abominate pork because barbarians especially abhor skin diseases like lepra and white scale, and believe that human beings are ravaged by such maladies through contagion. Now we observe that every pig is covered on the under side by lepra and scaly eruptions, which, if there is general weakness and emaciation, are thought to spread rapidly over the body. What is more, the very filthiness of their habits produces an inferior quality of meat. We observe no other creature so fond of mud and of dirty, unclean places, if we leave out of account those animals that have their origin and natural habitat there. People say also that the eyes of swine are so twisted and drawn down that they can never catch sight of anything above them or see the sky unless they are carried upside down so that their eyes are given an unnatural tilt upward. Wherefore the animal, which usually squeals immoderately, holds still when it is carried in this position, and remains silent because it is astonished at the unfamiliar sight of the heavenly expanse and restrained from squealing by an overpowering fear.[41]

Apart from the expression of his disgust of the pig's filthiness (which in his view even affects the quality of its meat),[42] Lamprias' explanation is remarkable because of its association of abhorrence of pork with lepra and white scale. This is obviously a faint echo of the Greek and Roman Exodus tradition, according to which the Jews were driven out of Egypt because of leprosy. The explanation is all the more significant as it lacks any negative tint (Lamprias actually agrees with it, underlining it by his mention of the filthiness of the pig), thus being in stark contrast with his contemporary Tacitus' use of the same motif. The strange description of the pig's inability to look up at the sky apparently was later used by Julian, who approves of the refusal to eat pork.

Tacitus, Plutarch's distinguished contemporary, lists the Jewish abstinence from pork among his negative catalogue of the "new religious practices" *(novos ritus)* introduced by Moses: the statue of the ass in the Temple (in memory of the herd of wild asses which led Moses in the wilderness to water); abstinence from pork, "in recollection of a plague *(sue abstinent memoria cladis),* for the scab to which this animal is subject once afflicted them"; frequent fasts (because of the "long hunger with which they were once distressed"); unleavened bread ("in memory of the haste with which they seized the grain"); and the Sabbath ("they say that they first chose to rest on the seventh day because that day ended their toils; but after a time they were led by the charms of indolence to give over the seventh year as well to inactivity").[43]

Tacitus' rationale for the Jewish abstinence from pork is that the "plague," transmitted by the pig, "once afflicted them." This refers to his account of the Exodus tradition where the Jews were expelled from Egypt because they were held responsible for a plague *(tabes)* "which caused bodily disfigurement" *(quae corpora foedaret)*.[44] Hence Tacitus leaves no doubt that the Jewish dislike of pork, although explained by their history, nonetheless denounces them as a despicable nation because it is they who were responsible for the plague in Egypt. And he makes it apparent that this plague was not a malady like any other affliction but created by a human genus *(genus hominum)* which was "hateful to the gods" *(invisum deis)*. Therefore, when the Jews abstain from pork in memory of the plague in Egypt, they ultimately commemorate and enforce their disastrous habits which make them hateful to the gods of any civilized nation.

De Abstinentia by the late-third-century scholar Porphyry was the only one of his many books to survive, obviously because of its decidedly ascetic standpoint.[45] In general, he views Judaism as superior to Christianity, and thus it is not surprising that he shows a certain understanding of the Jewish abstinence from pork (which may have been supported by his disapproval of eating any meat).

His first explanation of the Jews' abstinence from pork sounds very rational: the Jews don't eat pork for a very simple reason, "because in their places pigs were not to be found at all."[46] Otherwise, one might conclude, they gladly would have joined all civilized nations which abstain only from those animals "who live in association with men," like dogs, horses, or asses; pigs do not belong to this category (the tame ones are of the same species as the wild), and therefore are "of no use but for food."[47]

That this explanation is hardly satisfying, and especially does not justify why the Jews are so stubborn in refusing pork, is shown by his second answer: "For it would be a terrible thing, that while the Syrians do not taste fish and the Hebrews pigs and many of the Phoenicians and the Egyptians cows, and even when many kings strove to change them they preferred to suffer death rather than to transgress the law, we choose to transgress the laws of nature and the divine orders because of fear of men or some evil-speaking coming from them."[48] Although Porphyry refers here to the dietary customs of different peoples, he seems to be interested mainly in the

Jewish abstinence from pork (the "them" that "many kings" tried to reform seems to apply first and foremost to the Jews). Their abhorrence of pork is so fundamental that even persecutions cannot change their minds (it may well be that Porphyry alludes here to the persecution of Antiochus IV Epiphanes).

The explanation he offers this time is that the Jews refuse "to transgress the law" *(tēn tou nomou parabasin)*, most probably referring to the written law, the Torah, about which he was well informed and which he regarded as superior to the Christian New Testament. Most important is that he decidedly approves of the Jewish refusal to transgress the law because he compares it with his countrymen's option "to transgress the laws of nature *(tous tēs physeōs nomous)* and the divine orders" *(tas theias paraggelias)*. This meets with his general rule that it is "the greatest fruit of piety *(megistos karpos eusebeias)*, to respect the divine according to the customs of the forefathers" *(timan to theion kata ta patria)*.[49] This is very similar to Julian's argument some ninety years later; in his letter to Theodorus Julian actually uses the same expression *(ta patria)* and the same argument: "we" have forgotten all about the customs of our forefathers (or even more precisely: our national traditions), whereas the Jews follow them scrupulously, even at the risk of losing their lives.[50] Both Porphyry and Julian expressly admire the Jews for their rigor in keeping a firm hold on their traditional laws.

In a later passage in his *De Abstinentia*, Porphyry comes back to the Jewish custom of not eating pork. Here he opens a long digression about the Jews and their three forms of philosophy *(philosophiōn trittai ideai)*, which almost literally follows Josephus,[51] with the remark that these people "continued to abstain from many animals, and especially, even now, from pigs *(idiōs de eti kai nyn tōn choiriōn)*," although they had "suffered irremediably, first at the hands of Antiochus in the matter of their laws *(ta nomima)*, and then later at the hands of the Romans."[52]

Porphyry is remarkably sympathetic here to the suffering of the Jewish people which again is a consequence of their obeying their *nomima* (no doubt their *patria nomima*). The Jews are to be admired because they keep their national laws, up to the present time and despite persecution by the Seleucids and the Romans. Once more the abstinence from pork is singled out as the most characteristic and probably also most important of the Jewish laws.

After having summarized the three concepts of Jewish philosophy he explains their law in greater detail:

To all Jews it was forbidden to eat pork or unscaled fish, which Greeks call cartilaginous, and also any of the uncloven animals. Moreover, it was forbidden to them to kill animals which took refuge at their houses like supplicants, not to speak of eating them. Nor did the lawgiver allow to take away the parents together with the nestlings, and he enjoined that animals which are of help in work should be spared, even in enemy country, and not to slaughter them.[53]

This is a list of different laws which, with two exceptions, are to be found in the Bible.[54] Whereas the second part (the prohibition of killing animals which took refuge and those which are of help in work as well as of taking away parents with their nestlings) is taken from Josephus' *Contra Apionem*,[55] scholars agree that for the first part (the dietary laws) Porphyry relies on his own knowledge of the Bible.[56] Again it is noteworthy that this summary of the Jewish law starts with the prohibition against eating pork.

To sum up, most authors providing an ethnographic explanation for the Jews' abstinence from pork refer to the antiquity of this custom. This is in itself a favorable argument in the eyes of a pagan author. Except for Tacitus they all express open sympathy with the Jewish determination not to transgress the law and to follow their ancient customs *(ta patria nomima)*, contrasting it with the carelessness and irreligiosity of their own or other peoples. Plutarch even goes so far as to find it consistent if the Jews revered the pig because it taught them how to cultivate the soil.

LATIN SATIRISTS

From the authors who just mention or try to explain in one way or another the Jewish aversion to pork are to be distinguished the Latin satirists; they form a rather distinctive category with some common characteristics.

The first is Petronius, most probably Petronius Arbiter, the courtier at Nero's court (first century C.E.).[57] In one of the fragments of his poems he writes:

The Jew may worship his pig-god *(porcinum numen)*
and clamour in the ears of the heights of heaven *(summas caeli),*
but unless he cuts also back with a knife his foreskin *(inguinis oram),*
and unless he unlooses by art the knotted head *(nodate solverit arte caput),*

cast forth from the people he shall emigrate to Greek cities,[58]
and shall not tremble[59] at the fasts of Sabbath imposed by the law.[60]

Here we have a kind of satirical summary of what Petronius considered to be the most significant features of the Jews: a pig-god, prayer to the heights of heaven, circumcision, and the Sabbath; of these the pig-god, as far as I know, is unique and never mentioned by any other Greek or Latin author.

The four characteristics are obviously not on the same level. Worshipping the pig-god and praying to the heights of heaven are important but do not add up to the genuine Jew of whom circumcision is also required in order to be able to fulfill the law and to "tremble at the fasts of Sabbath." Hence circumcision is the most important prerequisite to be or to become a Jew.[61] One may argue that the distinction being made here refers to the status of the "God-fearers" *(sebomenoi)*, who only worship the pig-god and the heights of heaven, and the Jews in the full sense of the word, who are also distinguished by circumcision. Here Petronius may even be alluding to the question of whether one could be regarded as a full proselyte without having undergone circumcision.

Most remarkable are the characteristics of the first stage, worshipping the pig-god and clamoring in the ears of the heights of heaven. Both characteristics apparently attempt to summarize the Jewish belief in one (?) God, but whereas the identification of the Jewish God with the sky is well known and at least as early as Hecataeus,[62] the pig-god *(porcinum numen)* is absolutely new. The only remark which could be construed as similar is the one made by Petronius' younger contemporary Plutarch, who argues that it would be consistent if the Jews revered the pig (because it taught them sowing and plowing). But the difference is considerable. Plutarch does not say that the Jews actually worship the pig, although he would understand it if they did so, whereas according to Petronius the *porcinum numen,* together with *caeli summas, is* the Jewish God—and, unlike Plutarch, Petronius certainly is not in favor of such an idea. It seems questionable, therefore, that the pig-god is but another attempt to explain rationally why the Jews refrained from eating pork.[63] The elevation of the pig to a *porcinum numen,* and its association with the heights of heaven, clearly gives the poem a negative and, in the eyes of the Jews, obscene connotation. To be sure, the context is that of a satire; however, the point of this particular satire is not the *porcinum numen* but the requirement of circumcision in order to be able to "enjoy" the fasts of Sabbath. Thus, the pig-god seems to have been created by Petronius not in order to explain but to ridicule the Jewish rejection of pork, and simultaneously the fascination of the "God-fearers" with the Jewish God.

Juvenal, the last and greatest of the Roman satirists (ca. 60–130 C.E.), mentions the Jewish abhorrence of pork twice in his *Saturae*. In the first instance only the Sabbath and the pig are joined together in order to characterize the Jews: "It [a diamond of great renown] was given as a present long ago by the barbarian Agrippa to his incestuous sister [Berenice], in that country where kings celebrate festal sabbaths with bare feet, and where a long-established clemency suffers pigs to attain old age *(et vetus indulget senibus clementia porcis)*."[64] Juvenal refers here to Agrippa II and his sister Berenice,[65] whose alleged incestuous relationship is mentioned also by Josephus (but not by Tacitus,[66] Suetonius,[67] and Dio,[68] who only speak of her liaison with Titus).[69] The barefooted Sabbaths and the clemency toward pigs obviously aim at ridiculing Jewish customs, an effect which no doubt is meant to be intensified by the combining of these customs with the incestuous couple: these people are very scrupulous with regard to their strange ritual practices, but when it comes to things which really matter (like incest), they are much less rigid.[70]

In the next example Juvenal combines all the well-known features of the Jewish religion: "Some who have had a father who reveres the Sabbath *(metuentem sabbata patrem)*, worship nothing but the clouds *(nil praeter nubes)*, and the divinity of the heavens *(caeli numen)*, and see no difference between eating swine's flesh, from which their father abstained, and that of man; and in time they take to circumcision."[71] In focusing on Sabbath, heaven, pork, and circumcision, this poem closely resembles the one by Petronius discussed above. In fact, it gives the impression that Juvenal knew Petronius' *Fragmenta* and "responded" to this specific segment, or that both drew on the same strand in Roman perceptions of Jewishness. Reading Juvenal in conjunction with Petronius also augments the apprehension of the differences between and the respective peculiarities of the two writers.

First, as far as the pig is concerned, it is most noteworthy that in Juvenal it strictly remains within the realm of dietary laws (the Jews do not eat pork because they abhor it, as much as they abhor eating man's flesh). This certainly does not meet with Juvenal's approval, but there is also no particularly hostile overtone in this remark which only aims at emphasizing the grade of the Jews' abhorrence. This is quite in contrast to Petronius, who equates, as we have seen, the "heights of heaven" with the *porcinum numen;*

and it becomes even clearer when one compares the exact wording: whereas, according to Petronius, the Jew *porcinum numen adoret,* certain people, according to Juvenal, *caeli numen adorant.* Thus Juvenal restricts Jewish worship to the "heaven" (only qualifying *caeli numen* by *nil praeter nubes*), whereas Petronius has the *porcinum numen* as the object of Jewish worship (adding to this, somewhat unmotivated, the "heights of heaven"). This observation intensifies the particularly malicious tint of Petronius' Jewish "pig-god."

Second, Juvenal, like Petronius, distinguishes between two degrees of being Jewish, namely the stage of those who observe the Sabbath, worship nothing but the clouds and the divinity of heavens, and abstain from eating pork, and that of those who "in time" undergo circumcision. The former obviously are the *metuentes* or *sebomenoi/phoboumenoi ton theon,* "God-fearers," who kept some of the Jewish observances but did not go as far as to become proselytes; the latter are those who did undergo circumcision and thus became proselytes in the full sense of the word.[72] Thus both authors have circumcision as the main characteristic of the Jews. However, whereas the distinction between "God-fearers" ("sympathizers") and "full" Jews can only be suspected in Petronius, the "sympathizers" are the main target in Juvenal: they start with observing the Sabbath[73] and the dietary laws as well as with worshipping the divinity of heavens but unfortunately in the end they undergo circumcision and become full Jews.[74]

This is made very clear in the continuation of his poem when Juvenal laments that those who finally underwent the rite of circumcision "have been wont to flout the laws of Rome" *(Romanas contemnere leges)* and instead follow the Jewish law *(Judaicum ius),* "and all that Moses handed down in his secret tome *(arcano volumine),* forbidding to point out the way *(non monstrare vias)* to any not worshipping the same rites, and conducting none but the circumcised to the desired fountain."[75] Circumcision is the decisive criterion distinguishing between *metuentes* who adhere to strange customs (which may be mocked but in the end are harmless) and "complete" Jews who follow the *Judaicum ius* in its full sense, which will not be communicated to the non-initiates and, even more important, which is exclusive in its very essence because it not only is restricted to the circumcised but also consists mainly in excluding others from the (true) way and the desired fountain. Hence, the message of Juvenal is (similar to Petronius and even more so to his contemporary Tacitus): we may tolerate the strange but harmless "God-fearers" but we must know that in the second generation they almost inevitably become true Jews, thus by definition misanthropic and lost to humankind as we understand it; this is the real danger which should not be underestimated.

One final author who makes use of the Jewish custom of not eating pork in a satirical context is Macrobius (beginning of the fifth century C.E.) who attributes to Augustus the famous dictum: "I'd rather be Herod's pig than Herod's son *(melius est Herodis porcum esse quam filium)*."[76] Augustus is said to have made this remarkable statement when he heard "that among the boys under the age of two years whom in Syria Herodes the king of the Jews had ordered to be put to death was the king's own son."[77] Although this historical setting provided by Macrobius is anachronistic (it is obviously influenced by the massacre of the children in the New Testament),[78] Stern nonetheless believes that the original joke[79] "goes back substantially to an Augustan source."[80] However this may be, there can be no doubt that the target of this joke was Herod and not the Jewish abstinence from pork.

In conclusion, it is not surprising that the authors who most conspicuously use the motif of the pig with an anti-Jewish bias are the Roman satirists Petronius and Juvenal. To be sure, satirists by definition look for opportunities to ridicule, and one has to be cautious when using them for historical commentary. On the other hand, to ridicule something is not an end in itself but serves a purpose, a purpose, moreover, which was apparently well received by an audience.[81] In our case it is the close connection being made between abstinence from pork and circumcision: the abstinence from pork (Juvenal) and the worship of the pig-god (Petronius) belong to the stage of the "God-fearer" who in the end undergoes circumcision, and this is what worries our satirists and their audience.

All in all, however, the use of the motif of the Jews' abstinence from pork is remarkably free from anti-Jewish polemic; in some cases, it is even openly sympathetic. The exceptions are the tradition of the pig sacrifice in the Temple (second century B.C.E.), Tacitus, and the satirists. Whereas the beginning of this negative attitude seems to be connected with the successful Maccabean expansion, its renewed rise in the second half of the first and the beginning of the second century C.E. no doubt has to be regarded as an expression of increasing "Judeophobia" because of the success of proselytism.

CHAPTER FOUR

Sabbath

*T*HE HEBREW WORD *SHABBAT* derives from the verb *shavat*, which means "cease, abstain from work, rest": God "rested *(wayyishbot)* on the seventh day from all the work that He had done."[1] The Decalogue version of the biblical book Exodus takes this as the decisive precedent for the introduction of a Sabbath day on which Israel is expected to rest: "Remember the Sabbath day *(yom ha-Shabbat)* and keep it holy. Six days you shall labor and do all your work, but the seventh day is a Sabbath of the Lord your God: you shall not do any work . . . For in six days the Lord made heaven and earth and sea . . . , and He rested on the seventh day; therefore the Lord blessed the Sabbath day and hallowed it."[2]

Whether or not this rationale for the observation of the Shabbat is rather late (that is, exilic), there can be no doubt that the positive valuation of the Sabbath grew during and after the Exile. After the destruction of the Temple, violation of the Sabbath was regarded as an essential factor in the downfall of the kingdom;[3] observing the Sabbath became another preeminent mark, together with circumcision and abstinence from pork, of identification with the people of God,[4] and hence of distinction from the Gentiles. When Antiochus IV Epiphanes forbade circumcision and decreed the sacrifice of pigs and other unclean animals,[5] he also ordered the profanation of the Sabbath.[6] Those of the "enlightened" Jewish Hellenists in Jerusalem who welcomed his decrees as an opportunity to become like "all the nations" are said not only to have profaned the Sabbath but also to have sacrificed to the pagan idols.[7] Obviously, violation of the Sabbath was considered tantamount to idolatry.

DAY OF REST

The notion of the Sabbath as a day of rest is also prominent among pagan authors, albeit with different nuances and assessments. They vary from purely neutral statements to the awareness of the prohibition of business—even talking business—and traveling, and of the refusal to defend oneself. The first who mentions the Sabbath, the peripatetic Agatharchides of Cnidus (second century B.C.E.), refers to this connection, but with a very characteristic twist:

> The people known as Jews . . . have a custom of abstaining from work every seventh day; on those occasions they neither bear arms nor take any agricultural operations in hand, nor engage in any other form of public service, but pray with outstretched hands in the temples until the evening. Consequently, because the inhabitants, instead of protecting their city, persevered in their folly (anoian), Ptolemy, son of Lagus, was allowed to enter with his army; the country was thus given over to a cruel master, and the defect of a practice enjoined by law was exposed. That experience has taught the whole world, except that nation, the lesson not to resort to dreams and traditional fancies about the law, until the difficulties are such as to baffle human reason.[8]

The incident to which Agatharchides alludes is the conquest of Palestine by Ptolemy I Soter and the subsequent capture of Jerusalem, probably in 302 B.C.E.[9] The practice among Jews of not defending themselves as a consequence of their strict observance of the Sabbath is mentioned here for the first time. It is well attested about 150 years later when a group of the "pious" who rebelled against Antiochus IV were attacked by Seleucid troops and massacred without resistance on a Sabbath, because they regarded the observance of the Sabbath as more important than defending their lives.[10] According to the First Book of the Maccabees, the pious rebels immediately drew the conclusion that in future they had better defend themselves even on a Sabbath, because otherwise the Gentiles "will eradicate us from the earth."[11] The subsequent success of the Maccabees shows that they followed this advice.

We do not know whether Agatharchides, who is supposed to have spent some time in Alexandria during the reigns of Ptolemy VI Philometor (180–145 B.C.E.) and Ptolemy VII/VIII Euergetes II Physcon (170/145–116 B.C.E.),[12] may have already heard about this change of attitude among the early Maccabees. What is remarkable is not so much the fact that he reports the Jewish custom of not defending oneself on a Sabbath but the way he characterizes it. The immediate context in his History, according to Josephus, was the story of the Seleucid princess Stratonice who lost her life because, in her superstition *(deisidaimonia)*, she followed a divine dream *(enhypnion)* instead of human reason. Accordingly the Jews, in their folly *(anoia)*—in the shorter parallel version in *Antiquitates* Agatharchides is said to have used also the word *deisidaimonia*[13]—followed their dreams *(enhypnia)* as well as their "traditional fancies about the law" and lost their lives. The important distinction between the Jews and the other nations, however, is that the latter learned the lesson whereas the former maintained their unfortunate habit. Since the Jews are contrasted with the "whole world" *(tous allous pantas)*, Agatharchides' true subject is again the Jewish separateness and self-isolation which he attributes to superstition and folly. Hence, the at least potentially positive notion of a day of rest (instead of working the Jews pray in their synagogues) takes on a decidedly negative connotation: the Jews insist, against human reason, on being separated from the whole world by a stupid and superstitious custom.

It is true that during his stay in Alexandria Agatharchides "undoubtedly had an opportunity to meet many Jews, as they played a conspicuous part in the life and politics of second-century Egypt."[14] But it is very unlikely that he owes his special interpretation of the Sabbath to Jewish information.[15] It seems to reflect much more the spirit of the Alexandrian Greeks, whose malevolent interpretation of Jewish customs is notorious. Agatharchides reveals himself here as a worthy spokesman of an Egyptian-Greek anti-Jewish tradition which articulates itself within different contexts and uses different motifs.

Remarkably distinct from Agatharchides' comments on the Sabbath are those of the Latin writers of the Augustan period. Tibullus, for example, mentions the Sabbath in the first book of his *Elegiae,* published about 26/25 B.C.E. Here he regrets that he left his beloved Delia in Rome in order to follow M. Valerius Messalla Corvinus:[16]

> Yea, even I her comforter, after I had given my parting charge,
> sought still in my disquiet for reasons to linger and delay.
> Either birds or words of evil omen *(omina dira)* were my pretexts,
> or there was the accursed day of Saturn *(Saturni sacram . . . diem)* to
>   detain me.[17]

The "day of Saturn" no doubt is the Saturday = Sabbath; together with the "birds" and the "words of evil omen" it constitutes the portents which might have prevented Tibullus from undertaking his journey. Its qualification as "accursed"[18] is not meant to characterize the day or the Jewish custom itself, but refers to its function as an ill omen in this particular case:

being a day of rest it is supposed to prevent someone from traveling.[19] Tibullus' remark definitely displays, therefore, some familiarity with the essence of the Sabbath,[20] which obviously goes back to his knowledge of Jews and Jewish customs in Rome.

The same is true with regard to the only instance in which Horace mentions the Sabbath in his Satires. When pestered by a bore, Horace meets the poet Aristius Fuscus, by whom he desperately hopes to be saved:

> I begin to twitch his cloak and squeeze his arms . . . nodding and winking hard for him to save me. The cruel joker laughed, pretending not to understand. I grew hot with anger.
>
> "Surely you said that there was something you wanted to tell me in private."
>
> "I mind it well, but I'll tell you at a better time. To day is the thirtieth day, a Sabbath (hodie tricensima, sabbata). Would you affront the circumcised Jews (curtis Iudaeis)?"
>
> "I have no scruples," say I.
>
> "But I have. I am a somewhat weaker brother, one of the many. You will pardon me; I'll talk another day."[21]

There has been much discussion about the meaning of the "thirtieth day" and its combination with the Sabbath.[22] Horace may have been ignorant of the Jewish calendar, but he certainly knew what the Sabbath was considered to be, namely a day of rest on which the Jews are forbidden to talk business. The fact that neither of the protagonists is Jewish[23] reinforces the ironic effect of the episode, which does not bear any particular negative overtone. The Jews are marked by keeping the Sabbath free of business and by circumcision—one may take advantage of this fact in certain situations. Again, Horace obviously knew of Jews and their customs from his own experience.

Ovid refers to the Sabbath in his *Ars Amatoria* (published in 1 B.C.E.) as well as in *Remedia Amoris* (published shortly thereafter).[24] According to him, the seventh day is held sacred by the "Syrian Jew"[25] and "less fit for business";[26] in a piece which is reminiscent of Tibullus' *Carmina* he knows of the prohibition of traveling on the Sabbath:

> Yet the less you wish to go, the more be sure of going; persist, and
>   compel your unwilling feet to run.
> Hope not for rain, nor let foreign Sabbath stay you (nec te peregrina
>   morentur sabbata),
> nor Allia well-known for its ill-luck.[27]

The "foreign Sabbath" is the Sabbath of the Palestinian Jew, which prevents travel. Like his contemporaries Horace and Tibullus, Ovid is well aware of the Jewish custom of the Sabbath, which he refers to with no negative or polemical overtone whatsoever.[28]

A very peculiar interpretation of the Sabbath as a day of rest is given by Apion, spokesman of the Alexandrian Greeks. He connects the origin of the Sabbath with the expulsion of the leprous Jews from Egypt: "After a six days' march . . . they developed tumours in the groin, and that was why, after safely reaching the country now called Judea, they rested on the seventh day, and called that day *sabbaton,* preserving the Egyptian terminology; for disease of the groin in Egypt is called *sabbatosis.*"[29] This is a particularly malevolent explanation of the biblical law to rest on the seventh day: the lepers had developed tumors in their groins, and this disease,[30] not a divine law, forced them to rest. In connecting the word Sabbath with the Egyptian word for the disease, Apion makes it perfectly clear to his Greek readers that the Jews not only are of (humble) Egyptian origin but also carry with them an Egyptian illness which they commemorate every seventh day. This perfidious interpretation of the Sabbath is unparalleled and not repeated by any other pagan author, and it is certainly not by coincidence that it originated in Alexandria.

Quite different is the condemnation of resting on the Sabbath as idleness and indolence, which seems to be distinctively Roman (Seneca, Tacitus, Juvenal, Rutilius Namatianus). The Romans with their sense of efficiency and industry obviously had no sympathy for a day every week with no work. They must have disliked it as another prominent example of the intrusion of unwelcome and destructive foreign customs. Juvenal suggests how this uneasy feeling was connected with the phenomenon of proselytism, and Rutilius Namatianus' outburst leaves no doubt that at the beginning of the fifth century the idle Jewish God and his idle people were still regarded as the (in the end successful) enemies of the ancient Roman virtues.

Seneca, the Roman philosopher (end of the first century B.C.E.–65 C.E.), is the first to substantiate his criticism of the Sabbath with the denunciation of idleness. According to Augustine, he argues in his lost *De Superstitione* "that their practice [of the Sabbath] is inexpedient *(inutiliter),* because by introducing one day of rest in every seven they lose in idleness *(perdant vacando)* almost a seventh of their life."[31] By immediately adding that "by failing to act in times of urgency [the Jews] often suffer loss,"[32] he indicates that he knows of the Jewish habit of not defending themselves on a Sabbath. This notion, however, assumes a very different connotation if compared with Agatharchides and his followers: it is not the holiness of the day and the divine command which force them to refrain from self-defense but their inability "to act in times of urgency," that is, their laziness.

The reproach of idleness is taken over by Tacitus and his contemporary Juvenal and, much later, by Rutilius Namatianus. Tacitus in his digression on the Jews and their customs refers also to the Sabbath, which he counts among the religious practices "quite opposed to those of all other people": "They say that they first chose to rest on the seventh day (only) because that day ended their toils; but after a time they were led by the charms of indolence *(blandiente inertia)* to give over the seventh year as well to inactivity."[33] Tacitus shares with Apion the rationale for the introduction of the Sabbath (the seventh day ended their march through the wilderness after the expulsion from Egypt),[34] but he does not mention Apion's spiteful explanation. Instead, he puts the emphasis on Jewish "indolence": because of their inclination to idleness the Jews decided to rest not only on every seventh day but also on every seventh year—a charming interpretation of the Jewish sabbatical year, indeed.[35]

Juvenal concludes his poem on the "sympathizers" who unfortunately in the end become proselytes with the following sentence:

> For all which the father was to blame,
> who gave up every seventh day to idleness *(lux ignava)*,
> keeping it apart from all the concerns of life.[36]

As we have seen,[37] Juvenal distinguishes between three stages of sympathy with Judaism: reverence for the Sabbath together with abstinence from pork (that is, the beginning), worship of the clouds and the divinity of heaven and abhorrence of eating pork (the intermediary stage), and finally circumcision (the decisive step of becoming proselytes). For all this the "father" (the "God-fearer" whose son becomes a proselyte) was to blame because he was attracted to the idleness of the seventh day: idleness leads to the ridiculous worship of the clouds, the folly of equating swine's flesh with that of man, and the abnormal custom of circumcision.

That the Jewish God himself, who had to rest after completing the creation, is the model of this idleness, is emphasized by Rutilius Namatianus (beginning of the fifth century C.E.) in his fierce outburst against the Jews:

> Each seventh day is condemned to ignoble sloth *(turpi veterno)*,
> as 'twere an effeminate picture *(mollis imago)* of the god fatigued
> *(lassati dei)* . . .

And would that Judea had never been subdued
by Pompey's wars and Titus' military power!
The infection of this plague, though excised *(excisae pestis),* still
   creeps abroad to more:
and 'tis their own conquerors that a conquered nation[38] keeps
   down.[39]

Rutilius Namatianus' poem is known for its allusions to classical Latin literature, and it may well be that this particular passage with its peculiar combination of idleness and final triumph of the customs of the conquered nation has been influenced by Seneca.[40] The Jews, who out of idleness did not defend themselves on a Sabbath, infected with their idleness the entire world and in the end by this conquered their conquerors.[41]

While Pliny the Elder (23/24–79 C.E.)[42] and much later also Damascius (first half of the sixth century C.E.)[43] refer to the Sabbath as a day of rest without further comment, another group of authors connects the day of rest with the habit of not defending oneself, first mentioned by Agatharchides. Cassius Dio links this failing to Pompey's siege and subsequent capture of Jerusalem in 63 B.C.E.,[44] and Frontinus (40–104 C.E.) to Vespasian's or rather Titus' capture during the Great Revolt (70 C.E.).[45] In both cases modern historians agree that the Roman historians are mistaken in assuming that Jerusalem and the Temple were actually captured on a Sabbath, as the Jews had given up the principle of refraining from defending themselves on a Sabbath since the Maccabean Revolt.[46] Nevertheless, both authors testify to the widespread understanding of the Sabbath as a day of rest which could be explained in different ways. Frontinus' statement lacks any further qualification (except for the remark that it is "sinful" for the Jews "to do any business" on the Sabbath),[47] whereas Cassius Dio explicitly refers to the "religious excitement" *(ptoēsis)*[48] of the Jews, of which the Romans took advantage.

Precisely this assessment as superstition determines Plutarch's description of the Sabbath in his early work *De Superstitione* (written shortly after 70 C.E.?).[49] When explaining Euripides' dictum "Greeks discovering from barbarians evil things,"[50] he lists the following "superstitious" customs adopted by the Greeks: "smearing with mud, wallowing in filth, keeping of the Sabbath *(sabbatismous),* casting oneself down with face to the ground, disgraceful besieging of the gods, and uncouth prostrations."[51] Elsewhere in the same essay he refers to the Jewish abstention from self-defense on a Sabbath: "But the Jews, because it was the Sabbath day, sat in their places immovable, while the enemy were planting ladders against the walls and capturing the defences, and they did not get up, but remained there, fast bound in the toils of superstition *(deisidaimonia)* as in one great net."[52]

It is not entirely clear which conquest of Jerusalem Plutarch has in mind, but the close connection of the Sabbath with "superstition" gives rise to the assumption that he is thinking of the capture of Jerusalem by Ptolemy I Soter[53] and not by Titus, and that Agatharchides was his source. Although Plutarch by no means restricts the charge of superstition to the Jews,[54] one cannot overlook the tone of contempt which pervades the list of barbarian customs, and among them his evaluation of the "folly" of not defending oneself on a Sabbath (folly, foolishness, and uncultivated manner are probably the common denominator of the barbarian customs he assembles). This is all the more remarkable if one considers his rather positive assessment of the Jewish abstinence from pork and of the Jewish God.

FAST DAY

The view of the Sabbath as a day of fast seems to have been widespread among Greek and Latin authors. The first to mention it is Strabo of Amaseia, who maintains that Pompey captured Jerusalem on a fast day.[55] Most scholars agree that by this Strabo does not refer to the fast day par excellence, the Day of Atonement, but confuses the Sabbath with a fast day and follows the well-known tradition that Jerusalem and the Temple were captured on a Sabbath.[56]

The tradition of the six days' march in the wilderness which was followed by rest on the seventh day (Apion) is given a rather strange twist by some authors who connect the Exodus from Egypt with fasting. The first is Pompeius Trogus, according to whom Moses, the leader of the expelled lepers, "after having suffered together with his followers from a seven days' fast in the deserts of Arabia . . . , consecrated the seventh day, which used to be called Sabbath by the custom of the nation, for a fast-day *(ieiunio sacravit)*, because that day had ended at once their hunger and their wanderings."[57] A hint of this tradition may also be found in Lysimachus and in Tacitus. Lysimachus has the expelled lepers light up "a bonfire and torches" and keep a fast *(nēsteusantas)* during the night preceding their departure,[58] which may allude to the custom of the Sabbath. The same is possibly true with regard to Tacitus' remark that the Jews "by frequent fasts *(crebris ieiuniis)* even now . . . bear witness to the long hunger with which they were once distressed."[59] Tacitus obviously refers here to the six days' march through the wilderness, although, when describing the Exodus, he emphasizes the "scarcity of water" and does not mention the hunger at all.[60]

The alleged fast on the Sabbath is also the target of the Latin satirists. According to Petronius, it is the desired goal of the converts to Judaism to be allowed to "tremble at the fasts of Sabbath *(ieiuna sabbata)* imposed by the law,"[61] and Martial mentions among his impressive collection of bad smells which he prefers to that of Bassa "the breath of fasting Sabbatarian women" *(ieiunia sabbatariarum)*.[62] Whether or not this goes back to any actual knowledge of Jewish fasting habits is difficult to decide.[63] It seems more likely, however, that both Petronius and Martial make satirical use of a fundamental misunderstanding, namely that the Sabbath is a day of fast (which was probably nourished by some acquaintance with the Day of Atonement).[64] How widespread it was is shown by a remark of Suetonius (ca. 69 C.E.–first half of the second century C.E.) which is thought to be a direct quotation from a letter of Augustus to Tiberius: "Not even a Jew, my dear Tiberius, fasts so scrupulously on his Sabbaths *(sabbatis ieunium servat)* as I have to-day."[65]

LIGHT

The lighting of at least two candles every Sabbath eve immediately before the advent of the Sabbath is one of the most visible signs of its celebration; the Rabbis regarded it as one of the commandments reserved to women.[66] Among pagan authors the satirist Persius (34–62 C.E.) is the only one who gives a vivid and rather realistic description of the celebration of the Sabbath which also refers to the lighting of lamps:

> But when the day of Herod comes round,
> when the lamps wreathed with violets
> and ranged round the greasy window-sills
> have spat forth their thick clouds of smoke,
> when the floppy tunnies' tails are curled round the dishes of red
> ware,
> and the white jars are swollen out with wine,
> you silently twitch your lips,
> turning pale at the Sabbath of the circumcised *(recutitaque
> sabbata)*.[67]

The day of Herod most probably is the Sabbath and not the day of Herod's accession or his birthday. Apart from the practice of lighting lamps, Persius mentions also the customs of eating fish on Friday evening and of drinking wine. Not only is the tone of the whole piece clearly unfavorable, representing the disgust of a person of upper-class outlook toward the "cheap" entertainments of poorer people,[68] it also serves to demonstrate that the customs of the Jews are superstitious, like those of the Phrygians and the Egyptians.[69] The unexpected climax undoubtedly is the last verse, the silent twitch of the lips[70] and the turning pale: despite the opulent meal, the "hero" (a visitor?, a sympathizer?) is suddenly frightened by the overwhelming superstition of Jewish custom and belief.[70]

Superstition is precisely the context in which Seneca, Persius' older contemporary, puts the practice of lighting lamps on Sabbath: "let us forbid lamps to be lighted on the Sabbath, since the gods do not need light, neither do men take pleasure in soot."[72] For Seneca, the lighting of lamps is as superstitious as offering morning salutations and thronging the doors of temples, or as bringing towels and flesh-scrapers to Jupiter and proffering mirrors to Juno: God is worshipped adequately only by those "who truly know him," and he "seeks no servants" but himself does service "to mankind everywhere."[73]

WINE

The habit of drinking wine on the Sabbath was alluded to by Persius. The only other pagan author to refer to wine in connection with the Sabbath is Plutarch in his *Quaestiones Convivales,* when he argues that "the feast of the Sabbath is not completely unrelated to Dionysus."[74] One of his proofs for this is the wine: "The Jews themselves testify to a connection with Dionysus when they keep the Sabbath by inviting each other to drink and enjoy wine."[75] This may be a faint echo of the "custom of ushering in the Sabbath with benedictions over a cup of wine,"[76] but it may also allude to much more colorful drinking habits on the Sabbath than we would expect from our knowledge of contemporary Jewish literature. In any case, Plutarch's willingness to relate the custom of drinking wine on the Sabbath to Dionysus stands in remarkable contrast to his labeling the Sabbath as one of the superstitious practices the Greeks unfortunately learned from the barbarians. As a matter of fact, it is the only response which concedes the comparability of a pagan and a Jewish custom and admits that the two have something in common.[77]

COLD

The strange designation of the Sabbath as "cold" goes back to Meleager, one of the first pagan authors to mention the Sabbath (about 100 B.C.E.):[78] "White-cheeked Demo, some one hath thee named next him and is taking his delight, but my own heart groans within me. If thy lover is some Sabbath-keeper no great wonder! Love burns hot even on cold Sabbaths *(psychrois sabbasi)*."[79] In light of the much later authors of the fifth century C.E. one may suggest that it is indeed the prohibition of lighting fires on Shabbat and, as a result of this, of cooking, which gave rise to the notion of "cold Sabbaths." Thus, the anonymous author of the *Brevis Expositio in Vergilii Georgica* (first half of the fifth century C.E.) explains the "cold star of Saturn:" "It has been sufficiently known that the star of Saturn is cold, and therefore the food among the Jews on the day of Saturn is cold."[80] The only one to transfer the coldness of the day and the food to the coldness of the people is Rutilius Namatianus in his above-mentioned malicious poem:

> a root of silliness *(radix stultitiae)* they are:
> chill Sabbaths are after their own heart *(cui frigida sabbata cordi)*,
> yet their heart is chillier than their creed *(sed cor frigidius religione sua)*.[81]

CHAPTER FIVE

Circumcision

THE JEWISH PRACTICE OF circumcision, according to the Bible, goes back to God's covenant with Abraham as described in Gen. 17. It seals the covenant consisting of God's promise to make Abraham the father of many nations which in turn will possess "forever" the land of Canaan: "This is how you are to keep this covenant between myself and you and your descendants after you: circumcise yourselves, every male among you. You must circumcise the flesh of your foreskin, and it will be a sign of the covenant between us."[1] The failure to keep this covenant means being "cut off," "excised" *(karet)* from the "kin of his father."[2] In obeying God's order, Abraham circumcised himself (at the age of 99) and every male in his household: Ishmael, his son from Hagar, was 13 years old, and later, when Isaac, his son from Sarah was born, he circumcised him on the eighth day, "as decreed by God."[3]

Circumcision was thus the external sign of the covenant between God and Abraham/Israel, the nonobservance of which was considered as the ultimate break with this covenant, dissociation from the community of Israel. Although practiced also by other peoples,[4] it became, together with the Sabbath and the prohibition of eating pork, the most outstanding mark of the Jews in relation to other nations and religions. The Greeks disapproved of circumcision,[5] and hence it became more and more discredited among those Jews who regarded themselves as "enlightened" and hellenized.[6] Consequently, Antiochus IV Epiphanes forbade it when he issued his famous decrees against the Jewish religion (which apparently were inspired by the "enlightened" Jewish Hellenists in Jerusalem).[7]

EGYPTIAN ORIGIN

The early Greek writers are interested mainly in an ethnographic explanation of the custom of circumcision rather than in a judgment, be it favorable or disapproving. They all agree that circumcision is a very old custom, and that the Jews actually did not "invent" it but adopted it from the Egyptians. Probably the first to confirm this is Herodotus (fifth century B.C.E.), who explicitly states "that the Colchians and Egyptians and Ethiopians are the only nations that have from the first practised circumcision. The Phoenicians and the Syrians of Palestine acknowledge of themselves that they learnt the custom from the Egyptians, and the Syrians . . . say that they learnt it lately from the Colchians."[8] There has been much discussion on the question of who the "Syrians of Palestine" are,[9] but the most plausible answer still is the one suggested by Josephus,[10] namely that Herodotus refers to the Jews and that he owes this information to his visit to Egypt.

The next author to mention the custom is Diodorus, who apparently depends on Hecataeus:

> They [the Egyptians] say also that those who set forth with Danaus, likewise from Egypt, settled what is practically the oldest city of Greece, Argos, and that the nation of the Colchi in Pontus and that of the Jews, which lies between Arabia and Syria, were founded as colonies by certain emigrants from their country; and this is the reason why it is a long-established institution among these two peoples to circumcise their male children, the custom having been brought over from Egypt.[11]

The colonists who left Egypt in order to found Greece (under their leaders Danaus and Cadmus) and Judea respectively are also mentioned in Hecataeus' version of the Exodus story, quoted by Diodorus.[12] Thus it is very likely that Hecataeus is also Diodorus' source with regard to the custom of circumcision.[13] The information on the latter is very similar to Herodotus, the only difference being that the Colchians learned the custom, according to Hecataeus/Diodorus, from the Egyptians (like the Jews), whereas Herodotus has them among those nations who practiced it independently (together with the Egyptians).

The same argument, combining the Jewish practice of circumcision with their alleged origin from Egypt, is made by Strabo: "One of the customs most zealously observed among the Egyptians is that they rear every child that is born, and circumcise their males, and excise the females, as is also customary among the Jews, who are also Egyptians in origin, as I have already stated in my account of them."[14] The account of the Egyptian origin of the Jews, to which Strabo here refers, is his version of the Exodus story.

In our connection it is important to notice that the customs of circumcision and excision[15] as well as the abstinence from "flesh,"[16] according to him, are the result of the continuous decline of the Jewish state, and of the superstition *(deisidaimonia)* of its leaders. Superstition led to tyranny, and tyranny to robbery, "for some revolted and harassed the country, both their own country and that of their neighbours, whereas others, co-operating with the rulers, seized the property of others and subdued much of Syria and Phoenicia."[17]

Here Strabo refers no doubt to the Maccabean period, those who "revolted" most probably being the Jewish Hellenists in Jerusalem, and those who "co-operated with the rulers" being the Maccabees and Hasmoneans.[18] Strabo, therefore, does not conceal his dislike of the Jewish *deisidaimonia*, and particularly of the customs of circumcision/excision and abstinence from "flesh," because they are also an expression of the Jews' political degeneration and robbery. His explicit comment that the Jews abstain from "flesh" even today,[19] makes it clear that his dislike is very much directed toward the Jews of his own time. Thus, in Strabo's case, the antiquity of the custom of circumcision and its Egyptian origin do not speak in favor of the Jews.

This negative line of argument is continued by Celsus Philosophus, the only later author who is known to have mentioned the Egyptian origin of circumcision. Origen summarizes him as follows: "After this, though he does not attack the circumcision of the private parts which is the custom of the Jews, Celsus says that it came from the Egyptians."[20] Thus, according to Origen, Celsus has nothing against circumcision as such; he only wants to prove its Egyptian origin. That Origen interprets Celsus correctly becomes clear from the later passage in which Celsus explains why he is so concerned with proving the non-Jewish origin of circumcision:[21] the fact that the Egyptians and Colchians[22] practiced circumcision first, and that the Jews learned it from them, shows that the Jews' claim to be holier than other people is nothing but sheer arrogance *(alazoneia)*. Stern, therefore, is only partly right when he argues that Celsus is "only interested in proving that Jewish customs and institutions are not original but draw on the traditions of other people," and contrasts this with Strabo's connection of circumcision with superstition and the decline of the Jewish religion.[23] What is more important is the reason for Celsus' proof that circumcision is not original, namely his disclosure of Jewish "arrogance" which also guided his discussion of the belief in one God.

Despite the question of its origin, most authors of Greek and Roman antiquity take circumcision to be a distinctively Jewish custom which unmistakably identifies the Jews—although, to be sure, with different nuances and
assessments. The range of this perception varies from neutrality to irony to
derision and outspoken hostility.

There has been a lively debate among scholars over whether we may
find this view as early as the third century B.C.E., namely in the title of Naevius' otherwise lost comedy *Appella* (or *Apella*), which is supposed to mean
sine pelle, that is, *sine praeputio* ("without foreskin"), hence "The circumcised."[24] The advocates of this hypothesis refer to some other fancy titles of
plays written by Naevius, like *Testicularia* or *Triphallus,* as well as the mention of *Judaeus Apella* ("Apella, the Jew") in one of Horace's satires.[25] Con-
versely it has been argued, mainly by Stern: first, that there is no evidence
that in the third century B.C.E., even if *Apella* means "circumcised," the
Jews should be considered the circumcised par excellence; and second, that
the only two preserved lines of the play which curse the use of onions,[26] do
not necessarily allude to Jews (because of the alleged Jewish predilection for
onions). Stern therefore prefers to take *Apella* as the Greek name *Apelles,*
and does not infer from Naevius' play any reference to the presence of Jews
in Rome before 139 B.C.E., let alone to circumcision being considered as the
most characteristic mark of the Jews as early as the third century B.C.E.[27]

Neither argument is very convincing: the first is no less an assertion
than its opposite (in fact, the opposite does seem likelier: if *Apella* means
"The circumcised," it is very plausible that circumcision was regarded as
something typically Jewish). The second is certainly right but does not per-
tain to the question, because it is irrelevant whether the two known lines
refer to a Jew or not. Thus, although there is no definite proof, Naevius'
Apella may well be understood as rather early evidence for the pagan view
of circumcision as a distinctive Jewish custom.[28]

Apparently circumcision is something unmistakably Jewish for the
Greco-Alexandrian historian Timagenes (first century B.C.E.). According to
Josephus, Strabo relies on Timagenes when he writes of the Hasmonean
king Aristobulus I: "This man was a kindly person and very serviceable to
the Jews, for he acquired additional territory for them, and brought over to
them a portion of the Iturean nation, whom he joined to them by the bond
of circumcision."[29] Whatever particular territory Timagenes meant by the
"portion of the Iturean nation" conquered by Aristobulus,[30] there can be

no doubt that for him, circumcision was the decisive measure to incorporate members of a Gentile nation into the Jewish nation, and, for that matter, an absolutely natural measure. It has long been observed that Timagenes' sympathetic characterization of Aristobulus I lacks any hostile overtone, and this also holds true for his assessment of circumcision: it belongs to the Jews, and whoever wants to become a Jew, or in this case, whomever the Jews want to become a Jew, has to undergo this rite.

Josephus recounts of Apion, the anything but sympathetic Greco-Alexandrian author, that he "derides the practise of circumcision."[31] We do not have Apion's actual words but from all we know about his calumnies there can be little doubt that it was not just a remark in passing but one aimed at ridiculing the custom of circumcision as something specifically Jewish. In his answer, Josephus refers to the practice of circumcision among Egyptian priests and cannot refrain from regarding "the penalty which Apion paid for maligning his own country's laws as just and appropriate": an ulcer which rendered circumcision essential, and of which he finally died "in terrible tortures."[32]

In an interesting argument with a "colleague" who pretends to be a philosopher without practicing his profession, the Stoic philosopher Epictetus uses the example of a Jew:

> Do you not see in what sense men are severally called Jew, Syrian, or Egyptian? For example, whenever we see a man halting between two faiths,[33] we are in the habit of saying, "He is not a Jew, he is only acting the part." But when he adopts the attitude of mind of the man who has been baptized *(to pathos to tou bebammenou)*[34] and has made his choice *(hērēmenou)*,[35] then he both is a Jew in fact and is also called one. So we also are counterfeit "Baptists" *(parabaptistai)*,[36] ostensibly Jewish, but in reality something else, not in sympathy with our own reason, far from applying the principles which we profess.[37]

This text has been discussed in great detail with regard to the question of whether it can be taken as evidence for uncircumcised (that is, only "baptized") proselytes or whether it speaks of Christians because Epictetus may have confused Christianity with Judaism.[38] I do not wish to repeat that discussion here but accept the view most commonly held: that Epictetus does speak of Jews and apparently has taken a part of the conversion rites[39] to stand for all such rituals.[40]

If this is the case, Epictetus' example of "a man halting between two faiths" refers to someone who is attracted by Judaism but has not yet made the decisive step, that is, the "God-fearer," whom we know very well, for example from Petronius and Juvenal. The decisive step is "baptism" as *pars pro toto* for the conversion ritual which consisted ideally of baptism, circumcision, and an atonement offering followed by an immersion bath. Only by "baptism" does the would-be Jew become a "Jew in fact" and is rightly called a Jew; in the same way the would-be philosopher becomes a true philosopher only by practicing his philosophic profession. What is important in our context is the fact that Epictetus uses this example of the Jew, attesting not only to "baptism" as part of the conversion ritual but also to the phenomenon of proselytism as being connected mainly with the Jews.

The author who most vehemently and aggressively connects circumcision and Jewish separateness (together with misanthropy and impiety) is Tacitus. When he sets about to list the "base and abominable" Jewish customs, he mentions their eating and sleeping apart, as well as circumcision: "They adopted circumcision to distinguish themselves from other peoples by this difference *(circumcidere genitalia instituerunt, ut diversitate noscantur)*. Those who are converted to their ways follow the same practice, and the earliest lesson they receive is to despise the gods, to disown their country, and to regard their parents, children, and brothers as of little account."[41] Circumcision is the most characteristic mark of the Jews, and they chose it deliberately in order to "distinguish themselves from other peoples" and to express their "hate and enmity" against them *(adversus omnes alios hostile odium)*.[42] In addition, proselytes have to undergo the rite of circumcision, and once they have become Jews they disown their national gods, their country, and their family—the holy triad of ancient Rome's system of values. Insofar as circumcision determines and demarcates "Jewishness," it emphasizes the very essence of Judaism: otherness, exclusiveness, and misanthropy, which by definition cannot be accepted by any true Roman. Tacitus therefore has nothing but contempt for those who are attracted to Judaism, and calls them "the worst rascals among other peoples."[43]

That circumcision was considered to be the Jewish custom par excellence can be deduced also from Suetonius' reference to an incident of which he claims to have been an eyewitness, namely that "the person of a man ninety years old was examined before the procurator and a very crowded court, to see whether he was circumcised."[44] The context of this incident is the harsher enforcement of the levy of the *fiscus Iudaicus* by Domitian which will be discussed below.[45] Circumcision has become the definite sign, or rather stigma, of the Jews, and this is true for the further course of history. As late as the fourth century the Neoplatonic philosopher Sallustius mentions Jewish circumcision among the strange customs of the Massagetae who "eat their fathers" and the Persians who "preserve their nobility by begetting children on their mothers."[46]

As might be expected, those who use circumcision almost as a stereotype to characterize Jews are the Latin satirists. Horace, apart from the controversial "Apella, the Jew," also speaks of "the circumcised Jews" *(curtis Iudaeis)* in a rather self-evident and ironic way,[47] and Persius, when coining the phrase "Sabbath of the circumcised,"[48] does not even need to mention the Jews.

In Petronius' *Satyricon,* too, circumcision figures as the most prominent characteristic of the Jews. When Encolpius and his friends make plans to escape from their enemy, and he suggests that they dye themselves with ink in order to look like Ethiopian slaves, Giton adds: "Oh! yes, . . . and please circumcise us too so that we look like Jews *(ut Iudaei videamur),* and bore our ears to imitate Arabians, and chalk our faces till Gaul takes us for her own sons; as if this colour above could alter our shapes, and it were not needed that many things act in unison to make a good lie on all accounts."[49] Although Giton's proposal is meant ironically and he rather prefers "to plunge into the deep,"[50] there can be no doubt that for him and his friends circumcision is as typically Jewish as boring the ears is typically Arabian and chalking the face is typical of the Gauls. On the basis of this evidence, it is clear that the slave who annoys Encolpius by screeching Virgil and whom his master praises for being almost perfect, except for the fact that "he is circumcised *(recutitus est)* and snores,"[51] is also a Jew.[52] Hence it is only consistent that Petronius regards circumcision as the decisive step for the "God-fearer" in becoming a Jew: he may worship his "pig-god" and clamor in the ears of "high heaven"—unless he "cuts back his foreskin with the knife," he cannot "enjoy" the "fasts of Sabbath."[53] Most likely, Petronius' irony is not so much directed toward circumcision as such, but toward those fashionable would-be Jews who pretended to be Jewish by praying to the Jewish God but shied away from the decisive step. If this is the case, Petronius must have been as disturbed by the phenomenon of the increasing attractiveness of Judaism as were his slightly later contemporaries Tacitus and Juvenal.

No connection between circumcision and proselytism is made in the many references to the Jews by Martial, the author of the famous Latin epigrams (late first century C.E.).[54] Again, circumcision serves mainly to characterize the Jews (among other peoples), but acquires here a clearly sexual tinge. This is certainly true for the epigram on Caelia, who bestows her affections on everybody except her native Romans: whereas the representatives of the different nations are mentioned by the names of their respective nations only, it is said about the Jews that she does not "shun the loins *(inguina)*[55] of circumcised Jews *(recutitorum Iudaeorum)*."[56] It is hardly coincidental that the rather obscene *inguina* and "circumcision" are joined together.

The same applies to the epigram addressed to Laecania in which Martial complains that her slave is always present when she takes a bath, his "sexual organs *(inguina)* covered by a black piece of leather *(nigra aluta)*,"[57] and instead extols his slave (and himself) to her:

> but my slave, Laecania, to say nothing of myself,
> has the Jewish weight under (his) naked skin *(Iudaeum nuda sub cute pondus habet)*.[58]

To begin with, there can be no doubt that the "Jewish weight" is an obscene allusion to the alleged sexual potency of the Jews.[59] This is also apparent from the continuation of the epigram, in which he bluntly asks: "Or is it possible that solely the member[60] of your slave is real?"[61] which, of course, is to be answered with no: Take advantage, instead, of my "well equipped" Jewish slave, or even better, of myself,[62] and do not confine yourself to your slave!

The question, however, is whether Martial refers to Jewish sexual potency in a more general way, or whether he connects the sexual potency of the Jews with their circumcision in particular. Stern has taken it for granted, without explanation, that "Martial alludes to his Jewish slave as being circumcised,"[63] whereas H. J. Izaac in his French translation renders *nuda sub cute* simply as "à découvert,"[64] and by this contrasts Martial's naked slave with Laecania's slave who wears an *aluta*. The latter certainly being the case (there is obviously a play of words between *aluta* and *nuda*), one may still assume that the *Iudaeum pondus* in itself includes the notion of the circumcised Jew. However, the connection between sexual potency and circumcision becomes more explicit if one follows the variant reading *nulla sub cute* ("under no skin") which is substantiated by a considerable number of manuscripts.[65] According to this reading, the point of the epigram would be: my slave, in contrast to yours, is not only naked (because he does not wear an *aluta*), but also has "no skin," that is, no foreskin, and still, under his "no skin," is much better "endowed" than your slave.[66] This fits even better with the first line of the epigram (the play of words being *aluta* and *nulla*) as well as with the following line which also has *nudi*[67] (*nuda sub cute* immediately followed by *nudi* would be rather inelegant).[68]

In another epigram Martial refers to an actor or actually a singer who had his penis covered with a *fibula,* that is, a "sheath":[69]

> So large a sheath *(fibula)* covers Menophilus' penis
> that it would be enough by itself for all our comic actors.
> I had supposed (we often bathe together)
> that he was anxious to spare his voice, Flaccus.
> But while he was in a game in the middle of the sportsground with
>   everybody watching,
> the sheath slipped off the poor soul; he was circumcised *(verpus
>   erat)!*[70]

As the epigram itself explains, the *fibula* was used i.a. by singers because it was believed that their voices were impaired by sexual activity.[71] What is peculiar in this case is not only that the *fibula* fell off and revealed its owner as being circumcised, that is, Jewish,[72] but also that it was of an enormous size, thus covering, or better uncovering, an unusually big penis. Hence we have here the same correlation between being circumcised and "well-endowed" as in the above epigram to Laecania.

This becomes even more articulate if one considers the use of *verpus* for "circumcised." *Verpa* (= Greek *psōlē*) is the penis "with foreskin drawn back as a result of an erection," and is often used "when the performance of a sexual act is at issue," especially aggressive homosexual acts.[73] Consequently, the use of *verpus* for "circumcised"[74] equates the retraction of the foreskin with the excessive lustfulness associated with the Jews and their constant readiness, so to speak, to perform the sexual act.[75]

It is precisely the homosexual connotation of *verpus* which is the core of the following epigram:

> That you are excessively jealous of my books and disparage them on
>   every possible occasion,
> I forgive: you are sensible, circumcised poet *(verpe poeta).*
> Neither do I care about the fact that, although you criticise my
>   poems,
> you make up your own from them:
> there too you are sensible, circumcised poet *(verpe poeta).*
> But this crucifies me: that you even though you were born in
>   Jerusalem itself,

you bugger my boy *(pedicas puerum),* circumcised poet *(verpe poeta).*
Behold, you deny it and swear to me by the Thunderer's Temple.
I don't believe you.
Swear, O circumcised one *(verpe)* by Anchialus.[76]

The dramatic increase in this poem is marked by the three occurrences of *verpe poeta* and the final *verpe* only, with no *poeta* (because Martial has unmasked his opponent, finally, as being "circumcised" only and no "poet"). He ironically forgives him for disparaging his books and at the same time plagiarizing them, but he is tortured (lit. crucified) by the fact that he seduces[77] his beloved boy. The main offense of the false poet, therefore, is the seduction of Martial's boy; the punch-line being not so much the seduction itself, but the seduction by a circumcised Jew who could not be more Jewish (because he was born in Jerusalem). The "poet," who is not a rival at all as a poet, has become a rival, indeed, in his capacity as a lover—and this is what most annoys Martial. There is undoubtedly a trace of jealousy in Martial's anger about the Jew having been successful in seducing his boy (he wants it to be untrue),[78] and the repeated "circumcised" may even hint at his jealousy of the Jew's sexual potency. Thus, Martial's contempt for the Jew and his repulsion toward him may well be matched by his feeling of fear and jealousy of his sexual superiority. His obsession with the alleged sexual potency of the Jews gives the topic of circumcision a ring which is uncommon in the ancient world, but returns vehemently much later.

The last of the Roman satirists to be mentioned in this context is Juvenal. I have already analyzed his poem on the "God-fearers," who start with revering the Sabbath, worshipping the clouds, and abstaining from pork, and finally end up accepting circumcision and by this in becoming real Jews.[79] Here it suffices to point to the term *verpus* being used again for "circumcised" (as is the case in Martial), and to restate the close connection in this poem between the circumcised Jew and Jewish elitism.

A late heir of the Latin satirical tradition is again Rutilius Namatianus, the high Roman official and "probably the last non-Christian Latin writer to give vent to antipathy to Judaism."[80] In his description of his journey from Rome to Gaul he refers also to the *obscena gens* ("obscene, filthy people") of the Jews "that shamefully cuts off the genital head" *(quae genitale caput propudiosa metit),* that is, practices circumcision.[81] This seems to be a late echo of Tacitus' accusation that the Jews are "prone to lust," and especially of Martial's association of circumcision with lechery.

Much as the Greeks, and later the Romans, may have disapproved of circumcision, we have not found any pagan author who explicitly criticizes it as a custom which itself is to be discriminated against and detested. Some scholars, however, point to Hadrian's ban on circumcision, allegedly imposed sometime between 128 and 132 C.E.,[82] and take it as evidence for the emperor's dislike of circumcision. This understanding depends on two premises: first, that the ban was of "empire-wide application" and not merely a punishment for the so-called Bar Kokhba revolt, the second uprising against Rome (132–135 C.E.), and second, that the reason for it was Hadrian's "moral objection to the practice as a barbarous mutilation on a par with castration," and that "the laws aimed at stamping both practices out of civilized society were probably closely connected."[83] In order to evaluate this argument it is necessary to review briefly the evidence for the prohibition of circumcision and castration.

1. The only proof for Hadrian's ban on circumcision[84] is the short note in the *Historia Augusta:* "At this time also the Jews began war, because they were forbidden to mutilate their genitals *(quod vetabantur mutilare genitalia)*."[85] The historical credibility of this remark is controversial both because of the problematic literary character of the *Historia Augusta* in general[86] and because it contradicts Cassius Dio, who does not know of any prohibition of circumcision in connection with the Bar Kokhba revolt. Instead, Cassius Dio attributes the outbreak of the war to Hadrian's decision to rebuild Jerusalem as the Roman colony Aelia Capitolina.[87] Most scholars, however, combine Cassius Dio and the *Historia Augusta* and consider both the prohibition of circumcision and the foundation of Aelia Capitolina as decisive for the outbreak of the Jewish revolt.[88] It goes without saying that those who argue for a universal ban against circumcision issued by Hadrian must take the *Historia Augusta* very seriously.

2. Evidence for a universal ban on circumcision which applied to other peoples in the Roman empire is even more meager. Scholars mention the Arabs, the Egyptians, and the Samaritans but the references are dubious or late. That Origen "states expressly that in his own time circumcision was permitted only to Jews"[89] says nothing with regard to Hadrian. The same is true for the Egyptians: the alleged prohibition of circumcision is only a conclusion from the facts (a) that Egyptian priests were granted permission to perform circumcision during the reigns of Antoninus Pius and Marcus

Aurelius[90] and (b) that circumcision earlier in the Hellenistic period probably was also practiced by non-priests.[91] And finally, there is a Syriac passage, according to which the Romans abrogated all the ancient Arabic laws, especially the one concerning circumcision, when they conquered Arabia.[92] Whereas Drijvers applies this remark to the Arabian wars of Septimius Severus (195/96 C.E.) and Macrinus (217/18 C.E.),[93] Stern finds it "most natural" that it "alludes to the incorporation of the Nabatean kingdom into the Roman empire."[94] However, since the first conquest of Arabia took place in 106 C.E., that is, under Trajan, this would lead one to the rather strange conclusion (for the advocates of a universal ban on circumcision issued by Hadrian) that this universal ban in fact originated with Trajan.[95]

3. The situation is much different with regard to castration, which had been prohibited explicitly by Domitian and Nerva.[96] The ban on castration was enforced by Hadrian, who imposed on it the punishment of the *Lex Cornelia de sicariis et veneficis,* that is, the death penalty and confiscation of property.[97]

4. The earliest evidence for circumcision in Roman legislation is an edict by Antoninus Pius (138–161 C.E.), Hadrian's successor, which states: "Jews are permitted to circumcise only their sons *(circumcidere Iudaeis filios suos tantum)* on the authority of a rescript of the Divine Pius; if anyone shall commit it on one who is not of the same [Jewish] religion, he shall suffer the punishment of a castrator."[98] The advocates of a universal ban on circumcision maintain that this rescript exempted "the Jews alone" from Hadrian's earlier universal ban, by simultaneously restricting circumcision to the Jewish people proper, and prohibiting proselytism.[99] Since the latter is certainly the case, the former part of the argument stands in question. I have argued against it elsewhere,[100] and I still do not see any reason why the rescript should refer to "the Jews alone" in the sense that previously other peoples had been included in the ban on circumcision.[101] The most natural interpretation, as translated above, is that the first part of the rescript permits the Jews to circumcise *only their sons,* and that the second part determines the appropriate punishment for the transgressor. Since the punishment is precisely the one imposed by Hadrian on castration, namely the application of the *Lex Cornelia,* we have here, indeed, and not earlier, the first literary proof for the equation of circumcision with castration.[102]

Altogether, there is not much evidence either for a universal ban on circumcision issued by Hadrian or for Hadrian's rage to "stamp out" circumcision as if it were equivalent to castration. One finally may take refuge in psychology to connect the prohibition of circumcision with Hadrian's abhorrence of this practice. Hadrian, the most "Greek" of the Roman emperors, admired Greek culture and art.[103] There can be little doubt that he adhered to the standards of Greek aesthetic feeling, and this may well have been the case also with regard to the aesthetic judgment of the body, especially the male body. If the Greeks disliked circumcision, it was certainly not for moral reasons but because they regarded it as a mutilation of an otherwise perfect body. K. J. Dover has amply demonstrated that Greek artists, most notably vase-painters, were almost obsessed with the representation of the foreskin, and that they regarded the retraction of the foreskin and the exposure of the glans as ugly and crude, reserved for satyrs, ugly old men, barbarians, and comic burlesque.[104] Accordingly, it is not utterly impossible that Hadrian, guided not by "moral objection"[105] but by the ancient Greek ideal of beauty and perfection, indeed considered circumcision as a "barbarous mutilation" and tried to prohibit it. If this is the case, then we have here the most serious consequence of Greek and Roman disapproval of circumcision. However, this proposal cannot be more than a conjecture, and, of course, it does not solve the questions of when Hadrian issued the decree (before or during/after the Bar Kokhba war), and whether it was directed solely against the Jews or also against other peoples.[106]

CHAPTER SIX

Proselytism

THE QUESTION OF JEWISH proselytizing in antiquity, that is, whether the Jews were actively seeking converts to their religion, has occupied scholars for a long time. The main reason for this is the desire to explain the outburst of early Christian missionary activities in the first century C.E. which may, or may not, be rooted in the missionary zeal of contemporary Judaism.[1] I do not intend to deal here with the problem of Jewish proselytizing per se,[2] but rather with the evidence for *pagan responses* to proselytism. However, the results of this examination will also have some bearing on the broader question. The examination of the relevant sources clearly reveals in the pagan authors a dawning awareness of and reaction against Jewish proselytes. It ranges from the perception of a Jewish presence to familiarity with "Judaizers/sympathizers"[3] as well as proselytes (and with the distinction between these two categories) to open hostility toward proselytes.

THE EXPULSION FROM ROME IN 139 B.C.E.

The earliest evidence we possess refers to the presence of Jews and their cult in Rome. It may already, at this early stage, have evoked a sympathetic response on the part of some Romans, in turn leading to the expulsion of the Jews by the Roman authorities (139 B.C.E.). It is reported by Valerius Maximus via the late Byzantine authors Iulius Paris and Ianuarius Nepotianus.[4] The two epitomators agree that the Jews were expelled from Rome by the *praetor peregrinus* Cn. Cornelius Hispalus, that is, Cn. Cornelius Scipio Hispanus,[5] but they disagree about the cause. According to Paris they "attempted to infect Roman customs *(Romanos inficere mores conati erant)* with the cult of Jupiter Sabazius," whereas Nepotianus says, less specifically, that they "attempted to transmit their sacred rites to the Romans" *(Roma-*

nis tradere sacra sua conati erant); Nepotianus adds, however, that the *praetor* not only banished the Jews but also "cast down their private altars *(aras privatas)* from public places."[6]

It is not clear what a Jewish attempt "to transmit their sacred rites to the Romans" (Nepotianus) or "to infect the Roman customs" (Paris) might mean. Did the Jews actually seek to convert the Romans to Judaism, or did they merely try to introduce their native cult into Rome, in the sense that they wanted to practice it publicly? There is no definite answer to this question,[7] but I am inclined to favor the second possibility and to put less emphasis on a Jewish missionary zeal.[8] We have here, I suggest, the first evidence for a Jewish community in Rome which had become "visible" to the Roman authorities to such an extent that they felt disturbed or even threatened. This would indicate that it is not so much proselytizing which was at issue in 139 B.C.E. but the sheer Jewish presence in Rome.[9] The possibility cannot be excluded, however, that some Romans may have been attracted by Judaism and thus increased the feeling that the ancient Roman customs were in danger.[10]

HORACE

The next supposed allusion to Jewish proselytizing is found in the first century B.C.E. At the end of the fourth satire in the first book of his *Saturae*, Horace says:

> . . . when I find a bit of leisure, I trifle with my papers.
> This is one of those lesser frailties I spoke of,
> and if you should make no allowance for it *(cui si concedere nolis),*
> then would a big band *(multa manus)* of poets come to my aid
> (*auxilio*)—
> for we are the big majority—
> and we, like the Jews, will compel you
> to make one of our throng *(ac veluti te Iudaei cogemus in hanc concedere turbam).*[11]

Many scholars take the last line of this satire to refer to "strong Jewish missionary activity in Rome."[12] Feldman even sees this activity as "proverbial" and ponders the possibility that Horace might allude satirically to Ex. 23:2: "You shall not follow a multitude to do evil."[13] This interpretation takes it for granted that the point of comparison of "like the Jews" is to become "one of our throng": the Jews are known for compelling others to become members of their "throng"; in a similar fashion we (that is, Horace and his "big band of poets") will compel you to become a member of our "throng."[14]

This reading of the satire, however, is not the only possible one; in fact, the text is more complicated. To begin with, the subject of the satire is Horace's insistence on his "lesser frailty" of writing satires, and the last lines are meant to "convince" his opponent by force if his reasoned arguments fail; this force is stressed by the use of rather military language (*manus, auxilio,* cf. also *turba*).[15]

Such a reading of the last lines that yields the understanding "we will compel you to become part of our group" has been contested by J. Nolland in his thorough philological analysis of the final part of the satire.[16] According to his interpretation the meaning may be something similar to: "If you are not prepared to indulge it [the frailty of writing satires], . . . then we, like the Jews, will force you to indulge [it, namely the writing of satires] with regard to this throng [of poets]."

However this may be—I am not completely persuaded by the philological argument—the usual interpretation of this satire is problematical for another reason. Even if we translate "We will force you, like the Jews, to become part of our group," it is anything but self-evident that the point of comparison with the Jews is conversion to another group. I doubt that one would reach this conclusion without a prior preoccupation with the "zeal of Jewish missionary activity."[17] The more natural reading is to see the point of comparison in the *force* being exerted on Horace's opponent: "We will force you, as it is typical of the Jews, to become part of our group."[18]

On the basis of this understanding of the satire there is, indeed, nothing left of an alleged allusion to Jewish proselytizing in Horace, let alone of "proverbial" missionary activity. What may be proverbial is the forced compliance exerted by the Jews over their opponents. For a historical embedding of this suggestion, Nolland is certainly right in referring to Cicero's speech *Pro Flacco,*[19] delivered in 59 B.C.E., that is, one generation before Horace, which mentions the big "crowd"[20] of the Jews who "stick together" and who are so influential in "informal assemblies" that "every respectable man" must be careful not to incite them against him.[21] The Jews of Rome, as early as the middle of the first century B.C.E., seem to have been a kind of well-known, and feared, political "pressure group," and it is this political power to which Horace alludes satirically, not their religious persuasiveness or even force.

THE EXPULSION FROM ROME IN 19 C.E.

The second expulsion of the Jews from Rome by Tiberius in the year 19 C.E. is also explained by most scholars as a punishment for seeking proselytes.[22] The oldest Roman source is Tacitus, who reports:

> Another debate dealt with the proscription of the Egyptian and Jewish rites, and a senatorial edict directed that four thousand descendants of enfranchised slaves *(libertini generis)* tainted with that superstition *(ea superstitione infecta)* and suitable in point of age, were to be shipped to Sardinia and there employed in suppressing brigandage: "if they succumbed to the pestilential climate, it was a cheap loss." The rest had orders to leave Italy, unless they had renounced their impious ceremonial *(profanos ritus)* by a given date.[23]

To be sure, Tacitus does not speak explicitly about proselytes, nor does he give a reason for the expulsion. One may only suspect that the edict was aimed at the Egyptian and Jewish religions, because he mentions their respective "rites" and their "impious ceremonial." We do know of measures taken against the Egyptian religion, especially the cult of Isis,[24] but a fundamental attack of this severity against the Jewish religion would have been unprecedented and would have come very unexpectedly, to say the least, given the repeated guarantees of religious freedom.[25] For this reason alone one might assume that the conscription and expulsion did have something to do with Jewish proselytes.

There are two indications in Tacitus' text which support this supposition. First of all, Tacitus speaks of "descendants of enfranchised slaves" who were "tainted with that superstition," and the very use of the word "taint" or "infect," although it does not exclude native Jews,[26] strongly suggests converts to Judaism. This argument is enforced by the expulsion order which explicitly states that the rest had to leave Italy, "unless they had renounced their impious ceremonial by a given date." This detail of "renouncing" something makes it appear very probable that Tacitus is talking about converts and not about native Jews.[27] This does not mean, however, that the edict was directed against Jewish missionary activity: it only speaks of Jews, most likely converts, who were conscripted or expelled. The target is not proselytizing but proselytes, that is, people who converted to Judaism.[28]

The second author to mention the expulsion is Suetonius:

> He [Tiberius] abolished foreign cults, especially the Egyptian and the Jewish rites, compelling all who were addicted to such superstitions *(qui superstitione ea tenebantur)* to burn their religious vestments and all their paraphernalia. Those of the Jews who were of military age he assigned to provinces of less healthy climate, ostensibly to serve in the army; the others of the same people or of similar beliefs *(gentis eiusdem vel simila sectantes)* he banished from the city, on pain of slavery for life if they did not obey.[29]

Suetonius' account has the same structure as Tacitus', despite several differences in details. Like Tacitus, although he mentions both the Egyptian and the Jewish rites, he has only the Jews conscripted into military service, and he also distinguishes between the two categories of the conscripted and the "others." Unlike Tacitus, he mentions the measures specifically directed against the Egyptians,[30] he has the "others" banished from Rome (instead of Italy), and he knows of a punishment for those who refuse to leave Rome (slavery). Since he does not allow for the possibility of renunciation, he seems to imply that the whole Jewish community had to suffer either conscription or expulsion. More important, Suetonius explicitly includes among the expelled those "of similar belief" *(similia sectantes)*—more precisely: those "who followed the same practices"[31]—thus quite clearly referring to proselytes. Since he mentions, however, these proselytes together with "the others," he has not only proselytes expelled but all the remaining Jews. We cannot tell with certainty whether this is reliable historical information or an embellishment on the part of Suetonius. It seems hard to believe, though, that all members of the Jewish community were expelled from either Rome or Italy.

And finally, the third author to refer to Tiberius' ban is Cassius Dio, the historian of the early third century C.E.: "As the Jews flocked to Rome in great numbers and were converting *(methistantōn)* many of the natives to their ways, he [Tiberius] banished most of them."[32] Unlike Tacitus and Suetonius, Cassius Dio speaks only of the Jews (and not of the Egyptians), and only of an expulsion (he does not seem to know anything about the conscription), nor has he the entire Jewish community banished but only "most of them." In addition—and this is the most important difference—he is the only one who unambiguously gives Jewish missionary activities[33] as the reason for the banishment.

In order to evaluate the historical reliability of this particular detail, one has to take into account, as has been pointed out by M. Goodman, that the passage in question is not preserved in the manuscript tradition of Cassius Dio's Roman History, but in a "solitary quotation (not necessarily verbatim?) by the seventh-century Christian writer John of Antioch."[34] This may cause suspicion, but one should not argue, as Goodman at least implicitly does, with the late date of the source, and at the same time explain the motive for the expulsion "in terms of a new Roman awareness of the possibility of proselytism since the end of the first century [!], and perhaps as evidence for a real proselytizing mission in *his* [Cassius Dio's] day, the third century."[35] The latter seems to me very plausible, but I cannot see any reason for connecting Cassius Dio's remark (which may have been written at the beginning of the third century at the earliest and refers to an event of the *beginning* of the first century) with just the *end* of the first century—except for Goodman's tendency to postpone not only missionary activity but also real proselytes to the end of the first century C.E.

To sum up, the assumption is well founded that the expulsion of the Jews from Rome in 19 C.E. was a response to a growing number of Jewish proselytes in the full sense of the word[36] and thus to the attractiveness of the Jewish religion,[37] but not to actual missionary activities by the Jews.[38] Both Tacitus and Suetonius point to the former, whereas Cassius Dio's insinuation about active proselytizing seems to reflect the situation in his time rather than at the beginning of the first century.

SENECA

The next clue for Roman awareness of the continuing success of the Jewish religion is to be found in *De Superstitione,* the lost work of the Roman philosopher Seneca. It is known only from quotations, mainly by Augustine, and was probably written in the sixties of the first century C.E.[39] Augustine quotes Seneca as follows:

> But when speaking of the Jews he [Seneca] says: "Meanwhile the customs of this accursed people *(sceleratissimae gentis)* have gained such influence *(convaluit)* that they are now received throughout the world *(per omnes . . . terras)*. The vanquished have given laws to their victors *(victi victoribus leges dederunt)*." He shows his surprise as he says this, not knowing what was being wrought by the providence of God.—But he adds a statement that shows what he thought of their

system of sacred institutions: "The Jews *(illi)*, however, are aware of the origin and meaning of their rites *(causas ritus sui noverunt)*. The greater part of the people *(maior pars populi)* go through a ritual not knowing why they do so."[40]

This pronounced criticism, which for the first time in Roman literature "give[s] vent to deliberate animadversions on the Jewish religion and its impact on Roman society,"[41] is focused on Jewish customs (it follows Seneca's negative assessment of the Sabbath). Seneca is mainly concerned with the success of the customs of the *sceleratissima gens:* his helpless rage and his surprise[42] on this find vivid expression in his famous dictum about the "vanquished" who "have given laws to their victors."

There can be no doubt that Seneca is deeply troubled by this spread of Jewish customs among Gentiles. Whether he refers to Gentile "sympathizers" or "Judaizers" only ("God-fearers"), or to proselytes in the full sense of the word, cannot be decided with certainty. I do not see any reason, however, why full proselytes should be excluded; and even if he had mainly "sympathizers" in mind, I do not believe that the difference between "Judaizers," that is, people who followed certain Jewish customs but avoided the ultimate step, and "proselytes," that is, converts to Judaism, was important for him and for his assessment of the danger the Jews presented to Roman society.[43] On the other hand, the presence of proselytes should not just be identified with active proselytizing. To argue, as Stern does, that Seneca composed his works, which contain the references to the Jews, "at the height of the Jewish *proselytizing movement,*"[44] exaggerates and starts from the rash assumption that proselytes presuppose proselytizing activity. The latter is not maintained by Seneca nor can it be proved from the earlier sources.

Despite his dislike of the Jews, the second quotation displays a certain respect for their awareness of the "origin and meaning of their rites" *(illi* certainly referring to the Jews, as translated by Green). Respect for ancient customs—notwithstanding their content—and for those who uphold them, is a well-known motif in Greek and Roman literature; we find it even in Tacitus, although he makes every effort to downplay it. Their awareness of the origin and meaning of their rites actually distinguishes the Jews from "the greater part of the people" who are ignorant on that score. Stern wants to identify the latter with "the non-Jews who adopt Jewish customs," that is, "sympathizers,"[45] whereas Turcan sees here an implied contrast between the Jewish "priests" or "sages" and the ignorant Jewish masses.[46] Both interpretations are far-fetched: why should the "sympathizers" represent the "greater part of the people"? Nor is there any reason to identify *illi* with the "priests" or "sages." It seems much more probable to assume a contrast between the Jews (as part of the Roman populace) and the greater part of the *Roman* people.[47] *Populus,* indeed, most naturally refers to the Roman populace,[48] and there is nothing surprising in Seneca's criticism of his countrymen, even if it is to the advantage of the Jews.[49]

DOMITIAN AND PROSELYTES

A very peculiar attitude toward "sympathizers" and/or proselytes can be found during the reign of the Roman emperor Domitian (81–96 C.E.). In his account of the enforcement of the *fiscus Iudaicus* Suetonius says:

> Besides other taxes, the *fiscus Iudaicus* was administered with the utmost vigour *(acerbissime).* Persons who were either living a Jewish life without publicly acknowledging it *(inprofessi Iudaicam viverent vitam)* or, concealing their origins *(dissimulata origine),* did not pay the tribute that had been imposed on their people, were prosecuted. I recall being present in my youth when the person of a man ninety years old was examined before the procurator and a very crowded court, to see whether he was circumcised.[50]

The *fiscus Iudaicus* was the tax of two *drachmae* imposed after 70 C.E. by Vespasian "on all Jews, wheresoever resident . . . , to be paid annually into the Capitoline temple as formerly contributed by them to the temple of Jerusalem."[51] Thus it was rather a diversion of the original Temple tax of half a shekel, the only difference being that it was now to be paid not only by Jewish males of twenty years and upwards (including freed slaves and proselytes), but by "all Jews," including women, children and slaves.[52] Domitian no doubt enforced the administration of the tax, as Suetonius explicitly says, but the crucial question is, against precisely which groups of people the enforcement was directed.

To begin with, Suetonius clearly has two categories of people in mind, namely (a) those who lived a Jewish life without publicly acknowledging it (the *inprofessi*), and (b) those who concealed their origins. It is not entirely clear whether the reason given, that they did so to avoid the *fiscus Iudaicus,* applies only to the second category or to both categories, but the context strongly suggests the latter because also those who lived a Jewish life in secrecy in fact did avoid the tax (and it is the collection of the tax that Domitian's "decree" is about). The second category is the least controversial: it no doubt refers to ethnic but assimilated Jews who claimed not to be Jews any longer and thus not to be liable for the *fiscus Iudaicus,* probably also to Jewish Christians,[53] and to persons of other ethnic groups who happened to be circumcised.[54]

The first category is taken by most scholars to refer to proselytes and/or "Judaizers,"[55] indicating that Domitian extended the *fiscus Iudaicus* to these groups in order to increase the tax revenue. This interpretation has come under fierce attack by L. A. Thompson, according to whom "the first of Suetonius' categories of presumed tax-dodgers . . . also consisted of apostates[56] and non-Jewish *peregrini.* But, unlike the other category, these people had attracted the attention of informers, not by visible signs of circumcision, but by behaviour, such as abstention from pork, which could be construed as 'Jewish life.'"[57] He arrives at this rather surprising conclusion by a peculiar understanding of Suetonius[58] and by arguing that proselytes as well as "Judaizers" cannot be meant because this would involve a "fundamental contradiction": a "virtual legalization of conversion to Judaism" by imposing the tax on converts and at the same time punishing those Roman citizens who had "drifted into Jewish ways." By the latter he refers to a statement by Cassius Dio[59] which he takes as proof that Gentile converts to Judaism were accused of atheism and executed.[60]

Thompson's main argument, the alleged contradiction between subjecting converts to the *fiscus Iudaicus* and at the same time punishing them for being attracted to Judaism, is hard to comprehend. It may well miss, in its zeal to be logical, historical reality, because it takes for granted that the charge of "atheism"—which led to the death penalty under the law of *maiestas*—was Roman legislation, generally accepted and enforced under Domitian. This does not seem very likely because it is obvious from Cassius Dio's account[61] that Domitian, especially in his later years, deliberately used the charge of "atheism" to eliminate those rivals (and relatives) he deemed dangerous. This is most probably true with regard to the case of Flavius Clemens and Flavia Domitilla, reported by Cassius Dio, which took place about five years later than that of the old man, related by Suetonius.[62]

If Thompson's conclusion, that both categories mentioned by Suetonius refer to Jewish apostates, is untenable, what objection remains to seeing proselytes and/or "Judaizers" as the addressees of the first category? Smallwood argues for "Judaizers" only, and wants to exclude proselytes because they had been liable for the temple tax, "and there was no reason for Vespasian to exempt them from its successor" (that is, the *fiscus Iudaicus*), and because "they did formally profess Judaism."[63] Both arguments are certainly correct, but again, it is very doubtful that they are appropriate to the historical circumstances. Of course "well-established" proselyte families did profess their Judaism and were registered as taxpayers (both for the Temple tax and later for the *fiscus Iudaicus*), and there is no reason, indeed, why Domitian's enforcement should have been directed against this group. The harsh enforcement makes sense, however, if we are talking rather about *new* converts to Judaism, probably even a continuously growing number of proselytes, who did not want to be liable to the *fiscus Iudaicus* and kept their conversion secret in order to avoid it. This may have been precisely the situation confronting Domitian, and, of course, the group must have been large enough to seem likely to increase the tax revenues (together with the second group).

This interpretation fits very well with the specific case of "witch-hunting" depicted by Suetonius: it refers only to circumcision, not to any of the other characteristics of the Jewish way of life that Thompson mentions. According to the structure of Suetonius' account it even seems very likely that the search for circumcised Jews applies to both categories of Jews concealing their Judaism (in a different way) and not only to the second one.[64] This would mean that mainly real proselytes fall under that category and not merely "Judaizers" or "sympathizers." The "witch-hunters," encouraged by Domitian's measures, may also have put on trial many sympathizers, but the definite proof of whether or not they were Jews, and so liable for the tax, was circumcision. There can be no doubt, however, that the measures poisoned the atmosphere and that this was the reason Nerva abolished them.[65]

If this interpretation of Suetonius is correct, we have to regard Domitian's vigorous enforcement of the *fiscus Iudaicus* not as a measure against proselytes (he only wanted them to pay the tax) but as an indication of increasing proselytism (and, together with this, sympathy with Judaism) in Roman society during his reign. This is corroborated by Cassius Dio's account of the case of Flavius Clemens and his wife:

And the same year [95 C.E.] Domitian slew, along with many others, Flavius Clemens the consul, although he was a cousin and had to wife Flavia Domitilla, who was a relative of the emperor. The charge brought against them both was that of atheism *(atheotēs)*, a charge on which many others who drifted into Jewish ways *(es ta tōn Ioudaiōn ēthē exokellontes)* were condemned. Some of these were put to death, and the rest were at least deprived of their property. Domitilla was merely banished to Pandateria.[66]

The charge of "atheism" (*atheotēs* or *asebeia, impietas*) was raised by many pagan authors against the Jews, who did not participate in pagan cults. It did not have legal consequences, however, because—according to established Roman legislation—the Jews were exempted "from participation in state cults, including that of the emperor."[67] When Domitian used the charge of "atheism," that is, treason *(maiestas),* in order to eliminate people he deemed dangerous to his reign[68] or wanted to get rid of for other reasons, he most certainly did not abolish the ancient privileges. But the privileges were vulnerable and could be disregarded, especially where converts from the upper classes were concerned.[69] Cassius Dio does not say which stage of conversion had been reached by those who were persecuted by Domitian, but his reference to "many others who drifted into Jewish ways" makes it apparent that he has mainly "Judaizers" and "sympathizers" in mind. The explicit "many" certainly means that the phenomenon of sympathizers (and proselytes) must have become so common that Domitian could use it effectively for his purposes.

AUTHORS OF THE SECOND AND EARLY THIRD CENTURY C.E.

There can be no doubt that the Latin and Greek authors of the early second century C.E. were well aware of sympathizers and proselytes alike; this is not disputed even by those who claim "Roman ignorance about the concept of a proselyte" in the first century.[70] The first striking example is Epictetus, who takes a would-be Jew as the prime model of someone who is "halting between two faiths," that is, who is flirting with the idea of changing his faith, but does not have the courage to take the decisive step.[71] Tacitus, in his *Historiae,* also written in the first decade of the second century,[72] definitely speaks about proselytes when he complains that the "worst rascals among other peoples, renouncing their ancestral religions, always kept sending tribute and contributing to Jerusalem, thereby increasing the wealth of the Jews," and when he says that those "who are converted to their ways" learn as their first lesson to despise the gods, to disown their country, and to cut their family bonds.[73] And again, Juvenal in his fourteenth satire, written after 127 C.E.,[74] knows very well the difference between a mere sympathizer and a proselyte. Unlike Petronius, and unlike Epictetus, he puts the emphasis much more on the execution of the conversion: unfortunately, he argues, sympathizers normally become proselytes in the second generation. That this, indeed, has been the case becomes clear from the complaint expressed so vividly by authors of the later second and early third centuries, who deplore those, "even among the Romans," who have abandoned their native traditions because they are attracted by the customs of the Jews.[75]

To sum up, one has to distinguish carefully not only between sympathizers/Judaizers and proselytes but also between proselytes and proselytizing, in order to evaluate the respective pagan reactions to these phenomena. Both the scholars who argue in favor of early Jewish missionary activities and those who argue against it prematurely equate proselytes with proselytizing and start from the assumption that proselytes presuppose active proselytizing.[76] The sources I have analyzed do not give any reason for such an assumption: we find the whole range of pagans being attracted to Judaism, from sympathizers/Judaizers to, indeed, proselytes, but no evidence whatsoever for pagan response to proselytizing before the beginning of the third century C.E.

ROMAN LEGISLATION

Roman legislation against proselytes most probably starts with Hadrian's successor Antoninus Pius (138–162 C.E.). Although his decree[77] aimed primarily at revoking Hadrian's prohibition of circumcision (which had nothing to do with the question of proselytism), it also prohibited proselytism by restricting legitimate circumcision to ethnic Jews. The *Historia Augusta* records that, at the turn of the century, Septimius Severus (193–211 C.E.) forbade conversion to Judaism and imposed "heavy penalties" on converts.[78] Of his successor, Antoninus Caracalla (211–217 C.E.), the same source reports the following story: "Once, when a child of seven, hearing that a certain playmate of his had been severely scourged for adopting the religion of the Jews *(Iudaicam religionem),* he long refused to look at either his own father or the boy's father because he regarded them as responsible for the scourging."[79]

Whether this anecdote is historically reliable to the extent that it can be taken as a sign of his sympathy toward the Jews in general, is doubtful (even if reliable, it does not imply Caracalla's *general* sympathy for Judaism); but it nevertheless confirms that the prohibition of conversion to Judaism was in force at that time, and there is no indication in any source that Caracalla attempted to abolish it. On the contrary, the prohibition of proselytism seems to be a continuous feature of Roman legislation and jurisdiction from Antoninus Pius to the Christian emperors. At the end of the third century[80] the *Sententiae,* attributed to the jurist Paul, declare: "Roman citizens, who suffer that they themselves or their slaves be circumcised in accordance with the Jewish custom *(Iudaico ritu),* are exiled perpetually to an island and their property confiscated; the doctors suffer capital punishment. If Jews shall circumcise purchased slaves of another nation, they shall be banished or suffer capital punishment."[81] Despite the word "suffer," this passage clearly speaks of Roman citizens, who voluntarily underwent circumcision in order to become Jews, or had their slaves circumcised for the same purpose. Their punishment (exile and confiscation of property)[82] is less severe than that inflicted on the doctors who performed the act of circumcision (death), and on Jews who circumcised purchased slaves (banishment or death).[83]

Paul's *Sententiae* were highly appreciated, and all of his works were declared in 328 by Constantine the Great to possess legal authority.[84] When the Christian emperors from Constantine the Great (324–337 C.E.) to Theodosius II (408–450 C.E.) again and again reinforced the prohibition against conversion to Judaism, and especially against the circumcision of purchased slaves,[85] they simply took over and continued a tradition which had begun with Antoninus Pius' limitation of circumcision among the Jews.

PART II

Two Key Historical Incidents

CHAPTER SEVEN

Elephantine

THE FIRST RECORDED EVENT in Jewish history which may be understood as an outbreak of anti-Jewish feeling took place in the Egyptian military colony at Elephantine. The Jews of Elephantine were part of a culturally and ethnically mixed populace, dominated by native Egyptians, who lived, worked, and traded together relatively peacefully. This coexistence between Egyptians and Jews was forcibly interrupted (and probably brought to a complete end soon after) when the Egyptians, assisted by the local Persian authorities, destroyed the Jewish Temple at Elephantine. This chapter will review the evidence of this violent Egyptian-Jewish clash in its literary and historical context and with regard to the question of the origin of "anti-Semitism."

THE COURSE OF EVENTS

Jews settled in Egypt from biblical times, probably as early as the late eighth century B.C.E.[1] The settlement which is best known, thanks to some sensational papyrus discoveries at the end of the nineteenth and the beginning of the twentieth centuries,[2] is the one on the island of Elephantine on the southern border of Egypt. The origins of this settlement are debated but most scholars place them under the Egyptian king Psammetichus I (664–609 B.C.E.) and his contemporary, the Judahite ruler Manasseh (699–643 B.C.E.), in about 650 B.C.E. when Psammetichus was asserting his independence from Assyria.[3]

The archaeological and literary evidence leaves no doubt that the Jews of Elephantine belonged to the military colony which protected the southern border of Egypt against the Ethiopians (= Nubians). The center of their religious life was a Temple of the Jewish God who is called JHW (= Jahu) in the papyri. Since this Temple was located close to the temple of the Egyptian god Khnum,[4] the official lord of the region, permission to build the Jewish Temple must have been an exceptional privilege granted by the Egyptian king. Unfortunately we do not know anything about the relationship between the Jewish mercenaries and the native Egyptians during the first 200 years of their joint history at Elephantine,[5] if the Jews indeed came to the colony at about 650 B.C.E. We only know, thanks to the discovery of the papyri, that tension between Jews and native Egyptians came to a head in 410 B.C.E., and we can infer from the violence of these events that this tension must have been smoldering for some time past.

In 525 B.C.E. the Persian king Cambyses invaded Egypt and defeated Psammetichus III at Pelusion. For more than 100 years Egypt now formed part of the Persian empire, until Amyrtaeus of Saïs, the sole ruler of the Twenty-Eighth Dynasty (404–399 B.C.E.), asserted Egypt's independence under Artaxerxes II (404–361 B.C.E.).[6] It is the life of the Jewish colony under Persian supremacy (which extended also over Judah and Samaria) that the Aramaic papyri of Elephantine reflect. From the outset the Persian rulers must have been well disposed toward the Jews: they considered them a welcome pillar of their rule over Egypt. In one of the papyri the Jews of Elephantine boast that Cambyses, when he conquered Egypt, destroyed all the Egyptian temples (and certainly also the Khnum temple at Elephantine) but did no harm to the Jewish Temple.[7] Even if this remark is exaggerated, it clearly shows that the Jews regarded themselves (and were regarded by Persians and native Egyptians alike) as Persian allies. They served now under the command of Persian officers in the garrison of Elephantine and belonged, in the view of the Egyptians, to the oppressors of the Egyptian populace.

The basic military unit of the garrison *(ḥayla)* at Elephantine was the company *(degel)*, which was called after the names of its Persian commanders.[8] We know of two local officials stationed at Elephantine-Syene, the "commander of the garrison" *(rav ḥayla)* and the "Chief" *(frataraka:* literally "The Foremost"); the latter was a combined civil-military post and higher in rank than the commander. The names of four commanders and two *fratarakas* are mentioned in the documents: Rauka (495 B.C.E.),[9] Naphaina (ca. 435),[10] his son Vidranga (ca. 420–416),[11] and Vidranga's son Naphaina (410)[12] as commanders, and Ramnadaina (420)[13] and Vidranga (ca. 416–410),[14] the former garrison commander, as *fratarakas.* The main seat of the satrap, the governor of the Persian province of Egypt, was Memphis. The satrap of Egypt since 455/54 had been Arsames (Arsham), most probably a prince of the Achaemenid dynasty, who held this office for about half a century.[15]

After the death of Artaxerxes I (425 B.C.E.) political disturbances broke out, in the wake of which Arsames left Egypt to campaign for Darius II (425–405 B.C.E.). The Egyptians seem to have taken advantage of his absence and rebelled against the Persians, as can be inferred from the later remark of the Elephantine Jews in one of the papyri that when "detachments *(diglin)* of the Egyptians rebelled we did not leave our posts (and anything of) damage was not found in us."[16] In any case the Jews appear here on the side of the foreign Persian rulers.

The first clear evidence for tension between the Jews and the Egyptians is connected with a letter, the so-called Passover Letter, which is dated to the fifth year of Darius II, that is, 419 B.C.E. The letter was sent by a certain Hananiah to the Jewish garrison at Elephantine and deals with the celebration of Passover.[17] From another (undated) letter we learn that the arrival of this Hananiah and the contents of his letter did not escape the attention of the priests of Khnum: "It is known to you that Khnum is against us [the Jews] since Hananiah has been in Egypt until now."[18] What precisely caused the anger of the priests of Khnum will be discussed below. Nine years later, in 410 B.C.E., open conflict broke out and led to the destruction of the Jewish Temple. This happened after the satrap Arsames had left Egypt again, but this time his absence was not followed by a revolt of the Egyptians against Persian rule; on the contrary, the local Persian authorities (Vidranga, the *frataraka,* and his son Naphaina, the garrison commander) conspired with the Egyptians against the Jews. This conspiracy also proved unsuccessful because the Persian government backed the Jews. Whereas Vidranga and his followers were punished immediately for their crime by the Persian government,[19] it was three years before the Jews received permission to rebuild their Temple. Their first petition directed to Bagohi, the governor of Judah, and Johanan, the Jerusalem High Priest, remained unanswered.[20] Only another letter, about three years later (307 B.C.E.), to Bagohi and to Delaiah and Shelemiah, sons of Sanballat, the governor of Samaria,[21] yielded the desired result: Bagohi, the governor of Judah, and Delaiah, Sanballat's son, sent a messenger to Elephantine with an oral communication to be delivered to Arsames, instructing him to rebuild the Temple on its former site (the oral communication was recorded in a memorandum, obviously by the messenger himself).[22]

The subsequent destiny of the Jewish colony at Elephantine is lost in the mists of history. That the Temple had indeed been rebuilt, at least that "some structure was re-erected on the spot and a reduced sacrificial service reinstituted,"[23] can be deduced from a papyrus dated December 12, 402

B.C.E., in which "YHW the God who dwells in Elephantine the fortress" is mentioned.[24] Since the papyrus is dated according to the reign of Arta-xerxes II, the new Egyptian king Amyrtaeus (404–399) evidently only gained control of Egypt gradually and had not yet extended his rule as far as Elephantine at this time. The last dated document, from October 1, 399 B.C.E., alludes to the death or flight of Amyrtaeus and reports the accession to the throne of Nepherites I, the founder of the Twenty-Ninth Dynasty. Whether this marks the end of the Jewish garrison at Elephantine[25] or whether the Jews "rendered their services to the Egyptian crown as they had done before the Persian conquest,"[26] remains unknown.[27]

THE CELEBRATION OF PASSOVER AT ELEPHANTINE

The so-called Passover letter of 419 B.C.E. is a crucial document for any at-tempt to elucidate the relationship between the Jews and the Egyptians at Elephantine. It reads as follows (according to the reconstruction and trans-lation by Porten, who mainly follows P. Grelot):[28]

1 [To my brothers Je]daniah and his colleagues, the Jewish ga[rrison], your brother Hanan[i]ah. May God/the gods [seek after] the welfare of my brothers

2 [at all times]. And now, this year, year 5 of the king Darius, it has been sent from the king to Arsa[mes the

3 prince, saying: Keep away from the Jew]ish [garrison]. Now, you thus count four[teen

4 days in Nisan *and on the 14th at twilight* ob]serve [*the Passover*] and from the 15th day until the 21st day of [Nisan

5 *observe the Festival of Unleavened Bread. Seven days eat unleav-ened bread. Now*], be pure and take heed. [Do] n[ot] work

6 [*on the 15th day and on the 21st day of Nisan*]. Do not drink [*any fermented drink*. And do] not [eat] anything of leaven

7 [*nor let it be seen in your houses* from the 14th day of Nisan at] sunset until the 21st of Nisa[n at sun-

8 set. And b]ring into your chambers [*any leaven which you have in your houses*] and seal (them) up during [these] days.

9 [By order of the God of heaven and by order of the ki]ng.

10 [To] my brothers Jedaniah and his colleagues, the Jewish gar-rison, your brother Hananiah s[on of PN].

This letter contains a decree of the Persian king Darius concerning the celebration of Passover, conveyed to the Jewish community at Elephantine by a certain Hananiah. The rather enigmatic phrase in line 3 ("Keep away from the Jewish garrison") seems to hint at a conflict between the Jews and the local Persian governor which in a puzzling way was connected with the celebration of Passover. In order to understand it fully we have to discuss briefly the various interpretations of the letter that have been suggested.

Older studies assumed that the decree was initiated by the Jews who wanted to secure the proper implementation of the Passover laws throughout the diaspora, and that it therefore was directed toward all the Jews of the Persian empire. According to this interpretation our papyrus is nothing but the version of the decree sent by Hananiah to the satrap of Egypt and announced, on his instructions, to the Jews of Elephantine.[29] The force behind this argument is obviously the analogy of the Purim celebrations, introduced by Queen Esther and Mordecai (Est. 9:20ff.).[30] This explanation presupposes, however, a reconstruction of line 3 which is different from the one given above, namely that the decree of the king included an explicit instruction to keep Passover. According to this, the lacuna in line 3a has to be supplemented with something like "Let there be a Passover for the Jewish garrison"[31] or "[Let there be a festival for the Jew]ish [garrison in the month of Nisan]."[32] This interpretation is not very likely, not only because it does not explain why the king should be so concerned with the celebration of Passover all over his empire, but also and mainly because it disregards the internal structure of the letter (see below). In addition, there was definitely no new festival introduced by the king in the diaspora or in Elephantine because we have clear evidence that the Jews of Elephantine did celebrate Passover prior to the letter.[33]

Another suggestion has been made by Porten. It starts from the assumption that the letter is directed solely toward the Jews of Elephantine and proposes that the Hananiah of our letter might be identified with Hanani = Hananiah, the relative of the biblical Nehemiah (Neh. 1:2; 7:2) who was appointed governor of the fortress of Jerusalem and "by 419 may have replaced Nehemiah as governor of the province of Judah."[34] As the governor of Judah Hananiah's authority may have included the Jews of Egypt, and this responsibility may well have led him to remind the Elephantine soldiers of their duty to keep Passover. Hence the letter is simply a "reminder" and has nothing to do with a decree of the king introducing a new festival or new rites.[35]

This interpretation ignores the fact that since the Deuteronomic reform (622 B.C.E.) with its centralization of the cult in Jerusalem it was "not permitted to slaughter the passover sacrifice in any of the settlements that the Lord your God is giving you; but at the place where the Lord your God will choose to establish His name [Jerusalem], there alone shall you slaughter the passover sacrifice" (Deut. 16:5f.). If Hananiah was indeed the governor of Judah, he could hardly have been interested in imposing upon the Jews of Elephantine a ritual, the paschal sacrifice, which was meant to be performed in Jerusalem alone. Porten's ingenious solution to this dilemma addresses another problem of the letter which has long been observed: the instructions concerning Passover focus on the Festival of Unleavened Bread, one of the two components of Passover, and leave out almost completely the other component, the sacrifice of the paschal lamb (originally, each was a separate festival). According to Porten, this is precisely the intent of the letter—"to make but passing reference to the paschal sacrifice [in the phrase 'Observe the Passover', line 4, and possibly also in the injunction 'Be pure and take heed', line 5] and to concentrate on the Festival of the Unleavened Bread."[36]

This is too much of a psychological interpretation: to remind the Elephantine Jewish soldiers of a Passover which correctly consists of a paschal sacrifice and the Festival of Unleavened Bread but at the same time to let them know that the sacrifice is less desirable than keeping the Festival of Unleavened Bread because the former should be restricted to Jerusalem. What kind of conclusions should the poor Elephantine soldiers draw from this masterpiece of Jerusalem diplomacy?[37]

Hence, a third interpretation which is also suggested by Porten is to be preferred (actually Porten leaves it to his readers to decide which of his two interpretations he favors). This interpretation relies on K. Galling's reconstruction of line 3 (the above translation is based on Galling's brilliant reconstruction) and his analysis of the whole text.[38] It is the only one which fully takes into consideration the crucial line 3 and the structure of the letter. According to this interpretation we have to distinguish between two clearly recognizable parts of the letter, marked by the double "now" in lines 2 and 3, namely the decree of the king (lines 2–3a), and the instructions concerning Passover from Hananiah (lines 3b–8). Both, of course, are connected because they are conveyed to the Jews of Elephantine in one letter. This implies that the decree of the king must be interpreted in the light of the following instructions. Hence, if the reconstruction in line 3 is correct, the warning addressed to the satrap of Egypt, "Keep away from the Jewish garrison," must be related to the celebration of Passover.

This explanation correlates well with the historical context as we can reconstruct it. We have seen that the disturbances after the death of Arta-xerxes in 425 B.C.E. also led to an Egyptian rebellion against the Persians which was facilitated by the absence of Arsames, the satrap. It seems reasonable to assume that this rebellion was also directed against the Jews, who boasted of having been loyal to the Persians. The most obvious cause for tension between the Egyptians and the Jews is the sacrifice of the paschal lamb or ram (Num. 28:19) which is part of Passover. The priests of the ram-god Khnum may have petitioned Arsames to prevent the Jews from observing their festival and especially from offering the paschal sacrifice. Arsames obviously did not accede to the Egyptian demand (because the Egyptians had to wait for his absence to take action against the Jews), but he may have sent to the king for a formal ruling (it is also possible that the Jews of Elephantine appealed to their brethren in Jerusalem and/or Babylonia for help).[39] The decree in line 3 of the letter is the king's answer which says: "Keep away from the Jewish garrison," that is, do not interfere in Jewish affairs and let them sacrifice their paschal lamb! The details of the Passover festival are not the king's concern but are communicated by Hananiah, who accordingly should be regarded as the representative and messenger of the king. In any case, the Passover letter is not an unmotivated decree by the Persian king but a response to very specific historical circumstances.

This interpretation of the Passover letter as reflecting a conflict between the Elephantine Jews and the Egyptian priests because of the paschal sacrifice has been questioned. It is argued that Hananiah's instructions in the second part of the letter do not mention the sacrifice explicitly and that therefore the Passover of Elephantine consisted of the Festival of Unleavened Bread only.[40] Or, if indeed the sacrifice of the paschal lamb was the issue at stake, why did the conflict break out so late (the Passover letter did not introduce the paschal sacrifice for the first time)?[41] In addition, "the paschal sacrifice need not have been taken from the sheep," holy to the ram-god Khnum, but "could equally well have come from the goats" (cf. Ex. 12:5).[42] Porten therefore suggests that it was not so much the paschal sacrifice but "simply" the commemoration of the Jewish Exodus from Egypt celebrated at Passover which "served to antagonize the priests of Khnum, and perhaps other Egyptians."[43]

The first argument cannot be validated, if the reconstruction of line 3 of the letter is correct; it demands, as we have seen, a close connection with a form of Passover which was offensive to the Egyptians (and this cannot be said of the Festival of Unleavened Bread). In addition, the double instruction to keep Passover (line 4) and "observe the Festival of Unleavened Bread" (line 5) may well hint at both components of the Passover Festival. The second argument (why so late) is valid for any suggestion, certainly for Porten's recourse to the Exodus tradition—this must have been the constant thorn in the flesh of the Egyptians. As we have seen, the conflict had already been smoldering for some time, in any case before 425 B.C.E., and the final clash came only in 409 (when Arsames was again out of Egypt). There is also no reason to assume that the period before 425 was entirely peaceful, just because we do not have any information evincing conflict. And finally, the third argument (they could have taken goats) is an interesting exegesis of the biblical text the subtlety of which may well have escaped Jews and Egyptians alike.

The most likely solution, therefore, is the one put forward above, namely that the Passover letter points to a fundamental conflict between the Jews of Elephantine and the priests of Khnum. Not only the commemoration of the Exodus but also the presence of the Jewish God in his Temple among them, and in particular the sacrifice of the paschal lamb, was abhorrent to the Egyptian priests and their followers.

THE DESTRUCTION OF THE JEWISH TEMPLE

That the Temple of the Jewish God was destroyed nine years after the Passover letter, that is, in 410 B.C.E., is documented in two papyri (C 30/A4.7 and C 31/A4.8), both dated November 25, 407 B.C.E. (C 31/A4.8 is thought to be a copy of C 30/A4.7 or a "second draft" of the letter).[44] The decisive passage is as follows:

4 . . . In the month of Tammuz, year 14 of king Darius, when Arsames

5 had departed and gone to the king, the priests of Khnub the god who are in Elephantine the fortress, in agreement with Vidranga, who was Chief here, (said),

6 saying, "Let them remove from there the Temple of YHW the God which is in Elephantine the fortress." Then, that Vidranga

7 the wicked, sent a letter to Naphaina his son, who was garrison commander in Syene the fortress, saying, "The Temple which is in Elephantine

8 the fortress let them demolish." Then, Naphaina led the Egyptians with the other troops. They came to the fortress of Elephantine with their weapons,

9 broke into that Temple, demolished it to the ground, and the
stone pillars which were there—they smashed them . . .

12 . . . But the gold and silver basins and (other) things which
were in that Temple—all (of these) they took

13 and made their own . . .[45]

This letter, which is directed to Bagohi, the governor of Judah, clarifies that the destruction of the Jewish Temple was instigated by the priests of Khnum after the departure of the satrap Arsames, and that the Egyptians gained active support from the local Persian governor Vidranga (the parallel C 31/A4.8 reports explicitly that Vidranga was bribed):[46] Vidranga instructs his son Nafaina, the garrison commander, to carry out the destruction together with the Egyptians and with his own (Persian) troops (line 8).

Unfortunately, the letter does not give any reason for the destruction of the Temple. It cannot have been a spontaneous action because the Egyptians obviously waited until Arsames had left the country. This also implies that they were well aware that their activities could not claim any official Persian support but on the contrary were treasonable; subsequent punishment of Vidranga and "all the persons who sought evil for that Temple"[47] confirms this. Hence, it becomes clear that the destruction must have had to do with animosity between Egyptians (more precisely Egyptian priests) and Jews (more precisely the priests and devotees of the Jewish God and their ritual in the Temple) already smoldering for some time, a conflict moreover in which the central Persian government openly and undeniably sided with the Jews.

It is always dangerous, if one has only fragmentary evidence, to connect the scattered pieces in order to draw historical conclusions. In this context, however, it seems very likely that indeed the destruction of the Jewish Temple should be linked with the information we get from the Passover letter. In other words, the Egyptians took advantage of the absence of the Persian governor to eliminate once and for all the offense which had long angered them: Jewish worship, or, more precisely, sacrifice of lambs in their Temple, whether for Passover or for any other purpose. If the restoration and interpretation of the Passover letter are correct, it even appears that any action directed against the Passover ritual would be seen as offending an explicit royal decree, hence as *crimen maiestatis*.

Porten has developed a different theory to explain the historical background of the destruction of the Temple, although he apparently does not deny the suggestion made above.[48] Taking into consideration the building history of the area under discussion (the Khnum temple and the Jewish Temple were side by side) he proposes that some time between 434 and 420 B.C.E. the Egyptians erected on the border of the Jewish quarter "some sort of shrine" which "may have been a Khnumeum, a burial place of rams sacred to the god of the Cataract region."[49] In 410 they destroyed the Jewish Temple together with parts of the royal storehouse and built a wall[50] in order to provide a direct approach to this chapel or Khnumeum.[51] This much more prosaic explanation does not need to make play with the offering of lambs in the Jewish Temple. However, it is also a highly speculative theory which at best can be taken to supplement the more fundamental religious conflict between the Khnum priests and the Jews.

The details emerging from the papyri concerning the struggle of the Jews for permission to rebuild their Temple help to elucidate the historical background further. The two drafts of the letter of 407 B.C.E. to Bagohi, the governor of Judah (C 30/A4.7 and 31/A4.8), refer to an earlier letter of 410 to Bagohi and to Johanan, the High Priest of Jerusalem, which remained unanswered,[52] as well as to a separate letter sent in 407 to Delaiah and Shelemaiah, the sons of the governor of Samaria, Sanballat.[53] Both the fact that the Jews of Elephantine turned to the Persian governor of Judah (who most probably was also of Persian origin)[54] and the Jerusalem High Priest for help and the fact that they were only granted an answer (by Bagohi and Delaiah) after they had called in the authorities of Samaria are most revealing. As to the former, one need not resort to the highly dubious argument that Jerusalem was at that time already the center of "world Jewry";[55] it is sufficient to argue that the Jews of Elephantine most naturally turned to the Persian *and* Jewish authorities in the only other place where a Jewish Temple existed, a place, moreover, which obviously exercised at least a religious supremacy over the Jews of Elephantine and their Temple (of course, the letter had to be addressed to the governor, and one should also not forget that the governor of Egypt had left the country). As to the latter, it can be concluded that the Samaritan schism had not yet taken place,[56] and that the Jerusalem authorities were reluctant to grant the Jews of Elephantine permission to rebuild their Temple (hence, the Elephantine Jews were right in exercising pressure by turning also to Samaria).

The reason for this can be deduced from the memorandum issued jointly by Bagohi, the governor of Judah, and Delaiah, the son of the governor of Samaria (C 32/A4.9):

1 Memorandum of what Bagohi and Delaiah said
2 to me, saying: Memorandum: You may say in Egypt
3 before Arsames about the Altar-house of the God of
4 Heaven which was built in Elephantine the fortress,
5 formerly before Cambyses (and)
6 which that wicked Vidranga demolished
7 in year 14 of King Darius:
8 to (re)build it on its site as it was formerly
9 and they shall offer the meal-offering and the incense upon
10 that altar just as formerly
11 was done.[57]

Two details of this memorandum are important. First, it seems to presuppose that Arsames had returned to Egypt and that Bagohi and Delaiah were entitled to give instruction to Arsames, that is, that the satrap of Egypt was inferior in rank to the satrap of Judah (and Samaria); this may point not only to a religious but also to an administrative supremacy of the Persian province of Judah over the province of Egypt. If this is the case, it explains even better why the Jews of Elephantine turned to Bagohi.[58]

Second, all scholars agree that the mention of "meal-offering" and "incense" to be offered upon the altar of the Temple to be rebuilt is not accidental, that is, that the burnt offering, which is explicitly included in the request of the Elephantine Jews,[59] has been left out on purpose. The question, however, is why? If we ignore the very unlikely suggestion that the omission of the burnt offering was due to Persian susceptibilities (profaning of fire), two possibilities remain: the omission was a "concession to Egyptian susceptibilities (no more sacrifice of the ram),"[60] or it was a compromise between the extensive request of the Jews of Elephantine (meal offering, incense, *and* burnt offering) and the more restrictive attitude of their Jerusalem brethren (only meal offering and incense but no burnt offering).[61] The former presupposes the Egyptian-Jewish conflict the traces of which we have followed so far; the latter focuses on an internal Jewish point of view, namely the reluctance of the Jerusalem authorities, especially after the Deuteronomic reform, to come to terms with a Jewish Temple outside Jerusalem.[62] A variant of the internal Jewish explanation is the suggestion that the memorandum reflects a compromise between the liberal Samaritans (who did not at all reject the idea of Jewish Temples outside Jerusalem), and the conservative Judahites (who would have preferred to prohibit generally any Temple outside Jerusalem): the Samaritans concede that at least the sacrifice be forbidden in the Elephantine Temple, and the Judahites concede that a Temple may exist outside Jerusalem.[63]

Again, it seems hard to believe that the omission of the burnt offering in the memorandum echoes solely a Jewish controversy over the Temple, whether between the Elephantine Jews and their Jerusalem brethren or between the Judahites and the Samaritans. If the Jews of Jerusalem did not want to acknowledge a Jewish Temple outside Jerusalem, let alone agree to the rebuilding of a Temple the destruction of which from their point of view was fortunate, why should they agree to a "compromise" which allows meal offering and incense and prohibits burnt offering? Was burnt offering so much more important that its absence in Elephantine would allow the Jerusalem Temple to be seen as the only Jewish Temple in the full sense of the word? Moreover, why should the Persian governor of Jerusalem adopt these strange religious subtleties that a Temple without burnt offering is a Temple (good enough for the Elephantine Jews) and at the same time is not a Temple (from the point of view of the Jerusalem Jews)?

It is much more likely that the Persian governors of Judah and Samaria, instead of being concerned primarily with the peculiar interests of the Jerusalem Jews, were responding to the long-standing conflict between the Jews of Elephantine and the Egyptians; the other factor may have played a role in their deliberations but certainly not a prominent one.[64] In restricting the worship of the Jewish Temple to meal offering and incense they changed official Persian policy with regard to the Jewish cult in Elephantine, which, as we have seen, had tried to uphold the right of the Jews to perform their religious duties in their own way. This change, however, was not as radical as complete prohibition of the Jewish Temple cult. In the eyes of the Persians the prohibition of the sacrifice only may well have been a "fair compromise" from which they could expect the pacification of an otherwise insoluble, and politically dangerous, conflict. In any case, such a compromise makes much more sense from the point of view of Persian politics in Egypt than from that of internal Jewish religious quarrels which were hard to comprehend and politically irrelevant.

The draft of another letter (C 33/A4.10) shows that the Jews of Elephantine were aware of the problem which arose from burnt offerings in their Temple. The senders are five leaders of the Jewish community. The addressee is not mentioned, but must have been either Arsames or Bagohi. The letter asks for permission to rebuild the Temple, with the explicit qualification, however, that "sheep, ox, and goat are [n]ot made there as burnt-offering, but [*they offer there*] (only) incense (and) meal-offering."[65] Whether this is an answer to Bagohi's and Delaiah's memorandum and therefore the formal acceptance of the limitation of their rights,[66] or whether the relinquishing of burnt offering has been suggested by the Jews of Elephantine themselves in order to obtain permission to rebuild their Temple, it clearly shows that animal sacrifices of all kinds (and not only the paschal lamb) are the bone of contention.

ANTI-SEMITISM IN ELEPHANTINE?

The picture which emerges from all the available evidence concerning the Jews of Elephantine is that of an essentially political *and* religious conflict between Jews and Egyptians. The "religious" part of it takes place between the Jewish mercenaries and the priests of the ram-god Khnum who deny the claim of the Jews to worship their God Jahu and to offer sacrifices in their Temple. That this alone is not sufficient to explain the outburst of hatred as reflected in the sources but has to be supplemented by a "catalyst," can be deduced from the fact that we do not have any evidence of a religious conflict prior to the Persian conquest of Egypt, hence that the devotees of Khnum and Jahu seem to have lived together relatively peacefully during the time of undisturbed Egyptian supremacy. This "fact," however, has to be qualified because we do not have any information about the relationship between the Elephantine Jews and the Egyptians before Cambyses conquered Egypt; it may well be that there were indeed tensions and conflicts of which we simply know nothing.

The "catalyst" which intensified the conflict and gradually brought about the final eruption was Persian rule over Egypt, more concretely the cooperation between the Jews of Elephantine and the Persians.[67] It is the triangle between the Egyptians, the Persians, and the Jews, in all its religious and political dimensions and implications, within which the hatred of the Jews has to be defined. From the very beginning of this complicated relationship between native Egyptians, Persian oppressors, and Jewish mercenaries the Jews always appear on the side of the Persians.

When the Persians conquered Egypt in 525 B.C.E., they destroyed all the Egyptian temples but spared the Jewish Temple. It is irrelevant in this connection whether or not this is historically "correct";[68] on the contrary, even if the Jews only boast of something which cannot be validated, this is all the more revealing: the Jews claim to be on the side of the Persians!

Again, one hundred years later during the disturbances after the death of Artaxerxes I (425 B.C.E.), the Jews of Elephantine boast that they did not take part in the Egyptian rebellion against the Persians. The Passover letter of 419 B.C.E. attests to the fact that the Persian king takes the side of the Elephantine Jews against the Egyptians: he warns the Egyptians not to interfere in the religious affairs of the Jews, that is, to let them perform their ritual in their Temple the way they wish. And even the final stage, the destruction of the Jewish Temple in 410 B.C.E., is only at first glance achieved by the combined effort of Egyptians *and* Persians: on closer inspection it becomes clear that only the local Persian authorities join forces with the Egyptians and that both, Egyptians and Persians, are punished for challenging declared Persian policy regarding the Egyptian Jews.

The relationship between Jews, Egyptians, and Persians becomes even more complicated after the destruction of the Temple. While asking for the rebuilding of their Temple, the Jews of Elephantine turn to the Persian authorities of Judah and Samaria (probably because the satrap of Egypt had left the country and/or was inferior to the satrap of Judah) as well as to the Jerusalem High Priest (most obviously because they expected him to support their claim before the satrap). Again the Persians decide a matter of grave concern for the social life of Egyptians and Jews; and Jews outside Egypt interfere in what the Egyptians regard as internal Egyptian "interests." Whether or not this is symptomatic of the allegedly growing Jewish nationalism[69] (as we have seen, the Jerusalemites were quite reluctant to follow the request of their brethren in Elephantine), any real or imagined influence of the Jews of Jerusalem on the Persian authorities in favor of the Elephantine Jews will not have helped to ease the tension. This time the Persians (and the Jerusalemites) order a compromise which, in the eyes of the Persians, changes their previous policy only slightly but nevertheless supports the Jews of Elephantine in the face of their Egyptian opponents.

We will see in the next chapter that from an overall point of view the conditions in Elephantine are very similar to those in Alexandria. As in Elephantine, the Jews are the supporters of the hated foreign rule (Persians/Romans) and do not join with the native Egyptians in their struggle against the oppressors. Consequently the Egyptians fight not only against the Persians/Romans but also against the Jews, whom they try to "cut back" in what is essential for them (Temple worship/civil rights) and what affects the most sensitive part of their mutual relationship. At a moment that seems favorable, they (the Egyptians or the Egyptians and the Greeks respectively) plot with local Persian/Roman authorities (the Persian governor in Elephantine/the Roman governor in Alexandria) against the Jews—but the Persian/Roman supremacy protects the Jews and punishes the Persian/Roman governor. Even the intervention of "outside" Jewish authorities who have the support of the foreign rulers applies in both cases: in Elephantine it is the Jew Hananiah (the emissary of the Persian king) and the Jerusalem High Priest Johanan (who might influence the Persian governor of Judah); in Alexandria it is the Jewish king Agrippa (the "friend" of the Roman emperor). The religious element within this political constellation is more pronounced in Elephantine than in Alexandria, but one should not forget that the Alexandrian Egyptians (as well as the Greeks) take advantage of the Roman emperor's desire to be worshipped as a god.

What expresses itself most forcefully in Elephantine (as in Alexandria) is an Egyptian nationalism, nourished by religious sentiments, which is directed against the foreign oppressors and their Jewish "collaborators." The circles in which this nationalism is cultivated can clearly be identified: the patriotic priests who are not willing to tolerate the Jewish cult, or rather who use the Jewish cult as a pretext to act against the Jews. These Jews who are anything but religious purists (they intermarry with their Egyptian neighbors[70] and no doubt practice a peculiar religious syncretism)[71] are turned into the enemies of the Egyptian "nation" as a sociocultural organization which is threatened, politically and religiously, by "foreign elements." Although members of different ethnic origin were stationed at Elephantine,[72] it is solely the Jews against whom the Egyptian priests direct their animosity.[73] Since the sources reflect only the result of this dislike and the viewpoint of the victims, we have no evidence of the argument used by the Egyptians in this conflict. It is most likely, however, that the action against the Jews did not take place in a vacuum but was accompanied by political-religious propaganda. In Part III I will reconstruct the traces of this propaganda and connect the literary with the historical evidence.

Whatever term one chooses to designate the events in Elephantine, there cannot be any doubt that the first time in history that an anti-Jewish outburst becomes evident is at about 410 B.C.E. in the colony of Elephantine, that is, almost precisely 450 years before the riots in Alexandria. It is not the Egyptian-Greek city of Alexandria which is the mother of "anti-Semitism" but the very heart of Egypt itself.

CHAPTER EIGHT

Alexandria

THE MOST VIOLENT ERUPTION of anti-Jewish sentiment in antiquity is connected with the city of Alexandria.[1] According to Josephus, the Jews were allowed to settle in Alexandria by its founder Alexander and "obtained privileges on a par with those of the Macedonians."[2] Whether or not this is true,[3] there can be no doubt that the Jews in Alexandria had a long and for the most part peaceful history. Things changed, however, when the Romans gradually gained power in Egypt. The Greek and Egyptian population of Egypt was notoriously anti-Roman, and the support which the Egyptian Jews provided for Caesar during his campaign in Egypt (48/47 B.C.E.)[4] was certainly unlikely to make them popular with their Greek and Egyptian neighbors. When Augustus introduced (in 24/23 B.C.E.?) a capitation tax *(laographia)* from which only the Greek citizens of Alexandria were exempted completely,[5] the question of citizenship in Alexandria became acute and contributed a good deal to tension between the different and competing ethnic groups.

The accession to power in 37 C.E. of Gaius Caligula marked a decisive turning point in the history of the Jews in Alexandria. The prefect of Egypt, A. Avillius Flaccus, appointed by Gaius' predecessor Tiberius in 32 C.E., could expect the change of regime to result in his recall. His position may have been further weakened because of his friendship with Tiberius and with the praetorian prefect Q. Naevius Macro, who had helped Caligula to the throne but was driven to suicide late in 37 or early in 38 C.E.

In August 38 C.E. the newly appointed Jewish king Agrippa I (Gaius had conferred on him the former tetrarchy of Herod's son Philip) visited Alexandria; his arrival signaled the outbreak of unrest among the Greek and Egyptian population of Alexandria which led to murderous riots against the Jews. Flaccus' precise part in this is unclear; according to Philo he permitted the installation of Gaius' images in the synagogues, issued a decree against the Jewish rights of citizenship, and finally tolerated or even instigated the plundering of Jewish houses and the killing of the Alexandrian Jews. In September or October 38[6] Flaccus was suddenly recalled to Rome, banished to the island of Andros in the Aegean Sea, and subsequently executed. His successor was C. Vitrasius Pollio.

We do not learn much about the fate of the Jewish community after the riots of August 38. The peace established between the Jews and their fellow Alexandrians must have been an uneasy one because in the winter of 39/40[7] two delegations were sent to Rome to plead their case before the emperor. What precisely the case was is difficult to determine. As far as the Jews are concerned, Philo speaks of a document about their "sufferings and claims,"[8] the "sufferings" obviously hinting at the persecution of 38, and the "claims" probably referring to an improvement of their civic rights.[9] The Jewish embassy was led by Philo, the Greek one by Apion and included most probably Isidorus and Lampo and perhaps also Chaeremon.[10]

Gaius first received the delegations upon his return from his northern campaign, probably in the spring (May?) of 40 C.E.[11] This first audience was very brief and put the Jews off till another opportunity[12] which arose much later. It was not before the autumn of 40[13] that Gaius gave the two delegations another and longer hearing.[14] In the meantime he had issued the decree to set up a statue dedicated to himself in the Temple of Jerusalem,[15] and the Jews expected the worst. According to Philo's most vivid account the audience, which took place during an inspection of the gardens and villas of Maecenas and Lamia on the Esquiline,[16] centered on the issue of Gaius' deification. The emperor opened it with the question or rather accusation: "Are you the god-haters *(hoi theomiseis)* who do not believe me to be a god, a god acknowledged among all the other nations but not to be named by you?"[17] Apart from this he seemed to be interested only in the question of why the Jews refuse to eat pork.[18] When he finally allowed the Jewish delegation to substantiate their claims regarding their citizenship *(politeia)*,[19] he impatiently interrupted their explanations and dismissed them with the remark: "They seem to me to be people unfortunate rather than wicked and to be foolish in refusing to believe that I have got the nature of a god."[20] This was the last encounter between Gaius and the Jews; the emperor was assassinated on January 24, 41 C.E.

His successor Claudius' accession to power again changed things radically. When the news of Gaius' death reached Alexandria (end of February or beginning of March), the Alexandrian Jews armed themselves and attacked their fellow citizens.[21] According to Josephus, Claudius immediately commanded the prefect of Egypt to put down the unrest, and issued an edict to Alexandria and Syria[22] as well as to "the rest of the world"[23] determining the rights of the Jews. Josephus does not date the edicts but gives the impression that they were closely connected with the renewed outbreak of unrest in Alexandria in February or March 41 C.E.[24] Shortly after, on April 30 and May 1,[25] the leaders of the Alexandrian Greek faction, Isidorus and Lampo, were put on trial and sentenced to death. Not much later the Alexandrian Greeks sent a new delegation to Rome, to offer the emperor honors upon his accession to the throne and to reopen the question of citizenship. This becomes clear from the famous *Letter of Claudius to the Alexandrians,* published on November 10, 41 C.E., by the prefect L. Aemilius Rectus.[26] According to a cryptic remark in the same letter, the Jews decided to respond with two separate delegations[27] (the reasons for which are debated).[28] Claudius' letter dealt with both positions and settled the conflict[29]—until it broke out again in 66 C.E. during the reign of Nero, and in 115–117 C.E. during the revolt under Trajan.

THE COURSE OF EVENTS ACCORDING TO PHILO

Our only source to give a coherent description of what happened in Alexandria in 38 C.E. is Philo; Josephus unfortunately confines himself to stating that "Meanwhile, there was a civil strife *(stasis)* in Alexandria between the Jewish inhabitants and the Greeks,"[30] and proceeds immediately to the report on the two delegations in Rome.[31] Philo's accounts are preserved in his treatises *In Flaccum* and *Legatio ad Gaium,* which complement each other, although with different emphases.

In Flaccum, by far the most detailed account, has been described as a biography (of A. Avillius Flaccus)[32] with elements of a novel;[33] it certainly did not aim at giving a detailed historical account.[34] From the outset, it makes very clear who has to be regarded as the arch-villain of the whole affair: no less a person than the prefect himself, who, after having administered his province with outstanding judiciousness and excellence during the first five years of his office, unfortunately lost control and turned into one of the worst prefects ever. The reason for this was Gaius Caligula's accession to power and the subsequent assassination or rather enforced suicide of Tiberius Gemellus (Tiberius' grandson who had been appointed co-emperor together with Gaius in Tiberius' legacy) and of Macro (the praetorian prefect since 31 C.E.), both closely associated with Flaccus. Fearing that Gaius might designate for him the fate of his friend Macro, Flaccus desperately sought support and was offered help by his former enemies, the political leaders of the Alexandrian Greeks, the "popularity hunting" Dionysius, the "paper-poring"[35] Lampo, and most notably Isidorus, the "faction leader, busy intriguer, mischief contriver and . . . state embroiler."[36] They convinced him that he could not expect anything from the emperor and therefore should look for "a really powerful intercessor to propitiate Gaius": "Such an intercessor is the city of the Alexandrians which has been honoured from the first by all the Augustan house and especially by our present master [Gaius]; and intercede it will if it receives from you some boon, and you can give it no greater benefaction than by surrendering and sacrificing the Jews *(tous Ioudaious ekdous kai proemenos)*."[37]

This is the plot. Philo does not explain what precisely the Greeks expect Flaccus to do to the Jews but instead unfolds the plot in several dramatically composed stages. The first is the surprising visit to Alexandria of Agrippa I on his way to the kingdom to which Gaius had appointed him. Instead of traveling to Syria via Greece as he would have preferred (in order to avoid Alexandria and some possible diplomatic complications),[38] he followed Gaius' advise to take the shorter and much more comfortable route via Alexandria. Philo's account of Agrippa's stay in Alexandria is somewhat confusing. On the one hand he emphasizes that Agrippa wished to remain incognito,[39] but on the other hand he puts into the mouth of Flaccus' Alexandrian allies that "he is attracting all men to him by the sight of his bodyguard of spearmen, decked in armor overlaid with gold and silver."[40]

However unobtrusively Agrippa conducted himself, his presence in Alexandria obviously did not escape attention. The Egyptians, "jealous by nature," "were bursting with envy and considered that any good luck to others was misfortune to themselves, and in their ancient, and we might say innate hostility to the Jews *(dia tēn palaian kai tropon tina <physei> gegenēmenēn[41] pros Ioudaious apechtheian)*, they resented a Jew having been made a king just as much as if each of them had thereby been deprived of an ancestral throne."[42] Flaccus permitted the "lazy and unoccupied mob in the city" to assemble in the gymnasium and to vilify and gibe at Agrippa.[43] Their most spectacular action was to instigate a local lunatic named Carabas to parody the king and the court ceremonial.[44] Philo leaves no doubt that Flaccus, by failing to stop these activities (which were directed, after all, at a friend of the emperor), by even encouraging them, became mainly responsible. After this, Agrippa disappears from Philo's account; he apparently left Alexandria. The next stage of the unfolding drama is that Flaccus meets the demands of the mob to have images of the emperor installed in the synagogues[45] (an act which made them unfit for worship) and even to confiscate the synagogues.[46] The first climax is reached when he "issued a proclamation in which he denounced us as foreigners and aliens" *(xenous kai epēlydas)* in Alexandria, thus deliberately abolishing the Jewish "citizenship" *(politeia)* and "participation in political rights."[47] This decree no doubt is the fulfillment of Flaccus' part of the agreement with the Greeks: the surrender and sacrifice of the Jews.

The next "logical" step is the permission "to pillage the Jews as at the sacking of a city."[48] Having become "foreigners," the Jews lost their rights as legal "resident aliens" and were forced into one section of the city, the "Delta" quarter, "the first known ghetto in the world."[49] The abandoned houses and shops were pillaged; those who were herded together in the "ghetto" (which could not take all the Jews: many of them "poured out over beaches, dunghills and tombs"),[50] died of hunger or were lynched when they dared to leave the "ghetto" and to buy sustenance for their families. Philo's description of this first pogrom in Jewish history vividly recalls the much later accounts of the massacres during the crusader period (as much as both may be inspired by their respective traditions of narrative historiography):

> Poor wretches, they were at once seized by those who wielded the weapon of mob rule, treacherously stabbed, dragged through the whole city, and trampled on, and thus completely made away with till not a part of them was left which could receive the burial which is the right of all. Multitudes of others also were laid low and destroyed with manifold forms of maltreatment, put in practice to serve their bitter cruelty by those whom savagery had maddened and transformed into the nature of wild beasts; for any Jews who showed themselves anywhere, they stoned or knocked about with clubs, aiming their blows at first against the less vital parts for fear that a speedier death might give a speedier release from the consciousness of their anguish.
>
> Some . . . took the most effective at all, fire and steel, and slew many with the sword, while not a few they destroyed with fire. Indeed, whole families, husbands with their wives, infant children with their parents, were burnt in the heart of the city . . . And when they lacked wood for fire they would collect brushwood and dispatch them with smoke rather than fire, thus contriving a more pitiable

and lingering death for the miserable victims whose bodies lay promiscuously half-burnt . . .

Many also while still alive they drew with one of the feet tied at the ankle and meanwhile leapt upon them and pounded them to pieces. And when by the cruel death thus devised, their life ended, the rage of their enemies did not end, but continued all the same. They inflicted worse outrages on the bodies, dragging them through almost every lane of the city until the corpses, their skin, flesh and muscles shattered by the unevenness and roughness of the ground, and all the parts united to make the organism dissevered and dispersed in different directions, were wasted to nothing.[51]

This is undoubtedly the main climax of Philo's account. It is followed by a report on the humiliating scourging of thirty-eight members of the Jewish *gerousia*[52] and the subsequent scourging of three other members of this body.[53] What is conspicuous is that Philo takes care to explain why the scourging was so degrading. There were different scourges used for "Egyptians" (that is, the native Egyptian population) and for "Alexandrians" (the Greeks). The Alexandrian Jews, when sentenced to scourging, were ordinarily regarded as "Alexandrians," that is, "beaten with whips more suggestive of freemen and citizens."[54] This privilege was abrogated now by Flaccus who ordered the Jewish magistrates to be "treated like Egyptians of the meanest rank and guilty of the greatest iniquities."[55]

The next step taken by Flaccus is the search for weapons hidden in Jewish houses. This comes rather as a surprise at this point of the account: one would not expect, after the horrible massacres, any attempt on the part of the Jews to organize armed resistance. It goes without saying that the soldiers found nothing, "not even the knives which suffice the cooks for their daily use."[56] What is more important again is Philo's detailed attempt to prove that it is the "Egyptians" who should be searched because they have hoarded weapons on a huge scale and are to be regarded therefore as the true enemies of the state.[57]

The next paragraph, in which Agrippa suddenly reappears, belongs to Agrippa's visit to Alexandria. It deals with the Jewish resolution in Gaius' honor which was suppressed by Flaccus, obviously in order to denounce the Jews to the emperor as disloyal subjects. Agrippa, when informed by the Jews of Flaccus' malice, sends the resolution to Gaius, "apologizing also for the delay and stating that we had not been slow to learn the duty of piety to the house of our benefactors; on the contrary we had been eager to show it from the first but had been deprived of the chance of proving it in good time by the spite of the Governor."[58] Although chronologically misplaced, this particular piece of information is obviously being given deliberately at precisely this point in the dramatic unfolding of Philo's story because it marks the decisive turning point: fate begins to change, justice finally will triumph. Flaccus is arrested and brought to Rome, and "this was caused," says Philo explicitly, "I am convinced, by his treatment of the Jews, whom in his craving for aggrandisement he had resolved to exterminate utterly."[59] The prosecutors are none other than Isidorus and Lampo, his former allies who had persuaded him to attack the Jews. It also becomes clear only now that both had been his enemies all along, except for the short period when they used him for their conspiracy against the Jews. Indeed Isidorus, the chairman of most of the Alexandrian "clubs," "synods," and "divans," had once used his followers to instigate a plot against Flaccus and had to leave town temporarily when his slander became obvious.[60] That these enemies, whom Flaccus trusted blindly, now conduct his arraignment, proves according to Philo that justice "watches over human affairs."[61]

The last part of Philo's account deals with Flaccus' miserable life in exile on the island of Andros and his eventual execution—not without emphasizing that he finally recognized and regretted his injustice against the Jews.[62] Accordingly, the treatise concludes: "Such was the fate of Flaccus also, who thereby became an indubitable proof that the help which God can give was not withdrawn from the nation of the Jews."[63]

Like *In Flaccum*, the *Legatio ad Gaium* belongs to the last works written by Philo (after January 41 C.E., Gaius' death); because of its different literary character and purpose, however, the events of 38 C.E. play a different and less important role here than in *In Flaccum*. The main difference results from the different focus: the center of attention in the *Legatio ad Gaium* is Gaius Caligula, his madness and megalomania, especially his attempt at self-deification. Accordingly, it is he and not Flaccus who appears in the role of the arch-villain. When he decided to assume the guise of the gods and demigods everybody ("I might almost say the whole inhabited world") submitted to his madness, except for the Jews.

It is precisely at this point that Philo turns to the events in Alexandria: "The promiscuous and unstable rabble of the Alexandrians perceived this, and thinking that a very suitable opportunity had occurred, attacked us and brought to light the hatred which had long been smouldering, reducing everything to chaos and confusion."[64] "Perceived this" obviously refers to the fact that the Jews had fallen out of favor with Gaius, which gave the

Alexandrians the opportunity to give way to their hatred, long bottled up and suppressed.[65] The description of the events themselves is similar to, though much shorter than, *In Flaccum*. Some details are to be found, however, only in *Legatio ad Gaium*, for example the vandalizing and destruction of many of the synagogues.[66] Only those synagogues which could not be razed or burned down because they were situated in densely populated areas were desecrated by having images of Gaius set up in them.[67]

Philo leaves no doubt whom he has in mind, particularly when he talks about the "Alexandrians" and their hatred of the Jews. No one "among the Greeks and barbarians" fitted Gaius' vanity better in thinking that he was God than the Alexandrians, and these Alexandrians, although consisting of Greeks and Egyptians, are first of all the native Egyptians. This becomes clear when Philo argues that they do not regard the title of God very highly because they allow it "to be shared by the indigenous ibises and venomous snakes and many other ferocious wild beasts";[68] for them it was only natural to declare an emperor God (the only one who failed to see through this was Gaius). The majority of Gaius' courtiers were also Egyptians, most prominent among them a certain Helicon, "an abominable execrable slave."[69] He became the tool of the anti-Jewish party, having been reared "right from the cradle" in all kinds of calumnies against the Jews and their customs. In the following negotiations of the two embassies with Caligula he is a key figure.

To summarize, Philo draws a multilayered picture of the events, which is partly contradictory but nevertheless shows some clear outlines. It is first and foremost a political drama in the triangle of Flaccus, Gaius Caligula, and the Alexandrians. The Jews are the innocent victims of a political conflict of interests: Gaius' accession to the throne disturbs the balance of power in Alexandria. The Roman prefect, until then of unimpeachable reputation, suddenly has reason to fear falling out of favor with the new emperor and begins to run amok. He neglects his duties and finally, in his desperate search for allies, cooperates with his former enemies, the representatives of the Greek Alexandrians. They demand that he sacrifice the Jews, and in acquiescing to their demand he brings on a horrible pogrom. His political calculation, however, turns out to be wrong: he does fall out of favor, for whatever historical reason,[70] and is arrested, banished, and later executed.

That the Jews are not only passive players in this political game becomes evident from the episode with Agrippa. His appearance does not seem to have been as discreet as Philo wants us to believe, and the Jews at least succeed in using him to send their resolution (most probably an address of devotion on the occasion of Gaius' accession to the throne) to the emperor. Without a doubt, the Jews understand themselves as part of the constellation of political power.

Gaius Caligula, despite the account in *Legatio ad Gaium,* is the less active participant in this political conflict. Philo's attempt to connect his craving for deification with the outbreak of the anti-Jewish activities in Alexandria is rather artificial. The Alexandrians could certainly rely on his "indescribable hatred of the Jews,"[71] but there is no indication that he actively stirred up the unrest in Alexandria. The setting up of images in the synagogues takes place solely on the initiative of the Alexandrians, and the setting up of the statue "dedicated to himself under the name of Zeus" in the Jerusalem Temple[72] happens much later and has nothing to do with the events in Alexandria.

This is the level of "international" or "foreign" politics, Alexandria and its entanglements with the major power of Rome. Quite different from this is the level of domestic policies within Alexandria. It is expressed for the first time in Flaccus' decree which aimed at "the destruction of our citizenship" *(tēn tēs hēmeteras politeias anairesin)* by defining the Alexandrian Jews as "foreigners and aliens."[73] Philo unfortunately does not explain precisely what this means; he mentions only the abolishment of "our ancestral customs and our participation in political rights,"[74] probably referring to religious as well as to civic rights. There can be no doubt, however, that the edict pertained to the most essential elements of the social and political life of the Jews in Alexandria. Whatever the juridical basis of Jewish citizenship in Alexandria before the summer of 38, it becomes clear that the Alexandrians succeeded in changing radically the delicate and complicated balance between the different ethnic factions in Alexandria; Flaccus' decree is taken as a charter for anti-Jewish riots and paves the way for horrible massacres. Although Philo does not define the new civic status of the Jews, the episode of the scourging of the magistrates is a clear hint: being "treated like Egyptians of the meanest rank,"[75] they are placed on par with the native Egyptians.

The conflict over civic rights in Alexandria took place between the three ethnic groups of the Greeks, the Egyptians, and the Jews. Unfortunately, Philo is rather vague in references to the city's factions; he mostly speaks of the "Alexandrians" as the enemies of the Jews, without defining precisely which group he has in mind. No doubt Isidorus and Lampo, the arch-enemies, are the representatives of the Greeks; they instigate the idea of sacrificing the Jews. The gibes against Agrippa are concocted in the gymnasium,[76] clearly indicating that the Greek Alexandrians must have been an important factor in the struggle for civic rights in Alexandria. They obviously had a vital interest in degrading the Jews.

However, this is only part of the picture Philo provides. His references to the "Egyptians," that is, the native Egyptian population of Alexandria, place them at the bottom of the social ladder. From the outset he states clearly that they have an "innate hostility to the Jews";[77] they hoard weapons and therefore they, not the Jews, are to be regarded as political criminals and guilty of high treason;[78] and it is certainly no coincidence that the Egyptian courtier Helicon has been taught from the cradle "not by one person only but by the noisiest element in the city of the Alexandrians"[79] to vituperate the Jews and their customs. Hence, there is unambiguous evidence of a rivalry, an irreconcilable hostility, between the Egyptian and Jewish populations of Alexandria. The Egyptians are the arch-enemies of the Jews, they hate them and try to harm and to blacken them whenever possible. Philo does not explain this hostility, but obviously it is not a recent development but goes back to the past, most probably to the remote past. On the other hand, Philo leaves no doubt that he does not like the Egyptians either: they are jealous by nature and burst with envy,[80] "adepts at flattery and imposture and hypocrisy, ready enough with fawning words but causing universal disaster with their loose and unbridled lips."[81] More than the Greeks, this seems to be Philo's main message, it is the Egyptians who represent the hotbed of anti-Jewish resentment.[82] If we can safely assume that the mob who executed the pogrom consisted mainly of Egyptians, it even seems plausible that the Greek faction deliberately used the Egyptians in order to achieve their goal.

THE EDICT(S) OF CLAUDIUS

As we have seen, Philo refers several times to the question of civic rights as a potential source of unrest among the various ethnic groups in Alexandria. In order to evaluate the historical significance of this argument in the context of the anti-Jewish riots, we must analyze the different edicts (or the different versions of the edict) of Claudius which deal with this question. Josephus' version of Claudius' edict to Alexandria reads as follows:

> Tiberius Claudius Caesar Augustus Germanicus, of tribunician power, speaks. Having from the first known that the Jews in Alexandria called

Alexandrians *(Alexandreis)* were fellow colonizers from the very earliest times jointly with the Alexandrians *(Alexandreusi)* and received equal civic rights *(isēs politeias)* from the kings as is manifest from the documents in their possession and from the edicts; and that after Alexandria was made subject to our empire by Augustus their rights were preserved by the prefects sent from time to time, and that these rights have never been disputed; . . . and learning that the Alexandrians *(Alexandreis)* rose up in insurrection against the Jews in their midst in the time of Gaius Caesar, who through his great folly and madness humiliated the Jews because they refused to transgress the religion of their fathers *(tēn patrion thrēskeian)* by addressing him as a god; I desire that none of their rights *(tōn dikaiōn)* should be lost to the Jews on account of the madness of Gaius, but that their former privileges *(ta proteron dikaiēmata)* also be preserved to them, while they abide by their own customs *(tois idiois ethesin);* and I enjoin upon both parties to take the greatest precaution to prevent any disturbance arising after the posting of my edict.[83]

An unbiased reading of this text can hardly leave a doubt that with this edict Claudius settles the question of Jewish citizenship in Alexandria once and forever: the Jews in Alexandria are called "Alexandrians" and enjoy from the very beginning equal civic rights, that is, citizenship *(politeia)*, with their fellow citizens. This status has been maintained by the Ptolemaic kings as well as by the Roman administration, with the exception only of Claudius' predecessor, the "mad" Gaius Caligula, who wanted the Jews to address him as a god and allowed the Alexandrians to persecute the disobedient Jews. The edict does not say what precisely Gaius did to the "rights" of the Jews, but Claudius' desire to restore the "former privileges" clearly indicates that these "rights" had been restricted. It is conspicuous, however, that the edict, when describing positively the restitution of the Jewish rights, refers only to "their own customs" and does not return explicitly to the "civic rights."

This interpretation of the edict as affirming the right of the Jews to be called "Alexandrians" like the Greek citizens of Alexandria, enjoying *isopoliteia* in the sense of citizenship in the Greek *polis* of Alexandria, is in keeping with Josephus' other statements on the subject. This is apparent from his reference to Julius Caesar's bronze tablet for the "Jews in Alexandria" which declared that they were "citizens of Alexandria" *(Alexandreōn politai)*[84] as well as from his efforts to prove (against Apion) that Alexander had already granted the Alexandrian Jews "privileges on a par with those of the Macedonians,"[85] that is, *isopoliteia,* and that they are therefore rightly called "Alexandrians."[86] Josephus is obviously interested in claiming for the Jews of Alexandria the right of citizenship equal to the Greek citizens and in having Claudius confirm this privilege.

Against this has been argued, most notably by Kasher,[87] that "Alexandrians" and "Alexandrian *politai*" do not refer to citizens of the Greek *polis* but rather to members of the respective political organizations *(politeumata)* within the city of Alexandria;[88] accordingly, that *isopoliteia* does not refer to citizenship in the *polis* Alexandria but rather to equal political status for the Jewish *politeuma* on a par with the other ethnic communities.[89] This interpretation is certainly possible but nevertheless seems far-fetched, mainly because it presupposes a very clear idea of the legal and technical terminology on the part of Josephus and at the same time ignores Josephus' tendency to wishful thinking with regard to the Jewish civic rights in Alexandria. In any case, Kasher's interpretation does not see the Jewish striving for citizenship in Alexandria as a possible source of conflict; it is solely the attempt of the Alexandrians to abolish the established rights of the Jewish *politeuma* which leads to the unrest.[90]

The immediately following edict which was sent "to the rest of the world" does not help to clarify the question of citizenship. It grants the "same privileges to be maintained for the Jews throughout the empire under the Romans as those in Alexandria enjoy."[91] In defining these "privileges" as the right to "observe the customs of their fathers *(ta patria ethē)* without let or hindrance,"[92] it puts the emphasis, as is the case in the second part of the edict to Alexandria, on religious rather than civic rights. Moreover, the tone of the second edict is quite different from that of the first: whereas Claudius in the edict to Alexandria enjoins "upon both parties to take the greatest precautions to prevent any disturbance," the edict to the "rest of the world" is much less balanced: "I enjoin upon them [the Jews] also by these presents to avail themselves of this kindness in a more reasonable spirit, and not to set at nought the beliefs about the gods held by other peoples but to keep their own laws *(tous idious nomous).*"[93] This makes it seem that the Jews, dissatisfied with merely being allowed to observe their own laws, had expressed their disagreement or displeasure with the religious customs and beliefs of their neighbors, and that this was the only reason for tension between Jews and non-Jews.

A very different picture evolves from the third edict, the *Letter to the Alexandrians* which answers the request of the Alexandrian delegation:

(73) With regard to the responsibility for the disturbances and rioting, or rather, to speak the truth, the war *(tou polemou)*, against the Jews, although your ambassadors . . . argued vigorously and at length in the disputation, I have not wished to make an exact inquiry, but I harbor within me a store of immutable indignation against those who renewed the conflict. I merely say that, unless you stop this destructive and obstinate mutual enmity, I shall be forced to show what a benevolent ruler can be when he is turned to righteous indignation.

(82) Even now, therefore, I conjure the Alexandrians to behave gently and kindly towards the Jews who have inhabited the same city for many years, and not to dishonour any of their customs in their worship of their god *(tōn pros thrēskeian autois nenomismenōn tou theou)*, but to allow them to keep their own ways *(tois ethesin)*, as they did in the time of the god Augustus and as I too, having heard both sides, have confirmed.

(88) The Jews, on the other hand, I order not to aim at more than they have previously had and not in future to send two embassies as if they lived in two cities, a thing which has never been done before, (92) and not to intrude themselves *(mēde epispaiein)* into the games presided over by the *gymnasiarchoi* and the *kosmētai*, since they enjoy what is their own, and in a city which is not their own *(en allotria polei)* they possess an abundance of all good things. (96) Nor are they to bring in or invite Jews coming from Syria or Egypt, or I shall be forced to conceive graver suspicions. If they disobey, I shall proceed against them in every way as fomenting a common plague for the whole world *(koinēn teina tēs oikoumenēs noson exegeirontas)*.

(100) If you both give up your present ways and are willing to live in gentleness and kindness with one another, I for my part will care for the city as much as I can, as one which has long been closely connected with us.[94]

This document poses many problems which have occupied scores of scholars.[95] To begin with, there can be no doubt that it is authentic and that its indisputable authenticity has a bearing on the edict quoted by Josephus and discussed above. Most scholars agree that both the pronouncement quoted by Josephus and the papyrus are genuine edicts of the emperor Claudius, that they reflect "two imperial opinions on the same subject in the same year,"[96] the first issued soon after Claudius' accession, probably in March 41 (after a hearing of the first delegations led by Philo and Isidorus), the second probably issued in October and published in November 41 (after a hearing given to the second delegations mentioned in the letter during the spring or summer of 41).[97]

This chronological assumption does not say anything, however, about the contents of the two edicts, especially of the first one (in Josephus), which has to be read in light of the second (the papyrus) because of the latter's obvious historical significance. Tcherikover has argued that Josephus did not preserve the precise wording of the first edict but used a forged version adapted for a Jewish point of view. This pertains above all to the passages which are incompatible with the letter and therefore to be regarded as a forgery: the reference to the Jews as Alexandrians, the statement that the Jews have dwelt in Alexandria "from its earliest times," and the claim that the Jews enjoyed *isopoliteia* with the Alexandrians.[98] Some scholars, most notably Schwartz in his recent evaluation of the subject, have gone a step further and taken the more rigorous view that we are not dealing with two edicts but with two versions of one and the same edict, namely the papyrus letter of which Josephus' edict to Alexandria is a Jewish adaptation.[99] Without going into detail here, there is something to be said in favor of this view, mainly because the alleged first edict becomes almost meaningless if stripped of all the forgeries noticed by Tcherikover.

Whether Josephus' edict to Alexandria is a forgery of a first edict issued originally by Claudius or a forged version of the only edict, the papyrus letter, there can be no doubt that its claim of Alexandrian citizenship for the Jews, dating back to ancient times and being confirmed by Claudius, is an ideal construction which does not stand up to closer examination.[100] In contrast to Josephus, Claudius' letter distinguishes unequivocally between "Alexandrians" and "Jews" and explicitly warns the Jews "not to aim at more than they have previously had" and to be content with what they have "in a city which is not their own." This can hardly be interpreted differently from meaning that (a) Claudius did not want to grant or to confirm the Jews civic rights in Alexandria, and (b) the Jews did attempt to improve their civic status and this was one of the reasons for unrest in Alexandria.

Kasher's arguments against this interpretation are not very convincing. He maintains that it contradicts Philo and that *hē allotria polis* "should be understood literally, without the slightest relation to the civic status of the Jews," simply meaning "that Alexandria, like all of Egypt, was the private possession of the emperor, and they therefore could not do as they liked in it."[101] Philo is scarcely a historically reliable witness against

Claudius in this particular case, and the explanation that Alexandria was the private possession of the emperor and that the Jews should behave appropriately, of course, pertains to the Alexandrians as well. In the context of the long admonition to the Jews it is certainly not an adequate interpretation but another example of Kasher's forced attempt to play down any hint of civic rights.

This is also true for the directly related remark that the Jews should not "intrude themselves into the games presided over by the *gymnasiarchoi* and the *kosmētai*." What Tcherikover translates as "intrude" is based on an emendation of the Greek text, namely to correct the word *epispairein*—the reading the first editor of the papyrus suggested—to *epispaiein*.[102] Whereas the use of the verb *epispairein* is extremely uncommon[103] and its suggested meaning "to palpitate, to be in alarm" does not fit in the context of Claudius' letter, *epispaiein* = *epeispaiein* = *insilire* = "intrude" makes perfect sense. The Jews were prohibited from "intruding" or "forcing their way" into the games presided over by the gymnasiarchs and *kosmētai*, which were reserved for citizens of the *polis* only.[104]

This interpretation is also rejected by Kasher, who argues, following Radin[105] and Amusin,[106] that *epispairein* means "harass" and that Claudius warns the Jews "not to harass" *(mēde epispairein)* the games arranged by the gymnasiarchs and *kosmētai*. This, of course, gives the letter a completely different meaning: instead of prohibiting the Jews who aspire to citizenship in the *polis* from forcing their way into the games and thus into the gymnasium, it warns them not to disturb the games violently and not to create unrest. Kasher supports his reading of the letter by pointing to the fact that the emperor's warning is "part of a passage dealing with the disturbances and quarrel with the Jews of the city,"[107] that "the section in *Claudius' Letter* referring to the Jews was aimed entirely at restoring order and preventing the recurrence of the 'war against the Jews.'"[108]

The latter is a rather hasty and superficial conclusion. The section in the letter referring to the Jews (lines 73ff.) is divided into four clearly discernible parts: the first (lines 73 to the beginning of 82) deals with both opponents, the Jews and the Alexandrians. The emperor refuses to search for the causes of the conflict (obviously from the very beginning, 38 C.E.) but expresses his particular indignation against those who renewed it, that is, the Jews, in 41 C.E. He nevertheless makes clear that the conflict is a mutual one and that both sides must stop it immediately. The second paragraph (lines 82–88) deals with the Alexandrians alone (*eti kai nyn* obviously referring to the renewed outbreak of the hostilities for which the Jews were responsible: "even now," that is, although the Jews have renewed the conflict, I conjure the Alexandrians . . .),[109] admonishing them "not to dishonour any of their [the Jews'] customs in their worship of their god," that is, emphasizing the religious aspect of the quarrel and not touching on the question of the civic rights at all. The section addressing the Jews (lines 88–100), on the other hand, is dominated by the reproach that they aim at more than they have had and more than befits them: the enigmatic and much discussed two embassies have to be viewed under this heading as well as the crucial *epispairein/epispaiein* into the games, the bringing in of Jews from Syria or Egypt, and the final threat to proceed against them "as fomenting a common plague for the whole world." The fourth paragraph (lines 100 end–104; the last lines 105–109 seem to be a personal addition made by Claudius himself),[110] again addressing both parties and hence referring back to the first section, gives the whole piece a well-considered balance.

The context and theme of the third paragraph make highly unlikely Kasher's argument that it has to be interpreted in the framework of the "disturbances and quarrel with the Jews of the city, or rather with the 'war' against them."[111] This is the subject of the first paragraph only and clearly directed against the Alexandrians; it does not make any sense in a warning directed at the Jews. In addition, the order not *epispai(r)ein* into the games is obviously related to the beginning ("not to aim at more than they have previously had") and the immediately following "since they enjoy what is their own . . . in a city which is not their own." This leaves no doubt that *epispai(r)ein* into the games reflects a claim on part of the Jews which is rejected by the emperor.

The other elements in the third paragraph of the letter fit well in this context of an "improper" Jewish claim. The sending of two separate embassies which provokes the emperor's anger is framed by the order "not to aim at more than they have previously had" and "not to intrude themselves into the games." Hence it makes sense to argue that the two embassies represented two opposing parties within the Jewish community of Alexandria ("as if they lived in two cities," as the letter has it), one aggressively advocating the claim for civic rights and the other holding a more moderate view.[112] This is much closer to the context than Tcherikover's suggestion that the two factions stem from the riots: a militant faction had "captured the leadership of the Jewish community in Alexandria after their successful fight against the Greeks in 41" and opposed the more peaceful part of the community represented by Philo.[113] As we have seen, the section of the letter addressing the Jews does not deal at all with the riots and the responsibility for them; and apart from this, it seems hard to imagine in the political climate of the spring of 41 (after *the Alexandrian Jews* had attacked their fellow citizens) a Jewish embassy which argued in front of the emperor "in favour of the right of the Jews to fight back when attacked."[114]

The two remaining elements in the section dealing with the Jews also have to be interpreted in light of the general warning "not to aim at more than they have previously had." Taking this context into consideration, the prohibition of bringing Jews from Syria (= Palestine) or Egypt into Alexandria is not directed against Jewish attempts "to strengthen themselves [military] for their struggle against the Alexandrians"[115] but against attempts to strengthen the Jewish population of Alexandria in order to give vigor to their claim for civic rights.[116] The same is true for the sentence which concludes the whole section on the Jews: if they disobey the aforementioned detailed orders, Claudius will proceed against them "as fomenting a common plague for the whole world." By fomenting social disturbances in Alexandria, aiming at more than befits them, the Alexandrian Jews may give rise to unrest in other parts of the Jewish diaspora and threaten the *pax Romana*.[117]

The paragraph on the whole reflects a very active striving of the Alexandrian Jews for social advancement and the determined intent of the emperor to keep the *status quo* and not to give way to the Jewish demands. Kasher's conclusion that the Alexandrian Jews fought "only" for self-determination within the limits of their *politeuma* and that the Alexandrians "opposed that aim" cannot be substantiated by a closer reading of the letter. He does not answer the question of why the Jews had to fight for their right as a *politeuma* (which was granted) and why the Alexandrians queried this right. By emphasizing the active Jewish resistance against this unfair treatment ("the Jews did not sit by idly, but fought for their rights to the point even of initiating acts of revenge"), he reveals more than a little of his own political presuppositions.[118]

THE ACTS OF THE ALEXANDRIAN MARTYRS

The most vivid and colorful information we possess on Isidorus' and Lampo's trial are the so-called *Acta Isidori (et Lamponis)*, which have survived in four papyrus fragments.[119] They belong to a series of separate pamphlets, later collected under the title "Acts of the Alexandrian Martyrs." Most scholars agree today that the "Acts of the Alexandrian Martyrs" altogether as well as the individual pamphlets (which refer to different cases at different times) are not official protocols of the Roman authorities but belong to the category of "popular stories, fiction,"[120] or "historical novels"[121] written for the purpose of political propaganda. This does not mean, however, that they are historically worthless; on the contrary, they provide valuable and otherwise unattested historical information which has to be examined carefully.[122] They are all written from the point of view of the nationalist Alexandrian Greeks who oppose the Roman government embodied in the person of the respective emperor. The Jews are portrayed as representing the interests of Rome in this power struggle and hence as the natural enemies of the Alexandrians.

The *Acta Isidori* are among the earliest of these papyrus fragments. They are presented in the guise of a trial of king Agrippa in which Isidorus (and probably also Lampo) performed the task of the prosecutor(s).[123] The date of the trial is given as the fifth and sixth days of Pachon, which is the 30th of April and 1st of May, but the year is unfortunately missing. Depending on whether Agrippa I or II is the Agrippa of the trial, it took place in either 41 or 52/53 C.E.; most scholars agree now, however, on Agrippa I and accordingly on 41 C.E. as the date of the trial.[124] The historical circumstances of the "trial" itself are highly problematic. Schwartz has rightly pointed out that the text gives much more the impression of reporting a trial in which Isidorus (and Lampo) are the defendants rather than Agrippa, and that we ought to speak of a "'record' however literary and biased—of a debate between Agrippa and two Alexandrian spokesmen, after the latter had been condemned to death."[125]

The "trial," which takes place in an imperial garden in Rome in the presence of senators and "men of consular rank," is opened by Isidorus, who begins, strangely enough, not with his charges against Agrippa but with asking the emperor's permission to speak about "my native city's sufferings."[126] This sounds as if the "sufferings," which unfortunately are not explained, have something to do with the Jews, that is, as if the "trial" of Agrippa is a resumption of the public debate over the quarrel between "Jews" and "Alexandrians," the opponents being this time Agrippa and Isidorus. Claudius, after having agreed to hear Isidorus' account of the "sufferings" of Alexandria, immediately adds that he should not attack his "friend" Agrippa as he did in the cases of "Theon the exegete" and "Naevius, prefect of Egypt and prefect of the praetorian guard at Rome."[127] Isidorus answers with a blunt slander of Agrippa: "My Lord Caesar, what do you care for a twopenny-halfpenny Jew (*Ioudaiou triōboleiou*) like Agrippa?"[128] Whether the word *triōboleios* (lit. "amounting to three obols") is used here in the technical sense of referring to a prostitute's fee or "only" implies "nothing more than worthless,"[129] it is no doubt a "coarse insult" which was directed no less against Agrippa than against his "friend," the emperor. Unfortunately, the continuation of the text is badly damaged. We hear only of the outraged answer of Claudius ("What? You are the most insolent of men to speak")[130] but the rest of the exchange between Isidorus and the emperor cannot be reconstructed.

The third fragment (156c) comes back to Isidorus' charges against the Alexandrian Jews. Since Isidorus explicitly answers Agrippa, this can be taken as further evidence that the "trial" has to do with the quarrel between the Jews and the Alexandrians and that Agrippa is regarded as the spokesman of the Alexandrian Jews. Here we are presented with the following exchange between Isidorus and Agrippa.

> I accuse them [the Jews] of wishing to stir up the entire world *(hoti kai holēn tēn oikoumenēn epicheirousin tarassein)* . . . We must consider every detail in order to judge the whole people. They are not of the same nature as the Alexandrians *(Alexandreusin homoiopatheis)*, but live rather after the fashion of the Egyptians *(tropō de Aigyptiōn homoioi)*. Are they not on a level with those who pay the poll-tax *(isoi tois phoron telousi)*?
>
> Agrippa: The Egyptians have had taxes *(phorous)* levied on them by the rulers . . . But no one has imposed tributes on the Jews.[131]

To begin with, the accusation against the Alexandrian Jews of stirring up the whole world is reminiscent of Claudius' threat in his letter to proceed against them "as fomenting a common plague for the whole world." As in the letter, the disturbance *(tarachē)* of the Jews is connected with the civic rights in Alexandria. Isidorus subsequently formulates precisely the point of view of the "Alexandrians," that is, the Alexandrian Greeks, in this quarrel: the Jews are not equal to the "Alexandrians" but rather to the native Egyptians; consequently, they are subject to the "poll-tax" or "tribute" *(phoros)* like the Egyptians. Agrippa's answer denies exactly Isidorus' presupposition: the Jews are not subject to "tributes"; consequently, it is implied, they are equal to the (Greek) Alexandrians and entitled to full civic rights like the Alexandrian Greeks and unlike the native Egyptians.[132]

The tax or taxes of which both speak most probably refer to the poll-tax *(laographia,* lit. "numbering of the people") introduced by Augustus in about 24/23 B.C.E. It was valid for every Egyptian; only citizens of Greek cities, Roman citizens, and some minor groups were exempt. With regard to the taxes the Jews were treated as Egyptians, a fact which must have been taken by the hellenized Alexandrian Jews as a gross insult: "in their eyes the payment of *laographia* was not merely an additional expense but also a mark of extreme political and cultural degradation, putting them on the same level with the Egyptian fellahin."[133] The degradation may well be mirrored, as has long been observed, in the famous petition (dated 5/4 B.C.E.) of the Alexandrian Jew Helenos, son of Tryphon, who was compelled to call himself "a Jew of Alexandria" instead of "an Alexandrian" as he obviously had written originally.[134] It does not seem to be accidental that the *laographia* is mentioned several times in the petition. In maliciously insinuating that all the Jews live "after the fashion of the Egyptians" and *therefore* are subject to the "poll-tax," Isidorus is as provocative as Agrippa, who bluntly denies any tributes imposed on any Jew. Both statements have to be regarded as half-truths for the sake of propaganda,[135] because the Jews certainly did not identify themselves with the native Egyptians, and not all of the Jews paid the *laographia* although most did (in Alexandria as well as, especially, in the *chōra*). The discussion clearly reflects the "undefined status of the Jews"[136] in Alexandria, and both sides try to gain the best from it for their respective clientele. As we know from Claudius' letter to the Alexandrians, his decision to execute their spokesmen did not influence his assessment of the question of Jewish civic rights in Alexandria.

The last fragment of the *Acta Isidori et Lamponis* conveys a rather bizarre conversation between the emperor and Isidorus. Claudius again accuses Isidorus of having killed many friends of his. Isidorus replies that he merely fulfilled the wish of Claudius' predecessor and that he is only too willing "to denounce anyone you wish." Disgusted at this opportunism, the emperor exclaims, "Isidorus you are really the son of a girl-musician," whereupon Isidorus answers, no less insultingly, "I am neither a slave nor a girl-musician's son, but gymnasiarch of the glorious city of Alexandria. But you are the cast-off son of the Jewess Salome (*sy de ek Salōmēs tēs Ioudaias hyos apoblētos*)."[137] "Girl-musician," of course, means prostitute, and Isidorus returns this insult by calling the emperor Salome's illegitimate son. Whether such a dialogue could have happened in reality or must be considered a literary invention is of little importance. In any case, the dialogue reflects the tension and mutual dislike between Rome and its Alexandrian Greek subjects. The Alexandrian Greeks hate the Jews and project their hatred onto Agrippa who defends the Jews, and finally onto the emperor who defends Agrippa. The reason for this hatred is generally the tendency to identify the Jews with Roman rule and more concretely the Jewish desire to be equal to the Alexandrian Greeks.

ALEXANDRIAN ANTI-SEMITISM?

According to the evidence analyzed (Philo, Josephus, Claudius' letter, Acts of the Alexandrian Martyrs), there can be no doubt that the struggle between the different ethnic groups in Alexandria (Greeks, Jews, Egyptians) was the major factor which determined the events and led to the explosion in the summer of 38 C.E. The rivalry with regard to civic status is the *leitmotif* which runs through all our sources.

The precise significance of this struggle over civic rights is seen differently in the different sources. The least reliable witness is Josephus; he assumes that the Jews had "always" enjoyed full citizenship in Alexandria and that this was confirmed by Claudius' edict. Philo maintains that Flaccus deliberately abolished Jewish citizenship and thereby put the Jews on a level with the native Egyptians; he does not define the particular nature of this "citizenship" but it is obvious that Flaccus' decree is regarded as an act of arbitrary and humiliating degradation.[138] The most reliable witness is Claudius' letter, which clearly indicates that the Jewish claim for full citizenship as an expression of their active striving for social advancement and the Greek opposition against this demand were the main reasons for the unrest in Alexandria; "full citizenship" most probably means to become part of the *polis* Alexandria with equal rights with the Greek citizens and not to be limited to the restrictions of a *politeuma*. And finally, the *Acta Isidori* also seem to focus on the question of whether the Jews of Alexandria are to be legally identified with the Egyptians or with the Greeks.

The conflict between Jews, Greeks, and Egyptians in Alexandria was first and foremost a political conflict; there is no trace whatsoever of religious questions involved. It was triggered and nourished—this is most clearly seen in Philo's account—by shifts in the delicate balance of power between the competing ethnic groups: the accession to power of Gaius Caligula, which was construed by the Greeks as a chance to settle the question of civic rights in their favor; Agrippa's visit to Alexandria, which threatened to turn to the Jews' advantage and called for a counter-measure on part of the Greeks; and finally Claudius' accession to the throne, which demanded new efforts from both parties and led to a new though fragile balance of power.

Taking this as granted, the crucial question remains whether the recognition of the political dimension of the conflict (which has to be supplemented, of course, by the political dimension of the relationships between Rome and its Greek and Jewish subjects)[139] is sufficient to explain all aspects of the quarrel. In a recent article called "Kalkül oder 'Massenwahn'? Eine soziologische Interpretation der antijüdischen Unruhen in Alexandria 38 n.Chr.,"[140] Werner Bergmann and Christhard Hoffmann have taken precisely this view against almost all the relevant scholarly literature.[141] Over and again they insist that we are confronted in Alexandria with "real conflicts of interest,"[142] "concrete political competition,"[143] "clearly defined political goals,"[144] "rational"[145] and "purposeful, organized political action"[146] as opposed to alleged "mass hysteria,"[147] "real conflicts of interest and power."[148] Anti-Semitism figures in this scenario as the effect of the "real conflicts of interest" and not as their cause.[149] It is not motivated by a "basic cultural-religious contrast" but by a "situation of concrete political competition"; anti-Semitism is the consequence, not the cause of tension in Alexandria.[150] From this point of view it is unnecessary to assume a "deeply rooted hatred" or a "widely spread anti-Semitism"[151] among the Greek populace of Alexandria.

This is not the place to discuss Bergmann and Hoffmann's article in all its details, but some remarks are appropriate. To begin with, their explanation of the political nature of the conflict is hampered by their desire to stick to Kasher's thesis that the Alexandrian Jews did not aim at full citizenship within the *polis* but fought for equal rights and self-determination as a *politeuma*,[152] which in itself was regarded, according to Kasher, as "a thorn in the flesh of the *polis*."[153] This rather vague definition of the political conflict must rely heavily on the interpretation of the word *epispai(r)ein* in Claudius' letter as active harassments of the Greek gymnasium by Jewish gangs in order to account for the Jewish part of the conflict:[154] the Jews were active troublemakers, wanted a kind of "autonomous" *politeuma* (What is this? The right of being organized as a *politeuma* was granted, and why should the Jews aim at a new definition of the *politeuma?*), and the Greeks only reacted by trying to restrict and finally abolish the rights of the existing *politeuma*.

In addition, the way Bergmann and Hoffmann reject certain arguments which are often used to explain Alexandrian anti-Semitism but nonetheless employ them in order to determine the purely "political conflict" (without defining the relationship between what they call "political" and "anti-Semitic") is rather confusing. For example, the desire of the Jews to move up in social status, which threatens to downgrade the Alexandrian Greeks, is a political conflict with no anti-Jewish feelings involved on the part of the Greeks. When certain Greeks in the public discussion over the question of civic rights make use of certain anti-Jewish legends, this is the result of the presupposed political conflict and has nothing to do with its nature.[155] The same is true with regard to the argument of "demographic shift" in favor of the Jews (immigration of their countrymen from the *chōra* and from abroad), which was perceived by the Alexandrian Greeks as "foreign infiltration":[156] within the discussion of possible anti-Semitic models of explanation for the unrest they tend to prefer Tcherikover's interpretation that the alleged "immigration" had to do with the increase of military power during the Jewish reprisal in 41 C.E. and cannot be held responsible for any anti-Jewish feelings or measures on the part of the Greeks.[157] However, when the "clearly defined political goals" are discussed, the Jewish immigration plays a more prominent role, together with the political claims of the *politeuma,* and is not restricted to military intervention only.[158]

Most instructive is the role Bergmann and Hoffmann ascribe to the so-called anti-Semitic clubs in Alexandria. These are the *thiasoi* or *synodoi* ("synods") and *klinai* ("divans") which Philo mentions explicitly in connection with Isidorus' first plot against Flaccus[159] and which seem to have been essential also for the unrest in 38 C.E.[160] They convene in the gymnasium or the theater, where they jeer at Agrippa and demand the installation of images in the synagogues.[161] Since Isidorus is said to be the "president" of all or most of them and since they follow him blindly,[162] Bergmann and Hoffmann see the "anti-Semitic clubs" with their leader Isidorus as the political center of the Greeks which organizes and controls the activities against the Jews;[163] these activities are to be regarded, therefore, as a "rational answer on political opportunities"[164] rather than as the expression of "deeply rooted, militant hatred of the Jews" which leads to "spontaneous turmoil"[165]—although, to be sure, a "spontaneous participation on the part of the populace" cannot be excluded.[166]

It is obvious that a clear-cut distinction between "purely political" and something else (which is not defined but seems to be "cultural-religious")[167] forms the basis of Bergmann and Hoffmann's argument; the former is governed by "rational" the latter by "irrational" action. Anti-Semitism belongs solely to the "cultural-religious" and "irrational" realm; politics (and politicians?) are to be acquitted of any anti-Semitic feelings. At most, political tension and the political activities resulting from this tension may lead to anti-Semitism.

This interpretation of the events in Alexandria is highly problematic, to say the least. First of all, the distinction between "politics" and "culture/religion" is untenable for the ancient world. The effort Bergmann and Hoffmann make to separate these two areas, and especially the "political-rational" from the "irrational," is remarkable but leads to artificial results. Second, to limit anti-Semitism to the sphere of culture and religion as distinct from politics reveals a peculiar understanding of politics (as well as of anti-Semitism). What is, then, according to Bergmann and Hoffmann's criteria, the nature of the anti-Semitism which was the *effect* of the political competition? Was it "cultural-religious" and "irrational" if this is what defines anti-Semitism? Where do we find it in Alexandria after 38 C.E.? How does "political conflict" turn suddenly into "anti-Semitism?"

In distinguishing artificially between "political" and "cultural-religious,"[168] Bergmann and Hoffmann play down or even suppress pieces of information which do not fit with their theory of anti-Semitism. They ignore completely the Egyptian element within the power struggle in Alexandria, or rather declare Philo's Egyptians to be Greeks: when Philo speaks of the Egyptians' "ancient, and we might say innate hostility to the Jews,"[169] they maintain without giving any reason that he means the Greeks;[170] accordingly, it is also the Greek "anti-Semitic clubs" which have weapons at their disposal,[171] although Philo explicitly speaks of Egyptians.[172] As we have seen, Philo's account displays an ancient and deeply rooted hostility between Jews and Egyptians (from both sides) which cannot simply be explained away by Philo's contempt for the "mob" *(ochlos).*[173] This contempt certainly existed but is substantiated over and again by the anti-Jewish attitude of the Egyptians. No doubt the "clubs" which were used by their leaders for anti-Jewish agitation were Greek institutions, but no doubt either that the borderline between the clubs with their Greek clientele and the Egyptians was fluid. Just as there is little ground for claiming that "mainly members of the Greek upper class were organized in the anti-Semitic clubs,"[174] there is little reason for restricting the "mob" to the Greeks and excluding the Egyptians. Why should the "mob" who "streamed into the theatre" in order to "call out with one accord for installing images in the synagogues"[175] have consisted only of Greeks? The same is true for the "mob" who pillaged the Jewish houses and brutally killed those Jews who left their quarter in order to buy food.[176] If the Greek leaders of Alexandria looked for support in their "political" struggle against the Jews, they will hardly have omitted the Egyptians: they could rely even more securely on the Egyptians' anti-Jewish feelings than on those of their fellow Greeks.

This is all the more true as some of the prominent Greeks were of Egyptian origin. We know this from no less a person than Apion,[177] and there is no reason to believe that he was an exception. On the contrary, we learn form Josephus that the numbers of Greeks and Macedonians in Egypt "were swelled by a host of Egyptians," and it was only then that "sedition became chronic." It is not the Greeks and Macedonians but the "naturalized" Egyptians, "who originated these disturbances, because the populace, possessing neither the Macedonian's strength of character nor the Greek's sagacity, universally adopted the evil habits of the Egyptians and indulged their long-standing hatred *(antiquas inimicitias)* of us."[178] The dislike of the Egyptians which comes to expression here is very similar to Philo's attitude. As in Philo, the Egyptians are portrayed by Josephus as a nation of slaves[179] with a foolish religion[180] who always hated the Jews.

There can be no doubt, therefore, that the rivalry with regard to Alexandrian citizenship did not exist only between Jews and Greeks but also between Jews and "naturalized" (let alone native) Egyptians, and that the latter rivalry must have been by far the worst.[181] When demagogues like Apion and Isidorus addressed the mob for their "political" goals they certainly appealed to Greek as well as to Egyptian prejudices against the Jews, and we know from literary sources how effective these appeals were. Why should they have left out the stories about the humiliating expulsion of the Jews from Egypt because of leprosy or about the Jewish ass-worship or about the horrible Jewish custom of human sacrifice, all attributed by Josephus to Apion and all deeply rooted in the Egyptian (and Greco-Egyptian) tradition? It is too naive an approach to separate this "cultural-religious" from the purely "political" evidence and to argue that anti-Jewish resentments like those in the expulsion story are the result of the political conflict and manifest themselves only as part of the escalation of this conflict.[182] This may be the case, as far as the discernible stages of the conflict are concerned, but one cannot seriously distinguish between the "political" and the "cultural-religious" aspect in the sense that we have "at first" a political stage of the conflict which "later" becomes enriched by cultural-religious elements. Apion's cultural-religious argument does not create resentments against the Jews but makes deliberate use of instruments which had been ready for a long time. Cultural-religious and political aspects were inextricably interwoven in the conflict in Alexandria, and it is precisely this amalgam of political goals and (mainly) Egyptian hatred of the Jews which makes it unique and may allow us to speak of Alexandrian anti-Semitism.[183]

PART III

Centers of Conflict

CHAPTER NINE

Egypt

THE MOST FORCEFUL LITERARY propaganda in Egypt against the Jews is expressed, as we have seen above, in the story about their expulsion as lepers; the earliest witnesses are Hecataeus (about 300 B.C.E.) and Manetho (beginning of the third century B.C.E.). The *Vorlage* of this expulsion story was an *Egyptian* tradition about the invasion of Egypt and the suppression of its religion by "foreigners" and these foreigners' subsequent expulsion from the country. At some stage still to be determined, this originally Egyptian tradition was transferred to the Jews.

THE HISTORICAL SETTING OF THE EXPULSION STORY

There have been several attempts to locate the Egyptian expulsion story historically, the most prominent of which are those of Eduard Meyer and Raymond Weill.[1] Whereas Meyer wants to see the historical core in a combination of two different events, namely the turmoil at the end of the Nineteenth Dynasty (during and after the reign of Merneptah at about 1200 B.C.E.) and the much earlier disturbances associated with the "monotheistic reform" of Amenophis IV = Akhenaten (1377–1358 B.C.E.),[2] Weill is more skeptical about the validity of any one-dimensional historical reconstruction. Although he agrees to a historical "origin" for the story (namely the Hyksos tradition), the recurrence in Egyptian history of the motif of the "Asiatique impie,"[3] his invasion and later expulsion by the "savior king," lead Weill to conclude that any search for one concrete historical event in order to explain the Egyptian expulsion story is methodologically misguided. Instead, scholars should take into account the applicability of the motif to different historical situations.[4]

Here is not the place to enter into this discussion (which after all is the realm of the Egyptologists),[5] but there is certainly much to recommend

Weill's position.[6] What concerns us is the historical context of the second stage of the development: when, why, and by whom was the Egyptian expulsion story transferred to the Jews? As for "by whom," I have argued that the fusion of "original" Egyptian and "later" anti-Jewish motifs belongs to the very core of Manetho's Exodus tradition (if not Hecataeus') and cannot be relegated to a mysterious (and much later) Pseudo-Manetho. This does not answer the question, however, of whether Manetho himself is responsible for the anti-Jewish tenor of his version of the story or whether he relies on older material. Most of the scholars who claim that Manetho fabricated his anti-Jewish expulsion story want to see it in the context of the pro-Jewish policy of Ptolemy I Philadelphus (283–246 B.C.E.), more precisely as a response to the Greek translation of the Hebrew Bible instigated, according to the Letter of Aristeas, by the king. This view has been emphatically put forward by Kasher, according to whom the Egyptian priest Manetho "could very well have felt that the translation would dim the splendor of his motherland, particularly since the salvation of Israel in the Bible involved the defeat and humiliation of his people"; Manetho was forced, therefore, "to launch a mighty propaganda campaign against Jewry and the Jewish faith, hoping thus to redress the effects of the Septuagint."[7]

This reading of Manetho's expulsion story as the direct answer to the Septuagint version of the Exodus tradition is not likely. First of all, it overlooks that the earliest witness for the expulsion story is not Manetho but Hecataeus, who can hardly be seen as responding to the Greek translation of the Bible. And if one wants to focus on Manetho, it is difficult to explain the structure and the details of his story on the basis of the biblical *Vorlage*.[8] Nor is it by any means proven that the Bible (Pentateuch) was already translated when Manetho wrote his *Aegyptiaca*, or that a hellenized Egyptian author like Manetho, if the Septuagint (or part of it) did exist, had access to it and read it.[9] This does not exclude, of course, the possibility that the Passover ritual, which commemorates the biblical Exodus, was known one way or another to the Egyptians and especially to the Egyptian priests (be it as a literary text or as a festival). On the contrary, Egyptian knowledge of the Passover ritual is already apparent in the Elephantine papyri. But then we cannot use the Septuagint version of the Exodus as the trigger and *terminus a quo* of Manetho's expulsion story; the story need not have been fabricated by Manetho but may be much earlier, as early at least as any knowledge of the Exodus can be supposed.

If the expulsion story predates Manetho (and also Hecataeus because there is no reason to believe that he invented it), we have to look for elements within the narrative which might help in placing it in a historical context and explaining its application to the Jews. The analysis of both Hecataeus' and Manetho's versions has yielded two prominent motifs, the impiety motif and the *misoxenia,* that is, xenophobia, motif. The former is connected in Hecataeus with "foreigners" (who later become Jews) who practice in Egypt "different rites of religion and sacrifice," whereas Manetho castigates the impiety of first the *Egyptian* lepers with their leader Osarseph (they refuse to worship the Egyptian gods but sacrifice and consume the sacred animals) and second the Hyksos/Jerusalemites who, together with the lepers, treat the Egyptian people "impiously and savagely" and destroy their temples. It has been argued since Meyer[10] and Marquart[11] that the iconoclasm so vividly portrayed by Manetho is reminiscent of Akhenaten's religious reform or rather revolution which stamped out the traditional Egyptian cult in favor of the *one* principle out of which the world was created and is revived every day, the "living sun."[12]

Some features of the expulsion story seem to confirm this.[13] Most conspicuous is that the lepers in Manetho's version are Egyptians and that the priest Osarseph comes from Heliopolis, during the Old Kingdom the center of the sun god Atun-Re. In Chaeremon's version of the story, the Egyptian name of one of the leaders of the lepers is Tisithen, a name which clearly alludes to *iten,* the Egyptian word for the disc of the sun.[14] And it is certainly no coincidence that in most versions the name of the king, who "cleansed" Egypt of the lepers, is Amenophis, whose identification with Amenophis IV = Akhenaten suggests itself.[15] On the other hand is it obvious that no complete correspondence between the expulsion story and the Amarna period can be established. This has already been shown by Meyer, and Redford no doubt exaggerates in his zeal to explain the story solely out of the historical context of the Amarna period.[16] As I have argued above, any attempt to trace Manetho's story back to *one* historical event is methodologically problematic and does no justice to its complexity. This does not mean, however, that the demonstration of historical uncertainties and inconsistencies[17] provides sufficient grounds for denying any link between the traumatic experience of Akhenaten's short-lived revolution and the formation of the expulsion story. Such an attempt is similarly problematic in its one-sided and over-historical interpretation: it is precisely the multilayered complexity and versatility of the story which *also* allows for reminiscences of the Amarna experience.[18] These reminiscences are easily transferable to the Jews, whose monotheism may have evoked the memory of the strange reform introduced by the heretic king.[19] We should not forget that Hecataeus already describes the religion of the colonists, who settled in Jerusalem after they had been driven out of Egypt, as a cult without images because they were of the opinion "that God is not in human form."

Whereas one trace of the impiety motif in Manetho's account, the crime of the Egyptian lepers, leads back to Akhenaten's revolution, the other one, the impious and savage conduct of the "foreigners" (the Hyksos/Jerusalemites), cannot be connected with the Amarna period. Since both the Jerusalemites and the lepers combine forces and not only destroy the Egyptian temples but also slaughter the sacred animals, Manetho has obviously blended in one motif different historical allusions. In search of a historical context for the second trace, the invasion of foreigners who rage against the temples and the sacred animals, J. Yoyotte has pointed to the Persian conquerors of Egypt, first Cambyses (525 B.C.E.) and later Artaxerxes III Ochus (343 B.C.E.).[20] As we have seen above, Cambyses is purported to have destroyed all the Egyptian temples (except for the Jewish one at Elephantine), and both Cambyses and Artaxerxes III are reported not only to have killed the sacred Apis bull but also to have cooked and consumed it.[21] This is, indeed, reminiscent of the "foreigners'" and lepers' roasting of the sacred animals in Manetho's story.

It is very probable, therefore, that one layer of Manetho's impiety motif has to be seen in the context of the Persian period and is part of the Egyptian anti-Persian propaganda. To explain the second step, the motif's transference to the Jews, we may refer to the events in the Jewish colony at Elephantine, analyzed above: the Jews do slaughter sacred animals and are the allies of the hated Persian oppressors.[22] This is not to say that the events in Elephantine triggered the transference of the expulsion story in all its complexity to the Jews, in other words that Elephantine was the sole historical blueprint out of which Manetho developed his story. This again would be an oversimplification which does not account for the different historical layers in Manetho's story (especially the one connected with the Amarna revolution). But it does suggest the kind of confrontation between Egyptians and Jews in this period which could have caused the transfer of the originally Egyptian motif of the struggle against impious foreigners to the Jews. One might imagine, indeed, the nationalistic priests of Khnum exploiting this handy literary tradition in order to combat their enemies, Persians and Jews alike.[23]

XENOPHOBIA

The second motif, the alleged *misoxenia* = xenophobia of the Jews, is very complex in its treatment of the different authors. We are interested here in its Egyptian layer, that is, whether it originated in the peculiar Egyptian context, which is so striking with regard to the impiety motif, or whether it has to be relegated to predominantly Greek influence. Manetho, the Egyptian-Greek author, does not mention it at all in his first version of the expulsion story; he simply describes how brutally the foreign invaders "of obscure stock," that is, the Hyksos, act against the native Egyptians, how they burn their cities, raze their temples to the ground, and treat all the natives with cruel hostility. This is the classical Egyptian motif of the foreign oppressor, which has nothing to do with misanthropy, let alone xenophobia, on the part of the "foreigners"; if anyone, it is the Egyptians who are "xenophobic."[24]

The situation is different in Manetho's second version. Here the lepers, after king Amenophis had assigned to them Auaris, the deserted city of the Hyksos, are placed by their leader Osarseph, the former priest of Heliopolis, under the obligation neither to worship the Egyptian gods nor to have "intercourse with any save those of their own confederacy." The latter prohibition, which may be labeled xenophobia, comes very unexpectedly. Because it is closely related to the impiety motif one may be inclined to connect it with the foreign oppressors, but there is no reason for this, especially since it belongs to the literary layer of the *Egyptian* lepers. As a matter of fact, at this level of Manetho's story both the impiety and the xenophobia are the *result* of the lepers' position as the outcasts of Egyptian society, even before they finally are driven from Egypt.

This accords well with Hecataeus' version of the expulsion story. According to Hecataeus the foreigners who founded Jerusalem differ in their religion and in their way of life from all other nations: they adopt a way of life "which was somewhat unsocial and hostile to foreigners" because of their own expulsion from Egypt. Here the xenophobia motif belongs to the foreigners but is, as in Manetho, the result of their being outcasts. The same is true for Diodorus Siculus and especially Lysimachus, who is probably also of Egyptian origin: according to him the "impure and impious persons" (who are identified with the Jews from the outset) are driven into the wilderness and, having become outcast, decide "to show good will to no man, to offer not the best but the worst advice, and to overthrow any temples and altars of the gods which they found," a decision which they put into practice very efficiently on their way to Judea. This resembles Manetho's second version in that the xenophobia and impiety motifs are closely interwoven and are the immediate result of the outcast position. The "xenophobia," however, has become a more general "misanthropy," a development that may lead further away from the original Egyptian context.

It is hard to comprehend how the cruel maltreatment of the Egyptian populace by foreign oppressors and the resulting xenophobia of the Egyptians transforms into the xenophobia/misanthropy of the foreigners/ lepers/impious = Jews driven out of Egypt. If one does not wish to argue that the Egyptians transferred their own xenophobia to the Jews, a transfer which is not very likely, one must reckon with the possibility that the xenophobia motif indeed belongs more to the Greek adaptation of the expulsion story than to its original Egyptian background. To be sure, it is possible that the Greek Hecataeus may have adopted it together with the original version of the expulsion story during his visit in Egypt, but it is equally possible and even more probable that it is part of his specific Greek retelling of the story. And as far as the Egyptian Manetho is concerned, there is certainly no reason to believe that his version of the story has been taken in its entirety from the Egyptian tradition. After all he writes in Greek and for a Greek readership,[25] and it may well be that this particular piece of information on the Jews is directed toward the Greeks. Especially the very peculiar formulation "intercourse with none save those of their own confederacy," which belongs to the *coniuratio* motif, seems to point to this direction.

Apart from the expulsion story there is at least one other literary motif which is deeply rooted in the Egyptian anti-Jewish tradition. As we have seen above, alleged Jewish ass-worship goes back to an identification of the God of the Jews with Typhon-Seth, the arch-enemy of Osiris, which is no doubt of Egyptian origin. Since Seth later becomes the embodiment of evil and is identified with the hated Persian rule (Artaxerxes III Ochus is said not only to have slaughtered the sacred Apis bull,[26] which was believed to be the incarnation of Osiris, but also to have worshipped the ass who was associated with Seth and killed Osiris),[27] we are dealing here with another motif transferred to both the Jews and the Persians. Whether this means that the legend of Jewish ass-worship originated during the Persian period is an open question; it is striking, however, that this motif too first appears during the Persian occupation.

Altogether, there can be no doubt that chronologically and geographically Egypt has to be regarded the hothouse of the growth later labeled anti-Semitism, in its unique combination of religious and political aspects. This originally Egyptian "anti-Semitism," however, gained its historical power in a Hellenistic context.

CHAPTER TEN

Syria-Palestine

*I*F "ANTI-SEMITISM" ORIGINATED in the peculiar religio-political climate of ancient Egypt, what then is the Greek contribution to it? I have considered above the possibility that the charge of xenophobia is part of the Greek adaptation of originally Egyptian anti-Jewish traditions. In order to substantiate this argument it is necessary to examine the motifs of both xenophobia and misanthropy in their larger Greek context. Only then does it become possible to assess their impact on the Syrian-Palestinian center of conflict (with their roots in Hellenistic Egypt).

XENOPHOBIA: THE GREEK CONTEXT

Contemporary Greek literature provides good evidence for evaluating the force of the xenophobia/misanthropy argument. The expulsion of foreigners *(xenēlasia),* which is given by Hecataeus as the reason for the Jews' *misoxenia* ("as a result of their own expulsion from Egypt" they adopted their peculiar way of life), was not alien to the Greeks. As a matter of fact, the Spartans are well known, and by some condemned, for practicing it: according to Thucydides, Pericles, in his speech before the outbreak of the Peloponnesian war (431 B.C.E.), demands that the Spartans "cease passing laws for the expulsion of aliens *(xenēlasias)* so far as concerns us or our allies."[1] Plato in his *Protagoras* has Socrates refer to the custom rather ironically,[2] and Aristotle mentions it as widespread without commenting on it.[3] Later it becomes a peculiar feature of the barbarians in contrast to the civilized Greek world. "According to Eratosthenes," says Strabo, "the expulsion of foreigners is a common custom *(koinon . . . ethos tēn xenēlasian)* to all barbarians,"[4] and as outstanding examples he refers to the Egyptians, the Carthaginians (who "used to drown in the sea any foreigners who sailed past their country to Sardinia or to the Pillars"), and the Persians.[5] Obviously, the custom has become an ethnographic cliché, one which, however, was never applied to the Jews—most probably because they were regarded as the prototype of expelled foreigners.

Unlike the custom of *xenēlasia*, which is motivated mainly by "practical" concerns, *misoxenia* ("hatred of foreigners," "xenophobia") is connected with the "national character" of a people. Strikingly enough, this motif is not attested at all in Greek literature independent of the Jews; it appears for the first time in history in Hecataeus' peculiar description of the Jewish "unsocial and xenophobic mode of life." Hence it is connected, from the very outset, with the Jews, and also later seems never to be associated with any other people. No wonder that the Jews responded to it and, quite clearly in order to neutralize it, transferred it to other peoples, in particular to one other people, the Egyptians.

The apocryphal *Wisdom of Solomon* of uncertain origin (some scholars assign it to the beginning of the first century C.E., others want to date it earlier)[6] accuses the Egyptians of xenophobia because they enslaved their "guests," the people of Israel:

> They [the Egyptians][7] suffered justly for their own wickedness, because their hatred of strangers *(misoxenia)* was on a new level of bitterness. While others there had been who refused to welcome strangers when they came to them, these made slaves of guests who were their benefactors. There will indeed be a judgement for those whose reception of foreigners was hostile; but these, after a festal welcome, oppressed with hard labor men who had earlier shared their rights.[8]

Another strategy for neutralizing the charge of xenophobia is adopted by the historian Flavius Josephus at the end of the first century C.E. In his *Antiquitates* Josephus gives a remarkable account of the misconduct of the Sodomites. Whereas the Bible is quite clear about the kind of ill-treatment the Sodomites inflicted upon their foreign guests (namely that "the men of Sodom, both young and old, everyone without exception" wanted to have sexual intercourse with Lot's visitors),[9] Josephus does not mention the details of their "monstrous sins"[10] at all but is concerned only with their xenophobia:

> Now about this time the Sodomites, overwhelmingly proud of their numbers and the extent of their wealth, showed themselves insolent to men *(eis te anthrōpous ēsan hybristai)* and impious to the Divinity

(kai pros to theion asebeis), insomuch that they no more remembered the benefits that they had received from Him, hated foreigners *(einai te misoxenoi)* and declined all intercourse with others *(kai tas pros allous homilias ektrephestai).* Indignant at this conduct, God accordingly resolved to chastise them for their arrogance, and not only to uproot their city, but to blast their land so completely that it should yield neither plant nor fruit whatsoever from that time forward.[11]

It is the Sodomites' xenophobia (and their impiety: the two are connected, as in Hecataeus' and Manetho's expulsion stories) which deserves the severest punishment, not their notorious homosexuality. God himself disapproves of hatred of foreigners and, of course, of impiety, and accordingly uproots the Sodomites and their city from the earth. The message of this adaptation by Josephus of the Sodomite story is clear. It is quite obviously the Jewish answer to the accusation of xenophobia and separateness and tells its Greek and Roman readers: The Jews not only are not xenophobic and do not separate themselves from others, they very much disapprove of this "cardinal sin" of human behavior and fought against it in the earliest period of their history.

Closely related to the *misoxenia* motif is the accusation of *am(e)ixia.* *Am(e)ixia* means literally "unsociability," "want of intercourse," an unsociable and savage way of life, and can be used in many different contexts.[12] When applied to one ethnic group avoiding contact with another it comes very close to *misoxenia.* Although the word itself is not used in connection with the Jews, the concept is precisely the one expressed in Manetho's phrase that they "should have intercourse with none save those of their own confederacy."[13] Hence, it is again the Jews who appear for the first time in history *as a nation* refusing to have dealings with other nations. Unlike the alleged *misoxenia,* however, *am(e)ixia* is later also associated with other peoples. Plutarch mentions in his Life of Gaius Marius that the Teutones and Cimbri, who invaded Gaul and Italy in large numbers, "had not had [before this invasion] intercourse with other peoples *(amixia tē pros heterous).*"[14] One might argue, therefore, that the accusation of *am(e)ixia* also became an ethnographic cliché and was not attached solely to the Jews. But there are considerable differences between Manetho and Plutarch: whereas Manetho's account of the Jews is clearly hostile and describes an attitude which is deliberately and fundamentally directed against other peoples (actually against humankind), Plutarch's account of the Germans neither is hostile nor says that they avoid intercourse with other peoples intentionally. On the contrary, the Teutones and Cimbri are prime examples of barbaric tribes which lived so far from the civilized world that they just happened to have no contact with others; the want of intercourse is not a feature of tribal identity but rather explains how it is that nobody knows "what people they were nor whence they had set out."[15]

MISANTHROPY: THE GREEK CONTEXT

The *misanthrōpia* motif, which in Hecataeus appears as *apanthrōpos bios,* can also be traced back to a cultural context which originally has nothing to do with the Jews. The evidence available starts with Plato's dialogue *Phaedo,* written in about 384 B.C.E.[16] Here "misanthropy" *(misanthrōpia)* is compared most characteristically by Socrates with "misology" *(misologia),* the hating of arguments. Both originate from the lack of the appropriate skill: misanthropy develops "when without skill, one puts complete trust in somebody, thinking the man absolutely true and sound and reliable, and then a little later finds him bad and unreliable," and when this happens again and again with different persons, one ends up "hating everyone, thinking there's no soundness whatever in anyone at all."[17] The same is true for misology, which originates "when someone who lacks skill in arguments, trusts some argument to be true, and then a little later it seems to him false, sometimes when it is, and sometimes when it isn't, and then the same thing happens with one argument after the other"—he finally ends up "hating and abusing arguments."[18]

The misanthropist and the misologist suffer from lacking the skill *(technē)* to distinguish between good and bad people and between good and bad arguments, and are forced by their ignorance to draw the most extreme but wrong conclusion, namely that there are only bad people and bad arguments. It is obvious that Socrates uses the example of misanthropy only in order to explain misology, which he regards as the worst fate that can befall someone;[19] the point at issue is to convince Phaedo that he has to guard against believing "that there's probably nothing sound in arguments."[20] However, in drawing the analogy between misology and misanthropy, Socrates leaves no doubt that he regards misanthropy and misology as equally foolish (and probably also despicable).

This unfavorable connotation of misanthropy is also employed by Plato's contemporary, the orator Isocrates, in his *Antidosis,* a fictitious trial speech, written 354/53 B.C.E.[21] When defending the sophists, the professional teachers of true philosophy and oratory,[22] and distinguishing them from sycophants, demagogic politicians,[23] he conjures up the golden age of the ancestors. Unlike his fellow Athenians, they knew to distinguish between the two groups and put Solon, "who was the first of the Athenians to receive the title of sophist, at the head of the state, while they applied to the sycophants more stringent laws than to other criminals."[24] Whereas the "greatest crimes" were brought before one court only, charges against sycophants could be brought before different courts because their crimes "exceeded all other forms of villainy": "for other criminals, at any rate, try to keep their evil-doing under cover, while these flaunt their brutality (*ōmotēs*), their misanthropy (*misanthrōpia*) and their contentiousness (*philapechthēmosynē*) before the eyes of all."[25] Misanthropy, together with such flattering epithets as brutality and contentiousness, characterizes the sycophants, the worst rascals on Isocrates' social scale.

Only shortly after Isocrates' *Antidosis,* at about 351 B.C.E.,[26] the speech against Stephanus (Oration XLV, *In Stephanum* I) was written by another famous orator, Demosthenes.[27] Stephanus, the defendant, was charged by a certain Apollodorus with false testimony in a previous case against Phormio which Apollodorus lost; in this speech Demosthenes takes up the position of Apollodorus. He launches a venomous attack on Stephanus as well as on his patron Phormio (whom he had defended in the earlier case: Oration XXXVI). Stephanus is characterized in the most unfavorable way: as an opportunist, who evades his duties of the state and conceals his wealth, a merciless money-lender, "brutal and savage on all occasions,"[28] even toward his own family, in short "a common enemy of the whole human species (*koinon echthron tēs physeōs holēs tēs anthrōpinēs*)."[29] It is precisely in this context that the term *misanthrōpia* is used,[30] giving it the worst possible connotation. Again, the misanthrope is put on the lowest end of the social scale, this time representing the "rascals in wealth."[31]

This line of argument against misanthropy, established by the early Greek philosophers and orators, can be pursued further in ancient literature. Suffice it to mention the Stoic Chrysippus of Soloi (about 281–208 B.C.E.), who shortly after Hecataeus combines misanthropy with hatred of women (*misogynia*) and hatred of wine (*misoinia*) as "diseases,"[32] or the orator and popular philosopher of the first century C.E., Dio Chrysostom (Cocceianus) of Prusa, who regrets that most recipients of Fortune's blessing become filled immediately with "arrogance (*hybris*), and misanthropy (*misanthrōpia*) and effrontery (*thrasytēs*)."[33]

It does not come as a surprise, then, that Greek contempt for misanthropy is taken up by no less a person than the eminent Jewish philosopher

Philo. Most striking among the many instances in which Philo refers to misanthropy[34] is his furious attack on the Greek and Roman custom of exposing infants (infanticide), "a sacrilegious practice which among many other nations, through their ingrained inhumanity *(tēs physikēs apanthrōpias)*, has come to be regarded with complacence."[35] Parents who expose their children "are breaking the laws of Nature and stand self-condemned on the gravest charges, love of pleasure *(philēdonia)*,[36] hatred of men *(misanthrōpia)*, murder *(androphonia)* and, the most abomination of all, murder of their own children *(teknoktonia)*."[37] They are "men haters" *(misanthrōpoi)*, "for who could more deserve the name than these enemies, these merciless foes of their offspring? For no one is so foolish as to suppose that those who have treated dishonourably their own flesh and blood will deal honourably with strangers."[38]

Here Philo parallels misanthropy with xenophobia, making it very clear (like Josephus) that the two are closely related and that the Jews detest both.[39] In singling out infanticide as one of the worst examples of misanthropy and xenophobia, he implicitly seems to respond to the Greek and Roman accusation against the Jews and to argue that their accusers, not the Jews, are the misanthropists and xenophobes.

XENOPHOBIA / MISANTHROPY DIRECTED AGAINST THE JEWS

Against this background it becomes clear that the charge of xenophobia, "unsociability," and misanthropy directed against the Jews was a most powerful weapon in the Greco-Roman world. This holds true in particular for misanthropy, which took on two very peculiar and devastating characteristics: it was aimed at the Jews not so much as individuals but first and foremost as a nation, and it was understood not as hatred of all humankind, including their own kind, but as hatred of humankind, except for their own kind. In this meaning it is expressed for the first time around 300 B.C.E. (note that Hecataeus already combines the *apanthrōpos* and *misoxenos bios*) within the cultural milieu of Greek Egypt and obviously marks a specifically Greek tinge to an originally Egyptian tradition (the expulsion story). Its degree of bias against the Jews varies in different authors: whereas Hecataeus explains rather unemotionally and almost sympathetically why the Jews developed their xenophobic way of life, the tone becomes shriller with Manetho and especially Lysimachus.

The xenophobia/misanthropy motif takes on a completely new quality in the work of the Greek author Diodorus Siculus, who may depend on the philosopher Posidonius of Apamea. Diodorus combines both the stories of the expulsion from Egypt and of ass-worship with the "shock therapy" of defiling the Jewish Temple by offering a "great sow" and binds these different traditions together under the *leitmotif* of the Jewish misanthropy and xenophobia,[40] which is reinforced in an unparalleled way. The xenophobia, so characteristic of Hecataeus, appears only in the "xenophobic laws" which are the result of what stands in the center of the argument, the misanthropy. This misanthropy, to be sure, also means the refusal to share the table, that is, food, with other people, but it is more than that: it is pure and absolute hatred of all humankind. The horrified king cannot but uproot once and forever this monstrous product of evil which is an attack on the values of the whole civilized world.

The old misanthropy/xenophobia motif has become, as it were, independent; it is being utilized in a new geographic and historical context which may well be precisely the one the story itself pretends to: Syria/Palestine in the reign of Antiochus VII Sidetes, which saw the transition of power from the first to the second generation of the Maccabees—a mark of their political success.

The climax of Jewish misanthropy is reported in Apion's story about the fattening and subsequent sacrifice and consumption of a "Greek foreigner" in the Jewish Temple. I have argued above that the main point of this story lies in the oath of hostility toward Greeks, the essence of which is "to show no goodwill to a single alien, above all to Greeks."[41] Again, when rescuing the poor victim from the hands of the evil Jews, the king acts as the representative of the whole civilized, that is, Greek, world. No doubt the cruel custom of human sacrifice is the ultimate perversion of the Jews' misanthropy which offends all civilized humankind.

The emphasis put on Jewish misanthropy as directed mainly against Greeks makes it very likely that this particular revision of the misanthropy/xenophobia motif originated in a Greek context. Apion, at the same time nourished by his Egyptian anti-Jewish sentiments, used it in order to address his Greek audience. It has been argued that the possible Egyptian background of the story of human sacrifice is also to be seen in the Osiris myth, namely that the tearing apart of the victim which is mentioned in Damocritus' version is reminiscent of Osiris' dismemberment by Seth.[42] This is a tempting but rather far-fetched hypothesis which relies solely on the very late quotation of Damocritus in the *Suda,* the Byzantine lexicon of the tenth century C.E. If it could be validated, it would connect the motif of human sacrifice with that of ass-worship and neatly explain how Apion fabricated his story out of originally Egyptian elements. There can be no doubt, however, that the story gained its main power in its Greek adaptation.

XENOPHOBIA/MISANTHROPY AND THE ORIGIN
OF ANTI-SEMITISM

The indisputable fact that the accusation of misanthropy/xenophobia looms so large, in the literary guise of the stories of the expulsion from Egypt, of human sacrifice, and of ass-worship,[43] during the reign of Antiochus IV and the period subsequent to it has led to the very influential theory that the historical situation of Syria-Palestine in the second century B.C.E. was instrumental in the rise of ancient anti-Semitism. Elias Bickerman, who, as we have seen, relegates the motifs of human sacrifice and ass-worship to Seleucid propaganda of the second half of the second century B.C.E., has declared rather apodictically: "There is no anti-Jewish passage in Greek literature before the Maccabean struggle, nor any recorded anti-Jewish action."[44] This statement suggests, of course, that the Maccabean revolt with the successful expansionist policies of the Hasmoneans was the decisive trigger to release anti-Jewish sentiments on the part of the Greek populace. Isaak Heinemann, too, who in his famous article "Antisemitismus" distinguishes three "focuses of conflict" (Konfliktsherde), gives chronological priority to the "Syrian focus of conflict" (it is mentioned before the Egyptian and the Roman focus).[45] He places the first "Judenhetze," however, after 88/87 B.C.E. in Egypt, that is, after the unsuccessful attempt of Ptolemy Lathyrus and his mother Cleopatra to regain power in Palestine: "Prior to 88 B.C.E. there had in all likelihood been no Jew-baiting (*Judenhetze*) whatsoever in the diaspora and later only there where one takes offense at the power of Jewish settlements."[46] This is a rather strange choice of historical event to link with "Judenhetze" (the Hasmonean expansion would have been much more natural in view of his own argument), but the ideological background is the same: the "power of Jewish settlements" causes offense and leads to anti-Jewish riots.

Bickerman is followed by historians of antiquity like Martin Hengel, Christian Habicht, and Klaus Bringmann. Hengel's position is particularly instructive. On the one hand he sees in Jewish "separateness" (which is only the other side of misanthropy and xenophobia) the result of the forced assimilation under Antiochus IV and his Jewish collaborators: this tendency to separation together with the political expansion of the Hasmoneans aroused anti-Semitism;[47] the "anti-Semitic movement," therefore, belongs to the late second or early first century B.C.E.[48] On the other hand he does acknowledge that the earliest anti-Jewish account has a national-Egyptian bias and stems from Manetho, that is, from the beginning of the third century B.C.E.[49] He does not reconcile these two positions but simply states that an anti-Semitic tendency is first recognizable with Posidonius, that is, at the turn of the second century. Thereby, despite the Egyptian evidence, he implicitly regards the Seleucid era as decisive for the emergence of ancient anti-Semitism.[50]

Christian Habicht explicitly refers to Heinemann and Bickerman in his brief description of the origin of ancient anti-Semitism, thereby confirming the influence of both authors:

> If it seems paradoxical that the prohibition of the Jewish religion led this religion out of a state of crisis, then more than one result of the conflict is paradoxical. It was the descendants of Judas the Maccabee who increasingly distanced themselves from their previous goal. The Hasmoneans created a new Jewish state, they enlarged worldly power with spiritual power by seizing hold of the high priesthood. They violently expanded the borders of Israel in all directions at the expense of their neighbors. The new self-esteem born out of self-assertion became boundless and through the forced conversion of those of different beliefs exerted intimidation *(Gesinnungsterror)* similar to that to which the Jews themselves had been exposed. *This development led in the second century to the regrettable phenomenon we call anti-Semitism. Before the Maccabean period there is no anti-Jewish passage in Greek literature, no anti-Jewish act in history.*[51] However, immediately thereafter, we do hear such voices and see such conduct. Anti-Semitism is the poisonous fruit of the conflict between Judaism and Hellenism and its result.[52]

This is a very apt description of the trend of research inaugurated by Heinemann and Bickerman: the first sentence in italics refers in a note to Heinemann's article, the second is an almost verbatim quotation of Bickerman's apodictic statement quoted above. To be sure, the pungent formulation that the Hasmonean expansion and particularly the forced conversion of their neighbors produced anti-Semitism goes far beyond what Heinemann actually says, but it is no doubt in line with his and especially Bickerman's and Hengel's argument (see above). In any case, the conclusion is very clear: anti-Semitism is the "poisonous fruit" of the conflict between Judaism and Hellenism, that is, again in line with Hengel and Bickerman, of a mainly internal Jewish development.

Most recently Z. Yavetz has launched a ferocious attack on Habicht[53] which probably sees too much significance in Habicht's few sentences and ignores or rather plays down the scholarly tradition in which Habicht stands. This is particularly obvious in Yavetz's attempt to exonerate Bickerman and to insinuate that Habicht quotes Bickerman inaccurately.[54] The latter charge is simply a misrepresentation on the part of Yavetz;[55] the former is somewhat artificial in view of Bickerman's famous passage and of the fact that he, no matter how one looks at it, did not fully recognize the events at Elephantine.[56] Much more relevant is Yavetz's argument, first, that "no hint is made against the violent and aggressive expansion of the borders of the Jewish state at the cost of their neighbours, in any anti-Jewish text and the 'Gesinnungsterror' exercised by the Jews against Edomites and emphasized so strongly by Habicht, is conspicuous by its absence from the sources,"[57] and second, that instead all the slanderous stories of, for example, the expulsion from Egypt, human sacrifice, and ass-worship are repeated over and over.

With this we come full circle. The hypothesis of the emergence of anti-Semitism out of the historical context of the Maccabees and Hasmoneans collapses if one takes the age and origin of these stories seriously; most of them are considerably older than the second half of the second century B.C.E. and originated in Egypt. The misanthropy/xenophobia motif, which has become so powerful a weapon in the Hellenistic context, also appears first in Greek Egypt and much earlier than its reinforcement by "Seleucid propaganda." The Seleucid-Greek and the later Egyptian-Greek authors utilized this weapon for internal purposes in order to strengthen their own ranks as well as for external purposes: the misanthropic Jews are the outcasts of the Hellenistic world. The latter argument became particularly forceful when Rome was about to extend its influence over the Near East, and Greeks and Jews were competing with each other for Rome's favor.[58] Where this could lead can be studied in Hellenistic Alexandria.

CHAPTER ELEVEN

Rome

AS MUCH AS EGYPTIAN AND Greek attitudes toward the Jews are distinct and yet interrelated in a peculiar way, Rome again has its own agenda in regard to the Jews, and at the same time responds to some earlier traditions.

CICERO

The first voice to be heard, and one regarded as the first evidence of Roman "anti-Semitism,"[1] is that of the great orator of the late Republic, Cicero (106–43 B.C.E.), in his famous speech *Pro Flacco,* delivered in October 59 B.C.E. Cicero (together with Quintus Hortensius) defended the former governor of the Roman province of Asia, Lucius Valerius Flaccus, against the charge of corruption. Among the charges was the accusation that he had confiscated the "gold" collected by the Jews of his province for the Temple in Jerusalem, obviously the annual half-shekel = *didrachmon* payment.

Cicero begins the part of his speech dealing with the charge against the Jews by insinuating that Laelius, the prosecutor, had procured not only the particular place of the trial (the Aurelian Steps) but also "that crowd" *(illa turba)* of the Jews, because he knew "how vast a throng *(manus)* it is, how close-knit *(quanta concordia),* and what influence it can have in public meetings *(in contionibus).*"[2] This remark determines the context in which Cicero's assessment of the Jews must be judged. It is the Jews as a pressure group, influential in public assemblies, who are attacked by Cicero. Ironically Cicero continues that he wants to "speak in a whisper like—this—, just loud enough for the jury to hear; for there is no shortage of men to incite this crowd against me and all the best men *(in optimum quemque),* but I shall not help them by making it easier for them."[3] It is precisely in this context of withstanding the improper and indecent pressure of the Jews that he refutes the charge against Flaccus:

> It was the practice each year to send gold to Jerusalem on the Jews' account from Italy and all our provinces, but Flaccus issued an edict forbidding its export from Asia. Who is there, gentlemen, who cannot genuinely applaud this measure? The Senate strictly forbade the export of gold on a considerable number of previous occasions, notably during my consulship. To oppose this barbaric[4] superstition *(barbarae superstitioni resistere)* was an act of firmness, and to defy in the public interest *(pro re publica)* the crowd of the Jews *(multitudinem Iudaeorum)* that on occasion set our public meetings ablaze was the height of responsibility.[5]

Here Cicero is mainly concerned to disparage the disturbing "crowd of the Jews," and to praise Flaccus for having had the courage to do so. What annoys him is that this "crowd" had become so influential in the public meetings *(in contionibus)* that it was difficult to resist it.[6] But his main argument is that it is "in the public interest"[7] to defy this ever growing influence, and this "public interest," of course, is represented best by him and his friends, "all the best men."[8] In Cicero's view, then, the "crowd of the Jews" and "all the best men" are opposed. If one takes his political language into consideration, it does not seem far-fetched to assume that Cicero refers here to his own political group, the "Optimates," the "conservative senatorial group which stood for the retention of the traditional prerogatives of the aristocracy,"[9] and that he counts the Jews of Rome among his opponents, the "Populares," the "people's party which was finding a new and powerful leader in Julius Caesar."[10] Hence, what is primarily at stake here is a political conflict in which the Jews unfortunately belong to the wrong side.

This political conflict, however, has again a religious flavor. The Jews not only belong to the wrong group, they also represent an element within it which is most unwelcome and contrary to the values of Rome as Cicero understands them. They are the embodiment of *barbara superstitio,* and this "barbaric superstition" consists of more than just sending money to their Temple in Jerusalem. According to Cicero *superstitio* is opposed to *religio,* the latter being the essence of the political, cultural, and religious ideals of ancient Rome. If the Jews represent *superstitio,* they stand for everything which opposes these ancient values. "Religion *(religio)* has been distinguished from superstition *(superstitio)* not only by philosophers but by our ancestors *(maiores),"* he says in *De Natura Deorum.*[11] Applied to the situation of *De Flacco* this means that unfortunately this distinction of "our ancestors" is no longer maintained, that the Jewish *superstitio* has been allowed to enter the very heart of Rome.

That this precisely is the case—that the Jewish *religio* (= *superstitio*) is alien and in sharp contrast to the *religio* of Rome, and as such has to be fought—becomes clear from the end of the paragraph dealing with the Jews:

> Each state, Laelius, has its own religious canon *(religio)*, and we have ours. Even when Jerusalem was still standing and the Jews at peace with us, the practice of their sacred rites[12] *(istorum religio sacrorum)* was incompatible with the glory of our empire, the dignity of our name, and the institutions of our ancestors *(maiorum institutis);* and now that the Jewish nation has shown by armed rebellion what are its feelings for our rule, it is even more so; how dear it was to the immortal gods has been shown by the fact that it has been conquered, farmed out to the tax-collectors and enslaved.[13]

Cicero presents himself as the advocate of Rome's traditional values, the *mos maiorum.*[14] The Jewish *religio,* he argues, was always opposed to the *religio* of Rome because it is incompatible with ancestral customs and institutions. When it now is allowed to intrude in Rome's affairs, a deplorable state of confusion and a degeneration of the ancient customs results. With this very fundamental argument Cicero sets the tone of the Roman attitude toward the Jews and hence of a considerable part of the subsequent discussion.[15] It is directed against the influence of the Jews and the intrusion of customs regarded as foreign to and in the end destructive of the values of Rome.[16] As a matter of fact, from this point of view his speech is addressed no less to Laelius, the prosecutor, than to the Jews, because it is Laelius who gives in, by his irresponsible defense strategy, to the pressure of the Jews and thus helps in undermining the traditional Roman values. Hence, Cicero's argument displays dislike mingled with fear of the Jews. Cicero and the group he represents do not like the Jews, their behavior, their customs; and at the same time they are afraid of the Jews' growing influence, which will, in their opinion, destroy the traditional value system of Rome. This attitude, to be sure, is quite different from the fervent anti-Jewish outbursts of the Egyptian-Greek tradition of which Cicero could have known via his teacher Apollonius Molon.[17]

Varro, Cicero's slightly older contemporary who, however, outlived him by fifteen years, is similarly concerned with the customs of the "ancient Romans" *(antiquos Romanos),* but in a very different way. Varro regards the Jews as a people who were (and are) in agreement with the customs of ancient Rome; their imageless cult corresponds to what was also once the ideal of the original Roman religion but which has since degenerated into the idolatry of substituting statues for the true gods.[18] In other words, Varro is arguing here, quite in contrast to Cicero, that the Jewish cult has to be valued as true *religio,* whereas the Romans have resorted to *superstitio.* This is a remarkable statement to which no other Roman author ever comes close.[19]

The subsequent period, especially the first and early second centuries C.E., testifies to the growing influence of Jews in Rome and the dislike this provoked in Roman society. The attraction Judaism exercised must have developed to such a degree that Jews and Judaism were regarded as a threat to Rome and all that it stood for. Salient examples are Horace, the *senatus consultum* of 19 C.E. expelling the Jews from Rome, Seneca's startled discovery that the "vanquished have given laws to their victors," and Petronius' and particularly Martial's obsession with circumcision.

At the end of the first century C.E., during the reign of Domitian, sympathy with and conversion to the Jewish way of life must have become such a common "plague" in the eyes of the Romans that the emperor could make use of the increased number of new proselytes to increase his tax revenues.[20] Moreover, Domitian utilized the charge of "atheism" against the many "who drifted into Jewish ways," in order both to appropriate their properties and to eliminate prospective rivals. The latter purpose, exemplified by the case of Flavius Clemens and his wife Flavia Domitilla, clearly shows that the "virus" of Jewish life had infected even members of the highest class.[21] According to Tacitus, they cannot have been a rare exception. In referring to an event of 57 C.E., he mentions that Pomponia Graecina, the wife of Aulus Plautius, the conqueror of Britain, was "arraigned for alien superstition" *(superstitio externa)* and brought to trial before a family council.[22] The character of her alleged superstition, of which she was pronounced innocent, can only have been Judaism or Christianity, most likely the former.

JUVENAL

Special attention must be paid to Juvenal because we can compare his representation of the Jews with that of other ethnic groups. His deep concern with

Judaizing as a danger to the values of the Roman empire goes together with his contempt for oriental religions and his xenophobic attitude to foreigners in general, especially Egyptians and Greeks. His dislike of foreign language, customs, and physical appearance[23] is aptly summarized in *Saturae*, III, 62ff.: "The Syrian Orontes has long since poured into the Tiber, bringing with it its lingo *(linguam)* and its manners *(mores)*, its flutes and its slanting harp-strings; bringing too the timbrels of the breed *(gentilia tympana)*, and the trulls who are bidden ply their trade at the Circus. Out upon you, all ye that delight in foreign strumpets *(lupa barbara)* with painted headdresses!"[24]

An entire satire (XV) is devoted to the monstrous Egyptian religion which demands the worship of all kinds of animals but declares it an "impious outrage to crunch leeks and onions with the teeth: what a holy people *(o sanctas gentes)* to have such divinities springing up in their gardens!"[25] It also forbids eating "animals that grow wool"—but considers it lawful "to feed on the flesh of man."[26] No wonder that Egypt appears as the barbaric country par excellence[27] which made it a habit to devour its war-captives raw:[28]

> what calamity drove these Egyptians to the deed? What extremity of hunger, what beleaguering army, compelled them to dare so monstrous and infamous a crime? Were the land of Memphis to run dry, could they do aught else than this to shame the Nile for being loth to rise? No dread Cimbrians or Brittones, no savage Scythians or monstrous Agathyrsians, ever raged so furiously as this unwarlike and worthless rabble *(inbelle et inutile vulgus)*.[29]

Egypt is barbarism incarnate and is as such to be detested, its cults are to be ridiculed[30] because they do not belong to Rome,[31] but still they do not pose a serious threat to Rome.

It is different with the Greeks and the Jews, and a comparison between these two ethnic groups is particularly illuminating. As W. J. Watts has shown,[32] Juvenal's attitude to the Greeks is quite complex. Figures from the past can be viewed favorably or at least neutrally; "a Greek is rarely attacked explicitly *as* a Greek."[33] Only when the present day is in question can Juvenal "be shown as sometimes positively hostile,"[34] and this particularly in the context of economic competition. The Greeks are only too successful in entering Roman society, in transforming it into something of which Juvenal cannot approve because it does not conform to what he regards as the ancient Roman customs and virtues.

How then are the Jews different—if there is a difference between Juvenal's representations of the Greeks and the Jews? Watts has pointed out that the difference is the exclusiveness of the Jews: if the Greeks are blamed for integrating *too much* into Roman society, the Jews are blamed for *not* integrating *at all.*[35] This no doubt is correct; as we have seen, the accusation of exclusiveness and separateness stands at the very center of Juvenal's "argument." Watts' conclusion, however, that "Greek integration meant the disintegration of the Roman *mos maiorum*" whereas Jewish integration "meant disintegration of Judaism,"[36] is a wrong comparison, all the more so as by implication it wants to convey the message that the Jews were regarded as less dangerous. As Watts correctly notices (and explicitly says), the first sentence refers to the Roman and the second to the Jewish view. Yet what is at stake is solely the Roman view, that is, the way Juvenal regards the Greek and Jewish influence on Roman customs. And here, in contrasting "largely prejudice which leads Juvenal to dislike the Jews" with "pure prejudice which causes his dislike and resentment of the Greeks,"[37] Watts clearly does not do justice to Juvenal's argument against the Jews in *Satura* XIV.

Juvenal accuses only the Jews—not any other ethnic group, and certainly not the Greeks—of proselytism. And it is precisely the combination of proselytism and exclusiveness that alarms him. One can hardly think of a more serious attack on the customs of Rome's ancestors than the Jewish insistence that one has to abandon the "laws of Rome" *(Romanas contemnere leges)* in order to follow the "Jewish law" *(Judaicum ius)*. That the one had to be substituted for the other, could not be integrated into the other, was completely alien to a Roman; that this strange superstition could become successful in the very heart of the Roman empire was intolerable because it undermined the agreement upon which the Roman society was based and functioned. Hence one should not underestimate the threat the Jews posed in the eyes of Juvenal and his contemporaries, quite by contrast to the Greeks. The *misanthrōpia* motif, which was so characteristic for the Hellenistic writers, takes on its peculiar Roman tinge: these people, who adopt a way of life particularly alien and hostile to Roman (and Greek) culture, succeed, strangely and ominously enough, in entering Roman society and converting Romans to their religion of arrogant exclusiveness.

TACITUS

The grand synthesis of the Roman attitude toward the Jews is Tacitus' digression analyzed above;[38] it was written during the first decade of the second century C.E., and may well have been known to Juvenal.

The starting point, characteristic of the genre, is the origin of the Jews; it covers about half of the part dealing with Jewish customs and beliefs (*Historiae,* V, 2:1–4:4). The second part is devoted to other customs *(instituta)* of the Jews, independent of their origin (V, 5:1–5). They are: proselytism (sympathizers?); extreme loyalty among themselves and hatred toward others; sitting apart at meals, sleeping apart, and abstaining from intercourse with foreign women; circumcision; again proselytism (full converts); disapproval of infanticide (only in order to increase their numbers); burial customs (similar to the Egyptians); ideas about God (opposite to the Egyptians and, partly, to the Romans)[39]; and finally chanting in the Temple and wearing garlands of ivy—which does not make them devotees of Dionysus because, altogether, their ways *(mos)* are "preposterous and mean."

Whereas the rites referred to in the first part, which derive from the expulsion experience, are described in a rather moderate and "ethnographic" way (this is not true, however, of the Exodus story itself), the tone becomes much shriller when the "base and abominable" customs of the second part are presented (note that the former are called *ritus* and the latter *instituta*). It is certainly not by accident that Tacitus opens the list with the proselytes (or rather sympathizers?) who renounce their "ancestral religions" *(spretis religionibus patriis)* and send tribute to Jerusalem,[40] proceeds with a detailed description of the separateness and exclusiveness of the Jews who stick together but hate everybody else, and then comes back to the (full) converts, who distinguish themselves from other peoples by circumcision, despise the gods, disown their country, and leave their families. Quite clearly the same combination of exclusiveness and proselytism—intolerable behavior according to all accepted Roman standards and yet blatantly successful—that we encountered in Juvenal manifests itself here. Tacitus is certainly less amazed than Juvenal, much more aggressive, but the phenomenon is the same: the *misanthrōpia* motif in Roman guise, that is, the deep concern that a "religion" which in its exclusiveness is so contrary to all the cherished Roman values undermines and finally threatens to destroy them.

This can be further elucidated by Tacitus' use of language. As we have seen, the ancient Jewish customs which at least are understandable, though not to be approved, are called *ritus,* the others *instituta,* and the Jewish way of life is *mos* (like the Egyptian).[41] What is opposed, therefore, is the *mos Judaeorum* and the *mos maiorum,* the Jewish and the ancestral Roman customs. Moreover, what constitutes the Jewish way of life and value system is never called *religio,* but the sympathizers/proselytes abandon their ancestral *religiones* in order to enter the Jewish *mos.* In correlation with this, Tacitus expressly calls the Jewish "religion" in the same digression *superstitio,* thus following the line of argument introduced into Latin literature by Cicero.

To be sure, Cicero and Tacitus are not the only Latin (and Greek) authors who accuse the Jews of superstition, nor is this charge attributed only to the Jews.[42] To mention but a few examples: Livy calls the rites of the Samnites, the arch-enemies of the early Republic, "superstitious,"[43] and Statius (ca. 45–96 C.E.) speaks of the "dark cult *(nigra superstitio)* of Palaemon solemnized about the gloomy altars."[44] According to Quintilian (second half of the first century C.E.), Socrates was accused of "corrupting the youth and introducing new superstitions" *(novas superstitiones).*[45] A far more extensive and diversified use of the word "superstition" is made, however, by Tacitus.[46] It is not reserved for barbarians but can also be applied, in the more literal sense, to Romans: Roman soldiers are sometimes "pliable to superstition";[47] Vitellius finally accepts the title Caesar "from a superstitious feeling with regard to the name" *(superstitione nominis);*[48] and Vespasian, given his inclination to astrology, was not "wholly free from such superstitious belief" *(nec erat intactus tali superstitione).*[49]

Tacitus' favorite superstitious barbarians, except for the Egyptians and the Jews, are the Gauls, the Britons, and, especially, the Germans: "The Druids chant their prophecies with vain superstition" *(superstitione vana),*[50] and the Britons are similar to the Gauls with regard to their "ceremonies" *(sacra)* and "superstitious beliefs" *(superstitionum persuasio).*[51] When reporting the conquest of the island of Mona (Anglesey), he mentions with obvious satisfaction the demolition of the groves "consecrated to their savage superstitions *(saevis superstitionibus):* for they considered it a pious duty to slake the altars with captive blood and to consult their deities by means of human entrails."[52] According to ancient German custom *(mos)* women are endowed with "prophetic powers" *(faticidas)* and even, "as the superstition grows" *(augescente superstitione),* attributed divinity.[53] The Aestii (Estonians) on the east coast of the Baltic "worship the mother of the gods" and wear, "as an emblem of that superstition" *(insigne superstitionis),* the figures of wild boars.[54] Like the Britons, the Semnones (a tribe between the middle Elbe and the Oder, that is, of Brandenburg and Lausitz),[55] perform their "superstition" in a grove "after publicly offering up a human life."[56]

Whereas Tacitus' reports about the superstitious customs and beliefs of the "northern" barbarians are relatively dispassionate, he does not conceal his contempt when he refers to the Egyptians (in this he is quite similar to Juvenal). The province of Egypt had to be put "under the direct control of the imperial house," because it is "given to civil strife and sudden disturbances because of the fanaticism and superstition of its inhabitants, ignorant as they are of the laws and unacquainted with civil magistrates."[57] He regards the cult of the Egyptian god Serapis as particularly superstitious, quoting as an example an incident which happened to Vespasian in Alexandria: a blind citizen of Alexandria "threw himself before Vespasian's knees, praying him with groans to cure his blindness, being so directed by the god Serapis, whom this superstitious nation[58] worships before all others."[59] After some hesitation Vespasian heals not only the blind man but also another Alexandrian citizen with a lame hand, and takes this as a sign that the "favor of heaven" was bestowed upon him. This is less surprising, after what we have already heard about Vespasian, than the complete lack of criticism of Vespasian on the part of Tacitus: the Egyptian belief in the healing power of human beings is superstitious; the successful emperor is the favorite of the (true) gods.

The history of the charge of superstition directed against Jews in particular can be traced back to Agatharchides of Cnidus. According to Josephus, he is the first to have used the Greek equivalent of *superstitio, deisidaimonia,* connecting it with the custom of the Sabbath. At the beginning of the first century C.E., Strabo of Amaseia in his *Geographica* mentions the term again in order to determine the two essentially different stages of the Jewish nation: the first, dominated by Moses and his early successors "who acted righteously and were truly pious *(theosebeis)* toward God," and the second, dominated by "superstitious men," the period of superstition *(deisidaimonia),* when "abstinence from flesh," "circumcisions and excisions," and "other observances of that kind" were introduced.[60]

One may safely conclude from this that, according to Strabo, Judaism under Moses was a true *religio* but later became a *superstitio*—and unfortunately chose to remain so to Strabo's day.[61] In the second half of the first century C.E. Quintilian is less subtle and identifies the "Jewish superstition" *(Iudaica superstitio)* even with its founder Moses,[62] and Plutarch comes back to the *deisidaimonia* of keeping the Sabbath.

Again, also with regard to the Jews, Tacitus makes by far the most extensive and aggressive use of the charge of *superstitio.* He introduces it, even before the digression on the Jews, when referring briefly to Vespasian's siege of Jerusalem, which proved a task "difficult and arduous by the character of the mountain-citadel and the obstinate superstition of the Jews *(ob*

... *pervivaciam superstitionis)* rather than by any adequate resources which the besieged possessed to withstand the inevitable hardships of a siege."[63] *Superstitio* here applies to the fanatic and desperate[64] behavior of the besieged rather than to their religious customs.[65]

This is different in the digression. The Jewish superstition is mentioned there three times, clearly providing a kind of leitmotif. It makes its first appearance in a brief recapitulation of Jewish history:

> While the East was under the domination of the Assyrians, Medes and Persians, the Jews were regarded as the meanest of their subjects *(despectissima pars servientium):* but after the Macedonians gained supremacy, King Antiochus endeavoured to abolish Jewish superstition *(demere superstitionem)* and to introduce Greek civilization *(mores Graecorum dare);* the war with the Parthians, however, prevented his improving this basest of peoples *(taeterrimam gentem).*[66]

Here we have a clear confrontation of *superstitio* and *mores Graecorum:* the Jewish superstition in its full cultural and religious sense is in contrast with Greek civilization, that is, with the way of life accepted by the whole civilized world. Antiochus IV Epiphanes is idealized as the vanguard of this worldwide culture and religion, trying hard to include the Jews as part of civilized humankind, but unfortunately being prevented from this by external circumstances (a remarkable view of the struggle between the Seleucids and the Maccabees/Hasmoneans). The Jews embody here, indeed, the opposite of all the values of Greco-Roman culture.

This is enforced by the way Tacitus characterizes the Jewish nation as a whole. Jewish superstition as opposed to Greek civilization is framed by two most contemptuous sentences which are unprecedented in Tacitus' taxonomy in describing other peoples: both the superlative of *despectissima* and *taeterrima* appear here for the first time,[67] the latter only here,[68] and nowhere else in connection with a people. His portrayal of the Egyptians as *dedita superstitionibus gens* comes closest to this, but it is rather mild in comparison with the elaborately crafted outburst of dislike of and contempt for the Jewish nation.

Immediately after this fierce start he mentions Jewish superstition again, this time in connection with his description of the institution of the Jewish kings: despite the resistance of the "fickle mob" *(mobilitate vulgi)*[69] the Hasmoneans managed to remain in power by suppressing the populace, daring to "essay every other kind of royal crime without hesitation," and finally fostering the national superstition *(superstitionem fovebant),* "for they had assumed the priesthood to support their civil authority."[70] That the historical process was exactly the reverse (the Hasmonean high priests assumed the kingship, and this, as a matter of fact, earned them considerable internal criticism) is not important for Tacitus' argument. For him the merging of kingship and priesthood expressed the most impudent ambition of the Jews, namely to represent a true *religio,* in the political and religious sense, opposed to and in competition with the *religio* of the Greco-Roman world.

The climax of Tacitus' confrontation of (Jewish) *superstitio* and (Roman) *religio* is reached at the end of the digression when he describes the prodigies, interpreted by the majority of the Jews as announcing the advent of the Messiah but in fact heralding the destruction of their Temple and state: "Prodigies had indeed occurred, but to avert them either by victims or by vows is held unlawful by a people prone to superstition and opposed to religious rituals *(gens superstitione obnoxia, religionibus adversa)*."[71] As Moore, commenting on his translation of this passage, has noticed ("the word *religiones* probably refers to the formal ceremonies by which the Romans warded off [*procurare*] the evil effect of prodigies; but it may have a wider connotation here"),[72] *religiones* here is both the particular religious rituals to be performed in the case of bad prodigies, and the complete religious and cultural taxonomy of which the specific rituals are part. What is at stake, then, is the confrontation of the *national* Jewish *superstitio* and the *national* Roman *religio.* It is hardly by coincidence that Tacitus only here speaks of the Jewish *gens* which is opposed to the *religiones:*[73] in devoting themselves to their (national) superstition and in refusing to follow the appropriate religious practices, the Jews are the enemies of the (Roman) religion.[74] The natural consequence of this hubris could only be the destruction of their religious and political center, Jerusalem and the Temple. One may add that this did not put an end to the religious and national ambition of the Jews, on the contrary, and this precisely is Tacitus' problem.

This problem can further be elucidated by referring briefly to the famous paragraph in the *Annales,* in which Tacitus speaks about Nero's persecution of the Christians following the burning of Rome. Christus, he explains, who had given the sect of the Christians the name, "had undergone the death penalty in the reign of Tiberius, by sentence of the procurator Pontius Pilatus, and the pernicious superstition *(exitiabilis superstitio)* was checked for a moment, only to break out once more, not merely in Judea, the home of the disease *(originem eius mali),* but in the capital itself, where all things horrible or shameful in the world collect and find a vogue."[75] Although Tacitus was certainly aware of the distinction between Jews and Christians, his description of the Christian superstition closely resembles the Jewish one. Not only does he identify Judea as the "country of origin" of the "disease" (note the correspondence between *malum* and *exitiabilis*), what is even more revealing, he adds that the Christians were convicted "not so much on the count of arson *(in crimine incendii)* as for hatred of human mankind *(odio humani generis)*."[76] This is the well-known accusation of *misanthrōpia,* and precisely the language he used in his *Historiae* with regard to the Jews, namely that "toward every other people they feel only hate and enmity" (*adversus omnes alios hostile odium,* literally "hostile hatred").[77] Hence, one may conclude that for him the Christians in essence are Jews, only worse, because they were rightly persecuted and the Jews (so far) were not.

In any case, in arguing that the Christians were convicted for "hatred of human mankind," Tacitus clearly "does not give the juridical grounds for the condemnation of the Christians, which could hardly have been based on a hatred of humanity,"[78] but applies the old anti-Jewish misanthropy motif to the Christians, that is, makes the Christians inferior Jews and, what is even more important in this context, in the end holds the Jews responsible for the Christian atrocities. This is confirmed in a passage by Sulpicius Severus, which most probably draws on Tacitus' *Historiae,*[79] according to which Titus and his friends argue in favor of the destruction of the Temple, "in order to wipe out more completely the religion *(religio)* of the Jews and the Christians; for they urged that these religions *(religiones),*[80] although hostile to each other, nevertheless sprang from the same sources; the Christians had grown out of the Jews: if the root were destroyed *(radice sublata),* the stock would easily perish *(stirpem facile perituram)*."[81]

The Christians are the "worst rascals" among the Jews, to use Tacitus' words regarding the sympathizers/proselytes, and he makes it perfectly clear why he is so concerned about them: because the "disease" was not confined to Judea but has infected "the capital itself," that is, Rome. This is his main worry, that the Jewish and Christian superstition has entered Rome and finds followers among all classes of Roman society. As we have seen, he reports the expulsion of the freedmen, who were "tainted with that [Jewish] superstition" *(ea superstitione infecta),*[82] and the case of Pomponia Graecina, who was "arraigned for alien superstition" *(superstitio externa).*[83] It does not matter so much whether Pomponia Graecina's "alien superstition" was Jewish or Christian (or both), what matters is the fact that it is an *alien* superstition which is exceedingly successful in Rome.

This becomes clear also from another passage in the *Annales,* in which Tacitus quotes a request by Claudius, addressed to the senate, to found a college of diviners. Claudius complains that the art of divination, this "oldest art of Italy," had gone out of fashion and "was done (now) more negligently through the public indifference to all liberal accomplishments, combined with the progress of alien superstitions" *(externae superstitiones).*[84] It is again the success of alien superstitions which matters. Although Claudius most probably refers to the Jewish and Egyptian cults,[85] it is obvious that Tacitus is more concerned with the Jewish superstition: he uses here as well as in the case of Pomponia Graecina the phrase *externa superstitio,* and, as we have already observed, he goes into details only with regard to the expulsion of the "four thousand descendants of enfranchised slaves," that is, the Jewish proselytes in Rome (and Italy).

To sum up this brief survey of the charge of *superstitio* in general and in Tacitus in particular: Stern is certainly right in arguing that *superstitio* "is the common designation for Judaism by Tacitus."[86] This statement, however, needs to be qualified. If we try to determine more closely what distinguishes his description of Jewish superstition from that of other peoples, it is clearly the incomparably aggravated anger and contempt which characterizes Tacitus' attacks on the Jews. This, in turn, is an expression of his incomprehension of the paradox that the Jews refuse to be part of the Roman world and at the same time succeed in proselytizing, in infiltrating Roman society. The human sacrifices of the Britons and the Germans are horribly barbaric, the Egyptians are fanatical and awfully superstitious, but the true danger for Roman civilization is the Jews—and the Christians. The German superstition does not pose any danger to Rome; the Egyptian does to a certain degree, but it can be constrained (by contempt, proper education, and, if necessary, the appropriate intervention of the authorities); the Jewish/Christian superstition threatens to get out of control.

ATTRACTION AND REPULSION

Tacitus personifies most palpably the fear of the Roman upper class that the Jews might succeed, despite their political defeat. Since this fear reflects only too vividly the appeal Judaism had to Roman society, it is precisely the ambivalence between attraction and repulsion which characterizes not only Tacitus' but the overall Roman attitude toward Judaism. The Romans disliked the Jews *because* they were afraid of them, and they were afraid of them because of their growing appeal to Roman society. It is therefore too simple to label the attitude of the Romans toward the Jews—and in particular of Tacitus, the most outspoken representative of this attitude—as "Judenhass" or even "Judenhetze."[87] This takes into account only one side of the coin, namely the hatred, and disregards the other, complementary one, the fear and horror.[88]

The tension between appeal, fear, and hatred expressing itself in Roman Judeophobia can finally be illuminated from yet another angle. Not only do we have Roman authors who are strikingly sympathetic toward Jewish beliefs, like Varro; even the most outright opponents of the Jews cannot deny them respect. Good examples of the latter are Seneca and, especially, Tacitus, who, in a completely hostile context, appreciates on a philosophical level the Jewish belief in one God *(unum numen)* who is *summum et aeternum.*

This subliminal positive approach becomes all the more obvious if one compares the Roman and the Egyptian-Greek attitudes toward the Jews. The Romans are very concerned with the Jewish abstinence from pork, on the one hand because they cannot understand why one should dislike pork, and on the other hand because they look at it as the admission ticket to Judaism (Petronius and Juvenal). In the Greek tradition the abstinence from pork does not play a particular part—with the conspicuous exception of Antiochus IV's pig sacrifice in the Temple in order to exorcise Jewish misanthropy once and forever! Again, the Jewish custom of the Sabbath preoccupies the Romans very much, mainly because they associate it with undesirable idleness and indolence; the notion that by sticking to this superstitious "folly" the Jews separate themselves from the whole civilized world, however, is left to Agatharchides of Cnidus, and the explanation of it as a nasty disease to Apion. Circumcision, which interests the Greek authors mainly with regard to the question of its origin, worries most of the Roman authors as the decisive step in becoming a proselyte; accordingly, proselytism is a subject only in Roman, not in Greek literature.

Most remarkable are the differences in relation to the accusation of impiety and misanthropy, the prominent motifs in the Egyptian and Greco-Egyptian tradition. The Jewish belief in the divinity of heaven is immediately combined with their xenophobic way of life in Hecataeus, and Manetho and Apollonius Molon also inextricably link the atheism of the Jews with their misanthropy. The charge of atheism is much less common in Roman literature: one is not surprised that the annoyed emperor

Caligula calls the stubborn Jews, who refuse to worship him as a god, "god-haters," but apart from this outburst we have only Pliny the Elder's passing remark that the Jews hold in contempt the "divine powers," and much later Julian's statement, which needs to be interpreted in its proper context, that the Christians have gathered "atheism from the Jewish levity." On the other hand we observe not only the openly sympathetic comment by Varro and the implicitly positive reflection by Tacitus: Livy and Lucan introduce the learned concept of the *ignotus/incognitus/incertus deus,* and even Petronius and Juvenal, with all their contempt, cannot but refer to the *summum caelum* and *caeli numen.* The notion of a Jewish exclusiveness which is also intolerant of other gods is reintroduced in the second century C.E. by Numenius of Apamea, Celsus, and Cassius Dio, and reinforced in the fourth century by Julian.

The accusation of misanthropy is also much less dominant in Roman literature. Whereas the Greeks (and the Greco-Egyptians) seem to have been obsessed with it and gave it a particularly hostile and unsavory flavor, it was not until Tacitus and Juvenal that the idea entered Roman literature, and in a quite different guise. Both Tacitus and Juvenal view Jewish misanthropy and exclusiveness mainly in the context of proselytism, that is, not so much or not only as describing the essence of the Jewish nation as a whole but rather in its surprising capacity to recruit proselytes.

The difference between Egypt and Greece on the one hand and Rome on the other becomes even more apparent if we consider that the charge of human sacrifice, the prime example of Jewish misanthropy and xenophobia according to the Greek and Greco-Egyptian tradition, never occurs in Roman literature. This is all the more conspicuous as, for example, Tacitus seems to know all about the custom of human sacrifice among barbaric peoples like the Germans and the Britons. Also, the ass-worship, especially in the nasty form given to it by Apion, is absent from Roman literature or gets a very different tinge. The only Roman author proper[89] to mention it is Tacitus, who gives it a rather scholarly explanation, despite the negative context into which he puts it. And last but not least the Exodus tradition, the masterpiece of Egyptian and Greek *Judenfeindschaft:* only Tacitus adopts the hostile Egyptian and Greek version as the starting point of his description of the Jewish customs; the sole other Roman author to make use of it, Pompeius Trogus, completely changes its meaning by incorporating it into a decidedly positive context.

Altogether, the Roman attitude toward the Jews is much more complex than the Greek and, especially, the Egyptian. The Romans inherited and absorbed, no doubt, to a certain degree the blunt Egyptian hatred and the Greek contempt for the outcasts of humankind. In addition, however, they sensed an appeal to which they reacted either with sympathy and, indeed, conversion or with fear, dislike, and, indeed, hatred. But they did not remain impassive and even in their hatred paid tribute to the *sceleratissima, despectissima,* and *taeterrima gens* of the Jews.

Anti-Semitism

*I*T IS COMMONPLACE TODAY to point out that the term "anti-Semitism" is a mere anachronism and, taken literally, distorts rather than illuminates the phenomenon it is supposed to describe. Going back probably to Wilhelm Marr,[1] the term attempts to give the racist theory of an "eternal struggle" between the "Aryan" and the "Semitic" races a scientific-sounding name, wrongly transforming common linguistic features ("Semitic languages") into dubious racial categories ("Semitic race"). Its literal meaning, "hostility against Semites," reveals its absurdity, since it aims, in its original racist context, not precisely at all "Semitic peoples," but solely at the Jews.

One could readily avoid the term "anti-Semitism" and instead use less awkward and less misleading terms like "hostility against Jews" ("Judenfeindschaft"), "hatred of Jews" ("Judenhaß"), or "anti-Judaism." Things are not that easy, however, because historical problems are not solved by simply changing names, and the crucial historical questions are (a) whether there was always the same kind of hostility against and hatred of the Jews throughout history, and (b) whether there is something unique about this hostility directed at the Jews which distinguishes the Jews from other ethnic groups. Hitler's "Endlösung," which is the direct offspring of the racist theories of the nineteenth century, makes it all too clear that there is, indeed, something unique about "hatred of Jews," and that this "hatred," or "hostility," or "anti-Judaism" did express itself differently in different periods of history.

If this is the case, one should argue for a more specific vocabulary, reserving the more common and neutral terms "hostility," "hatred," and "anti-Judaism" for expressions of hostility which the Jews share with other ethnic groups, and the term "anti-Semitism," despite or precisely because of its anachronism, for this unique "hatred" which finally led to the

"Endlösung." But this is where the historical problem begins, because one then has to determine what defines the uniqueness of hostility against Jews as distinguished from other forms of hostility, and where in history "simple" anti-Judaism turns into actual and "unique" anti-Semitism. Unless one wants to attribute to the "Endlösung" a very dubious uniqueness—namely, that it had no roots in history except for the racist theories of the nineteenth century—one has indeed to look into previous periods to answer that question. And this is precisely the reason why we cannot avoid it and why we cannot be content with the easy assessment that the ancient Greco-Roman world, which certainly did not have any concept of race as we understand it, is too distant from our modern world to assign to it any notion of hostility against Jews comparable to what we now call, after the *Shoah,* anti-Semitism.

The most advanced theory of anti-Semitism has been developed by Gavin I. Langmuir in his article "Toward a Definition of Antisemitism," published in a revised form in a book of essays bearing the same title.[2] Langmuir discusses anti-Semitism in the context of current psychological and sociological theories of "ethnocentrism," "ethnic prejudice," and "xenophobia." He strongly emphasizes the functional context or structure of verbal communications about outgroups and distinguishes among three kinds of hostile assertions:

1. Realistic hostility. "Realistic assertions about outgroups are propositions that utilize the information available about an outgroup and are based on the same assumptions about the nature of groups and the effect of membership on individuals as those used to understand the ingroup and its reference groups and their members."[3] There is nothing special, and certainly nothing specifically anti-Jewish, about this first kind: "Since groups (including Jews) do have different values and do compete for scarce goods, these assertions may provide the basis for hostile attitudes and actions."[4]

2. Xenophobia. "Xenophobic assertions are propositions that grammatically attribute a socially menacing conduct to an outgroup and all its members but are empirically based on the conduct of a historical minority of the members; they neglect other, unthreatening, characteristics of the outgroup."[5] Most important about this second category is that it fits the "kernel of truth" theory of prejudice: some members of the outgroup "have in fact been involved in the events considered threatening."[6] What is wrong about the xenophobic assertion is the imputation that *all* members of the outgroup are responsible for the actions regarded as despicable. Of course, xenophobic assertions are not reserved for Jews alone, but Jews are a prime example of this category of hostility. The only two examples Langmuir provides refer to them: "Jews are Christ-killers," that is, some Jews did indeed kill Jesus, but the label "Christ-killers" is attached to all Jews of all generations; and usury, that is, some Jews are indeed usurers, but the label "usury" is attached to all Jews.

In fact, however, the link between reality, that is, the concrete actions of some members of the outgroup considered threatening, and the xenophobic assertion, is very loose. It is established by the ingroup, and then extended to all members of the outgroup, in order to avoid confronting the true causes of the social menace projected onto the outgroup: "xenophobes are not talking about real people but about something much more intangible, their sense of danger, of chaos."[7] One possible response to this deeply felt threat is to attack the outgroup in order to reduce the tensions caused by the menace.

3. Chimeria. "Chimerical assertions are propositions that grammatically attribute with certitude to an outgroup and all its members characteristics that have never been empirically observed."[8] The neologism "chimeria" is taken from the Greek "chimera" *(chimaira)* which refers to a fabulous fire-breathing monster. Hence, in contrast to xenophobia, "chimerical assertions present fantasies, figments of the imagination, monsters that, although dressed syntactically in the clothes of real humans, have never been seen and are projections of mental processes unconnected with the real people of the outgroup. Chimerical assertions have no 'kernel of truth.'"[9]

The latter, no "kernel of truth," is the first decisive criterion distinguishing chimerical assertions from xenophobic ones. The second is that chimerical assertions apply to "all real individuals who can somehow be identified as members of the outgroup."[10] Moreover, whereas xenophobia is a social phenomenon, chimeria belongs primarily to the realm of the individual: "xenophobic assertions seem to be reactions to ill-understood menaces to social organization, while chimerical assertions seem to be reactions to ill-understood menaces to individual psychic integration."[11] This does not mean, however, that chimeria is not socially significant. On the contrary, but in order to turn xenophobia into chimeria and personal chimeria into socially significant chimeria, another mechanism is needed: the ingroup has to make the outgroup powerless and inferior. Only then is the stage set for the stronger, that is, social, form of chimeria, which accuses the outgroup of "inhuman conduct," "a general conscious conspiracy," or "an unconscious conspiracy of nature or biology."[12] The prime example Langmuir adduces for chimeria is the assertion that the Jews commit ritual murder.[13]

It is only this last category of socially significant chimerical hostility against Jews which justifies—this is Langmuir's main thesis—the term "anti-Semitism." Xenophobia does not, because xenophobic hostility against Jews cannot be distinguished from hostility directed against other groups.[14] To be sure, socially significant chimeria is not reserved for Jews, its targets also include blacks (and in certain periods of history also witches), and one might question, therefore, the use of a specific term for chimeria directed against Jews. "Nonetheless," he argues, "socially significant chimeria is an aberration that has seriously affected very few groups but has afflicted them terribly. The use of a special name to designate the peculiarly horrifying example that marked European culture for seven centuries and killed millions of victims during the 'Final Solution' therefore seems justifiable."[15]

It is not my concern here to discuss Langmuir's view about modern anti-Semitism and its relation to similar assertions directed against witches and blacks. I should only like to point out that he does not deal at all with the contents of these assertions and does not substantiate his claim that they are "chimerical" in the same way as the assertions directed at Jews.[16] Moreover, and more important in our context, his justification for the use of the term "anti-Semitism" in the end comes down to the degree of quantity and intensity,[17] which certainly is a highly problematic criterion. The crucial question, however, is how his theory of anti-Semitism applies to the historical reality. Unfortunately, the article on the definition of anti-Semitism is purely synchronical and very rarely refers to historical events. It is only in the Introduction of the book that he puts his theory into a historical context.

According to this, the turning point in history which turns "simple" anti-Judaism into "irrational" or "chimerical" anti-Semitism is the twelfth and thirteenth centuries C.E. Only then does hostility against Jews acquire a new quality: "faulty overgeneralizations reflecting a central core of truth" developed into "the new accusations of ritual murder, host desecration, and well-poisoning," which "were not faulty and inflexible generalizations but false fantasies unsupported by evidence."[18] With this fits another essential component of his theory: "It starts where the Jewish population was smallest and most defenseless . . . Jews no longer had the power to act as they wished, to demonstrate the falsity of stereotypes about their character and potential, or to disprove the irrational accusations against them."[19]

Before this decisive turning point, which starts at about 1150 C.E., we find two major stages of hostility against Jews, namely the Greco-Roman period and the early Christian era, both falling into the category of anti-Judaism. The Greco-Roman hostility (to which, for no specified reason, the Persians also belong) is marked by a hatred of Jews "because of a real Jewish characteristic, their insistence on maintaining their Judaic identity as a separate people."[20] Quite clearly, although he does not say so explicitly, the ancient Greco-Roman-Persian hostility belongs to what he calls "realistic assertions" in his theory. It still lacks the menace essential for the second category, the "xenophobic assertions": because the Persians, Greeks, and Romans had developed their social identities independently of Judaism, they "could hate or ridicule Jews without feeling any threat . . . to the foundations of their own sense of identity . . . Their anti-Judaic hostility thus differed little from many other instances of ethnocentric hostility throughout history."[21]

Different from this is Christian anti-Judaism. Because of the "patriarchal connection" between Judaism and Christianity, "for Christians, the ability of Jews to maintain their own identity was not only annoying or hateful in the way ethnic differences so often are; it was an intimate and enduring threat to their sense of identity, a challenge built into their own religion."[22] Hence, (early) Christian anti-Judaism, which seems to fall neatly into the category of "xenophobic assertions," emerges as "an important precondition for European antisemitism, a halfway station between a very common kind of ethnocentric hostility and the peculiar irrational hostility of Hitler"[23]—which began, to be sure, at about 1150 C.E.

Let us now see how Langmuir's theory, with its historical application, concurs with our findings. At first sight it might seem attractive because, by so clearly determining the decisive point in history which marks the transition from anti-Judaism to anti-Semitism, it releases us from our concern about anti-Semitism in the Greco-Roman world: the Greeks and Romans were ethnocentric, and their ethnocentric attitude was the same toward Jews as toward other barbarians, because the Jews did not threaten their sense of identity any more than did any other barbaric people.

This is certainly a theory one may adopt (I will come back to it), but unfortunately it does not conform with Langmuir's own criteria. To begin with some more theoretical considerations, the emphasis and confidence Langmuir puts on empirical knowledge in order to define realistic, xenophobic, and chimerical assertions are appropriate for modern sociological case studies but highly dubious for the ancient world. To what extent assertions about Jews in antiquity (and not only then) were empirically based is questionable, and it is even more questionable whether empirical data had, and have, any influence on the degree of anti-Jewish feelings. Doesn't this rather rationalistic approach in the end fall into the well-known trap, which Langmuir tries so hard to avoid,[24] of finally holding the Jews themselves responsible for whether the non-Jews are "merely" anti-Jewish or genuinely anti-Semitic? As long as the famous "kernel of truth" can be found in the non-Jews' assertions, they are just anti-Jewish (because they have a *fundamentum in re*), but when the Jews never did what the non-Jews accuse them of, do we then detect anti-Semitism (because there is no empirical basis)?

When we apply Langmuir's three categories of realistic, xenophobic, and chimerical assertions to our sources, we immediately realize that the distinction is artificial and does not work in the sense of a linear, evolutionary historical development from "realistic" through "xenophobic" to "chimerical." As far as xenophobic assertions are concerned, the major feature he attributes to them is the threat, the social menace, felt by the members of the ingroup. Historically, he clearly wants to reserve this threat for the Christians and their peculiar form of anti-Judaism, whereas the Greco-Roman attitude toward the Jews is devoid of any sense of threat (hence, they are the prime example of an ingroup with "realistic" assertions about the Jews). This assumption is definitely mistaken. One of our main findings has been that it is precisely the feeling of being threatened by the Jews which informs many, if not most, anti-Jewish statements in antiquity. The Jews were regarded as a threat, although in different forms, to Egyptian, Greek, and, above all, Roman society alike. It is very doubtful whether the Egyptians, Greeks, and Romans felt less threatened in their "sense of identity" than the Christians, and the feeling of threat certainly cannot be used as a criterion to distinguish between two different categories of hostility against the Jews.

Furthermore, the proposition that xenophobic assertions originate from the conduct, or rather misconduct, of a minority among the Jews, and are then attributed to all Jews (unlike chimerical assertions which by definition point to all Jews), is also artificial and cannot be validated in our sources. Greek and Roman xenophobia directed against Jews quite obviously is not based on some concrete actions of some Jews (in contrast to the proper behavior of others) but from the very beginning aims at all Jews as Jews, in spite of what they do and what they do not do.

And finally, chimerical assertions—they are the weakest point of Langmuir's theory as far as the Greco-Roman world is concerned. "Irrational" or "chimerical" fantasies, "that have never been empirically observed,"[25] are also an essential part of the pagan anti-Jewish arsenal (and similarly of the early Christian). The most salient example, of course, is the alleged Jewish custom of human sacrifice and subsequent anthropophagy, which is hardly different from the ritual cannibalism Langmuir establishes as the decisive criterion that defines the turning point at about 1150 C.E. from anti-Judaism to anti-Semitism. Whether the Jews annually sacrifice and consume a foreigner or whether they kill Christian children in order to utilize their blood or to share their heart at Passover, is phenomenologically the same and does not allow us, therefore, to put one into the category of anti-Judaism, let alone of "realistic assertions," and the other into the category of anti-Semitism.

Moreover, the additional proposition that the essential inferiority and powerlessness of the outgroup, that is, the Jews, is a crucial factor in turning anti-Judaism into anti-Semitism, does not hold true for our evidence either. Whether the legend of human sacrifice is part of Seleucid propaganda or whether it belongs to the Greco-Egyptian anti-Jewish tradition, in neither case does it reflect weak and powerless Jews. On the contrary, it portrays Jews who not only represent a considerable menace to the society creating these legends but also are, and are regarded as, politically powerful during these particular periods of their history.

From this we may safely arrive at the conclusion that, according to Langmuir's theoretical model, anti-Semitism predates Christianity. At least the Greeks were anti-Semites, however not out of a position of power and utilizing a status of Jewish inferiority, but rather vice versa, responding to politically threatening Jews. Unfortunately, again, things are not that simple. If chimerical assertions are essential for the emergence of anti-Semitism, one would expect to find them only, or at least predominantly, in connection with Jews. But this is precisely not the case, and we face here the same problem which troubled Langmuir with regard to the "blacks" and the "witches," namely that the phenomenon (chimerical assertions) is not as uniquely anti-Jewish as required in order to qualify for the label "anti-Semitism." As Bickerman has made abundantly clear, the charge of human sacrifice and ritual cannibalism in antiquity was by no means restricted to the Jews.[26] He gives several examples of these "cannibalistic conspiracies," the most famous of which is the *coniuratio Catilinae:* according to Cassius Dio's account, Catiline sacrificed a boy, made his conspirators take an oath on the boy's entrails, and he and his friends subsequently consumed them as the sacrificial meal.[27] The charge of anthropophagy could be used against different rivals and enemies, in different historical and political contexts (by no coincidence it was later applied to the Christians as well),[28] and the least it needed was a "kernel of truth"—it is the classic (in the double sense of the word) example of Langmuir's "chimerical assertions."

With this we come full circle. Langmuir's theoretical model does not help us to distinguish anti-Judaism from anti-Semitism: his crucial chimerical fantasies are part and parcel of ancient hostility, but not only against Jews. If his model is not altogether worthless, one should opt for a much more dynamic interplay of its components (realistic, xenophobic, chimerical), instead of his linear pattern of development. There is obviously no clear-cut, absolute point in history at which anti-Judaism turns into anti-Semitism. The transitions between the different components are fluid, and this applies to all periods of history, certainly to the ancient world.

Should we, then, be content with the term "anti-Judaism" and forget about "anti-Semitism," at least in antiquity? Or, to phrase it differently because not the term but the definition is decisive, can we be content with the result that there is nothing special and unique about Greco-Roman hostility against Jews—whether or not we want to give it a specific name? A recent attempt to identify that "special" and "unique" has been made by S. Cohen in a short but illuminating article.[29] He starts by demonstrating that the term "anti-Semitism" is anachronistic and misleading, and then briefly reviews certain events of ancient Jewish history: neither the destruction of the Temple in 70 C.E. ("because the Romans had good reason to do what they did"),[30] nor the Antiochean and Hadrianic persecutions, nor even the Alexandrian pogroms were "anti-Semitic": "As Apion, the leader of the 'anti-Semitic' party, asked, 'If the Jews wish to become Alexandrian citizens, why don't they worship the Alexandrian gods?'—an excellent question. The Jews wanted equality with tolerance, to be allowed to be the same as everyone else while also being different from everyone else, and Apion rightly refused."[31] This bold statement becomes even bolder in a footnote saying: "If it be objected that I am following the 'anti-Semitic' interpretation of the events in Alexandria, I believe that the reconstruction is correct no matter what its origin."[32]

With this, however, the matter is not settled. In a second attempt Cohen asks, almost desperately, "Where is that elusive point that separates justifiable hatred from unjustifiable, legitimate opposition from illegitimate, and the 'anti-Jewish' from the 'anti-Semitic'?"[33] and reviews Apion and Hadrian again:

The former had good reason to dislike the Jews and to oppose their attempts to obtain civic equality, and the latter had good reason to suppress a Jewish rebellion and to forbid the practices of Judaism. But would Apion's policies have led to the creation of a Jewish ghetto, the profanation of Jewish synagogues, the looting of Jewish property, and anti-Jewish pogroms, had these policies not been motivated, at least in part, by hatred of Jews and Judaism? Would Hadrian's suppression of a rebellion have led to a three-year-long persecution of Judaism and the deaths of numerous martyrs had it not been motivated, at least in part, by hatred of Jews and Judaism? I indicated in the previous paragraph that the simple application of the term "anti-Semitic" to these incidents is neither justifiable nor helpful; but here, I concede, perhaps we must allow for a certain degree of "anti-Semitic" feelings to account for the scale and severity of the incidents. Both Apion and Hadrian crossed the point that separates the justifiable from the unjustifiable, but the precise location of this point is as elusive for historians of antiquity as it is for students of contemporary "anti-Semitism."[34]

This is a most revealing statement. The "elusive point" we are looking for and which distinguishes the justifiable from the unjustifiable, the legitimate from the illegitimate, anti-Judaism from anti-Semitism, seems to be, if I understand it correctly, the "scale and severity of the incidents." Both Apion and Hadrian had good reason to act against the Jews, but their grossly exaggerated hatred and "anti-Semitic feelings" led them to persecutions of a scale and severity which crossed the line and allow us to pinpoint the "elusive point." Here we are back to an argument which served also as Langmuir's final resort to determine the uniqueness of the socially significant chimeria directed against the Jews: the degree of brutality, atrocity, and horror to which the Jews were exposed (in contrast to the "blacks" and the "witches"). Nobody would want to question the seriousness of this argument—but can the "scale and severity" of a persecution be the decisive criterion for distinguishing an anti-Jewish from an anti-Semitic "incident?" Doesn't this introduce a dangerous, easily misunderstood, quantitative element?

I do not believe that Hadrian and the Hadrianic persecution is a case in point,[35] but Apion and Alexandria are good examples to further our discussion. As we have seen, Apion is the main propagandist of the particular Greco-Egyptian blend of hostility, composed of the elements "impiety," "xenophobia" and, above all, "misanthropy." Of these the "impiety" goes well back into Egyptian anti-Jewish prejudices, whereas the "xenophobia" and definitely the "misanthropy" seem to be the predominant Greek contributions. This explosive mixture reaches its climax in the alleged human sacrifice as part of the Jewish Temple worship, the "classical" literary form of which has been given by no one but Apion: the mysterious Jewish God demands the sacrifice of foreigners who happen to be Greeks. This unmasks the Jews and their religion as opposed to and, indeed, a constant threat to the civilized world, which by definition is Greek.[36]

The Jews as the "evil incarnate," denying and perverting in their xenophobic and misanthropic hatred all cherished values of humankind, conspiring against the civilized world—this, I would like to argue, is the allegation which crosses the line from the "justifiable" to the "unjustifiable," from "anti-Judaism" to "anti-Semitism." It is directed against "the" Jews, that is, not only some but all Jews, and it has no regard for what Jews do and do not do in reality—"the" Jews are identified as the outcasts of human civilization. To be sure, it has a "kernel of truth," in that the Jews do separate from others in certain circumstances, but it is precisely this conscious perversion of the "truth," the phobic mystification of the outgroup, which distinguishes the "anti-Semitic" from the "anti-Jewish" attitude. Since it is the peculiar result of the amalgamation of Egyptian and Greek prejudices, one might argue that only the idea of a world-wide Greco-Hellenistic civilization made it possible for the phenomenon we call anti-Semitism to emerge.

Hence, I would contend that Langmuir's "xenophobic" assertions do indeed incorporate the core of anti-Semitism, that it does not require "chimerical" assertions to release anti-Semitic feelings. Chimerical assertions may be combined with xenophobic ones (as is the case with the allegation of human sacrifice which is the peak of Jewish misanthropy) but not necessarily so: the accusation of xenophobia and misanthropy does not need the chimerical element of anthropophagy in order to become "anti-Semitic." The xenophobic assertion itself is sufficient, to be sure a very peculiar one which, ironically or paradoxically, transfers to the outgroup, the object of hostility, the grotesquely exaggerated projection of the ingroup's own hatred: the Jews are the xenophobes and misanthropes par excellence, and as such a menace to the entire world.

Neither does the accusation of xenophobia and misanthropy necessarily need to result in a severe persecution to become "anti-Semitic"—but it often did, and we have good examples for this. One is the riots in Alexandria. Apion, who obviously played a crucial part in these events, no doubt used his "theoretical" weapons against the Jews in order to fuel the political conflict. And as I have demonstrated above,[37] it is precisely the combination of theoretical "arguments" with political goals which makes up the specific situation in Alexandria. This, I would argue, already allows us to apply to it the term "anti-Semitic," not only the creation of the Jewish ghetto, the profanation of the synagogues, and the looting of Jewish property—all these are *results* of a pre-existing anti-Semitic "disposition," not what determines anti-Semitism. Whether the political conflict alone shows traits of what could be labeled "anti-Semitic" is another question. One might be inclined to see in the peculiar constellation of the Jews being a minority in a predominantly Egyptian-Greek city, yet at the same time regarded as closely allied with the hated foreign oppressor, an early manifestation of what later anti-Semitic stereotypes call "double loyalty." However, our analyses of the events in both Alexandria and Elephantine have made it abundantly clear that the "political" and the "cultural-religious" spheres are inextricably interwoven, and one should not look, therefore, at either component alone.

Another example is the advice given to Antiochus VII Sidetes by his counselors when he was laying siege to Jerusalem at the beginning of the rule of John Hyrcanus (around 134 B.C.E.).[38] The counselors strongly suggest that the king not only "take the city by storm" but also "wipe out completely the nation of Jews" (the importance of this "argument" is emphasized by its being repeated twice).[39] The justification for this genocide or ethnocide is nothing else but the impiety and misanthropy of the Jews because of which, as the counselors remind the king, they had been driven out of Egypt and had had to tolerate the deliberate sacrifice of a pig in their Temple, carried out by the king's predecessor Antiochus IV Epiphanes. This is a classic example of the conclusion, drawn from Jewish misanthropy, that the entire genos or ethnos of the Jews should be eliminated. Again, what makes it anti-Semitic is not the severity of the conclusion but its motive, the charge of a deeply rooted, essential misanthropy.

The earliest example of violent actions against the Jews in the diaspora is the destruction of the Jewish Temple at Elephantine. Here, however, it is much more difficult to reconstruct the ideological background. The contemporary sources only tell us that the Jews are regarded by the nationalistic Egyptian priests as impious foreigners who slaughter sacred animals and, moreover, are the allies of the hated Persian oppressors. There is nothing about Jewish xenophobia, let alone misanthropy, and also nothing about a persecution of the Jews which in the other examples is so closely related to the charge of misanthropy. Hence, if we follow our above definition, we should not call the events in Elephantine "anti-Semitic." It needed the Greek retelling of ancient Egyptian prejudices, and the Greek claim to a world-wide culture, to turn anti-Judaism into anti-Semitism. But since this Greek retelling was only made possible in Egypt and by using the specific kind of hatred of this particular group of foreigners provided by the Egyptian priests, since it was phrased unequivocally for the first time by the Egyptian priest Manetho, one may well maintain that anti-Semitism did, and could, emerge in Egypt alone.

If the accusation of xenophobia/misanthropy is the core of "anti-Semitism," its emergence in history can be traced back to the beginning of the third century B.C.E. (Manetho and probably Hecataeus) at the latest, with certain roots in the earlier Egyptian tradition. It is certainly not by coincidence that the Greek adaptation of the book of Esther emphasizes precisely Jewish misanthropy when quoting the anti-Jewish decree of the Persian king Ahasuerus. The Hebrew text, the date of which is controversial,[40] places in the mouth of the wicked Haman the famous words: "Dispersed in scattered groups among the peoples throughout the provinces of your realm, there is a certain people whose laws are different from those of every other people *(datehem shonot mikol-ᶜam)*. They do not observe the king's laws, and it does not befit your majesty to tolerate them. If it pleases your majesty, let an order be drawn up for their destruction."[41]

Whenever this originated, and whether it belongs to a Persian or Greek context,[42] the formulation of the accusation is relatively moderate (despite the cruel conclusion): the Jews have laws which differ from those of all others, and in particular, they do not observe the king's laws. Quite different is the Greek translation of the Septuagint which originated at the end of the second century/beginning of the first century B.C.E.[43] According to its version of the king's decree, the Jews are a "hostile" *(dysmenē)* people who are "opposed" *(antitheton)* in their laws "to any other people" *(pros pan ethnos)*. Moreover, they are the only people, who are in the state of military alertness *(en antiparagogē)*[44] "always (and) against everyone" *(panti anthrōpō)*, who follow with their laws a foreign way of life,[45] and who finally "commit, ill-disposed towards our affairs *(dysnooun tois hēmeterois pragmasin)*, the worst evil deeds *(ta cheirista kaka)*."[46]

Here, the biblical text takes the guise of the well-known allegation of an essential misanthropy, not only against the Persians but against all humankind, the answer to which can only be complete elimination: "they all—wives and children included—shall be utterly destroyed by the swords of their enemies . . . , so that those who have been hostile and remain so in a single day go down in violence to Hades, and leave our government completely secure and untroubled hereafter."[47] Only when all the threatening Jews have been exterminated can the Persian empire, and indeed humankind, be saved.

The fundamental hostility of the Jews toward humankind as the reason for their extinction becomes even clearer in Josephus' quotation of the Greek addition to Esther. According to Josephus, Haman brought the charge before the king,

> that there was a certain wicked nation (*ethnos ponēron*) scattered throughout the habitable land ruled by him, which was unfriendly and unsocial (*amikton asymphylon*) and neither had the same religion nor practiced the same laws as others, "but both by its customs and practices it is the enemy (*echthron*) of your people and of all mankind (*hapasin anthrōpois*). If you wish to lay up a store of good deeds with your subjects, you will give orders to destroy this nation root and branch and leave not a remnant of them to be kept either in slavery or in captivity."[48]

Here we have it all, the allegation of *amixia*, "unsociability," and of a way of life that is hostile to and, therefore, dangerous for all humankind; only the complete extinction of the Jews can avert this threat once and for all. Josephus clearly expresses through Haman, the arch-enemy of the Jews, the essence of Greek anti-Semitism, the Jewish *amixia* which leads to misanthropy and hatred of humankind.

This is not to say, however, that the "strangeness of the Jews midst ancient society" is the "most fundamental *reason*[49] for pagan anti-Semitism," as Sevenster has put it.[50] It is true that the allegation of the Jewish "separateness" and "strangeness" does have a *fundamentum in re*, but to argue that it is the *reason* for pagan anti-Semitism is to confuse cause with pretext,[51] to hold the Jews themselves responsible for what others do to them. Sevenster falls here into the same trap as Langmuir did, the only difference being that, according to Langmuir, Jewish separateness counts only for anti-Judaism (because of the "kernel of truth"), not for anti-Semitism in the true sense of the word. On the other hand, the attempt to refute Sevenster's position by the opposite observation, namely, that in the Greco-Roman world "most

Jews were not separate at all,"[52] is equally problematic because it follows the same line of argument as Sevenster. To what degree the Jews were separate is not important—they no doubt were to a certain extent, and Sevenster is right in pointing out that Jewish writers and especially Josephus took pride in this.[53] The only crucial question is what the Greco-Egyptian and Greek authors made out of it. They turned Jewish separateness into a monstrous conspiracy against humankind and the values shared by all civilized human beings, and it is therefore *their* attitude which determines anti-Semitism.

If early Egypt represents "anti-Semitism" *in statu nascendi,* Hellenistic Egypt and the Greek East "anti-Semitism" coming to full blossom, what about Rome? As we have seen, the picture is more complex in Rome than in Egypt and Greece. Beginning with Cicero and Seneca, and reaching its climax with Juvenal and Tacitus, there is an ambivalence between dislike and fear, criticism and respect, attraction and repulsion, which responds to the peculiar combination of exclusiveness and yet success that characterizes Judaism in the eyes of the Roman authors. The deeply felt threat that the Jewish superstition might succeed in finally destroying the cultural and religious values of Roman society is the very essence of Roman hostility against Jews. It is the Roman version of the Greek charge of misanthropy, and it is what distinguishes Jews from other barbarians. Other barbarians may be savages and may do loathsome things, other barbarians may be despicable, but other barbarians were never seen as being so dangerous and threatening as the Jews.[54]

Also the consequences of the Romans' dislike and hatred are different from, and more complex than, those of the Egyptians and, especially, the Greeks. There are no persecutions of Jews—except for the persecutions of the Christians which, as we have seen,[55] are almost indistinguishable in motivation *(odium humani generis)* from the classic charge against the Jews *(adversus omnes alios hostile odium).* Hence, the Roman hatred of Jews could, indeed, reach a degree which would make one inclined to use the term "anti-Semitism" in the sense described above in the Greek context. On the whole, however, the peculiarity of the Roman attitude toward the Jews seems better expressed by the term "Judeophobia" in its ambivalent combination of fear and hatred. One may argue, of course, that "anti-Semitism" also carries, and always carried with it, an element of fear. This is certainly the case, but the Roman fear is peculiar not only in that it projects onto the Jews an irrational feeling of being threatened by some mysterious conspiracy but also, and mainly, in that it responds to the very real success of the Jews in the midst of Roman society, that it is the distorted echo of sympathy.

As the course of history shows, *this* fear was well-founded. The vanquished did succeed in giving laws to their victors: at first as Jews and later, and most effectively, in the guise of Christianity.

Abbreviations

AJSL	American Journal of Semitic Languages and Literatures
ANRW	Aufstieg und Niedergang der römischen Welt
ARW	Archiv für Religionswissenschaft
BAR	Biblical Archaeology Review
CPJ	V. Tcherikover et al., Corpus Papyrorum Judaicarum
CRAI	Acádemie des Inscriptions et Belles-Lettres. Comptes Rendus
EJ	Encyclopaedia Judaica
GLAAJ	M. Stern, Greek and Latin Authors on Jews and Judaism
JBL	Journal of Biblical Literature
JJS	Journal of Jewish Studies
JR	Journal of Religion
JRS	Journal of Roman Studies
JSJ	Journal for the Study of Judaism
JSS	Jewish Social Studies
LCL	Loeb Classical Library
NT	Novum Testamentum
PW	Paulys Real-Encyclopädie der Classischen Altertumswissenschaft
RAC	Reallexikon für Antike und Christentum
REJ	Revue des Etudes Juives
RHR	Revue de l'Histoire des Religions
ThWNT	Theologisches Wörterbuch zum Neuen Testament
TRE	Theologische Realenzyklopädie
VT	Vetus Testamentum
ZPE	Zeitschrift für Papyrologie und Epigraphik

Notes

INTRODUCTION

1. Cf. L. Wickert, *Theodor Mommsen. Eine Biographie*, vol. 3: *Wanderjahre*, Frankfurt a.M. 1969, p. 664.

2. C. Hoffmann, *Juden und Judentum im Werk Deutscher Althistoriker des 19. und 20. Jahrhunderts*, Leiden etc. 1988, p. 222.

3. A. G. Sperling, *Apion der Grammatiker und sein Verhältnis zum Judentum. Ein Beitrag zu einer Einleitung in die Schriften des Josephos*, Dresden 1886 (Programm des Gymnasiums zum heiligen Kreuz in Dresden, erste Abteilung), p. IV.

4. K. Zacher, "Antisemitismus und Philosemitismus im klassischen Altertum," *Preußische Jahrbücher* 94, 1898, pp. 1–24; quotation from p. 1.

5. 5, 1921, pp. 472–483.

6. *Juden und Judentum*, p. 224.

7. Antisemitismus, pp. 1, 24. My emphasis.

8. E. Meyer, *Ursprung und Anfänge des Christentums*, vol. 2: *Die Entwicklung des Judentums und Jesus von Nazaret*, Stuttgart and Berlin 1921 (^{5}1925), pp. 31–32.

9. *Deutschlands Erneuerung* 5, 1921, p. 483.

10. F. Staehelin, *Der Antisemitismus des Altertums in seiner Entstehung und Entwicklung*, Winterthur 1905, p. 23.

11. *EJ*, vol. 2, Berlin 1928, col. 957.

12. *Verus Israel*, Oxford 1986 (the original French version appeared under the same title in Paris in 1948, ^{2}1964), p. 202. On the same page he quotes approvingly Mommsen's dictum.

13. V. Tcherikover, *Hellenistic Civilization and the Jews*, Philadelphia 1959 (New York 1979), p. 358.

14. J. N. Sevenster, *The Roots of Pagan Anti-Semitism in the Ancient World*, Leiden 1975, p. 89. For a critique of Sevenster see J. Mélèze Modrzejewski, "Sur l'antisémitisme païen," in M. Olender, ed., *Pour Léon Poliakov. Le racisme: Mythes et sciences*, Brussels 1981, pp. 411–439. Many modern scholars come to similar conclusions. See, e.g., E. M. Smallwood in her classical study *The Jews*

under Roman Rule. From Pompey to Diocletian, Leiden 1976, p. 123, or H. Castritius, "Die Haltung Roms gegenüber den Juden in der ausgehenden Republik und der Prinzipatszeit," in T. Klein et al., eds., *Judentum und Antisemitismus von der Antike bis zur Gegenwart,* Düsseldorf 1984, p. 32.

15. *Juden und Judentum,* p. 224. The confrontation of the "substantialist" and the "functionalist" approaches also plays an important role in other disciplines, e.g. in the discussion about "magic" in Religious Studies. See, e.g., Charles R. Phillips, "The Sociology of Religious Knowledge in the Roman Empire to A.D. 284," in *ANRW* II, 16.3, 1986, pp. 2677–2773; Hendrik S. Versnel, "Some Reflections on the Relationship Magic-Religion," *Numen* 37, 1991, pp. 177–197.

16. *Festgabe zum Zehnjährigen Bestehen der Akademie für die Wissenschaft des Judentums 1919–1929,* Berlin 1929, pp. 76–91.

17. Supplementband V, Stuttgart 1931, cols. 3–43.

18. Ursprung und Wesen, p. 85.

19. Ibid., pp. 79ff.; Antisemitismus, cols. 5f.

20. Ursprung und Wesen, pp. 79, 80.

21. See also the passing remark by A. Funkenstein that "the anti-Jewish arguments of pagan antiquity . . . were political and ethnic in origin, born in part out of the aggressive Hasmonaean policies against the Greek population of the land of Israel," in *Perceptions of Jewish History,* Berkeley, Los Angeles, and Oxford 1993, p. 313.

22. A. Giovannini, "Les origines de l'antijudaïsme dans le monde grec," *Cahiers du Centre G. Glotz* 6, 1995, pp. 41–60.

23. Ibid., p. 59.

24. His reductionist approach is also evident in his explanation of "Greek anti-Judaism" as a "phenomenon totally independent of the hypothetical Egyptian anti-Judaism" (ibid., p. 41, n. 1). He arrives at this conclusion by merely proclaiming that Manetho "was, incidentally, an Egyptian priest and not a Greek," who, of all things, bequeathed us a "rather neutral version" recounting the expulsion of the Jews from Egypt (p. 42). Although it is certain that Manetho was indeed an Egyptian priest familiar with Egyptian national traditions, he nevertheless did write his *Aegyptiaca* as a devout follower of Ptolemy's religious policies. As for his version of the expulsion story, opinions may, of course, differ; however, arguing that it is "neutral" is surprising indeed.

25. *Jésus et Israël,* Paris 1948 (*Jesus and Israel,* New York 1971); *Genèse de l'Antisémitisme,* Paris 1956.

26. *Verus Israel,* passim. For an evaluation of Simon's criticism of Isaac (ibid., pp. 489–493) see J. G. Gager, *The Origins of Anti-Semitism,* New York and Oxford 1983, p. 17.

27. *Histoire de l'antisémitisme,* vol. 1: *Du Christ aux Juifs de cour,* Paris 1955 (*The History of Anti-Semitism,* vol. 1: *From Roman Times to the Court Jews,* New York 1965; London 1974).

28. *Faith and Fratricide: The Theological Roots of Antisemitism,* Minneapolis 1974.

29. *Origins,* p. 40.

30. Ibid., p. 36.

31. Princeton, N.J., 1993, p. 84.

32. See, e.g., Gager, *Origins,* p. 8.

33. Z. Yavetz, "Judeophobia in Classical Antiquity: A Different Approach," *JJS* 44, 1993, pp. 1–22. As a matter of fact, the French version (judéophobie) had already appeared in an article by J. Halévy published in 1903: "Le Calembour dans la judéophobie alexandrine," *Revue Semitique* 11, 1903, pp. 263–268.

34. The latter deserves a study of its own: no doubt Christian anti-Judaism followed its own agenda, but also no doubt it developed in a historical setting which was infused with anti-Jewish sentiments and had found distinctive ways to express them.

35. That the subject of "pagan anti-Semitism" can be addressed adequately only in the broader context of the encounter between Jews and Gentiles (and Christians) in antiquity has been emphasized also by N. de Lange in his brief article "The Origins of Anti-Semitism: Ancient Evidence and Modern Interpretations" (in S. L. Gilman and S. T. Katz, eds., *Anti-Semitism in Times of Crisis,* New York and London 1991, pp. 21–37).

36. This has been pointed out also by Gager, *Origins,* p. 31; Yavetz, Judeophobia, p. 5.

37. *Greek and Latin Authors on Jews and Judaism,* ed. with introductions, translations and commentary by M. Stern, vols. 1–3, Jerusalem 1974–1984, henceforth abbreviated *GLAJJ.* All translations from Greek and Latin sources are, where available, from the Loeb Classical Library, followed by the respective number in *GLAJJ.* Deviations from the Loeb translations have been indicated, except for the word "race" (the equivalent of *genos, ethnos, genus, gens*) which has been tacitly replaced by "people," "nation" or "origin." Although I am aware that the usage of the word "race" in English is different from the German "Rasse," I couldn't bring myself to use it in connection with the Jews.

38. Yavetz, Judeophobia, p. 19; Funkenstein, "Anti-Jewish Propaganda: Pagan, Christian and Modern," *Jerusalem Quarterly* 19, 1981, p. 56.

39. Judeophobia, pp. 2 and 20.

40. Tacitus, *Historiae,* V, 8,2.

41. Dan. 11:21; 11:36–39.

42. E. Bickermann, *Der Gott der Makkabäer*, Berlin 1937, pp. 117ff.; M. Hengel, *Judentum und Hellenismus*, Tübingen ²1973, pp. 515ff.

43. Egypt is considered to be the "wellsprings of pagan anti-Semitism" also in Joseph Mélèze Modrzejewski's recent monograph *The Jews of Egypt: From Ramses II to Emperor Hadrian*, Philadelphia and Jerusalem 1995, pp. 135–157 (the French original of the book appeared 1992 in Paris). This chapter of an otherwise highly stimulating book is somewhat unbalanced. The author briefly reviews the story of the lepers and the Elephantine thesis put forward by Yoyotte (which he does not find very convincing), deals at great length with the legend of the "miracle at the Hippodrome" in the Third Book of Maccabees (only to conclude that it doesn't have to do anything with anti-Semitic feelings on the part of the Egyptian king, that is, either Ptolemy IV Philopator or Ptolemy VIII Euergetes II Physkon), and finally discusses two private letters dated to the second and the first centuries B.C.E. respectively. Of these he regards only the latter, which mentions people who "loathe the Jews" (V. A. Tcherikover and A. Fuks, eds., *Corpus Papyrorum Judaicarum*, vol. 1, Cambridge, Mass., 1957, p. 141), "convincing proof of the reality of popular hostility toward Jews in the Ptolemaic kingdom" (p. 157). This conclusion is no doubt correct, but one wonders whether this is all that streams from the "wellsprings of pagan anti-Semitism" in Egypt.

44. An excellent study of the use of Egyptian motifs in Western literature is being prepared by Jan Assmann, to be entitled "Moses the Egyptian: The Image of Egypt in Western Monotheism. An Essay in Mnemohistory."

1. EXPULSION FROM EGYPT

1. For the earlier literature see M. Stern, "Nevuah miṣrit-yewanit wehamasoret ʿal gerush ha-yehudim mi-miṣrayim be-historiyah shel Chaeremon," *Zion* 28, 1962/63, pp. 223–227, and his respective commentaries in *GLAJJ*; J. Gager, *Moses in Greco-Roman Paganism*, Nashville and New York 1972, pp. 113ff. ("Moses and the Exodus"); id., *The Origins of Antisemitism*, New York and Oxford 1983, passim; C. Aziza, "L'utilisation polémique du récit de l'Exode chez les écrivains alexandrins (IVᵉᵐᵉ siècle av. J.-C.—Iᵉʳ siècle ap. J.-C.)," in *ANRW*, II, 20.1, pp. 41–65 (a broad overview). See also the M.A. thesis of my student Lucia Raspe, *Die ägyptischen Exodustraditionen und die Entstehung des antiken Antisemitismus*, FU Berlin, Berlin 1994.

2. On Hecataeus see W. Spoerri, art. "Hecataios von Abdera," in *RAC*, XIV, Stuttgart 1988, cols. 278–286, and G. E. Sterling, *Historiography and Self-Definition: Josephos, Luke-Acts and Apologetic Historiography*, Leiden, New York, and

Köln 1992, pp. 59–91. Sterling argues for the dating of Hecataeus' *Aegyptiaca* between 321 and 304 B.C.E., and between these parameters for a date "as early as possible" (p. 78).

3. Diodorus Siculus, *Bibliotheca Historica*, 40,3,1–3 = *GLAJJ*, vol. 1, no. 11 (trans. F. R. Walton, *LCL*).

4. *GLAJJ*, vol. 1, p. 21.

5. Gager, *Moses*, p. 37.

6. Ibid., p. 28.

7. Ibid.

8. "The many" in Greek writers can have a derogatory overtone, as e.g. in the distinction made by Pseudo-Xenophon (the "Old Oligarch") in his *Athēnaiōn Politeia* between the *chrēstoi* ("useful," "good," "decent," "respectable people"), who are rich, and the *ponēroi* ("troublesome," "evil," "worthless," "masses"), who are poor. On this see J. M. Moore, *Aristotle and Xenophon on Democracy and Oligarchy*, London 1975, pp. 22, 48, and G. E. M. De Ste. Croix, *The Class Struggle in the Ancient Greek World from the Archaic Age to the Arab Conquests*, London 1981, pp. 71ff.

9. Ibid.

10. Diodorus Siculus, 40,3,4; the translation follows F. R. Walton and Gager, whose rendering of *misoxenos* is more accurate (Walton has "intolerant").

11. 40,3,1–2.

12. F. Jacoby, *Die Fragmente der griechischen Historiker*, vol. 3a (Kommentar), Leiden 1954, p. 50; Gager, *Moses*, p. 37; Stern, *GLAJJ*, vol. 1, p. 29.

13. Sterling, *Historiography and Self-Definition*, p. 73, has shown convincingly "that the native Egyptian data passed through a Greek sieve as Hekataios wrote."

14. *Contra Apionem*, I, 73–91 = *GLAJJ*, vol. 1, no. 19, and *Contra Apionem*, I, 228–252 = *GLAJJ*, vol. 1, no. 21.

15. *Contra Apionem*, I, 76 (trans. W. G. Waddell, *Manetho*, Cambridge, Mass., 1940, *LCL*, Fr. 42).

16. *Contra Apionem*, I, 239f. = *GLAJJ*, vol. 1, no. 21 (trans. W. G. Waddell, *Manetho, LCL*, Fr. 54).

17. *Contra Apionem*, I, 248f. (trans. W. G. Waddell, *Manetho, LCL*, Fr. 54).

18. E. Meyer, *Aegyptische Chronologie*, Berlin 1904, pp. 71–79; F. Jacoby, *Fragmente*, vol. 3c, p. 84; R. Laqueur, art. "Manethon (1)," *PW*, XXVII, 1928, cols. 1071ff.; W. G. Waddell, *Manetho*, pp. XVII–XIX (summary of Laqueur's *PW* article); J. Heinemann, Antisemitismus, col. 27; some hesitation has been expressed by R. Weill, *La Fin du Moyen Empire Égyptien*, vols. 1–2, Paris 1918, pp. 70–76 and 104–111, and V. Tcherikover, *Hellenistic Civilization*, pp. 362f. See also J. Mar-

quart, "Chronologische Untersuchungen," *Philologus*, Suppl. 7, Leipzig 1899, pp. 667–673; J. Yoyotte, "L'Égypte ancienne et les origines de l'antijudaïsme," *RHR* 163, 1963, pp. 133–143.

19. Gager, *Moses*, p. 118.

20. See also Gager, *Moses*, p. 120.

21. See also J. Yoyotte, L'Égypte ancienne, p. 141.

22. "tends to confirm our view that the expulsion story itself, in its pre-Mosaic [Egyptian] form, is the source for the themes of sacrilege and misanthropy in Moses' advice to his people" (*Moses*, p. 120). Gager combines here in an inappropriate way the themes of sacrilege and misanthropy.

23. Gager, *Moses*, p. 119.

24. Levy, Divre Tacitus (below, n. 88), p. 25., n. 146, points out that the *misanthrōpia/odium generis humani* motif is attested quite frequently in Greek and Latin literature, but the examples he provides refer only to individuals, not to a whole people.

25. *GLAJJ*, vol. 1, p. 64. See also D. Mendels, "The Polemical Character of Manetho's *Aegyptiaca*," in H. Verdin, G. Schepens, and E. de Keyser, eds., *Purposes of History: Studies in Greek Historiography from the 4th to the 2nd Centuries B.C.*, Lovanii [Löwen] 1990, p. 109.

26. Ibid.

27. Even this is no definite proof since, e.g., Arrian also uses *legetai* or similar expressions when referring to his main (acknowledged) source; see A. B. Bosworth, *From Arrian to Alexander: Studies in Historical Interpretation*, Oxford 1988, p. 39. (I owe this reference to T. Spawforth.)

28. This particular element of Manetho's account may indicate that the impiety motif not only is connected with "foreigners" but also reflects internal Egyptian controversies. As to the latter one may speculate about the religious revolution of the Amarna period. See below, Chapter 9.

29. See on this in greater detail Raspe, *Die ägyptischen Exodustraditionen*, and P. Schäfer, "Die Manetho-Fragmente bei Josephus und die Anfänge des antiken 'Antisemitismus,'" in *Aporemata*, I, in press.

30. This is Gager's translation: *Moses*, p. 117.

31. When dealing with Manetho, Gager leaves it open whether the *misoxenia* motif in #238 belongs to Manetho or to Pseudo-Manetho and explicitly only assigns the identification of Moses and Osarseph in #250 to Pseudo-Manetho (*Moses*, p. 117f.). When dealing with Lysimachus, however, he states that it is Pseudo-Manetho according to whom "Moses forbade his followers to associate with any except members of their own group" (ibid., p. 119).

32. Although he did not point to this specific aspect of the story, Stern is right in arguing that it is not Manetho, and certainly not Pseudo-Manetho, who "invented" the combination of the story of the polluted people and their allies with that of the Jews and Moses. Weill had already argued (*La Fin du Moyen Empire Égyptien*, p. 104) that the fusion of Egyptian and Jewish elements belongs to Hecataeus' version of the story. Gager (*Moses*, p. 116, n. 6) mentions this and even concludes that "this would undermine Meyer's argument that Manetho *could* not have referred to the Jews in his history of Egypt." This does not prevent him, however, from boldly concluding: "there is general agreement that the underlying stories themselves, of which there were many versions . . . reach far back into Egyptian history and that their application to the Jews is a secondary phenomenon." The application to the Jews may well reach back at least into Hecataeus after all.

33. *Contra Apionem*, II, 148 (trans. H. St. J. Thackeray, *LCL*).

34. *GLAJJ*, vol. 1, pp. 148ff.

35. Eusebius, *Praeparatio Evangelica*, IX, 19,1 = *GLAJJ*, vol. 1, p. 150.

36. *Contra Apionem*, II, 16.

37. Ibid., II, 148.

38. Dislike of foreigners and all human beings is more or less the same because *misanthrōpia* most likely is directed toward foreigners and not toward members of their own kin.

39. *Bibliotheca Historica*, I, 28,2 = *GLAJJ*, vol. 1, no. 55.

40. Ibid., I, 28,3 and I, 55,5 = *GLAJJ*, vol. 1, no. 57.

41. *GLAJJ*, vol. 1, p. 167.

42. *Bibliotheca Historica*, 40,3,1–3; see above.

43. *Bibliotheca Historica*, 34/35,1,1f., preserved in Photius' *Bibliotheca*, ed. Bekker, cod. 244, p. 379 = *GLAJJ*, vol. 1, no. 63 (trans. F. R. Walton, *LCL*).

44. See the discussion in *GLAJJ*, vol. 1, pp. 142ff. and 184. Stern, ibid., p. 142, and Gager, *Moses*, p. 126, have expressed some reservations.

45. Unfortunately, neither Gager nor Stern deals with this version of the Exodus story in Diodorus in any detail, mainly because they are preoccupied with Moses and the ass. Gager in his chapter on Moses and the Exodus (*Moses*, pp. 124ff.) refers to it only very briefly, leaving out of his quotation the most important parts, and maintains that "Diodorus stands closest to Lysimachus" (*Moses*, p. 124, n. 27). In his book *The Origins of Anti-Semitism* he does not deal with this version at all but only with Diodorus' first-mentioned two passages on the Egyptian origin of the Jews, taking these as evidence "that this claim [the Egyptian origin] was separable from and perhaps ultimately secondary to the

framework of anti-Jewish polemic" (*Origins*, p. 126), the latter being "definitely of Alexandrian origin" (*Moses*, p. 126).

46. Gager, *Moses*, p. 132.

47. A "forceful capture of Judea," Gager's last common feature between Diodorus and Lysimachus, is doubtful in both.

48. *Geographica*, 16,2,35f. = *GLAJJ*, vol. 1, no. 115 (trans. H. L. Jones, *LCL*). Cf. also *Historica Hypomnemata*, cited in Josephus, *Antiquitates*, 14, 118 = *GLAJJ*, vol. 1, no. 105.

49. *Origins*, p. 73.

50. Trans. Gager, ibid.

51. Cf. *GLAJJ*, vol. 1, p. 264. Stern himself is very reserved with regard to this question and even ponders the possibility "that Strabo is not merely derivative" (ibid., p. 266). Cf. Gager, *Origins*, p. 74: "No one would wish to deny that Strabo made use of sources, but neither does it seem plausible any longer to assume that his own contribution amounted to nothing more than superficial redaction."

52. *Aegyptiaca*, cited in Diodorus Siculus, *Bibliotheca Historica*, 40,3,4 = *GLAJJ*, vol. 1, no. 11.

53. Ibid.

54. *GLAJJ*, vol. 1, p. 305.

55. Strabo, *Geographica*, 16,2,36 (trans. Gager, *Origins*, p. 73).

56. Ibid., 37.

57. Hecataeus, *Aegyptiaca*, 40,3,8.

58. Gager, *Origins*, p. 73.

59. Ibid., p. 73f.

60. Justin, *Historiae Philippicae*, Libri XXXVI Epitoma, 2,1ff. = *GLAJJ*, vol. 1, no. 137 (trans. J. S. Watson, *LCL*).

61. Ibid., 2,8.10.

62. Ibid., 2,15.

63. Gager, *Origins*, p. 71.

64. Strabo likes the Jews of the remote past and does not mention the *misoxenia* motif in connection with their expulsion from Egypt, but he does not esteem very highly the contemporary Jews, who are characterized by their *deisidaimonia*; Pompeius does mention the *misoxenia* motif but changes it considerably—certainly not because of the Jews of ancient Egypt but rather to explain the behavior of contemporary Jews (it is not by coincidence that he also explains the Sabbath).

65. See A. Güdemann, art. "Lysimachos (20)," *PW*, XXVII, 1928, cols. 32ff.

66. I, 304–311 = Stern, *GLAJJ*, vol. 1, no. 158 (trans. H. St. J. Thackeray, *LCL*).

67. Ibid., I, 309.

68. The king's name (Bocchoris vs. Amenophis) and the oracle (the oracle of Ammon vs. the diviner Amenophis).

69. *Contra Apionem*, I, 305. Lysimachus runs into contradiction when he distinguishes between the lepers and the impure persons and identifies the Jews with the lepers only, because the lepers are being drowned and only the unclean people are banished to the wilderness and thus "saved." See also *GLAJJ*, vol. 1, pp. 385f.

70. Stern, *GLAJJ*, vol. 1, p. 382.

71. To use Stern's words with regard to Strabo, *GLAJJ*, vol. 1, p. 266.

72. *Contra Apionem*, II, 10 = *GLAJJ*, vol. 1, no. 164 (trans. H. St. J. Thackeray, *LCL*).

73. Ibid., II, 15.

74. Which is, as Stern notices, in accord with Lysimachus' account; see *GLAJJ*, vol. 1, pp. 385 and 397.

75. Which is, according to Josephus himself, in accord with Lysimachus. When he quotes Lysimachus (*Contra Apionem*, I, 304–311) he doesn't mention this number, however, but speaks only of the "victims of disease being very numerous."

76. *Contra Apionem*, II, 21.

77. Gager, *Origins*, p. 45.

78. On human sacrifice see below, Chapter 2.

79. *Moses*, p. 123.

80. E. Schwartz, art. "Chaeremon," *PW*, III, 1899, cols. 2025ff.

81. H. I. Bell, *Jews and Christians in Egypt*, London and Oxford 1924, pp. 34ff.; *Corpus Papyrorum Judaicarum*, ed. V. A. Tcherikover, A. Fuks, and M. Stern, Cambridge, Mass., 1957–1964, vol. 2, no. 153.

82. *Aegyptiaca Historia*, cited in Josephus, *Contra Apionem*, I, 289–292 (trans. H. St. J. Thackeray, *LCL*) = *GLAJJ*, vol. 1, no. 178. Cf. P. W. van der Horst, *Chaeremon: Egyptian Priest and Stoic Philosopher*, Leiden 1984 (²1987), pp. 8f. and 49f.

83. Ibid.

84. *GLAJJ*, vol. 1, pp. 417 and 420; Gager, *Moses*, p. 121.

85. On the motif of Isis' anger which resulted in an expulsion of the Jews see the fragment of the papyrus of the third century C.E.: *CPJ*, vol. 3, no. 520; M. Stern, Nevuah, pp. 223–227; id., *GLAJJ*, vol. 1, p. 420. The papyrus refers to the Jews with much more hostility than Chaeremon in his account of the Exodus tradition.

86. *Moses*, p. 121.

87. Stern, *GLAJJ*, vol. 2, p. 1.

88. *Historiae*, V, 3:1–4:2 (trans. C. H. Moore, *LCL*) = *GLAJJ*, vol. 2, no. 281. I refer only to those elements of Tacitus' account which are pertinent to the Exodus tradition. On Tacitus and the Jews see H. Lewy, "Divre Tacitus 'al qadmoniut ha-yehudim," *Zion* 8, 1942/43, pp. 1–34 and 61–84; J. Lévy, "Tacite et l'origine du peuple juif," *Latomus* 5, 1946, pp. 331–340; A. M. A. Hospers-Jansen, *Tacitus over de Joden. Hist. 5,2–13,* Groningen 1949; B. Blumenkranz, "Tacite antisémite ou xénophobe? (A propos de deux livres récents)," *REJ* 111, 1951–52, pp. 187–191; B. Wardy, "Jewish Religion in Pagan Literature during the Late Republic and Early Empire," in *ANRW*, II, 19.1, Berlin-New York 1979, pp. 613–635. H. Heinen, "Ägyptische Grundlagen des antiken Antijudaismus. Zum Judenexkurs des Tacitus, Historien V 2–13," *Trierer Theologische Zeitschrift* 102, 1992, pp. 124–149, also emphasizes the Egyptian provenance of Tacitus' attacks on the Jews.

89. Moore has "all other *religions*," which is a quite inaccurate translation of *ceteris mortalibus*.

90. See Stern, *GLAJJ*, vol. 2, p. 2, and Gager, *Moses*, p. 127.

91. Pace Stern, *GLAJJ*, vol. 2, p. 35, who argues that "Tacitus' version regards the emergence of the Jewish people as resulting from the expulsion of the contaminated rabble."

92. *Aegyptiaca*, cited in Josephus, *Contra Apionem*, I, 310 = *GLAJJ*, vol. 1, p. 384f. He leaves it open, however, whether this applies also to Judea, but one might well get the impression from Lysimachus' account that the former inhabitants of Judea were maltreated by the Jews.

93. See Lewy, Divre Tacitus, pp. 32ff., and *GLAJJ*, vol. 2, p. 41. Lewy also points out that Tacitus describes the Jewish customs as a kind of *coniuratio* which threatens the *pax Romana* (pp. 69ff.).

94. *Historiae*, V,5,2.

95. Gager, *Moses*, p. 127f.

2. THE JEWISH GOD

1. Deut. 5:7; 6:4; Ex. 20:3.

2. Ex. 20:4; Deut. 5:8.

3. With regard to the Persians it is found in Herodotus even earlier; see Herodotus, I, 131.

4. *De Pietate*, cited in Porphyry, *De Abstinentia*, II, 26 = *GLAJJ*, vol. 1, no. 4 (trans. M. Stern).

5. W. Jaeger, "Greeks and Jews," *JR* 18, 1938, p. 133; Stern, *GLAJJ*, vol. 1, p. 11.

6. Hengel, *Judentum und Hellenismus,* p. 466.

7. Some scholars argue that Theophrastus' description of the Jews in *De Pietate* depends on Hecataeus; see Jaeger, *Diokles von Karystos,* Berlin 1938, pp. 134ff.; id., Greeks and Jews, pp. 131ff.; Hengel, *Judentum und Hellenismus,* p. 466, n. 4; against this Stern, *GLAJJ,* vol. 1, pp. 8f.

8. *Aegyptiaca,* cited in Diodorus Siculus, *Bibliotheca Historica,* XL, 3:4 = *GLAJJ,* vol. 1, no. 11 (trans. F. R. Walton, *LCL*).

9. It may reflect the criticism of polytheism by Xenophanes; see Hengel, *Judentum und Hellenismus,* p. 466.

10. *Aegyptiaca,* ibid.

11. Above, Chapter 1.

12. Ezra 1:2.

13. Ezra 5:11 (God of heaven and earth); 5:12; 6:9; Neh. 1:4.5; 2:4.20; cf. A. Cowley, *Aramaic Papyri of the Fifth Century B.C.,* Oxford 1923 (30:15): *mara she-mayya* ("sovereign of heaven").

14. Dan. 2:18f.37.44 and more often; see Hengel, *Judentum und Hellenismus,* p. 544, n. 239. Even "Heaven(s)" alone can stand for "God"; see, e.g., Dan. 4:23.

15. Cf. A. Vincent, *La Religion des Judéo-Araméens d'Éléphantine,* Paris 1937, pp. 116ff.

16. Vincent, *Religion,* pp. 119ff.; Hengel, *Judentum und Hellenismus,* pp. 542ff.

17. Hengel, *Judentum und Hellenismus,* pp. 541ff.

18. *Aegyptiaca,* cited in Josephus, *Contra Apionem,* I, 239 = *GLAJJ,* vol. 1, no. 21; see above, Chapter 1.

19. Manetho, the Egyptian priest who was well acquainted with Greek culture, may have considered the Jewish refusal an attack on the very principle of traditional religious values.

20. See above, Chapter 1.

21. Cited in Augustine, *De Civitate Dei,* IV, 31 = *GLAJJ,* vol. 1, no. 72a (trans. W. M. Green, *LCL*).

22. Cited in Augustine, *De Consensu Evangelistarum,* I, 22:30 = *GLAJJ,* vol. 1, no. 72b (trans. M. Stern).

23. See also Varro, cited in Augustine, *De Consensu Evangelistarum,* I, 23:31 = *GLAJJ,* vol. 1, no. 72c, and ibid., I, 27:42 = *GLAJJ,* vol. 1, no. 72a.

24. Many references in Jesus Sirach, Daniel, the Genesis Apocryphon, Jubilees, 1 Henoch, Judith, Tobit, and the Scroll of Psalms from Qumran; see Hengel, *Judentum und Hellenismus,* p. 544, n. 240.

25. It is somewhat rushed, therefore, to say the least, to argue that "even Varro . . . says nothing about Jewish monotheism but seems, by implication, to

look on the Jewish religion as a kind of henotheism, that is, a belief in one god as supreme without denying the existence of other gods" (Feldman, *Jew and Gentile*, p. 150); see also the following quotation from Varro.

26. Augustine, *De Civitate Dei*, IV, 9 (trans. W. M. Green, *LCL*).

27. Hengel, *Judentum und Hellenismus*, p. 471; Stern, *GLAJJ*, vol. 1, p. 305.

28. See the full text quoted above, Chapter 1.

29. Feldman, *Jew and Gentile*, p. 150.

30. *Scholia in Lucanum*, II, 593 = *GLAJJ*, vol. 1, no. 133 (trans. M. Stern).

31. *GLAJJ*, vol. 1, p. 330.

32. Lydus, *De Mensibus*, IV, 53 = *GLAJJ*, vol. 1, no. 134 (trans. M. Stern).

33. See the thorough study by P. W. van der Horst, "The Altar of the 'Unknown God' in Athens (Acts 17:23) and the Cult of 'Unknown Gods' in the Hellenistic and Roman Periods," in *ANRW*, II, 18.2, Berlin and New York 1989, pp. 1444ff.; *GLAJJ*, vol. 1, p. 331. However, as has been mentioned also by van der Horst, one should not forget that the term *agnōstos* in relation to the Jewish God is already attested by Josephus (*Contra Apionem*, II, 167).

34. The concept of *di incerti* itself, with no relation to the Jews, is found in Varro (cf. E. Norden, *Agnostos Theos*, Leipzig and Berlin 1923, pp. 61f.; G. Wissowa, "Die Varronischen *Di Certi* und *Incerti*," *Hermes* 56, 1921, pp. 113–130); whether Virgil also has it in mind when he refers to "this grove . . ." as "a god's dwelling, though whose we know not": *hoc nemus . . . (qui deus incertum est) habitat deus* (*Aeneis*, VIII, 351f.; trans. J. W. Mackail, *The Aeneid of Virgil*, London 1885, p. 180), seems to be doubtful, pace Stern, *GLAJJ*, vol. 1, p. 439.

35. *Pharsalia*, II, 592f.: "and Judea given over to the worship of an unknown god *(et dedita sacris incerti Iudaea dei)*"; *GLAJJ*, no. 191 (trans. J. D. Duft, *LCL*). The Greek term for *incertus* is *adēlos;* see Lydus, *De Mensibus*, IV, 53 = *GLAJJ*, vol. 2, no. 367: "In conformity with Livy Lucan says that the Temple of Jerusalem belongs to an uncertain god *(adēlou theou)*."

36. M. Schanz and C. Hosius, *Geschichte der römischen Literatur*, vol. 2, München ⁴1935, p. 499.

37. *Contra Apionem*, II, 65.

38. Ibid., II, 66. See also ibid., I, 224f.: "since our religion is as far removed from that which is in vogue among them as is the nature of God from that of irrational beasts" (trans. H. St. J. Thackeray, *LCL*).

39. Ibid., II, 68.

40. *Historiae*, V, 5:4 = *GLAJJ*, vol. 2, no. 281 (trans. C. H. Moore, *LCL*).

41. Heubner and Fauth translate, probably more correctly, "Mischwesen aus Mensch und Tier"; see H. Heubner and W. Fauth, *P. Cornelius Tacitus: Die Historien. Kommentar*, vol. 5: *Fünftes Buch*, Heidelberg 1982, pp. 79f.

42. See esp. E. Wolff, "Das geschichtliche Verstehen in Tacitus Germania," *Hermes* 69, 1934, pp. 134ff.; R. T. Scott, *Religion and Philosophy in the Histories of Tacitus,* Rome 1968, pp. 82f., n. 79; Stern, *GLAJJ,* vol. 2, p. 43.

43. *Germania,* 9 (trans. M. Hutton and E. H. Warmington, *LCL*).

44. Cf. R. T. Scott, *Religion,* p. 82, n. 79: "The Roman consistently envisaged the divine as forces intruding into history, not as anthropomorphic. In the performance of ritual, not in the physical representations of gods, was the ethos and essence of Roman religion."

45. See Stern, *GLAJJ,* vol. 2, p. 43, following E. Wolff, *Das geschichtliche Verstehen,* p. 135.

46. Varro (see above) and later Cassius Dio (see below).

47. See above, Chapter 1.

48. It is most revealing that Feldman in his chapter "Attacks on Jewish Theology" (*Jew and Gentile,* pp. 149–153), where he discusses the pagan response to the Jewish belief in one God, does not mention this paragraph of Tacitus (he only refers to the passage in which Tacitus opposes the identification of the Jewish God with Dionysus). But see his "Pro-Jewish Intimations in Tacitus' Account of Jewish Origins," *REJ* 150, 1991, pp. 331–360.

49. *Saturae,* VI, 544f. = *GLAJJ,* vol. 2, no. 299 (trans. G. G. Ramsay, *LCL*). The first of these three parodistic titles probably refers to the Rabbinic interpreters of Jewish law, the second to the High Priest (Johanan [Hans] Levy, *Studies in Jewish Hellenism,* Jerusalem 1960 [in Hebrew], p. 202), and the third to the prophets. Some consideration has been devoted to the question of exactly why Juvenal calls the Jewess a high priestess "of the tree," but most exegetes of this passage agree that it is a reference to the trees outside the Porta Capena in Rome where the Jews were allowed to stay (see *Saturae,* III, 13ff., and J. D. Duff, ed., *D. Iunii Iuvenalis Saturae XIV. Fourteen Satires of Juvenal,* Cambridge 1898 [reprint 1970], pp. 247f.; *GLAJJ,* vol. 2, p. 101). In addition to this, it has been suggested that the tree could be "a sneering allusion to the fact that the Jewish Temple was destroyed, so that the Jews had now to worship under the trees instead" (Duff, *Saturae,* p. 248). This is possible, but one may also consider the simpler explanation that Juvenal introduces the tree in order to describe the nature of the worship of "highest heaven," i.e. that it took place in groves (see Tacitus, *Germania,* 9) under trees.

50. Chapter 3.

51. *Saturae,* XIV, 97.

52. It is probable that Juvenal alludes here to Aristophanes' criticism of Socrates and his followers who abandoned the gods of Greece and instead worshiped the clouds. See Aristophanes, *Nephelai,* 253f., 269, 291, 328f., 365, 423f., and Duff, *Saturae,* p. 415; Hengel, *Judentum und Hellenismus,* p. 486; *GLAJJ,* vol. 2, p. 107.

53. *Apotelesmatica*, II, 3:31 = *GLAJJ*, vol. 2, no. 336a.

54. Stern, *GLAJJ*, vol. 2, p. 163.

55. Origen, *Contra Celsum*, I, 15 = *GLAJJ*, vol. 2, no. 364b (trans. H. Chadwick).

56. Lydus, *De Mensibus*, IV, 53 = *GLAJJ*, vol. 2, no. 367 (trans. M. Stern).

57. The reference by Stern (*GLAJJ*, vol. 2, p. 215) to Sap. Sal. 14:21, "they [the idolaters] confer on sticks and stones the name that none may share *(to akoinōnēton onoma)*," does not elucidate Numenius' use of the term *akoinōnētos*.

58. The most remarkable example of this is the advice of Antiochus VII's counselors "to wipe out completely the nation of the Jews" because they are *akoinōnētoi*.

59. See, e.g., the famous dictum: "For what is Plato, but Moses speaking in Attic?" (Numenius, cited in Clemens Alexandrinus, *Stromata*, I, 22:150:4 = *GLAJJ*, vol. 2, no. 363a; trans. M. Stern).

60. Stern, *GLAJJ*, vol. 2, p. 225.

61. The *Alēthēs Logos* was written, according to most scholars, between 177 and 180 C.E.; see the summary by Stern, *GLAJJ*, vol. 2, p. 224, n. 1.

62. Following the line of tradition of the early Egyptian writers; see above, Chapter 1.

63. *Alēthēs Logos*, cited in Origen, *Contra Celsum*, I, 2:24 = *GLAJJ*, vol. 2, no. 375 (pp. 233f. and 265; trans. H. Chadwick). The "Most High" *(hypsistos)* is mentioned again in VIII, 69 (= *GLAJJ*, vol. 2, pp. 263 and 292).

64. He was the first pagan writer who drew extensively upon the Bible; see Stern, *GLAJJ*, vol. 2, p. 228.

65. *Alēthēs Logos*, cited in Origen, *Contra Celsum*, V, 2:41 = *GLAJJ*, vol. 2, no. 375 (pp. 256 and 286).

66. *Alēthēs Logos*, ibid.

67. *Alēthēs Logos*, ibid., V, 2:59 (= *GLAJJ*, vol. 2, pp. 258 and 287).

68. *Historia Romana*, XXXVII, 16:5–17:2 = *GLAJJ*, vol. 2, no. 406 (trans. E. Cary). The *Historia Romana* was compiled between 197 and 207 C.E. and written down between 207 and 219 C.E.; see F. Millar, *A Study of Cassius Dio*, Oxford 1964, p. 30.

69. Stern, *GLAJJ*, vol. 2, p. 353.

70. Ibid., p. 347.

71. For the meaning of *arrētos* as "ineffable" see also H. Lewy, *Chaldaean Oracles and Theurgy*, Cairo 1956, reprint Paris 1978, p. 77, n. 38, and p. 328, n. 59.

72. *Historia Romana*, XXXVII, 17:4. He goes on to explain the custom of referring the days to the seven planets, apropos of his remark that the Jews dedicate the day of Saturn to their God.

73. Lydus, *De Mensibus*, IV, 53 = *GLAJJ*, vol. 2, no. 452 (trans. M. Stern). It is uncertain whether Lydus quotes here from Porphyry's *De Philosophia ex Oraculis Haurienda* or from an otherwise unknown commentary by Porphyry on the Chaldaean Oracles. While earlier research was in favor of the former, more recent research advocates the latter; see *GLAJJ*, vol. 2, p. 433.

74. *Chaldaean Oracles*, p. 77.

75. Ibid., p. 319.

76. Lewy, ibid.

77. Lewy, ibid., pp. 117ff., 318ff.

78. See also Lewy, ibid., p. 9, n. 23.

79. In contrast with this stands the remark in *De Philosophia ex Oraculis Haurienda* (cited in Augustine, *De Civitate Dei*, XIX, 23), ascribed to an oracle of Apollo: "In one truly God *(Deum vero)*, the creator and the king prior to all things *(generatorem et in regem ante omnia)*, before whom tremble heaven and earth and the sea and the hidden places beneath, and the very divinities *(ipsa numina)* shudder; their law is the Father *(Pater)* whom the holy Hebrews greatly honour" (= *GLAJJ*, no. 451; trans. W. C. Greene, *LCL*). Stern, who favors the assumption that the quotation from Lydus is taken from a different and later work by Porphyry, argues that Porphyry in his former work, *De Philosophia ex Oraculis Haurienda*, "had no difficulty in admitting that the God worshipped by the Hebrews was both the Creator God and the Highest God" (ibid., p. 433). But since the quotation from *De Philosophia* also displays Neoplatonic and Chaldaean terminology (the "Father" and the "King" are mythical designations of the supreme God as distinguished from the demiurge, employed earlier by Plato and also by Numenius and Plotinus as well as by the Chaldaean Oracles; see Lewy, *Chaldaean Oracles*, pp. 76ff., 327f.), the difference between the two quotations becomes even more conspicuous. Neither solution (two quotations from one and the same work; quotations from two different works) answers the question of why Porphyry in one case identified the Jewish God with both the Supreme Being and the demiurge, and in the second case with the demiurge only as opposed to the first God and the Good. In *De Philosophia ex Oraculis Haurienda* (cited in Eusebius, *Praeparatio Evangelica*, IX, 10:4 = *GLAJJ*, no. 450; trans. E. H. Gifford) he attributes to the Oracle of Apollo the enigmatic saying: "Only Chaldees and Hebrews wisdom found in the pure worship of a self-born God."

80. Lydus, *De Mensibus*, IV, 53 = *GLAJJ*, vol. 2, nos. 467, 544, and 545: "But the schools of Iamblichus, Syrianus and Proclus consider him [the god worshiped by the Jews] to be the demiurge *(dēmiourgon)*, calling him the god of the four elements" (trans. M. Stern).

81. Stern, *GLAJJ*, vol. 2, p. 545.

82. *Contra Galilaeos,* 42E/43B = *GLAJJ,* vol. 2, no. 481a (trans. W. C. Wright, *LCL*); see also 238B.

83. Ibid., 93E; cf. 106E.

84. Ibid., 155C/D.

85. Ibid., 155D/E.

86. Ibid., 96C, where he distinguishes between "the immediate creator of this universe" and "the gods who are superior to this creator."

87. Ibid., 49E. He proves this with an interpretation of Gen. 1:2 which comes very close to certain Rabbinical exegeses or refutations of exegeses respectively; cf. Gen. R. 1:9 on Gen 1:1 (J. Theodor and C. Albeck, eds., *Bereshit Rabba,* Jerusalem ²1965, p. 8).

88. Ibid., 106D–E.

89. Ibid., 138C–D.

90. Ibid., 194D.

91. Ibid., 201E.

92. Ibid., 201E–202A.

93. Ibid., 238B–C.

94. Ibid., 306B.

95. Cf. ibid., 253B: "Moses . . . very many times says that men ought to honour one God only *(hena theon monon),* and in fact names him the Highest *(epi pasin)*"; according to 290E Moses taught "that there was only one God *(hena kai monon . . . theon),* but that he had many sons who divided the nations among themselves."

96. *Contra Galilaeos,* 354B = *GLAJJ,* vol. 2, no. 481a (trans. W. C. Wright, *LCL*).

97. *Ad Theodorum,* 453C-454B = *GLAJJ,* vol. 2, no. 483 (trans. W. C. Wright, *LCL*).

98. Ibid.

99. On the authenticity of the letter see Stern, *GLAJJ,* vol. 2, pp. 508ff.

100. See Stern, GLAJJ, vol. 2, p. 508, and n. 9.

101. *Ad Communitatem Iudaeorum,* 396D–398 = GLAJJ, vol. 2, no. 486a (trans. W. C. Wright, *LCL*).

102. See the references in *GLAJJ,* vol. 2, p. 567. It should be noticed, however, that *hoi kreittones* can mean "the Higher Powers" = "the Gods" in classical Greek.

103. However, according to Lydus, *De Mensibus,* IV, 53, Julian also used the older term *hypsistos theos.* Whether this is Julian's original language or due to Lydus' linguistic usage cannot be decided with certainty.

104. The use of the term *dēmiourgos* in *Fragmentum Epistulae,* 292C (= *GLAJJ,* vol. 2, no. 484), has no specific connotation.

105. *Scriptores Historiae Augustae, Divus Claudius,* 2:4 = *GLAJJ*, vol. 2, no. 526.

106. The Jewish author of the Letter of Aristeas had already identified Zeus with the God of the Jews (Ep. Arist. 16).

107. *De Civitate Dei,* IV, 11 (trans. W. M. Green, *LCL*); cf. ibid., VII, 13: "But why should I say more about this Jupiter, to whom perhaps all the other Gods are to be carried back?"

108. Hengel suggests that Varro depends on his "oriental teachers, the stoicizing platonist Antiochus of Ascalon, and the platonizing stoic Poseidonius of Apamea"; *Judentum und Hellenismus,* p. 477.

109. Ibid.

110. Diogenes Laertius, *Vitae Philosophorum,* VII, 135 (trans. R. D. Hicks, *LCL*).

111. Cf. F. Cumont, "Les Mystères de Sabazius et le Judaïsme," *CRAI,* 1906, pp. 63–79; id., "A propos de Sabazius et du Judaïsme," *Musée Belge* 14, 1910, pp. 55–60; R. Reitzenstein, *Die hellenistischen Mysterienreligionen,* Leipzig-Berlin ³1927, pp. 104ff.; M. P. Nilsson, *Geschichte der griechischen Religion,* vol. 2, München ²1961, pp. 660–667; Hengel, *Judentum und Hellenismus,* pp. 479f.; Stern, *GLAJJ,* p. 359 (with some reservations); a very good summary is provided by S. E. Johnson, "The Present State of Sabazios Research," in *ANRW,* II, 17.3, Berlin and New York 1984, pp. 1538–1613, esp. pp. 1602–1607.

112. Cf. Stern, *GLAJJ,* vol. 1, p. 357.

113. On the names of the praetor and the consuls and the corresponding date cf. Stern, *GLAJJ,* vol. 1, pp. 358f.

114. Valerius Maximus, *Facta ed Dicta Memorabilia,* I, 3:3 (Epitoma Iulii Paridis) = *GLAJJ,* vol. 1, no. 147b. (trans. M. Stern).

115. Nilsson, *Geschichte,* pp. 662ff.

116. References to earlier literature in *GLAJJ,* vol. 1, p. 359, to which should be added M. Simon, "Jupiter-Yahvé. Sur un essai de théologie pagano-juive," *Numen* 23, 1976, pp. 40–66 = id., *Le christianisme antique et son contexte religieux: Scripta Varia,* vol. 2, Tübingen 1981, pp. 622–648.

117. Nilsson, *Geschichte,* p. 662 (Sabbaths as events of convivial drinking could also foster the identification with Dionysus); H. Solin, "Juden und Syrer im westlichen Teil der römischen Welt," in *ANRW,* II, 29.2, Berlin and New York 1983, p. 606, n. 25.

118. Schürer, *History,* vol. 3, p. 19; Friedländer, *Sittengeschichte,* vol. 3, p. 209; H. J. Leon, *The Jews of Ancient Rome,* Philadelphia 1960, pp. 2ff.; Reitzenstein, *Mysterienreligionen,* pp. 106f., n. 1; Hengel, *Judentum und Hellenismus,* p. 479.

119. See Stern, *GLAJJ*, vol. 1, p. 359.

120. This possibility is mentioned but not favored by Hengel, *Judentum und Hellenismus*, pp. 478f.

121. E. N. Lane, "Sabazius and the Jews in Valerius Maximus: a Re-examination," *JRS* 69, 1979, pp. 35–38.

122. This has been suggested also by Johnson, Present State, p. 1603. The similarity of "Sabazius" with "Sabaoth/Sabbath" of course works in both directions, a Jewish syncretistic cult and pagan theocrasy.

123. Nepotianus' epitome, which does not mention the Jupiter Sabazius but only an attempt of the Jews "to transmit their sacred rites *(sacra sua)* to the Romans," speaks in favor of this assumption (Stern, *GLAJJ*, vol. 1, no. 147a).

124. The date of Cornelius Labeo is controversial and varies between the beginning of the second and of the third centuries; see Nilsson, *Geschichte*, p. 477, n. 8, who advocates the later date. More recently P. Mastrandrea, *Un Neoplatonico Latino: Cornelio Labeone,* Leiden 1979, p. 193, opts for the second half of the third century.

125. Cf. Nilsson, *Geschichte*, pp. 475ff.

126. Following Nilsson's conjecture (*Geschichte*, p. 478, n. 1), reading *Iakchon,* i.e. Dionysus, instead of *Iaō*. This fits in with the line of Macrobius' (Cornelius Labeo's) argument according to which the four gods of the Orphic verse (Zeus, Hades, Helios, Dionysus) are to be identified with Iao.

127. Cornelius Labeo, *De Oraculo Apollinis Clarii,* cited in Macrobius, *Saturnalia,* I, 18:18–21 = *GLAJJ,* vol. 2, no. 445 (trans. M. Stern); and see Mastandrea, *Un Neoplatonico Latino,* pp. 159ff.

128. Iao as the name of the Jewish God is first mentioned by Diodorus Siculus (*Bibliotheca Historica,* I, 94:2) and by Varro (cited in Lydus, *De Mensibus,* IV, 53). It is an original Jewish term which is well attested by the Aramaic papyri from Elephantine from the Persian period (A. Cowley, *Aramaic Papyri of the Fifth Century,* Oxford 1923, pp. 16, 66, 70, 85, 99, 112f., 119f., 125, 135, 149, 162; E. G. Kraeling, *The Brooklyn Museum Aramaic Papyri,* New Haven 1953, pp. 84f., 132, 142, 154, 168, 192, 236, 238, 248, 250, 270, 272). It does not occur in the *textus receptus* of the Septuagint, "having become a *vocabulum ineffabile* for the Jews" (Stern, *GLAJJ,* vol. 1, p. 172), but it does appear on a fragment of the Septuagint version of Leviticus, probably from the first century B.C.E., thus exactly from the same time as Diodorus (O. Eissfeldt, *Einleitung in das Alte Testament,* Tübingen ³1964, p. 960). In addition, the name is most extensively used in magical texts of almost any provenance and language. Hence it seems that it has gone out of fashion gradually on "official" documents and has been favorably adopted by pagan writers and by literary genres (magical papyri, amulets, etc.) which tend to be syncretistic.

129. Nilsson, *Geschichte,* p. 478.

130. While I agree, therefore, with Nock that Clarus stands for "une tendance systématique à une unité de foi qui pouvait comprendre jusqu'au dieu du judaïsme," I am not convinced that it aimed particularly at the Jewish God and at realizing "la conciliation du monothéisme et du polythéisme"; cf. A. D. Nock, "Oracles Théologiques," *Revue des Études Anciennes* 30, 1928, p. 286.

131. *Quaestiones Convivales,* IV, 5:3 = *GLAJJ,* vol. 1, no. 258 (trans. H. B. Hoffleit, *LCL.*)

132. Ibid., IV, 6:2.

133. Ibid.

134. See Deut. 16:13ff. for the connection with the ingathering of the produce from the threshing-floor and the winepress and for the merry character of the feast; Neh. 8:15 mentions the booths made of "branches of olive and wild olive, myrtle and palm, and other leafy boughs."

135. This has been suggested by Stern, *GLAJJ,* vol. 1, p. 561.

136. Stern, ibid.

137. By this he probably alludes to much more "convivial" Sabbath celebrations than one might imagine from Rabbinic literature.

138. *Quaestiones Convivales,* ibid. To be sure, the identification of the Jewish God with Dionysus is Plutarch's, not the Jews' suggestion, and there is no evidence for a Jewish reaction to it. The only historical piece of information we have is that the Jews were forced to participate in the cult of Dionysus during the reign of Antiochus IV Epiphanes (2 Macc. 6:7) but this, of course, was abolished by the Maccabees, and there is no reason to believe that Plutarch had access to this information or that he relied on any other evidence of a syncretistic Jewish-Dionysian cult at his time; rather his digression seems to be the result of learned speculation. On the Dionysus cult in Jerusalem, see Hengel, *Judentum und Hellenismus,* pp. 546ff.

139. See below, Chapter 3.

140. *Historiae,* V, 5:5 = *GLAJJ,* vol. 2, no. 281 (trans. C. H. Moore, *LCL*).

141. See, e.g., Hecataeus, *Aegyptiaca,* cited in Diodorus Siculus, *Bibliotheca Historica,* XL, 3:3–8.

142. See Tertullian, *Ad Nationes,* I, 14, and *Apologeticus,* XVI, 1–3; Minucius Felix, *Octavius* IX, 3, and the Palatine mockery crucifix: B. H. Stricker, "Asinarii," *Oudheidkundige mededelingen uit het Rijksmuseum van Oudheden te Leiden* 46, 1965, pp. 52–75; I. Oppelt, art. "Esel," in *RAC,* VI, Stuttgart 1966, cols. 592–594.

143. Josephus, *Contra Apionem,* II, 112–114; *GLAJJ,* vol. 1, no. 28 (trans. H. St. J. Thackeray, *LCL*).

144. See the commentary by Stern, *GLAJJ*, vol. 1, p. 101.

145. "Ritualmord und Eselskult. Ein Beitrag zur Geschichte antiker Publizistik," in id., *Studies in Jewish and Christian History*, vol. 2, Leiden 1980, p. 255.

146. *Antiquitates*, XIII, 275.

147. A. Jacoby, "Der angebliche Eselskult der Juden und Christen," *ARW* 25, 1927, p. 281.

148. Stern, *GLAJJ*, vol. 1, p. 100, with reference to Ecclesiasticus (Siracides) 50:25f.

149. Stern, *GLAJJ*, vol. 1, pp. 100f. and 97f. See E.Meyer, *Ursprung und Anfänge*, vol. 2, p. 33; W. Bousset and H. Gressmann, *Die Religion des Judentums im späthellenistischen Zeitalter*, Tübingen 1926, p. 76, n. 1.

150. See above, n. 145.

151. Ritualmord und Eselskult, p. 246.

152. Cf. Plutarch, *De Iside et Osiride*, 30, p. 362F; ibid., 50, p. 371C ("they assign to him the most stupid of the domesticated animals, the ass").

153. Ibid., 33, p. 364A.

154. Ibid., 39, p. 366C.

155. Ibid., e.g., 33, p. 364A; 36, p. 365B.

156. See H. Kees, art. "Seth," in *PW*, IV^2, 1923, col. 1919.

157. Kees, ibid., cols. 1905–1908; see Plutarch, *De Iside et Osiride*, 31, p. 363C, with regard to Artaxerxes Ochus: "This is also the reason why, since they hated Ochus most of all the Persian kings because he was a detested and abominable ruler, they nicknamed him 'the Ass'; and he remarked, 'But this Ass will feast upon your Bull', and slaughtered Apis [i.e. the incarnation of Osiris; cf. ibid., 29, p. 362D]"; see also ibid., 11, p. 355C, and Aelian, *Varia Historia*, IV, 8; id., *De Natura Animalium*, X, 28.

158. Ibid., 31, p. 363C-D = *GLAJJ*, vol. 1, no. 259 (trans. F. C. Babbitt).

159. See T. Hopfner, *Plutarch über Isis und Osiris*, vol. 2, Prague 1941, pp. 143ff.; J. G. Griffiths, *Plutarch, De Iside et Osiride*, [Cardiff] 1970, pp. 418f.; M. Wellmann, "Aegyptisches," *Hermes* 31, 1896, pp. 221–253 (Apion as Plutarch's possible source); K. Ziegler, *Plutarchos von Chaironeia*, Stuttgart 1949, p. 208 = *PW*, XXI, 1951, col. 845; Stern, *GLAJJ*, vol. 1, p. 563.

160. Ritualmord und Eselskult, pp. 247f. But not of the type "Rechtleitung durch Tiere" (guidance and rescue by animals) like Tacitus' etiology. The ass is not mentioned because it guided Typhon to Jerusalem but simply because it is the animal associated with Typhon.

161. Bickerman, ibid., p. 247.

162. See also Stern, *GLAJJ*, vol. 1, p. 563.

163. Manetho, *Aegyptiaca,* cited in Josephus, *Contra Apionem,* I, 228–250 = *GLAJJ,* vol. 1, no. 21; see above, Chapter 1.

164. Ibid., I, 237.

165. One may even speculate that they brought the worship of Typhon-Seth to Jerusalem.

166. One therefore need not take refuge in the explanation that the name Iao "is similar in sound to the Egyptian word for ass"; Stern, *GLAJJ,* vol. 1, p. 98, referring to Jacoby, Eselskult, pp. 265ff. See also S. Bochart, *Hierozoicon,* Frankfurt a.M. 1675, Lib. II, cols. 181. 220–228; Halévy, Calembour, p. 263; D. Simonsen, "Kleinigkeiten," in *Judaica. Festschrift zu Hermann Cohens Siebzig-stem Geburtstage,* Berlin 1912, p. 298; Bickerman, Ritualmord und Eselskult, p. 245.

167. See Stern, *GLAJJ,* vol. 1, p. 98 (with reference to Laqueur, *PW,* XV, p. 2251): "It is hardly to be supposed that Mnaseas invented either the original fable or its association with Palestinian conditions. He must have taken it over from his sources, in accordance with his usual procedure."

168. In addition to the Exodus motif.

169. *Contra Apionem,* II, 79 (trans. H. St. J. Thackeray, *LCL*).

170. See Stern, *GLAJJ,* vol. 1, p. 142 (with the relevant literature).

171. Diodorus Siculus, *Bibliotheca Historica,* XXXIV–XXXV, 1:3 = *GLAJJ,* vol. 1, no. 63 (trans. F. R. Walton, *LCL*).

172. The very location in the "innermost sanctuary" may be a clue.

173. *GLAJJ,* vol. 1, p. 143.

174. That Diodorus is independent of Posidonius here has already been suggested by F. M. T. de Liagre Böhl, *Opera Minora,* Groningen-Djakarta 1953, p. 124.

175. "Es ist wohl zu vermuten, daß Poseidonios, der auch sonst eine hohe Meinung über die jüdische Religion sowie über Moses äußerte, diesmal eine krasse und alberne Geschichte, wie von der der Anbetung des Eselskopfes, die er in seiner Quelle vorfand, durch die angeführte ersetzt hat" (Bickerman, Ritual-mord und Eselskult, p. 251).

176. "Ist das so, dann reichen wir mit der Eselsfabel dicht an die Zeit der Makkabäerkämpfe," ibid. Before this procedure he had reached only to about 100 B.C.E., simply by declaring, with no evidence, that Apollonius Molon's (lost) work *De Iudaeis* was Apion's direct *Vorlage,* and thus identifying Apion's version with Apollonius Molon; ibid., p. 250.

177. Ibid., p. 251.

178. Josephus, *Contra Apionem,* II, 80 (trans. H. St. J. Thackeray, *LCL*).

179. Ibid., II, 81–88.

180. Stern, *GLAJJ*, vol. 1, p. 141.

181. One should not forget the Egyptian origin of Apion.

182. The mention of Antiochus IV's entering the Temple could suggest his familiarity with Diodorus, but he also may have combined the well-known tradition of the spoliation of the Temple with the golden asinine head.

183. See Stern, *GLAJJ*, vol. 1, p. 531.

184. Suda, s. v. *Damokritos* = *GLAJJ*, vol. I, no. 247 (trans. M. Stern).

185. Tacitus, *Historiae*, V, 3:2 = *GLAJJ*, vol. 2, no. 281 (trans. C. H. Moore, *LCL*).

186. Bickerman, Ritualmord und Eselskult, p. 247.

187. IV, 5:2: "they honour the ass *(ton onon)* who first led them to a spring of water."

188. Bickerman, Ritualmord und Eselskult, p. 247: "Sie ist keineswegs, wie man gewöhnlich meint, 'antisemitisch', vielmehr eine gelehrte ätiologische Hypothese, die den Eselskult wissenschaftlich erklären soll."

189. *Historiae*, V, 4:2.

190. I do not think, therefore, that the "'effigies' here implies only an *anathēma* and not an object of worship" (Stern, *GLAJJ*, vol. 2, p. 37).

191. This is also made very clear by the immediately following sentence: "They likewise offer the ox, because the Egyptians worship Apis."

192. Josephus, *Contra Apionem*, II, 89.

193. The only other witness is Damocritus, who gives a slightly different account. The main differences are "every seventh year" instead of "annually," and the more precise description of how the "foreigner" was killed: "by carding his flesh into pieces."

194. *Contra Apionem*, II, 91–96 (trans. H. St. J. Thackeray, *LCL*).

195. Ritualmord und Eselskult (above, n. 145), pp. 225–245. See also D. Flusser, "'Alilot ha-dam' neged ha-yehudim le-'or ha-hashkafot shel ha-tequfah ha-hellenisṭit," in *Sefer Yoḥanan Lewy. Meḥqarim be-Hellenismus yehudi*, ed. M. Schwabe and J. Gutman, Jerusalem 1949, pp. 104–124.

196. His main proof, however, comes from the ancient Mexicans; ibid., pp. 236f.

197. "Einen schon Toten zu opfern, ist etwas zu spät"; Bickerman, ibid., p. 238.

198. Bickerman's claim that the sacrifice in our story is not consumed because its remains are thrown into a pit is also not very convincing. It rests on his assumption that *viscera* means "entrails," which obviously is influenced by the *coniuratio* stories he quotes. But *viscera* more precisely seems to be "flesh," i.e. all remains of the human body, "except skin, bones and

blood" (Thackeray, ad loc.)—there is therefore enough left to be thrown into a pit.

199. Ibid., p. 226.

200. There is some reason to believe that the whole passage (paragraphs 121–124) is misplaced and belongs after paragraph 99; see Thackeray, ad loc.

201. *Contra Apionem,* II, 121.

202. See above, Chapter 1.

203. That the *misoxenia* motif indeed was absent from Apion's version of the Exodus tradition known to Josephus may be inferred from the latter's remark on the oath of hostility: "Having once started false accusations, he should have said, 'show no goodwill to a single alien, above all to Egyptians'; for then this reference to the oath would have been in keeping with his original fiction, if, as we are given to understand, the cause of the expulsion of our forefathers by their Egyptian 'kinsmen' was not their malice, but their misfortunes."

204. *Contra Apionem,* II, 90–91.

205. Ritualmord und Eselskult, pp. 238ff.

206. This has also been emphasized by Flusser, ᶜAlilot ha-dam, p. 121 with n. 87.

207. A similar argument against Bickerman has been made by Stern, *GLAJJ,* vol. 1, p. 412: "However, we may suggest with no less reason that the writers whom Josephus describes as *volentes Antiocho praestare* are anti-Semitic Alexandrians, who regarded Antiochus as the prototype of a champion of Hellenic anti-Semitism against the enemies of mankind." Whether Apion is the representative here of the "anti-Semitic Alexandrians" only or of a broader Egyptian anti-Semitic or anti-Jewish tradition, there is no doubt that his target is the Jews as the "enemies of mankind."

3. ABSTINENCE FROM PORK

1. Lev. 11:7; Dtn. 14:8.

2. Isa. 65:4.

3. See Hengel, *Judentum und Hellenismus,* p. 534, n. 210.

4. See Sextus Empiricus, *Hypotyposes,* III, 220 (E. Pappenheim, *Erläuterungen zu des Sextus Empiricus Pyrrhoneïschen Grundzügen,* Leipzig 1881, p. 257); Theophrastus, *De Pietate,* cited in Porphyry, *De Abstinentia,* II, 25:4; about Egypt see Herodotus, II, 47.

5. 1 Macc. 1:45ff. (verse 47: "pagan altars, idols and sacred precincts were to be established, swine and other unclean beasts to be offered in sacrifice"). Cf. 2

Macc. 6:18.20; 7:1 (the martyrdom of Eleazar and the mother with her seven sons who were forced to eat pork).

6. *Antiquitates*, XII, 253f. ("he then commanded them to build sacred places in every city and village, and set up altars on which to sacrifice swine daily").

7. *Antiquitates*, XIII, 243; cf. ibid., XII, 253.

8. See the discussion in *GLAJJ*, vol. 1, pp. 142ff. Stern is much more cautious; ibid., and p. 168.

9. That is Moses, seated on an ass, as mentioned before; see above, Chapter 2.

10. Diodorus, *Bibliotheca Historica*, XXXIV–XXXV, 1:3f. = FGrHist, II, A 87 (Poseidonios von Apameia) F 109 = *GLAJJ*, vol. 1, no. 63 (trans. F. R. Walton, *LCL*).

11. 2 Macc. 5:15.

12. 1 Macc. 1:21–24.

13. E. Bickerman, *The God of the Maccabees*, Leiden 1979, p. 45. See Josephus, *Antiquitates*, XII, 246f.

14. The two different sources being used by Josephus may well be recognized from his accounts in *Contra Apionem*, II, 83 (where he mentions Antiochus' "iniquitous raid on the temple," caused by "impecuniosity"), and in *Antiquitates*, XII, 253f. (where he mentions the king's slaughtering a swine on the newly built pagan altar upon the Temple-altar and the subsequent decree "to build sacred places in every city and village, and to set up altars on which to sacrifice swine daily").

15. Bickerman calls this version the "anti-Jewish version," in contrast to the "Seleucid version" which is distinctively political: "Here, the persecution does not appear as a deliberate action against the Jewish faith, but as a punitive measure against the rebels" (*God of the Maccabees*, p. 12).

16. Diodorus, *Bibliotheca Historica*, XXXIV–XXXV, 1:1.

17. Ibid., 1:5.

18. Bickerman suggests that the "anti-Jewish version" originated "soon after the death of Epiphanes" (*God of the Maccabees*, p. 14), which seems to be rather arbitrary, but actually argues for the period of time between 150 and ca. 135 B.C.E., i.e. the period of the beginning of Maccabean expansion.

19. Josephus, *Contra Apionem*, II, 137 = *GLAJJ*, vol. 1, no. 176 (trans. H. St. J. Thackeray, *LCL*).

20. Stern, *GLAJJ*, vol. 1, p. 445.

21. *Vocum Hippocraticarum Collectio cum Fragmentis*, F33 = *GLAJJ*, vol. 1, no. 196.

22. Epictetus, cited in Arrianus, *Dissertationes,* I, 11:12–13 = *GLAJJ,* vol. 1, no. 252.

23. Ibid., 22:4 = *GLAJJ,* vol. 1, no. 253.

24. See Sextus Empiricus, below (Egyptian priests); Plutarch, *De Iside,* 8, p. 353F–354A; Celsus, *Alēthēs Logos,* cited in Origen, *Contra Celsum,* V, 2:41 (see below); Aelian, *De natura animalium,* X, 16 (Egyptians in general); and see also Josephus, *Contra Apionem,* II, 141: "and all [the Egyptian priests] abstain from swine's flesh."

25. Only the late remark by Damascius, *Vita Isidori,* cited in *Suda,* s.v. *Domninos = GLAJJ,* vol. 2, no. 549.

26. *Hypotyposes,* III, 223 = *GLAJJ,* vol. 2, no. 334 (trans. M. Stern). A very similar statement is made by Sextus Empiricus' contemporary Celsus; see above, Chapter 2. However, this is much less neutral because the context, as we have seen, is the Jews' belief that they are different from and superior to other people.

27. Ibid., III, 222.

28. Ibid., III, 226 (trans. R. G. Bury, *LCL*).

29. See above, Chapter 2.

30. M. Stern's translation according to the text of Bidez-Cumont.

31. *Ad Theodorum,* p. 453D (Wright, *LCL,* no. 20) = *GLAJJ,* vol. 2, no. 483 (trans. W. C. Wright, *LCL*).

32. Ibid., p. 453C.

33. "They act, as is right and seemly, in my opinion, if they do not transgress the laws" (ibid., p. 453D).

34. *Orationes,* V, p. 177C (trans. W. C. Wright, *LCL*). The reasons he gives ("because by its shape and way of life, and the very nature of its substance—for its flesh is impure and coarse—it belongs wholly to the earth . . . For this animal does not look up at the sky, not only because it has no such desire, but because it is so made that it can never look upwards") obviously depend on Plutarch; see below.

35. *Vita Isidori,* cited in *Suda,* s.v. *Domninos = GLAJJ,* vol. 2, no. 549 (trans. M. Stern). The story recalls the cure for epilepsy mentioned by Erotianus; see above.

36. *GLAJJ,* vol. 2, p. 672.

37. Cf. Stern, *GLAJJ,* vol. 1, p. 545, n. 2.

38. *Quaestiones Convivales,* IV, 5:2 = *GLAJJ,* vol. 1, no. 258 (trans. H. B. Hoffleit, *LCL*).

39. This is also mentioned by the Roman sophist Aelian (ca. 170–235 C.E.), who quotes Eudoxus: *Historia Animalium,* X, 16.

40. Plutarch, ibid.

41. *Quaestiones Convivales,* IV, 5:3 = *GLAJJ,* ibid.

42. Lamprias had argued earlier that in his view "of all delicacies the most legitimate kind is that from the sea" and that he disagrees, therefore, with his grandfather who "used to say on every occasion, in derision of the Jews, that what they abstained from was precisely the most legitimate meat" (ibid., IV, 4:4). The Romans in general, on the other hand, seem to have been very fond of pork: "Indeed, the abstinence from their national dish must have struck the Roman nationalists much as a deliberate abstention from roast beef would have affected an English citizen in our day who believes that patriotism and roast beef are somehow connected" (Feldman, *Jew and Gentile,* p. 167).

43. *Historiae,* V, 4:1–4 = *GLAJJ,* vol. 2, no. 281 (trans. C. H. Moore, *LCL*).

44. Ibid. V, 3:1.

45. See J. Bernays, *Theophrastos' Schrift ueber Frömmigkeit,* Breslau 1866 (Jahresbericht des jüdisch-theologischen Seminars "Fraenckel'scher Stiftung," 28. Januar 1866) = Berlin 1866 (separate edition with notes), p. 2.

46. *De Abstinentia,* I, 14 = *GLAJJ,* vol. 2, no. 453 (trans. M. Stern).

47. Ibid.

48. *De Abstinentia,* II, 61 = *GLAJJ,* vol. 2, no. 454 (trans. M. Stern).

49. *Ad Marcellam,* 18 (cf. W. Pötscher, ed., *Porphyrios Pros Markellan,* Leiden 1969, p. 23, and his commentary, pp. 85f.).

50. See above, Chapter 2.

51. See J. Bernays, *Theophrastos' Schrift,* pp. 22ff.

52. *De Abstinentia,* IV, 11 = *GLAJJ,* vol. 2, no. 455 (trans. M. Stern).

53. Ibid., IV, 14.

54. The pig: Lev. 11:7 and Deut. 14:8; uncloven animals: Lev. 11:4–6 and Deut. 14:7; unscaled fish: Lev. 11:10–12; Deut. 14:10; not to take away the parents with their nestlings: Deut. 22:6f. The exceptions are the prohibitions of killing those animals which took refuge and those which are of help in work.

55. II, 213.

56. Bernays, *Theophrastos' Schrift* (edition Berlin 1866), p. 154; Stern, *GLAJJ,* vol. 2, p. 443.

57. See the literature on his identification and the date discussed by Stern, *GLAJJ,* vol. 1, p. 441, n. 1.

58. Reading *exemptus populo Graias migrabit ad urbes* instead of *exemptus populo sacra migrabit ab urbe* ("he shall emigrate from the holy city cast forth from the people"); see the variant readings in *GLAJJ* and *LCL,* ad loc.

59. Reading *tremet* instead of *premet;* see *GLAJJ* and *LCL,* ad loc.

60. *Poemata,* ed. Baehrens, *Poetae Latini Minores,* vol. IV, no. 97 = F. Bücheler, *Petronii Satirarum Reliquiae,* Berlin 1862, no. 47 = *LCL* (M. Heseltine), no. 24. The translation follows largely (but not always) M. Heseltine.

61. As a matter of fact, circumcision is so important that Petronius describes it most eloquently: it consists of cutting back the foreskin and by doing so "unloosing the knotted head," that is, removing the knot = foreskin from the head of the penis. This is the plausible explanation of this strange line given by S. Cohen, *Diasporas in Antiquity*, Atlanta, Georgia, 1993, p. 14 (Stern, *GLAJJ*, vol. 1, p. 444, leaves the line out of his English translation).

62. See above, Chapter 2. One may take this as another allusion to the *sebomenoi* which in Hebrew are *yere'e shamayyim* ("Fearers of Heaven").

63. Stern, *GLAJJ*, vol. 1, p. 444, n. 1.

64. *Saturae*, VI, 157–160 = *GLAJJ*, vol. 2, no. 298 (trans. G. G. Ramsay, *LCL*).

65. For the suggestion that the reference is not to Agrippa and Berenice but to the last of the Ptolemies and Cleopatra VII, see Stern, *GLAJJ*, vol. 2, p. 100.

66. *Historiae* II, 2.

67. *Titus*, 7.

68. *Historia Romana*, LXV, 15, and LXVI, 18.

69. *Antiquitates*, XX, 145.

70. See also E. Courtney, *A Commentary on the Satires of Juvenal*, London 1980, pp. 281f.

71. *Saturae*, XIV, 96–99 = Stern, *GLAJJ*, vol. 2, no. 301 (trans. G. G. Ramsay, *LCL*).

72. On the question of the *metuentes* in Juvenal see J. Bernays, "Die Gottesfürchtigen bei Juvenal," in *Commentationes philologae in honorem Theodori Mommseni*, Berlin 1877, pp. 563–569 = *Gesammelte Abhandlungen von Jacob Bernays*, vol. 2, ed. H. K. Usener, Berlin 1885, pp. 71–80; Courtney, *Commentary*, p. 571; Stern, *GLAJJ*, vol. 2, pp. 103–106.

73. According to Juvenal observing the Sabbath is the starting point of the *metuentes*, whereas according to Petronius only those may keep the Sabbath who have undergone circumcision.

74. Feldman (*Jew and Gentile*, p. 347), while noticing a "progression of observance" here in Juvenal, makes the distinction between the first generation which "observes the Sabbath and the dietary laws," and the second generation which "accepts the Jewish view of G-d and goes even further in their observance of the dietary laws and eventually adopts Judaism in the fullest sense by undergoing circumcision." This distinction is not covered by the text because those who accept "the Jewish view of G-d" clearly belong to the first category.

75. *Saturae*, XIV, 100–104.

76. *Saturnalia*, II, 4:11 = *GLAJJ*, vol. 2, no. 543 (trans. M. Stern).

77. Ibid.

78. Matth. 2:16.

79. Which, of course, makes sense in Greek only: *hyos—hys.*

80. *GLAJJ*, vol. 2, p. 666 (because it is "generally agreed that Macrobius drew on ancient sources").

81. Hence I agree with S. H. Braund's carefully phrased view (*Roman Verse Satire*, Greece and Rome. New Surveys in the Classics, no. 23, Oxford 1992, p. 1): "First, it is important to notice that the approaches to satire which are based upon a biographical interpretation . . . and which typically present the satirist as a moral crusader or social reformer are now slowly, and rightly, being rejected in favour of approaches which emphasize the artistic aspect of the satirist's work. Such approaches take satire seriously as poetry and offer analysis of satire as the artistic products of the culture and intellectual milieu of the time." The artistic aspect, important as it is (and fashionable as it has now become among classicists), is not an end in itself but an expression, indeed, of the "culture and intellectual milieu of the time," and it is precisely the latter which has to be explored by the interpreter.

4. SABBATH

1. Gen. 2:2.

2. Ex. 20:8–11. The Deuteronomic version of the Decalogue gives another reason: God has commanded the observation of the Sabbath because he liberated Israel from the slavery in Egypt (Dtn. 5:12–15).

3. Jer. 17:19–27; Ez. 20:13.

4. Ez. 20:12: "Moreover, I gave them My Sabbaths to serve as a sign (of the covenant) between Me and them, that they might know that it is I the Lord who sanctify them."

5. 1 Macc. 1:47f.

6. 1 Macc. 1:46.

7. 1 Macc. 1:43.

8. Agatharchides of Cnidus, cited in Josephus, *Contra Apionem,* I, 209–211 = *GLAJJ*, vol. 1, no. 30a (trans. H. St. J. Thackeray, *LCL*); cf. the shorter version in *Antiquitates,* XII, 5f.

9. See Stern, *GLAJJ*, vol. 1, p. 108.

10. 1 Macc. 2:29–38.

11. 1 Macc. 2:40.

12. Cf. Stern, *GLAJJ*, vol. 1, p. 104.

13. *Antiquitates,* XII, 5–6 = *GLAJJ*, vol. 1, no. 30b. In *Contra Apionem,* I, 205, he uses the word *euētheia* ("simplicity," "silliness").

14. Stern, *GLAJJ*, vol. 1, p. 104.

15. I also find it difficult to accept Stern's judgment that he "refers to the superstition of the Jews in the same spirit as to that of Stratonice" (ibid., p. 105); after all, Stratonice belongs to "the whole world" which finally learned the lesson, whereas the Jews, by refusing to give up their strange practice, cut themselves off from the civilized society which follows human reason rather than superstition.

16. About him see E. Groag, art. "Corvinus (5)," in *PW*, IV, 1901, col. 1662.

17. Tibullus, *Carmina*, I, 3:15–18 = *GLAJJ*, vol. 1, no. 126 (trans. J. P. Postgate, *LCL*).

18. *Sacer* means "holy" as well as "accursed." Hence, G. Lee, *Tibullus: Elegies*, Liverpool ²1982, p. 37, translates "Saturn's sacred day."

19. However, one also has to consider that Saturn in astrology was regarded to be of "maleficent influence, and when he ruled hours and days everything was supposed to be unlucky and dubious and journeys to turn out badly" (P. Murgatroyd, *Tibullus I: A Commentary on the First Book of the Elegies of Albius Tibullus*, Pietermaritzburg 1980, p. 107).

20. Stern's comment (*GLAJJ*, vol. 1, p. 320) that "Tibullus' reference to Saturday implies no more real understanding of the Jewish Sabbath than that shown by Fuscus Aristius" (see the following quotation by Horace), seems to me unfounded.

21. *Sermones*, I, 9:63–72 = *GLAJJ*, vol. 1, no. 129 (trans. H. Rushton Fairclough, *LCL*).

22. See the summaries by Stern, *GLAJJ*, vol. 1, p. 326; Goldenberg, "The Jewish Sabbath in the Roman World," in *ANRW*, II, 19.1, pp. 437ff.; Feldman, *Jew and Gentile*, pp. 509f., n. 103.

23. The assumption that Horace was Jewish belongs to the "realm of pure conjecture" (Stern, *GLAJJ*, vol. 1, p. 322).

24. W. Kraus, art. "Ovidius Naso," in *PW*, XVIII, 1942, cols. 1934 and 1936.

25. *Ars Amatoria*, I, 76 = *GLAJJ*, vol. 1, no. 141.

26. Ibid., I, 415f. = *GLAJJ*, vol. 1, no. 142 (trans. J. H. Mozley, *LCL*).

27. *Remedia Amoris*, 217–220 = *GLAJJ*, vol. 1, no. 143 (trans. J. H. Mozley, *LCL*).

28. It is conspicuous, however, that in both cases in *Ars Amatoria* he explicitly speaks of the seventh day of the "Syrian Jew" or the "Syrian of Palestine" respectively, and in *Remedia Amoris* of the "*foreign* Sabbath." This does not seem to allude to his own experience in Rome (Stern is convinced that his references "testify to the impression made on the Roman society of the Augustan period by the presence of a vast Jewish community in Rome"; *GLAJJ*, p. 347)—or does he want to emphasize that the Jewish cult in Rome is "foreign?"

29. Apion, *Aegyptiaca*, cited in Josephus, *Contra Apionem*, II, 21 = *GLAJJ*, vol. 1, no. 165 (trans. H. St. J. Thackeray, *LCL*, with Stern's correction; *GLAJJ*, vol. 1, p. 396, n. 1).

30. M. Scheller, "*Sabbō* und *Sabbatōsis*," *Glotta* 34, 1955, pp. 298–300, suspects that the allusion is to a venereal disease.

31. Augustine, *De Civitate Dei*, VI, 11 = *GLAJJ*, vol. 1, no. 186 (trans. W. M. Green, *LCL*).

32. Ibid.

33. *Historiae*, V, 4:3 = *GLAJJ*, vol. 2, no. 281 (trans. C. H. Moore, *LCL*).

34. Ibid., V, 3:2.

35. This interpretation of Tacitus is followed by another one, held by "others," that the Sabbath honors Saturn (ibid., V, 4:4).

36. *Saturae*, XIV, 105f . = *GLAJJ*, vol. 2, no. 301 (trans. G. G. Ramsay, *LCL*).

37. In Chapter 3.

38. J. Wight Duff and A. M. Duff translate *natio* as "race," unintentionally using dubious terminology which belongs to the arsenal of modern anti-Semitism.

39. *De Reditu Suo*, I, 391–398 = *GLAJJ*, vol. 2, no. 542 (trans. J. Wight Duff and A. M. Duff, *LCL*).

40. Cf. A. Cameron, "Rutilius Namatianus, St. Augustine, and the Date of the *De Reditu*," *JRS* 57, 1967, pp. 31f.

41. This, of course, is also a *topos* (as with Virgil's *Graecia capta* conquering Rome), which belongs to Rome's discourse about "national decline." A similar one is luxury (*luxus*) and the vice of being soft (*mollis*) as imported vices from the east.

42. *Naturalis Historia*, XXXI, 24 = *GLAJJ*, vol. 1, no. 222: "In Judea is a stream that dries up every Sabbath." The reason for this, of course, is that the stream rests on Sabbath.

43. *Vita Isidori*, cited in *Suda*, s.v. *Zēnōn* = *GLAJJ*, vol. 2, no. 550.

44. *Historia Romana*, XXXVII, 16:1–4 = *GLAJJ*, vol. 2, no. 406; cf. *Historia Romana*, XLIX, 22:4f. (the day of Saturn).

45. *Strategemata*, II, 1:17 = *GLAJJ*, vol. 1, no. 229.

46. Cf. the commentary by Stern, *GLAJJ*, vol. 1, pp. 510f., and vol. 2, p. 252; R. Goldenberg, The Jewish Sabbath, pp. 430ff.

47. *Strategemata*, ibid.

48. *Historia Romana*, XXXVII, 16:3. E. Cary, *LCL*, translates "superstitious awe."

49. Cf. Ziegler, *Plutarchos von Chaironeia*, p. 72; H. A. Moellering, *Plutarch on Superstition*, Boston ²1963, pp. 19ff. ("rather early" but no connection

with 70 C.E.). M. Smith contests the attribution of *De Superstitione* to Plutarch; see his article "De Superstitione (Moralia 164E–171F)," in H. D. Betz, ed., *Plutarch's Theological Writings and Early Christian Literature*, Leiden 1975, pp. 1–35.

50. Euripides, *Troades*, 764.

51. *De Superstitione*, 3, p. 166A = *GLAJJ*, vol. 1, no. 255 (trans. F. C. Babbitt, *LCL*, with Stern's correction).

52. Ibid., 8, p. 169C = *GLAJJ*, vol. 1, no. 256 (trans. F. C. Babbitt, *LCL*).

53. Moellering, *Plutarch on Superstition*, p. 19 (referring to G. Abernetty, *De Plutarchi qui fertur de Superstitione Libello*, Diss. phil. Königsberg 1911, pp. 45ff.). Babbitt, *LCL* (*Plutarch's Moralia*, vol. II, Cambridge, Mass./London 1956 [reprint], p. 481, n. f) favors the capture of Jerusalem by Pompey in 63 B.C.E., or by Antony in 38 B.C.E.

54. Cf. Stern, *GLAJJ*, vol. 1, p. 547. The Jews' folly of not defending themselves on Sabbath is similar to the conduct of the Athenian general Nicias, who delayed his army's departure from Syracuse because of an eclipse of the moon (*De Superstitione*, 8, p. 169A–C).

55. *Historia Hypomnemata*, cited in Josephus, *Antiquitates*, XIV, 66 = *GLAJJ*, vol. 1, no. 104, and *Geographica*, XVI, 2:40 = *GLAJJ*, vol. I, no. 115.

56. Cf. Stern's comment, *GLAJJ*, vol. 1, pp. 276f.

57. Cited in Justinus, *Historiae Philippicae*, Libri XXXVI Epitoma, 2:14 = *GLAJJ*, vol. 1, no. 137 (trans. J. S. Watson, London 1902).

58. *Aegyptiaca*, cited in Josephus, *Contra Apionem*, I, 308 = *GLAJJ*, vol. 1, no. 158.

59. *Historiae*, V, 4:3 = *GLAJJ*, vol. 2, no. 281.

60. Ibid., V, 3:2. When he continues that the "seventh day . . . ended their toils" he implies that the "toils" consisted of hunger and not of thirst. From a very close and literary reading of V, 3:2 and V, 4:3 one may infer that the six days' march itself was marked by hunger (they found the water *before* they set about the march), and that indeed the commemoration of the hunger gave reason to the introduction of the Sabbath as a fast day.

61. *Fragmenta*, no. 37 = *GLAJJ*, vol. 1, no. 195.

62. *Epigrammata*, IV, 4 = *GLAJJ*, vol. 1, no. 239.

63. The attempts made by Goldenberg (The Jewish Sabbath, pp. 439ff.) to revive the theory of a Sabbath-fast are not convincing. His main evidence comes from "medieval practices" which "are quite possibly rooted in older traditions which have left no clearer trace" (ibid., p. 440). Feldman rightly points out that the notion of the Sabbath as a fast day is particularly strange in view of the Rabbis' provision for the joyful character of the day (*Jew and Gentile*, p. 162). His

own suggestion, however, that the Jewish custom of waiting for the midday meal on Sabbath until approximately noon may have provoked the pagan misunderstanding of the Sabbath as a fast day, is very far-fetched.

64. The ban especially on food and wearing sandals on the Day of Atonement (cf. M. Yom 8:1) seems to stand behind Juvenal's ironical allusion to the "country where kings celebrate festal Sabbaths (*festa sabbata*) with bare feet (*mero pede*)" (*Saturae*, VI, 159); cf. H. Lewy, "Philologisches aus dem Talmud," *Philologus* 84, 1929, p. 391. The references to the "Jewish custom of ascending the Temple Mount barefoot" (Stern, *GLAJJ*, vol. 2, p. 100, following Friedländer) or to "the fact that the Hasmonean kings also assumed the high priesthood for themselves and hence went barefoot in the Temple, as required for priests" (Feldman, *Jew and Gentile*, p. 164) are less likely (the "kings" are mentioned by Juvenal because his subject is the diamond which was given by "the barbarian Agrippa" to Berenice, "his incestuous sister").

65. *Divus Augustus*, 76:2 = *GLAJJ*, vol. 2, no. 303 (trans. J. C. Rolfe, *LCL*).

66. M. Shab. 2:6f.

67. *Saturae*, V, 179–184 = *GLAJJ*, vol. 1, no. 190 (trans. G. G. Ramsay, *LCL*, with Stern's correction). Cf. the detailed commentary by W. Kißel, *Aules Persius Flaccus. Satiren*, Heidelberg 1990, pp. 743ff.

68. Kißel, *Persius Flaccus*, pp. 746f., argues painstakingly but not convincingly against the shabbiness of the whole setting. Feldman, *Jew and Gentile*, p. 164, sees the references to the "coarsest part of the fish" and to the "red earthenware dishes" as indication that Persius "may be satirizing the poverty of the Jews."

69. Cf. *Saturae*, V, 186 (the cults of Isis and Cybele).

70. This is explained by Kißel, *Persius Flaccus*, p. 748, as "unheimliches, magisches Murmeln" because of the allegedly Jewish custom of praying (in this case the Kiddush) in a low voice ("kennt die jüdische Sitte auch das kaum hörbare Gebet"). This comes unfortunately close to an anti-Semitic cliché.

71. Very similar to Petronius' "and shall not tremble (*tremet*) at the fasts of Sabbath imposed by the law." Kißel, *Persius Flaccus*, p. 749, refers to Juvenal's "father who reveres (*metuentem*) the Sabbath" with the double meaning of reverence and fear. Very far-fetched and inappropriate seems Feldman's explanation, following J. H. Michael ("The Jewish Sabbath in the Latin Classical Writers," *AJSL* 40, 1923–24, p. 120): "Perhaps the reference is to the fear of a candidate for political office that he will offend the Jews on their Sabbath" (*Jew and Gentile*, p. 164).

72. *Epistulae Morales*, XCV, 47 = *GLAJJ*, vol. 1, no. 188 (trans. R. M. Gummere, *LCL*).

73. Ibid.

74. *Quaestiones Convivales,* IV, 6:2.

75. Ibid.

76. Stern, *GLAJJ,* vol. 1, p. 562, with reference to M. Ber. 8:1.

77. Therefore it is a moralizing modern judgment to argue that Plutarch's "comparison of the Sabbath to a bacchanalian orgy, at which the participants ply each other with wine until they are drunk, is no more flattering" (Goldenberg, The Jewish Sabbath, pp. 435f.).

78. According to L. A. Stella, *Cinque poeti dell' antologia palatina,* Bologna 1949, pp. 232ff., he belongs as early as the third century B.C.E.

79. A. S. F. Gow and D. L. Page, eds., *The Greek Anthology: Hellenistic Epigrams,* vol. 1, Cambridge 1965, p. 223 (Meleager, no. XXVI) = *GLAJJ,* vol. 1, no. 43 (trans. W. R. Paton, *LCL*).

80. *Brevis Expositio in Vergilii Georgica,* I, 336 = *GLAJJ,* vol. 2, no. 537c (trans. M. Stern).

81. *De Reditu Suo,* I, 389f. = *GLAJJ,* vol. 2, no. 542 (trans. J. Wight Duff and A. M. Duff, *LCL*).

5. CIRCUMCISION

1. Gen. 17:10f.

2. Gen. 17:14.

3. Gen. 21:4; cf. Gen. 17:12.

4. Herodotus, II, 36.37 and 104: Colchians, Egyptians and Ethiopians; the Phoenicians, the "Syrians of Palestine" (see below), and the Syrians learned it from the Egyptians and the Colchians respectively. It was also practiced among the Arabs; see Stern, *GLAJJ,* vol. 1, p. 4; vol. 2, p. 620. In later Egypt it seems to have been confined to priests only; Stern, ibid., p. 620; Hengel, *Judentum und Hellenismus,* p. 137.

5. Herodotus, II, 36f.; see R. Meyer, art. *"peritemnō,"* in *ThWNT,* vol. 6, Stuttgart 1959, p. 78.

6. See *CPJ,* vol. 1, pp. 125ff. (no. 4), and Hengel's interpretation, *Judentum und Hellenismus,* pp. 488ff.; 1 Macc. 1:15; Jub. 15:33f.; Josephus, *Antiquitates,* XII, 241 (the so-called *epispasmos,* the restoration of the foreskin: "they also concealed the circumcision of their private parts in order to be Greeks even when unclothed"). On the "assimilated" Jews during the reign of Hadrian who practiced the *epispasmos,* see P. Schäfer, *Der Bar Kokhba-Aufstand,* Tübingen 1981, pp. 43ff.; id., "Hadrian's Policy in Judaea and the Bar Kokhba Revolt: a Reassessment," in *A Tribute to Geza Vermes: Essays on Jewish and Christian Literature and History,* ed. P. R. Davies and R. T. White, Sheffield 1990, pp. 293–297.

7. 1 Macc. 1:48.6of.; 2:46; 2 Macc. 6:10.

8. II, 104:2–3 = *GLAJJ*, vol. 1, no. 1 (trans. A. D. Godley, *LCL*).

9. See the summary by Stern, *GLAJJ*, vol. 1, pp. 3ff.

10. *Antiquitates*, VIII, 262; *Contra Apionem*, I, 168–171.

11. Diodorus, *Bibliotheca Historica*, I, 28:2–3 = *GLAJJ*, vol. 1, no. 55 (trans. C. H. Oldfather, *LCL*); see also ibid., I, 55:5 = *GLAJJ*, vol. 1, no. 57.

12. *Bibliotheca Historica*, XL, 3:1–8.

13. See Stern, *GLAJJ*, vol. 1, pp. 3 and 167.

14. *Geographica*, XVII, 2:5 = *GLAJJ*, vol. 1, no. 124 (trans. H. L. Jones, *LCL*); cf. ibid., XVI, 4:9, where he maintains that the Creophagi males "have their sexual glands mutilated" and excise their women "in the Jewish fashion."

15. We have no evidence that excision of females has ever been practiced by the Jews, and it is mysterious from what source Strabo (who is the only evidence) has taken this information; see also Stern, *GLAJJ*, vol. 1, p. 306.

16. This obviously refers to the abstinence from pork.

17. *Geographica*, XVI, 2:37 = *GLAJJ*, vol. 1, no. 115 (trans. H. L. Jones, *LCL*).

18. See also Hengel, *Judentum und Hellenismus*, p. 471, n. 15, and Stern, *GLAJJ*, vol. 1, p. 306. One is inclined, at first sight, to favor the opposite possibility, but the explanation that the "others" who cooperated with the rulers "seized property of others and subdued much of Syria and Phoenicia" clearly hints at the Hasmoneans.

19. *Geographica*, ibid.

20. *Alēthēs Logos*, cited in Origen, *Contra Celsum*, I, 22 = *GLAJJ*, vol. 2, no. 375 (trans. H. Chadwick, *Origenes: Contra Celsum*, Cambridge 1953).

21. Ibid., V, 41.

22. Celsus obviously depends here on Herodotus; see above.

23. *GLAJJ*, vol. 2, p. 294.

24. See the detailed discussion of the pros and cons by Stern, *GLAJJ*, vol. 3, pp. 13ff.

25. *Sermones*, I, 5:100 = *GLAJJ*, vol. 1, no. 128.

26. Naevius, *Appella*, cited in Priscian, *Institutiones Grammaticae*, VI, 11 = *GLAJJ*, vol. 3, no. 559.

27. Stern, *GLAJJ*, vol. 3, pp. 13f.

28. Recently, J. Geiger has strongly argued in favor of Naevius' *Appella* being a Jew and taking this as evidence for the appearance of Jews in Latin literature "long before the establishment of a Jewish community in Rome" ("The Earliest Reference to Jews in Latin Literature," *JSJ* 15, 1984, pp. 145–147); see also Feldman, *Jew and Gentile*, p. 155, and n. 75.

29. *Antiquitates,* XIII, 319 = *GLAJJ,* vol. 1, no. 81 (trans. R. Marcus, *LCL*).

30. Northern Galilee or the whole of Galilee: see the discussion of the relevant literature by Stern, *GLAJJ,* vol. 1, pp. 225f.

31. *Contra Apionem,* II, 137.

32. Ibid., 143.

33. G. Long, *The Discourses of Epictetus,* London 1890, p. 126: "inclining to two sides."

34. Long, ibid.: "who has been imbued with Jewish doctrine."

35. Long, ibid.: "and has adopted that sect."

36. Long, ibid.: "falsely imbued (baptized)."

37. *Dissertationes,* II, 9, 20–21 = *GLAJJ,* vol. 1, no. 254 (trans. W. A. Oldfather, *LCL*).

38. See the summary of this discussion by Stern, *GLAJJ,* vol. 1, pp. 543f., and J. Nolland, "Uncircumcised Proselytes?" *JSJ* 12, 1981, pp. 173–194.

39. For the Rabbinic evidence that baptism was part of a complex ritual, see m Pes. 8:8; m Ed. 5:2; Mekhilta de-Rabbi Shimᶜon b. Yoḥai on Ex. 12:48 (ed. Epstein-Melamed, p. 37) = b Kerit. 9a; b Yev. 46a–b.

40. See most recently also M. Goodman, "Jewish Proselytizing in the First Century," in J. Lieu, J. North, and T. Rajak, eds., *The Jews among Pagans and Christians in the Roman Empire,* London and New York 1992, p. 68; id., *Mission and Conversion. Proselytizing in the Religious History of the Roman Empire,* Oxford 1994, pp. 81, 134.

41. *Historiae,* V, 5:2 = *GLAJJ,* vol. 2, no. 281 (trans. C. H. Moore, *LCL*).

42. Ibid., 5:1.

43. Ibid. Feldman, following Reinach, wonders why Tacitus, "despite his marked anti-Jewish prejudice, does not, when he mentions circumcision, . . . indicate that it was borrowed from the Egyptians." As a possible reason for this he suggests that Tacitus "wishes to indicate that the Jews do everything that is opposed to their Egyptian origin" (*Jew and Gentile,* p. 154). The latter is certainly correct, and as a matter of fact Tacitus does not need the Egyptian origin of circumcision in order to express his anti-Jewish feelings.

44. *Domitianus,* 12:2 = *GLAJJ,* vol. 2, no. 320 (trans. J. C. Rolfe, *LCL*).

45. Chapter 6.

46. *De Deis et Mundo,* IX, 5 = *GLAJJ,* vol. 2, no. 488 (trans. A. D. Nock).

47. See above, Chapter 4.

48. See above, ibid.

49. *Satyricon,* 102:13f. = *GLAJJ,* vol. 1, no. 194 (trans. M. Heseltine, *LCL*).

50. Ibid.

51. Ibid., 68:8 = *GLAJJ*, vol. 1, no. 193. The Jewish prince Tobias, in the middle of the third century B.C.E., when sending four slaves to the Ptolemaic "minister" Apollonius in Egypt, emphasizes that five of them are not circumcised, probably referring by this to their higher value: *CPJ*, vol. 1, no. 4 (pp. 125ff.); cf. Hengel, *Judentum und Hellenismus*, pp. 488f.

52. Heseltine translates *recutitus* as "he is a Jew." For *recutitus* = "circumcised" see also Persius and Martial.

53. See above, Chapter 3.

54. Stern has noticed that these references are "second only to those concerning the Phrygian cults of Cybele and Attis, which were connected with the institution of the castrated Galli"; *GLAJJ*, vol. 1, p. 521.

55. *Inguen*, literally "loin," "groin," is used in obscene graffiti, epigrams, and satires for "sexual organs"; see J. N. Adams, *The Latin Sexual Vocabulary*, Baltimore 1982, p. 47.

56. *Epigrammata*, VII, 30 = *GLAJJ*, vol. 1, no. 240 (trans. D. R. Shackleton Bailey, *LCL*).

57. *Aluta*, "thong," "strap," is a kind of suspensory to cover the penis.

58. *Epigrammata*, VII, 35 = *GLAJJ*, vol. 1, no. 241. D. R. Shackleton Bailey, *LCL*, following the reading *nulla sub cute* (see below), translates: "But my slave, Laecania, to say nothing of me, has a Jewish weight under his lack of skin" (Stern does not translate the epigram into English but quotes the older Italian translation by W. C. A. Ker, *LCL:* "Ma il mio servo . . . ha il giudaico peso sott'un nudo cuojo"). An epigram with a similar subject is XI, 75.

59. *Pondus*, literally "weight," refers here to the enormous "weight" of the sexual organs of the Jewish slave: "the allusion is to someone *bene mentulatus*, and the weight is primarily that of the *mentula* [penis]" (Adams, *Vocabulary*, p. 71).

60. *Mentula* = penis.

61. D. R. Shackleton Bailey, *LCL*, translates: "Is your slave's cock the only genuine article?"

62. By which he, of course, does not want to suggest that he is also Jewish. The point of comparison between Martial and his slave is the endowment, not the nakedness.

63. *GLAJJ*, vol. 1, p. 525.

64. H. J. Izaac, *Martial. Épigrammes*, vol. 1, Paris 1961, p. 220: "Mais mon esclave . . . porte à découvert une masse d'organes digne d'un juif."

65. See the *apparatus criticus* in Izaac's edition, p. 220.

66. This is also the interpretation suggested by A. E. Housman, "Praefanda," *Hermes* 66, 1931, pp. 409f. Izaac, *Martial*, p. 268, suggests that in *nulla sub*

cute, "cute désigne l'*aluta* du vers l," thus "under no *aluta*" = "not wearing an *aluta.*" He is followed recently by S. Cohen, *Diasporas in Antiquity,* Atlanta 1993, p. 42, who wants "to take *cutis* as synonymous with *aluta,* meaning 'leather.'" This not only is a strange translation (*cutis* always means "skin," and not the "second skin" of a suspensory) but also underestimates Martial's wit according to which the Jewish slave is naked in the double sense that he wears no *aluta* and has no foreskin.

67. "But the naked, young and old ones, bathe with you" *(sed nudi tecum iuvenesque senesque lavantur).*

68. I owe this interpretation of *nulla sub cute* to a discussion with Glen Bowersock, who also suggests that *nulla sub cute* may allude to *Appella = sine pelle.* D. Gilula ("Did Martial Have a Jewish Slave?" *Classical Quarterly* 37, 1987, pp. 532f.) comes to the opposite conclusion, also for stylistic reasons: "This *nulla sub cute* variant is unacceptable for two reasons: (a) It disregards the emphatic anaphora *sed . . . nuda* (3–4), *sed nudi* (5) . . ., (b) it overlooks the comparison of Martial to his slave."

69. A *fibula* "was a simple metal ring attached to the foreskin to make erection impossible, or at least painful enough to avoid" (N. M. Kay, *Martial Book XI, a Commentary,* London 1985, p. 229), but this *fibula* must have been different because it was meant to cover the whole penis. Therefore the question of how the supposedly circumcised Menophilus managed to affix a *fibula* cannot be taken as evidence that the epigram possibly has nothing to do with circumcision; see Cohen, *Diasporas,* pp. 42f.

70. *Epigrammata,* VII, 82 = *GLAJJ,* vol. 1, no. 243 (trans. D. R. Shackleton Bailey, *LCL*).

71. See Kay, *Martial,* p. 230, who refers to Aristotle, and who mentions also the *infibulatio* of athletes for similar reasons.

72. J. Friedlaender (*M. Valerii Martialis Epigrammaton Libri,* vol. 1, Leipzig 1886, p. 515, n. 6) suggests that Menophilus tried to conceal the circumcision because of the poll tax *(fiscus Iudaicus)* imposed on the Jews after the destruction of Jerusalem in 70 C.E. This is possible (in VII, 55:8, Martial mentions the tribute), but it may also be that he felt embarrassed to be exposed as Jewish.

73. Adams, *Vocabulary,* p. 13; see also Kay, *Martial,* pp. 169 and 258.

74. Which is attested only by Martial (see also the next epigram) and by Juvenal.

75. See Adams, *Vocabulary,* p. 13, who also refers to *Epigrammata,* VII, 55: "If you give presents in return to no man, Chrestus, give and return none to me either . . . But if you give them to Apicius, and Lupus and Gallus and Titus and Caesius, you shall assault, not my person . . ., but the one that comes from

Solyma now consumed by fire, and is lately condemned to tribute." Tacitus says explicitly that the Jews "are prone to lust *(proiectissima ad libidem gens),*" see *Historiae,* V, 5:2.

76. *Epigrammata,* XI, 94 = *GLAJJ,* vol. 1, no. 245 (trans. N. M. Kay).

77. *Pedicare* is a technical term for homosexual intercourse; see Adams, *Vocabulary,* pp. 123ff.

78. He does not accept his oath by the Thunderer's, i.e. Jupiter's, temple (because he is Jewish), and wants him to swear by Anchialus. The meaning of the latter is an unsolved enigma; see the discussion by Friedlaender, *Libri,* vol. 2, pp. 209f., n. 8; Izaac, *Martial,* vol. 2, p. 287, n. 1; Stern, *GLAJJ,* vol. 1, p. 528; Kay, *Martial,* pp. 259f. Friedlaender suggested (following a remark in a letter by Schürer) that Anchialus was a wealthy Roman Jew and the demanded oath would have been something like "Schwöre beim Sanct Rothschild!" This means to read one anti-Semitic stereotype in the light of another (see also Kay, *Martial,* p. 260). Only in order to extend the list of suggestions of how to explain the strange "Anchialus," I would like to propose a corruption of "Archelaus," i.e. Archelaus II.

79. Chapter 3.

80. Stern, *GLAJJ,* vol. 2, p. 660.

81. *De Reditu Suo,* I, 387f. = *GLAJJ,* vol. 2, no. 542.

82. 128 C.E. is taken as terminus *post quem* because Juvenal in *Saturae,* XIV, 99, which is dated around 128 C.E., speaks about circumcision and proselytes "without any hint that the operation was illegal"; see Smallwood, *Jews,* p. 429, and n. 5. 132 C.E. is the date of the outbreak of the Bar Kokhba war which is supposed to be connected with the ban on circumcision; see the summary in P. Schäfer, *Bar Kokhba-Aufstand,* pp. 38ff.

83. Smallwood, *Jews,* p. 431, and id., "The Legislation of Hadrian and Antoninus Pius against Circumcision," *Latomus* 18, 1959, p. 340, where she speaks of the "superficially similar operation of castration"; also recently A. Linder, *The Jews in Roman Imperial Legislation,* Detroit and Jerusalem 1987, p. 101, n. 8. See also G. Bowersock, "Old and New in the History of Judaea," *JRS* 65, 1975, p. 185 (without linking, however, circumcision and castration): "Hadrian simply considered the practice abhorrent."

84. Apart from Rabbinic sources which are difficult to date and which for the most part refer to the period after the Bar Kokhba war; see Schäfer, *Bar Kokhba-Aufstand,* pp. 43ff. and 194ff.

85. *Historia Augusta,* Hadrianus, 14:2 = *GLAJJ,* vol. 2, no. 511.

86. See Schäfer, *Bar Kokhba-Aufstand,* p. 38. Hohl, the German translator of the *Historia Augusta,* stated very clearly: "Ein ausdrückliches Verbot der Beschneidung ist erst für Antoninus Pius nachweisbar (Dig. 48, 8, 11 pr.);

Hadrian erließ lediglich ein allgemein gültiges Reskript gegen die Kastration (Dig. 48, 8, 4, 2)"; see E. Hohl et al., *Historia Augusta. Römische Herrschergestalten,* vol. 1, Zürich and München 1976, p. 383, n. 48.

87. Cassius Dio, *Historia Romana,* LXIX, 12:1–14:3.

88. E.g. Smallwood, *Jews,* pp. 437f.; Schürer, *History,* vol. 1, p. 540; Stern, *GLAJJ,* vol. 2, pp. 401f. and 619f.

89. Stern, *GLAJJ,* vol. 2, p. 620, with reference to Origen, *Contra Celsum,* II, 13.

90. See P. Teb. II 292 and 293, BGU I 347, P. Straßb. graec. 60 = U. Wilcken, *Chrestomatie,* in L. Mitteis and U. Wilcken, *Grundzüge und Chrestomatie der Papyruskunde,* Erster Band, Zweite Hälfte, Leipzig and Berlin 1912, nos. 74–77.

91. See the summary by Stern, *GLAJJ,* vol. 2, p. 620, and above, no. 4.

92. H. J. W. Drijvers, *The Book of the Laws of Countries,* Assen 1965, pp. 65f.

93. Id., *Bardaiṣan of Edessa,* Assen 1966, p. 92, n. 3.

94. *GLAJJ,* vol. 2, p. 620.

95. Or was it introduced by Trajan and gradually enforced by Hadrian?

96. Suetonius, Domitianus, 7:1; Cassius Dio, *Historia Romana,* XLVII, 2:3; see also Martial, *Epigrammata,* II, 60 and VI, 2.

97. Ulpian, *Digesta,* XLVIII, 8, 4:2.

98. Modestinus, *Digesta,* XLVIII, 8:11 (trans. A. Linder, *Roman Imperial Legislation,* p. 100).

99. See esp. Smallwood, *Legislation,* p. 334: "It would appear from it that before the issue of Antoninus' rescript there was in existence a universal prohibition of circumcision, which affected not merely Jews and would-be converts to Judaism, but also other races in the empire which followed this practice, and that Antoninus made an exception to it in favour of Jewish families, allowing them to circumcise their sons although still forbidding them to admit converts by means of this rite." The emphasis on the "Jews alone" is to be found in her book *The Jews under Roman Rule,* pp. 469f.

100. *Bar Kokhba-Aufstand,* pp. 40ff.

101. As a matter of fact, Smallwood concedes that the Egyptian priests were also exempted from the ban by Antoninus, hence it is not "the Jews alone." But, of course, she can resort to the argument that "Jews were the only people who were allowed the free and unconditional resumption of the practice" (*Jews,* p. 470).

102. In her book, Smallwood is somewhat warier: "It is not clear whether Hadrian as well as Antoninus equated circumcision completely with castration

by imposing the same penalties on both. It is possible that Hadrian had imposed a milder penalty on circumcision and that Antoninus increased the punishment for non-Jewish circumcision when he exempted the Jews" (*Jews*, p. 469, n. 6). The latter, of course, is mere speculation. Linder, *Roman Imperial Legislation*, p. 101, n. 8, takes it for granted that the "assimilation of circumcision to castration was a common theme in the antisemitic literature of the Graeco-Roman world." As evidence for this he refers to Juvenal, *Saturae*, XIV, 104, and to Martial, *Epigrammata*, VII, 82:6, and XI, 94: these are the three cases discussed above, in which *verpus* is used, but there can be no doubt that it means "circumcised" and not "castrated." Linder's discussion of Modestinus, on the whole, lacks the knowledge of the more recent relevant literature.

103. See A. Garzetti, *From Tiberius to the Antonines: A History of the Roman Empire AD 14–192*, London 1974, pp. 431ff.

104. *Greek Homosexuality*, Cambridge, Mass., 1978, pp. 125ff.; see esp. p. 127: "Even when the penis is shown erect there is not, as a rule, any retraction of the foreskin."

105. Smallwood, *Jews*, p. 431. The "moral objection" may fit with castration but certainly not with circumcision.

106. If it was only his sense of aesthetic beauty which led him to the decree, then it would have been directed almost certainly against anybody (whoever it may have been) who practiced circumcision. But in this case it is very hard to understand how he could so completely underestimate the Jewish reaction to such a prohibition. If the prohibition was mainly a punishment for the Jewish revolt, then it is more understandable that a primarily political measure was also motivated by other considerations.

6. PROSELYTISM

1. See the summaries by Feldman, *Jew and Gentile*, pp. 288ff.; Goodman, Jewish Proselytizing, pp. 53–78; E. Will and C. Orrieux, *"Prosélytisme Juif"? Histoire d'une erreur*, Paris 1992, pp. 101–115.

2. See now M. Goodman's recent monograph *Mission and Conversion*, esp. chap. 4: "Judaism before 100 C.E.: Proselytes and Proselytizing," pp. 60–90.

3. These terms are used to designate in the broadest sense what is called in scholarly literature "God-fearers" *(sebomenoi, phoboumenoi, theosebeis, metuentes)* without wishing to argue that they were a clearly and uniformly defined group throughout antiquity. I do maintain, however, that the distinction between "Judaizers/sympathizers" and full proselytes was made and known as

early as the first century C.E. For the discussion which evolved around the Aphrodisias inscription with its distinction between *prosēlytoi* and *theosebeis* see R. S. MacLennan and T. Kraabel, "The God-Fearers—a Literary and Theological Invention," *BAR* 12.5, 1986, pp. 46–53; L. H. Feldman, "The Omnipresence of the God-Fearers," ibid., pp. 58–69; F. Millar, in Schürer, *History,* vol. 3.1, pp. 150ff. (esp. p. 166); P. R. Trebilco, *Jewish Communities in Asia Minor,* Cambridge 1991, pp. 145ff., esp. pp. 152–155; Feldman, *Jew and Gentile,* pp. 362–369; H. Botermann, "Griechisch-Jüdische Epigraphik: Zur Datierung der Aphrodisias-Inschriften," *ZPE* 98, 1993, pp. 184–194 (arguing for a rather late date, i.e., the fourth century C.E.).

4. I have analyzed the text above, Chapter 2, with regard to Jewish syncretism.

5. See Stern, *GLAJJ,* vol. 1, p. 358.

6. Valerius Maximus, *Facta et Dicta Memorabilia,* I, 3:3 = *GLAJJ,* vol. 1, no. 147a and 147b (trans. M. Stern).

7. Goodman, Jewish Proselytizing, pp. 69f., seems to advocate the latter possibility and definitely argues against missionary activities; Feldman, *Jew and Gentile,* p. 301, considers both possibilities (and even adds a third, namely that the Jews "sought merely to get the Romans to observe certain Jewish practices") and argues against Goodman, but remains rather vague as to which he prefers (his hint at "aggressive tactics" may speak in favor of the former). See also Solin, Juden und Syrer, pp. 606f., who argues that "der Hauptgrund für die Maßnahme des Hispanus ist wohl vielmehr in der Gefahr zu sehen, welche der römische Staat in der Verbreitung eines orientalischen Kultes vermutete."

8. The removal of the "private altars" in Nepotianus is no argument against either possibility (Goodman, Jewish Proselytizing, p. 69)—it may well be an imprecise way of referring to Jewish places of worship = synagogues—nor is the late date of the two epitomes (which has been emphasized by Goodman, ibid.), nor the fact that "there is no other evidence for a Jewish community in Rome in the second century BC" (Goodman, ibid). The latter, of course, is a circular argument, which may just as well be used the other way around.

9. Feldman, *Jew and Gentile,* p. 302, rightly points out that the expulsion must have been short-lived because again in 59 B.C.E. Cicero speaks of the big Jewish crowd in Rome (*Pro Flacco,* 28:66); see below, and Chapter 11.

10. This comes close to Goodman, Jewish Proselytizing, p. 70, who, after having expressed his skepticism with regard to the reliability of almost every detail of Nepotianus/Paris, graciously concedes: "What may have happened is that some Romans, impressed by Jews, chose to express their admiration in conven-

tional Roman fashion by setting up of altars within the city." So we have here at least some kind of sympathizers.

11. *Saturae*, I, 4:138–143 = *GLAJJ*, vol. 1, no. 127 (trans. H. Rushton Fairclough, *LCL*).

12. See Stern, *GLAJJ*, vol. 1, p. 323.

13. *Jew and Gentile*, p. 299. In a footnote (p. 558, n. 37), he finds "another allusion to proselytes in Horace's description (*Satires* I.4.10) of a poet scribbling bad verses while 'standing on one foot,' which was the phrase used by the proselyte who approached Rabbi [*sic*] Hillel, Horace's contemporary (*Shabbath* 31a), and asked to be taught the entire Torah while standing on one foot." That the notion of doing things insufficiently or inadequately while standing on one foot may be a cross-cultural topos, did not occur to him.

14. All current translations suggest this interpretation. Cf. N. Rudd, *The Satires of Horace and Persius*, London 1973, p. 48: "and, like the Jews, we make you fall in with our happy band"; K. Büchner, *Horaz. Die Satiren*, Bologna 1970, p. 127: "und wie die Juden zwingen wir dich, zu unserm Haufen zu wechseln"; S. P. Bovie, *The Satires and Epistles of Horace*, Chicago and London 1959, p. 57: "like the Jews, we'll make you join us and join in our views"; F. Villeneuve, *Horace. Satires*, Paris 1958, p. 67: "à entrer dans notre troupe"; Will and Orrieux are somewhat more cautious, "*Prosélytisme Juif*"? p. 104: "et, comme les Juifs, nous te pousserons à te ranger à l'avis de cette foule." A. Kiessling and R. Heinze, *Q. Horatius Flaccus. Satiren*, Berlin 1957, p. 88, comment: "Die Proselytenmacherei der Juden ist bekannt . . .; der Schlußsatz wirkt aber nicht recht schlagend, wenn man nicht in Rom Fälle von Bekehrung früherer heftiger Antisemiten belacht hatte."

15. In addition, it is worth noting that Horace twice uses the word *concedere* ("indulge"), but in a different construction, namely (a) independently ("if you are not prepared to indulge the frailty of satire writing"), and (b) *concedere* + *in* with the accusative, which is normally translated "to pass (into a new state or condition)" or "to go over, transfer (to a policy, party etc.)," *Oxford Latin Dictionary*, Oxford 1985, p. 384.

16. "Proselytism or Politics in Horace Satires I, 4, 138–143?" *Vigiliae Christianae* 33, 1979, pp. 347–355. Nolland mainly argues that one should sever the close connection of *concedere* with *in hanc turbam* and understand *concedere* in both cases in exactly the same way (namely "indulge"), whereas *in* + accusative should be translated, as usual, as "in reference to, respecting, with regard to" (pp. 350f.).

17. Feldman, *Jew and Gentile*, p. 299.

18. This argument has also been used by Nolland, Proselytism, p. 349, but he relies mainly on his translation of *concedere*. Feldman's argument against this interpretation ("In any case, the passage in Horace speaks clearly of forcing oth-

ers, that is, non-Jews, *to join the Jews in their activities": Jew and Gentile*, p. 558, n. 39; italics mine) is based on a mistranslation of the Latin text: *in hanc turbam*, of course, does not refer to the crowd of Jews but to the crowd of poets.

19. Proselytism, pp. 352f. He is followed by Goodman, Jewish Proselytizing, p. 64; *Mission and Conversion*, p. 74.

20. It is hardly coincidental that Cicero uses for "crowd" the words *turba* and *manus*, which both are used by Horace for the "crowd" of poets.

21. *Pro Flacco*, 28:66 = *GLAJJ*, vol. 1, no. 68; see below, Chapter 11.

22. See esp. the summary by Smallwood, *Jews*, pp. 202ff.; also Stern, *GLAJJ*, vol. 2, pp. 69ff., 365; Feldman, *Jew and Gentile*, pp. 302f.

23. *Annales*, II, 85:4 = *GLAJJ*, vol. 2, no. 284 (trans. J. Jackson, *LCL*).

24. See Smallwood, *Jews*, p. 203, n. 7, and Stern, *GLAJJ*, vol. 2, p. 72.

25. Smallwood, *Jews*, p. 203.

26. Smallwood, *Jews*, p. 208, does not even rule out the possibility that "there were four thousand Jews of military age descended from Pompey's prisoners-of-war in Rome in 19."

27. See also Solin, Juden und Syrer, pp. 686f.; M. H. Williams, "The Expulsion of the Jews from Rome in A.D. 19," *Latomus* 48, 1989, pp. 770ff., who argues, however, that Tacitus, in his well-known anti-Jewish mood, has made up the story. Her suggestion that Jews by birth and not proselytes were expelled and that the reason was political unrest because of a deficiency in Rome's corn supply (ibid., p. 782) is not very convincing. It does not explain just why the Jews (and Egyptians!) were expelled. Moreover, like most scholars she uncritically equates proselytes and proselytism with missionary activities on the part of the Jews (cf. ibid., p. 779).

28. This is also emphasized by Will and Orrieux, *"Prosélytisme Juif?"* p. 106.

29. *Tiberius*, 36 = *GLAJJ*, vol. 2, no. 306 (trans. J. C. Rolfe, *LCL*).

30. The burning of the religious vestments and the paraphernalia seems to refer solely to the cult of Isis; see Stern, *GLAJJ*, vol. 2, p. 113.

31. This is the translation of Smallwood, *Jews*, p. 205.

32. *Historia Romana*, LXVII, 18:5a = *GLAJJ*, vol. 2, no. 419 (trans. E. Cary, *LCL*).

33. Which appears to be the result of a Jewish "invasion" of Rome instead of being instigated by the "native" Jewish community in Rome.

34. Goodman, Jewish Proselytizing, p. 70.

35. Ibid.

36. E. L. Abel, "Were the Jews Banished from Rome in 19 A.D.?" *REJ* 127, 1968, pp. 338–386, even argues that the edict was directed against proselytes alone, a conjecture which may be supported by Tacitus (see above) but not by Sueto-

nius; H. Moehring, "The Persecution of the Jews and the Adherents of the Isis Cult at Rome A.D. 19," *NT* 3, 1959, pp. 293–304.

37. L. V. Rutgers, "Roman Policy towards the Jews: Expulsions from the City of Rome during the First Century C.E.," *Classical Antiquity* 13, 1994, pp. 56–74, opts for straightforward political causes as opposed to religious reasons. As helpful as his article is in clarifying the matter, the opposition between "political" and "religious" issues is an oversimplification. It is true that "[Roman] intervention was not generally aimed at suppressing religious practices as such" (ibid., p. 70), but it is equally true that the Romans were well aware of the political implications of religious practices.

38. Josephus, *Antiquitates*, XVIII, 81–84, who mentions the expulsion, also seems to imply a connection with proselytes: as a reason for the expulsion he gives the embezzlement by "four wicked Jews" of a donation to the Temple in Jerusalem of "Fulvia, a woman of high rank who had become a Jewish proselyte." Stern, *GLAJJ*, p. 71, rightly points out that the edict "is important evidence for the wide diffusion of Judaism among the various strata of the Roman population at the beginning of the first century, C.E., ranging from freedmen (as testified by Tacitus) to the upper classes (the case of Fulvia)."

39. K. Münschel, *Senecas Werke*, Leipzig 1922, pp. 80ff. (the very last years of Seneca); Stern, *GLAJJ*, vol. 1, p. 429. R. Turcan, *Sénèque et les religions orientales*, Bruxelles 1967, pp. 12ff., dates it at 40–41 C.E.

40. *De Superstitione*, cited in Augustine, *De Civitate Dei*, VI, 11 = *GLAJJ*, vol. 1, no. 186 (trans. W. M. Green, *LCL*).

41. Stern, *GLAJJ*, vol. 1, p. 429.

42. "Surprise" is Augustine's comment who, of course, sees the success of the Jewish religion fulfilled in the final triumph of the Christian church.

43. Quite in contrast to his younger contemporary Petronius, who is well aware of the distinction between "Judaizers" and full converts; see above, Chapter 3.

44. *GLAJJ*, vol. 1, p. 429 (italics mine).

45. *GLAJJ*, vol. 1, p. 432.

46. *Sénèque*, p. 23: "Sénèque peut avoir voulu dire: 'Eux (= les prêtres, les docteurs de la loi, d'où l'emploi du démonstratif *illi*, au sens emphatique du terme) savent le sens, l'origine, la raison d'être du rituel, tandis que la masse ignare des Juifs se conforme grégairement et sans discuter à l'usage en tant qu'usage.'"

47. By this I am not suggesting, of course, that all these Jews were part of the *populus Romanus* in the technical sense of *cives Romani*.

48. As has been noticed also by Turcan, *Sénèque*, p. 23. See also M. Lausberg, *Untersuchungen zu Senecas Fragmenten*, Berlin 1970, p. 205, who argues against Turcan: "Es ist jedoch wohl unwahrscheinlich, daß Seneca ein Interesse

daran gehabt haben sollte, einen Unterschied unter den Juden selbst zu beto-
nen." The same applies to Stern's interpretation.

49. For Petronius' attitude toward proselytism see above, Chapters 3 and 5.

50. Suetonius, *Domitianus*, 12:2 = *GLAJJ*, vol. 2, no. 320 (the translation follows only partly J. C. Rolfe, *LCL*).

51. Josephus, *Bellum*, VII, 218.

52. Cf. Smallwood, *Jews*, p. 373.

53. Thus Smallwood, *Jews*, p. 376.

54. Thus L. A. Thompson, "Domitian and the Jewish Tax," *Historia* 31,
1982, pp. 339f. Stern, *GLAJJ*, vol. 2, p. 130, vaguely alludes only to "Jews by birth"
who "tried to evade the tax by concealing their origin."

55. Smallwood, *Jews*, pp. 276f., argues for "Judaizers" (see below). Stern
again is rather vague when he speaks of those "who were not Jews by origin but
adhered to the Jewish life" (*GLAJJ*, vol. 2, p. 130). He probably thinks of sympathizers rather than of proselytes.

56. That is, people of Jewish origin (ethnic Jews) who disowned their "Jewishness" in public but secretly adhered to it or at least to some Jewish customs.

57. Jewish Tax, p. 340.

58. Jewish Tax, pp. 337 and 340: the two subjunctives *(viverent . . . pependis-
sent)* imply that "'people who *allegedly* were either living a Jewish life in secrecy
or concealing their Judean origins' were persecuted." But the witch-hunt of the
informers is based on different "evidence." With regard to people of the first category they were attracted "by behaviour, such as abstention from pork," with regard to the second they looked for "visible signs of circumcision." I do not see
any basis for this distinction in Suetonius.

59. *Historia Romana*, LXVII, 14:1–3; see below.

60. Jewish Tax, p. 335; also pp. 336 and 337. M. Goodman ("Nerva, the *Fiscus Judaicus* and Jewish Identity," *JRS* 79, 1989, pp. 40–44), following Thompson
in his interpretation of Cassius Dio, applies both of Suetonius' categories to apostate (ethnic) Jews. He puts the emphasis slightly differently, however, by stressing
that the former group "failed to admit openly to their Jewish practices," thus distinguishing between their "customs" and their "Jewish ethnic origins" (ibid.,
pp. 40f.). When Nerva, Domitian's successor, revoked Domitian's calumnies, he
in fact "may unwittingly have taken a significant step towards the treatment of
the Jews in late antiquity more as a religion than as a nation" (ibid., p. 40). This
introduction of a group of "apostate" Jews who declared their Jewish "religion"
to be a kind of "private matter" is difficult to accept. It imposes modern categories on Suetonius and suffers in addition from a vague and blurred interpretation of Suetonius' two clear-cut categories of Jews who evaded taxation.

61. See below.

62. The episode of the old man (Suetonius) is dated by Smallwood, *Jews*, p. 377, in the early 90s, and the Flavius Clemens/Flavia Domitilla case occurred, according to the date given by Cassius Dio himself, in 95 C.E., thus toward the very end of Domitian's reign.

63. *Jews*, pp. 376f.

64. As Smallwood, *Jews*, p. 377, wants it.

65. As commemorated on his early coins: *fisci Iudaici calumnia sublata* ("the wrongful accusations in regard to the Jewish tax were suppressed"); see H. Mattingly and E. A. Sydenham, *The Roman Imperial Coinage*, vol. 2, London 1926, pp. 227 (no. 58), 228 (no. 82); H. Mattingly, *Coins of the Roman Empire in the British Museum*, vol. 3, London 1936, pp. 15, 17, 19. See also Cassius Dio, *Historia Romana*, LXVIII, 1:2 (Xiphilinus) = *GLAJJ*, vol. 2, no. 436: "no persons were permitted [under Nerva] to accuse anybody of *maiestas* or of adopting the Jewish mode of life" (trans. E. Cary, *LCL*).

66. *Historia Romana*, LXVII, 14:1–2 = *GLAJJ*, vol. 2, no. 435 (trans. E. Cary, *LCL*).

67. Smallwood, *Jews*, p. 379.

68. It is hardly by coincidence that Flavius Clemens' sons, as Smallwood (*Jews*, p. 378) notes, were "nominated as heirs to the throne."

69. Smallwood, *Jews*, p. 380.

70. Goodman, Nerva, p. 43.

71. See above, Chapter 5. The discourses of Epictetus are dated at about 108 C.E.; see F. Millar, "Epictetus and the Imperial Court," *JRS* 55, 1965, p. 142.

72. See M. Schwabe, art. "Cornelius Tacitus (395)," in *PW*, VII, 1900, col. 1575.

73. *Historiae*, V, 5:1–2.

74. See F. Vollmer, art. "Iunius (Iuvenalis)," in *PW*, XIX, 1918, col. 1042.

75. See Celsus and Cassius Dio; above, Chapter 2.

76. An exception is Will and Orrieux, who distinguish very clearly between sympathizers/proselytes and proselytizing = missionary activity: although rejecting the latter, they acknowledge the former.

77. See above, Chapter 5.

78. *Historia Augusta*, Septimius Severus, 17:1 = *GLAJJ*, vol. 2, no. 515 (*Iudaeos fieri sub gravi poena vetuit*).

79. *Historia Augusta*, Antoninus Caracallus, 1:6 = *GLAJJ*, vol. 2, no. 517 (trans. D. Magie, *LCL*).

80. The similarity between the measures mentioned by Paul and those imposed by Antoninus Pius, as recorded by Modestinus, makes it appear unlikely that Paul reflects the later legislation of Constantine II (M. A. de' Dominicis, "Di

alcuni testi occidentali delle 'Sententiae' riflettenti la prassi postclassica," *Studi in Onore di Vincenzo Arangio-Ruiz,* vol. 4, Naples 1953, p. 540, n. 66; contra: E. Levy, "Rehabilitierung einiger Paulussentenzen," *Studia et Documenta Historiae et Iuris* 31, 1965, pp. 7–9.

81. Paulus, *Sententiae,* V, 22:3–4 (trans. Linder, *Roman Imperial Legislation,* p. 118).

82. Both *perpetual* exile and the confiscation of property were an aggravation which usually were not part of the punishment of exile *(relegatio);* see Linder, ibid., p. 119, n. 5.

83. Banishment *(deportatio)* was regarded as harsher than exile (Linder, ibid., p. 119, n. 7), but the specifications given here for "exile" come very close to what was defined as "banishment." The infliction of two alternative penalties reflects, according to Linder (ibid., p. 119, n. 8), the distinction made between *honestiores* ("upper classes") and *humiliores* ("lower classes").

84. Linder, ibid., p. 117, with reference to *Codex Theodosianus,* I, 4:2.

85. See the evidence collected by Linder, ibid., Index, s.v. "Proselytism."

7. ELEPHANTINE

1. Cf. B. Porten, *Archives from Elephantine: The Life of an Ancient Jewish Military Colony,* Berkeley and Los Angeles 1986, p. 13.

2. The most important are the archives of (a) the Temple official Ananiah, acquired in 1893 by C. E. Wilbour and published in 1953 by Kraeling, *The Brooklyn Museum Aramaic Papyri* (quotation by K and the number of the papyrus); (b) the woman Mibtahiah, acquired in 1904 in Aswan and published in 1906 by A. H. Sayce and A. E. Cowley, *Aramaic Papyri Discovered at Assuan,* London 1906; (c) the communal leader Jedaniah, discovered in 1906 by O. Rubensohn and published in 1907 and 1911 by E. Sachau, *Aramäische Papyrus und Ostraka aus einer jüdischen Militärkolonie zu Elephantine,* vols. 1–2, Leipzig 1911. The Sayce-Cowley and Sachau papyri were republished in 1923 by Cowley, *Aramaic Papyri,* which has become the standard edition (quotation by C and the number of the papyrus). In 1945 S. Gabra discovered at Hermopolis eight letters of an Aramean family which were published in 1966 by E. Bresciani and M. Kamil, "Le lettere aramaiche di Hermopoli," *Atti della Accademia Nazionale dei Lincei,* Classe di Scienze Morali, Memorie, ser. VIII, 12, 1966, pp. 357–428. All these collections have been republished, together with English and Hebrew translations, by B. Porten in collaboration with J. C. Greenfield, *Jews of Elephantine and Arameans of Syene,* Jerusalem 1984 (in Hebrew), and again in *Textbook of Aramaic Documents from Ancient Egypt,* newly copied, ed. and trans. into Hebrew

and English by B. Porten and A. Yardeni, vol. 1: *Letters*, Jerusalem 1986; vol. 2: *Contracts*, [Jerusalem] 1989 (quotation by A and B respectively, followed by a new number). All translations (except for Kraeling) are according to Porten and Yardeni. Square brackets indicate restored text, italics within square brackets probable restoration, and parentheses additions required by the English style.

3. Porten, *Archives*, p. 12. This date is based on a remark in the Letter of Aristeas (13) according to which Jewish "troops had been dispatched [from Judah] to fight with Psammetichus against the king of the Ethiopians." Although this may refer as well to Psammetichus II (593–589 B.C.E.), preference is given to Psammetichus I, primarily because the erection of a Jewish Temple outside Israel seems to be more likely before the Josianic reform of 622 B.C.E. with its limitation of the sacrificial cult to Jerusalem (cf. Kraeling, *The Brooklyn Museum Aramaic Papyri*, pp. 43f., who considers also some other connections: with the Deuteronomic reform itself, that is, priests fleeing the reform of 622 B.C.E. which abolished all sanctuaries outside Jerusalem; with Psammetichus II; with the fall of Jerusalem and the destruction of the Temple in 587 B.C.E.; Porten, *Archives*, p. 13; Mélèze Modrzejewski, *Jews of Egypt*, p. 25, who opts for the end of the seventh century B.C.E., "perhaps during Josiah's time or, better yet, during the reign of his successor Jehoiakim [609–598 B.C.E.]"). Moreover, Manasseh is known for a policy of "paganization" and dissemination of foreign cults in Judah (2 Reg. 21:2ff.; 23:4; 2 Chron. 33:1ff.) which may have led some priests to flee to Egypt and to join the Jewish garrison at Elephantine (Porten, *Archives*, pp. 119ff.).

4. See the map in Porten, *Archives*, p. 112.

5. The earliest Aramaic document dates from 495 B.C.E., but most of the papyri concern internal Jewish affairs only.

6. Kraeling, *The Brooklyn Museum Aramaic Papyri*, pp. 111ff.

7. C 30/A4.7:13f.

8. For the following see Porten, *Archives*, pp. 28ff.

9. C 1/B5.1:3.

10. C 16/A5.2:7.

11. C 20/B2.9:5; C 25/B2.10:2.4; C 38/A4.3:3; K 8/B3.9:2f.; cf. Porten, *Archives*, p. 279.

12. C 30/A4.7:7.

13. C 20/B2.9:4.

14. C 27/A4.5:4; C 30/A4.7:5; C 31/A4.8:5.

15. C 32/A4.9:3 is the last papyrus which mentions his being in office in Egypt; see also G. R. Driver, *Aramaic Documents of the Fifth Century B.C.*, Oxford 1957, pp. 12ff.

16. C 27/A4.5:1f.

17. C 21/A4.1; see below.

18. C 38/A4.3:7.

19. C 30/A4.7:16f.; C 31/A4.8:15f.

20. C 30/A4.7:18; C 31/A4.8:17.

21. The letter to Bagohi is preserved in two copies or drafts (C 30/A4.7 and C 31/A4.8); the letter to the sons of Sanballat is mentioned in this letter (C 30:29; C 31:28). It is explicitly emphasized in the letter that "of all this which was done to us Arsames knew nothing" (C 30:30; C 31:29).

22. C 32/A4.9.

23. Porten, *Archives*, p. 295.

24. K 112:2.

25. As has been suggested by Kraeling, *The Brooklyn Museum Aramaic Papyri*, p. 113, because the new dynasty came from Mendes, also known for the worship of the ram-god: "It stands to reason that this circumstance gave new power and influence to the Khnum priesthood and at the same time boded ill for the Temple of Yahu and its adherents."

26. Porten, *Archives*, p. 296.

27. According to Mélèze Modrzejewski, *Jews of Egypt*, p. 43, "the Temple, which seems to have been rebuilt at some date between 406 and 401 B.C.E., was to be destroyed a very few years later, once and for all."

28. P. Grelot, "Études sur le 'papyrus pascal' d'Éléphantine," *VT* 4, 1954, pp. 349–384. The translation follows Porten and Yardeni; the reconstruction of lines 3 and 9, which is not included in Porten and Yardeni, is taken from Porten, *Archives*, pp. 129 and 311ff.

29. See, e.g., E. Meyer, *Der Papyrusfund von Elephantine*, Leipzig 1912, p. 96.

30. So explicitly Porten, *Archives*, p. 130.

31. This is Cowley's translation (C 21), *Aramaic Papyri*, p. 63.

32. This is the reconstruction proposed by H. L. Ginsberg; see Porten, *Archives*, p. 129, n. 55.

33. Porten, *Archives*, pp. 131f. (three ostraca).

34. Ibid., p. 130, following C. G. Tuland, "Hanani-Hananiah," *JBL* 77, 1958, pp. 157–161.

35. Ibid., p. 133.

36. Ibid.

37. And, of course, this interpretation totally ignores the fact that the Hananiah of the Passover letter was present in Egypt (C 38/A4.3:7).

38. K. Galling, *Studien zur Geschichte Israels im persischen Zeitalter*, Tübingen 1964, pp. 152ff. In his translation, as well as in Porten, *Archives*, line 3 is line 4.

39. The latter has been suggested by Porten, *Archives*, p. 281.

40. Kraeling, *The Brooklyn Museum Aramaic Papyri*, pp. 95f., 103.

41. Porten, *Archives*, p. 280.

42. Ibid.

43. Ibid., p. 281.

44. C 27/A4.5, of 410 B.C.E., refers to this event too, but the lines reporting the actual destruction of the Temple are missing.

45. C 30/A4.7 (cf. C 31/A4.8).

46. C 31/A4.8:5, which clearly shows that C 31/A4.8 is not a copy of C 30/A4.7 in the literal sense of the word; a "second draft" (Porten, *Jews of Elephantine*, p. 95) is more appropriate. Cf. C 27/A4.5:4.

47. C 30/A4.7:16f.; C 31/A4.8:15f. On the question of what precisely happened to Vidranga, scores of researchers have given their opinion; cf. the summary by Porten, *Archives*, p. 288, n. 19.

48. Porten, *Archives*, p. 286.

49. Ibid.

50. This results from C 27/A4.5:5.

51. Porten, *Archives*, pp. 284ff.; cf. id., "The Jews in Egypt," in *CHJ*, vol. 1, pp. 389f. ("It would seem that the expansion of the interests of the god Khnum brought his priests into conflict with the Jewish temple.")

52. C 30/A4.7:17f.; C 31/A4.8:16f.

53. C 30/A4.7:29; C 31/A4.8:28.

54. Galling, *Studien*, p. 162.

55. Porten, *Archives*, p. 293, n. 29. Yoyotte, L'Égypte ancienne, p. 143, refers to "nationalisme juif."

56. See Galling, *Studien*, p. 163, and the discussion of the different opinions by Porten, *Archives*, ibid.

57. C 32/A4.9.

58. Galling, *Studien*, p. 163, avoids this conclusion by referring to Arsames' representative, i.e. Hananiah ("der Sprecher bei Arscham [wohl der in EP 21 genannte Hananja] möge sagen"). I do not think that the phrase *lememar qodam Arsham* renders this interpretation possible.

59. C 30/A4.7:25f.: "And they will offer the meal-offering and the incense, and the holocaust on the altar of YHW the God in your name"; C 31/A4.8:24f.

60. Porten, *Archives*, p. 293, n. 29.

61. For this view see esp. Kraeling, *The Brooklyn Museum Aramaic Papyri*, p. 107: "The recommendation to disallow bloody sacrifice at Elephantine may represent a concession to the wish of the high priest and his colleagues to reserve such sacrifices for the Jerusalem Temple alone, and reflects some degree of alle-

giance to Deuteronomic principles." Porten also seems to opt for this alternative (*Archives,* p. 292).

62. Mélèze Modrzejewski, *Jews of Egypt,* p. 42, opts for both: "The high priest of Jerusalem would henceforth have the unique privilege of presiding over this rite, and the ministers of the god Khnum were to be spared what they conceived as an offense."

63. This last view has been put forward by E. Mittwoch, "Der Wiederaufbau des jüdischen Tempels in Elephantine—ein Kompromiß zwischen Juden und Samaritanern," in *Judaica. Festschrift zu Hermann Cohens Siebzigstem Geburtstage,* Berlin 1912, pp. 227–233.

64. This is also the opinion of Galling, *Studien,* p. 164.

65. C 33/A4.10:10f.

66. Porten, *Archives,* p. 292.

67. See also Yavetz, Judeophobia, p. 21.

68. See Porten, *Archives,* p. 291.

69. Yoyotte, L'Égypte ancienne, p. 143.

70. Porten, *Archives,* pp. 200ff.

71. Ibid., pp. 173ff.

72. Ibid., pp. 28ff.

73. Mélèze Modrzejewski, *Jews of Egypt,* p. 141, plays down the impact which the destruction of the Jewish Temple at Elephantine had for the question of the origin of "anti-Semitism" by stating that it "would be an overstatement as well as an anachronism . . . to label it an 'explosion of anti-Semitism.'" This is certainly correct, but to label it "simply a local incident, rather to be ascribed to Egyptian nationalistic feelings than to a specifically anti-Jewish brand of hatred" and to reserve "outright violence against the Jews in Egypt" for the riots in Alexandria, is dubious. What determines that one is simply local and only an expression of nationalistic feelings, and the other a "brand of hatred" causing "outright violence"? As the history of anti-Semitism has taught us, nationalistic feelings are very often combined with hatred, and there is no reason to believe that this was not the case with the nationalistic Egyptian priests in Elephantine who directed their hatred solely at the Jews.

8. ALEXANDRIA

1. A good summary of the events in Alexandria is provided by Mélèze Modrzejewski, *Jews of Egypt,* pp. 161–183, under the unfortunate title "The 'Jewish Question' in Alexandria."

2. *Contra Apionem,* II, 35.

3. In *Antiquitates*, XII, 8, Josephus states that it was Ptolemy I Soter who "gave them equal civic rights with the Macedonians in Alexandria."

4. *Antiquitates*, XIV, 127ff.

5. See Smallwood, *Jews*, p. 231.

6. Philo, *In Flaccum*, 116, gives as the date the feast of Tabernacles in the autumn 38 C.E.

7. Or 38/39, but most scholars opt for 39/40; see Smallwood, *Jews*, p. 243; Schürer, *History*, vol. 1, p. 392.

8. *Legatio*, 178f. This document is said to be an epitomized version of the letter which was sent to Gaius earlier (that is, in the summer of 38 C.E.) through Agrippa; see below. This causes some chronological problems if the "sufferings" indeed refer to the persecutions which *followed* Agrippa's visit to Alexandria; see F. H. Colson, *LCL*, pp. 92f.

9. See Smallwood, *Jews*, p. 243.

10. Apion is mentioned by Josephus, *Antiquitates*, XVIII, 257; regarding Chaeremon see the letter of the emperor Claudius to the Alexandrians (below, n. 94, and van der Horst, *Chaeremon*, test. 5, with the notes on pp. 47 and 83). According to Josephus, ibid., each delegation consisted of three envoys; Philo, *Legatio ad Gaium*, 370, mentions five members of the Jewish delegation.

11. The exact chronology of the two audiences is uncertain. Schürer, *History*, vol. 1, p. 393, n. 167, argues for the autumn of 40 C.E. for the first hearing because Caligula was absent from Rome on his expedition to Gaul and Germany from the autumn of 39 C.E. until his ovation on August 31, 40 C.E. However, the embassies were received in the gardens on the right bank of the Tiber, that is, outside the boundary *(pomerium)* of Rome (*Legatio*, 181). This allows for a return to *Italy* before August 41.

12. *Legatio*, 180f.

13. A. Kasher, *The Jews in Hellenistic and Roman Egypt: The Struggle for Equal Rights*, Tübingen 1985, p. 22, dates the last and most important meeting to January 41, without giving a reason.

14. *Legatio*, 351–367.

15. Ibid., 188, 207f. According to Josephus, *Antiquitates*, XVIII, 257ff., the erection of the statue follows the second audience as a result of Caligula's anger at the Jews. Smallwood rightly argues that Philo's eyewitness account "can be assumed to be basically more authentic" than Josephus (*Jews*, p. 245, n. 97).

16. *Legatio*, 351.

17. Ibid., 353.

18. Ibid., 361.

19. Ibid., 363.

20. Ibid., 367.

21. The only source for this is Josephus, *Antiquitates,* XIX, 278.

22. Josephus quotes only the former, *Antiquitates,* XIX, 280–285.

23. Ibid., 286–291.

24. See also Smallwood, *Jews,* p. 246, n. 101.

25. The date of the trial is uncertain, that is, whether it took place on April 30/May 1, 41 or 53. Most scholars prefer 53 C.E. but strong arguments have been brought in favor of 41 C.E.; see Tcherikover, *CPJ,* vol. 2, pp. 68f.; Smallwood, *Jews,* p. 253, with n. 127; most recently D. Schwartz, *Agrippa I: The Last King of Judaea,* Tübingen 1990, pp. 96ff.

26. *CPJ,* vol. 2, no. 153 (Papyrus London 1912), pp. 36–55.

27. Ibid., lines 90–91.

28. Tcherikover, ibid., pp. 50ff.; Smallwood, *Jews,* p. 248; Kasher, *Jews,* p. 23.

29. I do not see any reason for accepting Kasher's argument that the Alexandrians' disappointment on the execution of Isidorus and Lampo led to "renewed acts of hostility late in September and early in October of 41," which is based on a very peculiar reading of the letter (*Jews,* pp. 23 and 272f.).

30. *Antiquitates,* XVIII, 257; cf. the similar formulation in XIX, 278.

31. Ibid., 257–260.

32. *In Flaccum,* 2.

33. *Philo von Alexandria. Die Werke in deutscher Übersetzung,* ed. by L. Cohn, I. Heinemann, M. Adler, and W. Theiler, vol. 7, Berlin 1964, pp. 125f.

34. Ibid, p. 124.

35. *Grammatokyphōn*—"porer over records" (Liddell-Scott, ad loc.); "paper-poring" is F. H. Colson's translation in the *LCL* (all translations from *In Flaccum* and *Legatio ad Gaium* follow Colson) who also ponders "'paper-nosing,' if that is not too slangy." The German translation has "Bücherbüffler" or "Papierkrieger" (*Philo von Alexandria,* p. 133, n. 1). In *In Flaccum,* 132, he is called "pen-murderer," "Schreibtischtäter."

36. *In Flaccum,* 20; and see also ibid., 131 and 137.

37. Ibid., 22f.

38. He had borrowed a large amount of money from Philo's wealthy brother, the *alabarch* (customs official) Alexander (*Antiquitates,* XVIII, 159f.), and was most probably not eager for an encounter; see also Smallwood, *Jews,* p. 238.

39. *In Flaccum,* 27f.: "he wished if possible to slip out of the city quietly and unobserved by the whole population."

40. Ibid., 30.

41. Colson, ad loc., reads *syngegenēmenēn* or *engegenēmenēn.*

42. Ibid., 29.

43. Ibid., 33f.

44. Ibid., 36–39.

45. Ibid., 41.

46. Ibid., 53.

47. Ibid., 53f.

48. Ibid., 54.

49. Ibid., 55; the quotation is from Smallwood, *Jews,* p. 240.

50. Ibid., 56.

51. Ibid., 65–71.

52. Ibid., 74f.

53. Ibid., 76ff.

54. Ibid., 80.

55. Ibid.

56. Ibid., 90.

57. Ibid., 92–94.

58. Ibid., 103.

59. Ibid., 116.

60. Ibid., 135–145.

61. Ibid., 146.

62. Ibid., 170–175.

63. Ibid., 191.

64. *Legatio ad Gaium,* 120.

65. Ibid., 132, is reminiscent of the description in *In Flaccum* and focuses instead on Flaccus as the arch-villain.

66. Ibid.

67. Ibid., 134.

68. Ibid., 163.

69. Ibid., 166.

70. According to A. N. Sherwin-White ("Philo and Avillius Flaccus: a Co-nundrum," *Latomus* 31, 1972, pp. 820–828), Flaccus' arrest signaled a new phase of Gaius' politics in the autumn of 38 after the death of his sister Drusilla: vengeance on the enemies of the imperial house. See also *In Flaccum,* 185.

71. *Legatio ad Gaium,* 133.

72. Ibid., 188.

73. *In Flaccum,* 54.

74. Ibid., 53.

75. Ibid., 80.

76. Ibid., 34.

77. Ibid., 29.

78. Ibid., 92–94.

79. *Legatio ad Gaium,* 170; ibid., 205, he is called a "scorpion in form of a slave" who "vented his Egyptian venom on the Jews."

80. *In Flaccum,* 29.

81. *Legatio ad Gaium,* 162.

82. See also K. Goudriaan, "Ethnical Strategies in Graeco-Roman Egypt," in *Ethnicity in Hellenistic Egypt,* ed. P. Bilde et al., Aarhus 1992 (Studies in Hellenistic Civilization, III), pp. 74–99 (p. 87).

83. *Antiquitates,* XIX, 280–285; trans. L. H. Feldman *(LCL).*

84. Ibid., XIV, 188.

85. *Contra Apionem,* II, 35.

86. Ibid., 38.

87. For a summary of the vast literature on the subject see L. H. Feldman, *Josephus and Modern Scholarship (1937–1980),* Berlin and New York 1984, pp. 331–338.

88. A *politeuma* is a "corporate body of citizens" resident in a foreign city (cf. Liddell-Scott, s.v.), that is, designates separate ethnic bodies within Greek cities. The members of such *politeumata* were granted certain rights, especially to follow their own traditions and customs, but they were not formally recognized as citizens of their city. A case in point is the *politeuma* of the Jewish residents in Antioch (which Josephus calls "Antiochenes": *Contra Apionem,* II, 39) and in Sardis (*Antiquitates,* XIV, 235 and 259: in both cases the Jews are called *politai*). See the careful and cautious article by G. Lüderitz, "What Is the Politeuma?" in J. W. van Henten and P. W. van der Horst, eds., *Studies in Early Jewish Epigraphy,* Leiden, New York, and Köln 1994, pp. 183–225.

89. Kasher, *Jews,* pp. 275ff., 278ff.

90. See his summary, *Jews,* pp. 356f.

91. *Antiquitates,* XIX, 288.

92. Ibid., 290.

93. Ibid.

94. *CPJ,* vol. 2, no. 153, lines 73–104 (trans. V. A. Tcherikover).

95. See the bibliography provided by Tcherikover, ibid., pp. 36f.; Smallwood, *Jews,* pp. 246ff.; Kasher, *Jews,* pp. 310ff.; Schwartz, *Agrippa I,* pp. 100f.

96. This is a formulation by Schwartz, ibid., p. 100, who nevertheless disagrees with this view.

97. This chronology is aptly summarized by Smallwood, *Jews*, pp. 246ff; cf. Tcherikover, *CPJ*, vol. 2, pp. 49ff. It rests, i.a., on the remark in the letter (line 88) that "I [Claudius] too, having heard both sides, have confirmed."

98. *CPJ*, vol. 1, p. 70 with n. 45; II, p. 50.

99. Schwartz, *Agrippa I*, pp. 100ff. He considers Josephus' second edict "to the rest of the world" to be authentic, "with perhaps some light Jewish editing" (ibid., p. 105).

100. See also P. M. Fraser, *Ptolemaic Alexandria*, Oxford 1972, pp. 54ff.

101. *Jews*, p. 326.

102. The first editor was H. I. Bell, *Jews and Christians*, p. 37. Bell notes that the letter *rho*, though damaged, can be distinguished. The correction was first suggested by E. Schwartz, review of Bell, *Jews and Christians in Egypt*, in *Deutsche Literaturzeitung für Kritik der internationalen Wissenschaft* 45, N.F. 1, 1924, col. 2094. The emendation has also been accepted by Bell, "Bibliography: Graeco-Roman Egypt," *Journal of Egyptian Archaeology* 11, 1925, p. 95, n. 2.

103. It is only attested in Plutarch, *De Alexandri magni fortuna aut virtute*, I, 3 (327C).

104. See Tcherikover, *CPJ*, vol. 2, p. 53. J. H. Oliver, *Greek Constitutions of Early Roman Emperors from Inscriptions and Papyri*, Philadelphia 1989 (Memoirs of the American Philosophical Society, vol. 178), p. 88, suggests the reading *epeisperein* which should be explained by metathesis for *epeiserpein*, meaning "to enter unlawfully in addition," or "to intrude."

105. In his review of Bell's book, *Classical Philology* 20, 1925, p. 370: *epispairein* = "to jeer," "to scoff" at the public games.

106. I. D. Amusin, "Ad P. Lond. 1912," *Journal of Juristic Papyrology* 9–10, 1955–56, pp. 169–209: *epispairein* = "to disturb" the games; cf. G. De Sanctis, "Claudio e i giudei d'Alessandria," *Rivista di Filologia* 52, N.S. 2, 1924, p. 507; id., "I Giudei e le fazioni dei Iudi," *Rivista di Filologia* 53, N.S. 3, 1925, pp. 245f.

107. *Jews*, p. 316.

108. Ibid., p. 320.

109. See also Tcherikover, *CPJ*, vol. 2, p. 49.

110. See Tcherikover, ibid., p. 55.

111. *Jews*, p. 316.

112. Without labeling the one as "hellenized" and the other as "orthodox": H. Willrich, "Zum Brief des Kaisers Claudius an die Alexandriner," *Hermes* 60, 1925, pp. 482–488; and see Tcherikover's criticism in *CPJ*, vol. 2, pp. 50ff.

113. Tcherikover, *CPJ*, vol. 2, p. 52.

114. Ibid. This interpretation also contradicts Tcherikover's own (and correct) analysis of the passage addressed to the Jews; ibid., p. 54.

115. Tcherikover, *CPJ*, vol. 2, p. 54, following Bell.

116. Bickerman, review of Stephan Lösch, *Epistula Claudiana*, Rottenburg a.N. 1930, in *Deutsche Literaturzeitung* 52, 3. Folge 2, 1931, cols. 321f.; Tcherikover, *CPJ*, vol. 2, p. 54.

117. Tcherikover, ibid., p. 55.

118. Kasher, *Jews*, p. 321.

119. *The Acts of the Pagan Martyrs. Acta Alexandrinorum*, ed. H. A. Musurillo, Oxford 1954; those referring to the Jews are republished by Tcherikover, *CPJ*, vol. 2, nos. 154–159. My quotations are according to *CPJ*.

120. Tcherikover, *CPJ*, vol. 2, p. 56.

121. Smallwood, *Jews*, p. 250.

122. Tcherikover, ibid.: "the AAM, though not borrowing their material directly from official protocols, are nevertheless based in some way on historical documents"; Smallwood, *Jews*, ibid.: "the episodes are almost certainly basically historical"; see also Mélèze Modrzejewski, *Jews of Egypt*, pp. 173–179, who gives a very vivid summary of the *Acta*.

123. Cf. *CPJ*, vol. 2, no. 156a, col. II, lines 2–4: "Claudius Caesar Augustus hears the case of Isidorus, gymnasiarch of Alexandria *v.* King Agrippa" (all translations quoted from the papyri are by Tcherikover).

124. See the convenient summary by Schwartz, *Agrippa I*, pp. 96–99.

125. Schwartz, ibid., p. 99.

126. *CPJ*, vol. 2, no. 156a, col. II, lines 11f. = no. 156b, col. I, lines 6–8.

127. *CPJ*, vol. 2, no. 156a, col. II, lines 17–19 = no. 156b, col. I, lines 12–15. Theon is unknown but Naevius is Q. Naevius Cordus Sertorius Macro, who had been forced to commit suicide by Gaius Caligula; cf. Tcherikover, *CPJ*, vol. 2, p. 77.

128. Ibid., no. 156b, col. I, lines 17–18.

129. Mélèze Modrzejewski, *Jews of Egypt*, p. 177, suggests "a reference to the prodigality of the debt-ridden King Agrippa."

130. Ibid., line 20. Tcherikover is convinced "that such a coarse insult could not be uttered in a judgement-hall; it was the author of the AAM who put it into the mouth of Isidorus in order to amuse his readers" (*CPJ*, vol. 2, p. 77). However, with regard to the no less coarse insult in no. 156d, lines 11f. (see below), he does not want the possibility to be denied (ibid., p. 81).

131. *CPJ*, vol. 2, no. 156c, col. II, lines 22–30.

132. Although Agrippa speaks generally of "the Egyptians" and "the Jews," it is clear that he refers to the citizens of Alexandria.

133. Tcherikover, *CPJ*, vol. 1, p. 61.

134. *CPJ*, vol. 2, no. 151, line 2; Mélèze Modrzejewski, *Jews of Egypt*, pp. 164f.

135. Kasher, *Jews*, p. 344 (criticizing Tcherikover, *CPJ*, vol. 2, p. 79).

136. Kasher, ibid.

137. *CPJ*, vol. 2, no. 156d, lines 7–12, according to Tcherikover's and his predecessor's reconstruction.

138. Flaccus obviously not only put an end to any Jewish aspirations for advancement but also deprived them, in declaring them "aliens and foreigners," of their *politeuma* status.

139. See esp. S. Davis, *Race-Relations in Ancient Egypt*, New York 1952, pp. 116f., who argues that Augustus' confirmation of the Jewish privileges and the simultaneous deprivation of the Greeks of their privileged position were the causes of Alexandrian anti-Semitism.

140. In *Antisemitismus und jüdische Geschichte. Studien zu Ehren von Herbert A. Strauss*, ed. R. Erb and M. Schmidt, Berlin 1987, pp. 15–46.

141. Cf., e.g., H. I. Bell, "Anti-Semitism in Alexandria," *JRS* 31, 1941, pp. 1–18; A. Segré, "Antisemitism in Hellenistic Alexandria," *JSS* 8, 1946, pp. 127–136; R. Marcus, "Antisemitism in the Hellenistic-Roman World," in K. S. Pinson, ed., *Essays on Antisemitism*, New York ²1946; R. Littmann, "Anti-Semitism in the Greco-Roman Pagan World," in Y. Bauer et al., eds., *Remembering for the Future: Working Papers and Addenda*, vol. 1: *Jews and Christians during and after the Holocaust*, Oxford 1989, pp. 825–835; but see already Heinemann, Antisemitismus, cols. 9f., who also gives priority to the political conflict (without, however, completely ignoring the religious dimension).

142. Bergmann and Hoffmann, Kalkül, p. 20.

143. Ibid., p. 24.

144. Ibid., p. 30, n. 69.

145. Ibid., p. 32.

146. Ibid., p. 33.

147. Ibid.

148. Ibid., pp. 35 and 46.

149. Ibid., p. 20.

150. Ibid., p. 24.

151. Ibid., p. 46. This does not prevent Bergmann and Hoffmann, however, from frequently talking about "anti-Semitic clubs" (sometimes with, sometimes without quotation marks) or about the "anti-Semitic party leaders Isidorus and Lampo" (ibid.).

152. Ibid., p. 22f.

153. *Jews*, p. 356.

154. Bergmann and Hoffmann, Kalkül, ibid.

155. Ibid., pp. 21ff.

156. Ibid., p. 25: "Überfremdungsfurcht," a term deliberately taken from the modern anti-Semitic arsenal.

157. Ibid., p. 25.

158. Ibid., p. 30, n. 69.

159. *In Flaccum,* 136ff.

160. Ibid., 33 and 41, although Philo does not use the technical term here. According to *In Flaccum,* 4, Flaccus had made an attempt earlier to dissolve the "sodalities and clubs" *(tas te hetaireias kai synodous)* but obviously without success.

161. Ibid., 33f., 41; see also 139.

162. Ibid., 137: "When he wished to get some worthless project carried out, a single call brought them together in a body and they said and did what they were bidden."

163. Kalkül, pp. 29, 35.

164. Ibid., p. 29.

165. Ibid., p. 35.

166. Ibid., pp. 39f.; see also p. 44.

167. See ibid., p. 24.

168. It is certainly no coincidence that they see in Bringmann with his "political" interpretation of the so-called religious persecution by Antiochus IV Epiphanes an ally for their interpretation (ibid., p. 46, n. 167). This is not to say that I wish to argue in favor of a persecution under Antiochus IV which is to be explained by religious motifs only.

169. *In Flaccum,* 29.

170. Kalkül, p. 32.

171. Ibid., p. 35.

172. *In Flaccum,* 92ff.

173. Bergmann and Hoffmann, Kalkül, pp. 15f., with reference to R. Barraclough, "Philo's Politics: Roman Rule and Hellenistic Judaism," in *ANRW,* 21.1, Berlin and New York 1984, pp. 444ff. and 524ff.

174. Bergmann and Hoffmann, ibid., pp. 28f. If the "mob" (*In Flaccum,* 33, 35, 41) is identical at all with the "clubs" as is presupposed.

175. *In Flaccum,* 41.

176. Ibid., 56, 64ff.

177. Josephus, *Contra Apionem,* II, 69.

178. Ibid.

179. Ibid., II, 128.

180. Ibid., I, 225.

181. Josephus, ibid., II, 71: "The majority of them [the Egyptians] hold their position as citizens of Alexandria under no regular title; yet they call those

[the Jews] who notoriously obtained this privilege from the proper authorities 'aliens' *(peregrinos)!*"

182. Bergmann and Hoffmann, Kalkül, p. 24; see also the revealing sentence on pp. 18f. ("there may have been occasionally an expression of literary hatred of the Jews . . .").

183. Pace Goudriaan's reservations (Ethnical Strategies, p. 94).

9. EGYPT

1. E. Meyer, *Aegyptische Chronologie,* pp. 89–95; cf. id., *Geschichte des Altertums,* vol. 2.1., *Die Zeit der ägyptischen Großmacht,* Stuttgart and Berlin ²1928, pp. 420–426; R. Weill, *La Fin du Moyen Empire Égyptien. Étude sur les monuments et l'histoire de la période comprise entre la XIIᵉ et la XVIIIᵉ dynastie,* Paris 1918, pp. 22–145.

2. *Geschichte des Altertums,* vol. 2.1, p. 423.

3. *La Fin du Moyen Empire Égyptien,* p. 102.

4. Ibid., pp. 37–68, 133.

5. See more recently Donald B. Redford, "The Hyksos Invasion in History and Tradition," *Orientalia* 39, 1970, pp. 1–51; id., *Pharaonic King-lists, Annals and Day-books. A Contribution to the Study of the Egyptian Sense of History,* Mississauga, Ont., 1986. An excellent summary (and critique) of the discussion is provided by Raspe, *Exodustraditionen,* pp. 75ff.

6. See also Yoyotte, L'Égypte ancienne, p. 137: "En définitive, bien que toutes les théories soient soutenables à certains égards, on en vient à se demander si le souvenir vague de plusieurs calamités ne se mêle pas dans l'*Histoire des Impurs,* voire à nier l'existence de toute base historique aux origines de cette histoire."

7. Kasher, *Jews,* pp. 328f. See also M. Radin, *The Jews among the Greeks and Romans,* Philadelphia 1915, p. 100, Tcherikover, *CPJ,* vol. 1, p. 25, and more recently Aziza, L'utilisation polémique, p. 54; Mendels, Polemical Character, pp. 108f.; Funkenstein, *Perceptions of Jewish History,* pp. 36f., 313f.; Yavetz, Judeophobia, p. 21. That the link between Manetho and the Septuagint is taken more or less for granted can be seen from a formulation like the following: "Die jüdische Religion war Manetho, der zur Zeit der Septuaginta-Übersetzung lebte, zweifellos in ihren Grundzügen bekannt. Offenbar empfanden die Ägypter die jüdische Lebensform als antiägyptischen Affront, worin ihnen der starke antiägyptische Impuls der hebräischen Texte, vor allem der Exodus-Überlieferung, ja auch sehr entgegenkam" (Jan Assmann, *Monotheismus und Kosmotheismus. Ägyptische Formen eines "Denkens des Einen" und ihre europäische Rezeptionsgeschichte,* Sitzungsberichte

der Heidelberger Akademie der Wissenschaften, Philosophisch-historische Klasse, Jahrgang 1993, Bericht 2, Heidelberg 1993, p. 22).

8. Pace Radin, *Jews*, p. 101, and Kasher, *Jews*, p. 329.

9. Raspe, *Exodustraditionen*, pp. 50f.; on the Letter of Aristeas and the Greek translation of the Bible in general see recently G. Veltri, *Eine Tora für den König Talmai*, Tübingen 1994, and Mélèze Modrzejewski, *The Jews of Egypt*, pp. 99ff.

10. *Geschichte des alten Aegyptens*, Berlin 1887, pp. 276f.

11. *Chronologische Untersuchungen*, pp. 669ff.

12. See D. B. Redford, *Akhenaten, the Heretic King*, Princeton 1984; C. Aldred, *Akhenaten, King of Egypt*, London 1988; Assmann, *Monotheismus und Kosmotheismus*, pp. 25ff.

13. See Meyer, *Geschichte*, and esp. Redford, The Hyksos Invasion, pp. 44–51; id., *Pharaonic King-lists*, pp. 292–294.

14. Marquart, *Chronologische Untersuchungen*, p. 672.

15. See esp. Redford, The Hyksos Invasion, p. 49f.; *Pharaonic King-lists*, pp. 292ff.

16. This has been brilliantly demonstrated by Raspe, *Exodustraditionen*, pp. 82ff.

17. E.g., that the Egyptologists do not agree about whether the Amenophis of our story is Amenophis III, Akhenaten's father, or Amenophis IV = Akhenaten, the heretic king; or that it is by no means proven that Manetho's Amenophis can be identified with any historical Amenophis, and that he may be a later addition; or that Redford cannot make up his mind whether the "lepers" are supporters of Akhenaten or of his enemies, the devotees of the ancient Egyptian religion, etc.; see Raspe, *Exodustraditionen*, pp. 82ff.

18. See also Assmann, *Monotheismus und Kosmotheismus*, pp. 24f.: "Es scheint mir offensichtlich, daß sich hier vage Erinnerungen an die in den offiziellen Quellen totgeschwiegene Amarna-Religion in Form einer mündlichen Überlieferung erhalten haben . . . In der Volksüberlieferung hatten sich legendäre Erinnerungen an diese traumatische Epoche um so eher bilden und erhalten können, als ja die Folgen der totgeschwiegenen Amarna-Revolution an den Denkmälern im Lande allenthalben zu sehen waren, trotz der ramessidischen Restaurierungsarbeiten."

19. That Akhenaten's monotheism is cosmological, in contrast to the historical, political, and ethical monotheism of the Bible, of course does not matter here; the common ground of both forms of monotheism is the "anti-polytheistic impulse" (Assmann, *Monotheismus und Kosmotheismus*, pp. 34f.).

20. L'Égypte ancienne, pp. 139ff.

21. Herodotus, III, 27–29; Plutarch, *De Iside et Osiride*, 11, p. 355C; 31, p. 363C-D; 44, p. 368F; Aelian, *De Natura Animalium*, X, 28.

22. Yoyotte, L'Égypte ancienne, pp. 142f.; and above, Chapter 7.

23. Pace Emilio Gabba, "The Growth of anti-Judaism or the Greek Attitude towards Jews," in *The Cambridge History of Judaism*, ed. W. D. Davies and L. Finkelstein, vol. 2, *The Hellenistic Age*, Cambridge etc. 1989, p. 633; see earlier Jochanan (Hans) Lewy, "Tequfat ha-bayyit ha-sheni le-'or ha-sifrut ha-yewwanit we-ha-romit," in *Sefer Yoḥanan Lewy*, p. 8 = *Studies in Jewish Hellenism*, Jerusalem 1960 (in Hebrew), p. 10 = "Die Epoche des Zweiten Tempels im Lichte der griechischen und römischen Literatur. Ursachen und Aspekte der Juden-feindschaft in der Antike," translated into German by M. Brocke, in *Freiburger Rundbrief* 24, 1972, p. 24. Lewy wants to see, however, an influence of the biblical Exodus story on the Egyptian priests "at the end of the Persian Period."

24. This is precisely Gager's misunderstanding; see above, Chapter 1. See also Raspe, *Exodustraditionen*, p. 137, who speaks of an originally "aktive, gegen die Umwelt gerichtete Misanthropie, wie die ägyptische Tradition sie dem asiati-schen Feind unterstellt."

25. See also R. M. Errington, "Die Juden im Zeitalter des Hellenismus," in Thomas Klein et al., eds., *Judentum und Antisemitismus von der Antike bis zur Gegenwart*, Düsseldorf 1984, p. 7.

26. Plutarch, *De Iside et Osiride*, 31 (363 C).

27. Aelian, *De Natura Animalium*, X, 28.

10. SYRIA-PALESTINE

1. Thucydides, I, 144:2 (trans. C. Forster Smith, *LCL*); see also I, 77:6, where the institutions *(nomima)* of the Spartans are described as "incompatible *(ameikta)* with those of other peoples," and II, 39:1, where Pericles argues that the Athenians, in contrast to the Spartans, "never by exclusion acts *(xenēlasiais)* debar any one from learning or seeing anything which an enemy might profit by observing." Cf. also Xenophon, *Res publica Lacedaemoniorum*, 14,4; Aristo-phanes, *Aves*, 1013; Polybius, 9,29.4; Plutarch, *Agis et Cleomenes*, 10:2; id., *Apoph-thegmata Laconica*, 226D; 237A; 238E.

2. *Protagoras*, 342c (the Spartans as the model of true philosophers, who expel foreigners when they want to "consult their wise men openly"); cf. *Leges*, 950b; 953e.

3. *Politics*, 1272b, 17: "distance has here [in Crete] the same effect which is achieved elsewhere by laws for the expulsion of aliens" (trans. E. Barker, *The Politics of Aristotle*, Oxford 1946, p. 83).

4. Strabo, *Geographica*, XVII, 1:19 (trans. H. L. Jones, *LCL*).

5. Probably for this reason, Diodorus Siculus finds it noteworthy that the Atlantians and Celtiberians behave humanely toward strangers (*Bibliotheca Historica*, III, 56:2; V, 34:1).

6. See Eissfeldt, *Einleitung*, p. 744; Y. M. Grintz, art. "Solomon, Wisdom of," in *EJ*, vol. 15, col. 120.

7. The text speaks clearly about the Egyptians, and not about the Sodomites, as Thackeray suggests (Josephus, *Antiquitates*, I, 194, n. a ad loc., *LCL*). The Sodomites are hinted at in Sap. 19:17 as another example of people struck with blindness.

8. Sap. 19:13–16 (trans. REB, 1989).

9. Gen. 19:4ff.

10. Gen. 13:13.

11. *Antiquitates*, I, 194f. (trans. H. St. J. Thackeray, *LCL*).

12. See Liddell-Scott, s.v. *am(e)ixia* and *amiktos*.

13. See also Tacitus' accusation that the Jews "abstain from intercourse with foreign women" (*Historiae*, V, 5:2).

14. Plutarch, *Gaius Marius*, XI, 3 (trans. B. Perrin, *LCL*).

15. Ibid.

16. See D. Bostock, *Plato's Phaedo*, Oxford 1986, pp. 3f. R. Hackforth, *Plato's Phaedo*, Cambridge 1955, opts for "387 or a little later" (p. 7). Most scholars agree that it belongs to Plato's middle period and was written before the *Republic* and probably also before the *Symposium* (or is about contemporary with the latter); see Bostock, *Phaedo*, and also R. S. Bluck, *Plato's Phaedo*, London 1955, pp. 144f.

17. *Phaedo*, 89d/e (trans. D. Gallop, *Plato. Phaedo*, Oxford 1975, p. 40).

18. Ibid., 90b/d (trans. Gallop).

19. See also R. Burger, *The Phaedo: A Platonic Labyrinth*, New Haven and London 1984, pp. 116f.

20. *Phaedo*, 90d/e.

21. Isocrates, *Antidosis*, 9 (*LCL*). Cf. G. Norlin, *Isocrates*, vol. 2, London and New York 1929, p. 183.

22. See Norlin, *Isocrates*, vol. 2, p. 184, n. d (*LCL*).

23. See Norlin, ibid., p. 360, n. a.

24. *Antidosis*, 313 (trans. G. Norlin).

25. Ibid., 315 (trans. G. Norlin).

26. See A. T. Murray, *Demosthenes,* vol. 5, *Private Orations XLI–XLIX,* Cambridge, Mass., and London 1964, p. 177 *(LCL).*

27. On the question of whether Demosthenes can be assumed to be the author of this speech or rather Apollodorus, the plaintiff in this particular case, see Murray, *Demosthenes,* vol. 5, pp. 175ff.

28. *In Stephanum,* I, 70 (all translations by A. T. Murray).

29. Ibid., 65.

30. Ibid., 68.

31. Ibid., 67. In his speech *De Corona,* delivered in 330 B.C.E., he speaks of a "law so compact of iniquity *(adikia)* and misanthropy *(misanthrōpia)*" which drags an honest man "before the sycophants" (*De Corona,* 112; trans. C. A. and J. H. Vince, *LCL*), thus establishing, like Isocrates, a connection between the sycophants and misanthropy; see above.

32. H. von Arnim, ed., *Stoicorum Veterum Fragmenta,* vol. 3, *Chrysippi Fragmenta Moralia,* Leipzig and Berlin 1923, fragment 421 (p. 102f.).

33. Dio Chrysostomus, *Orationes,* Oration 65, 5 *(LCL).*

34. *De posteritate Caini,* 142; *De Abrahamo,* 22; *De Josepho,* 19; *De vita Mosis,* I, 58; *De Decalogo,* 111; *De Specialibus Legibus,* II, 16; ibid., III, 112f.; ibid., III, 138; *De Virtutibus,* 94; ibid., 141; *Quod omnis probus liber sit,* 90; *De vita contemplativa,* 20.

35. *De Specialibus Legibus,* III, 110 (trans. F. H. Colson, *LCL*).

36. Because they have intercourse with their wives, "not to procreate children" but "in quest of enjoyment" only; ibid.

37. Ibid., 112.

38. Ibid., 113.

39. In *De Specialibus Legibus,* II, 146, he accuses the Egyptians of "inhumanity" *(apanthrōpia)* because of their practice of expelling strangers *(xenēlasia),* that is, the Jews.

40. See above, Chapters 1 and 3.

41. Josephus, *Contra Apionem,* II, 121; see above, Chapter 2.

42. Raspe, *Exodustraditionen,* pp. 128ff., following a short remark by Yoyotte, L'Égypte ancienne, pp. 141f.

43. Diodorus Siculus has adapted the motif of ass-worship by identifying the man seated on the ass with Moses who gave the Jews their misanthropic customs.

44. "The Historical Foundation of Postbiblical Judaism," in Louis Finkelstein, ed., *The Jews: Their History, Culture, and Religion,* New York 1949, p. 102.

45. *PW,* suppl. V, Stuttgart 1931, cols. 5f.

46. Ibid., col. 19; see also col. 7. For the event see P. Schäfer, *The History of the Jews in Antiquity: The Jews of Palestine from Alexander the Great to the Arab Conquest,* Luxembourg 1995, p. 74.

47. *Judentum und Hellenismus,* p. 559.

48. Ibid., p. 464.

49. Ibid, p. 464, n. 1. This inconsistency has been noticed also by Yavetz, Judeophobia, p. 8, n. 48.

50. See also K. Bringmann, *Hellenistische Reform und Religionsverfolgung in Judäa,* Göttingen 1983, pp. 101 with n. 7, 147, who follows the same line of argument and simply declares: "Die feindselige Schilderung der Juden durch den ägyptischen Priester Manetho—sie stammt aus dem frühen dritten Jahrhundert v. Chr.—ist nationalägyptisch gefärbt . . .; für die Einstellung der griechischen Oberschicht innerhalb und außerhalb Ägyptens ist Manethos Judenfeindlichkeit nicht repräsentativ" (p. 101, n. 7).

51. My italics.

52. "Hellenismus und Judentum in der Zeit des Judas Makkabäus," in *Jahrbuch der Heidelberger Akademie der Wissenschaften für das Jahr 1974,* Heidelberg 1975, p. 109.

53. Judeophobia, pp. 8f.

54. Ibid., p. 8.

55. Bickerman speaks clearly both of "no anti-Jewish passage in Greek literature" and of "nor any recorded anti-Jewish action"; see above.

56. Judeophobia, ibid. Also the second argument that Habicht, had he really followed Bickerman, "could not have written that after the establishment of the Jewish state, the Jews did to others what had only recently been done to them" (ibid., p. 9), is a bit too sophisticated: Habicht does not claim here to follow Bickerman (but Heinemann), and, more important, the "terror of mind which the Jews themselves had experienced" (Habicht, ibid.) is the persecution of Antiochus IV in all its complexity, that is including its intra-Jewish components, and cannot simply be reduced (and certainly is not by Habicht) to Antiochus alone.

57. Ibid., p. 9.

58. This has also been emphasized by Yavetz, Judeophobia, pp. 21f.

11. ROME

1. See, e.g., S. Luria (Lur'e), *Antisemitizm v drevnem mire (Der Antisemitismus in der alten Welt),* Berlin, Petersburg, and Moscow 1923, pp. 93f.

2. *Pro Flacco,* 66 (trans. C. Macdonald, *LCL*).

3. Ibid.

4. Macdonald, ad loc., has "outlandish."

5. *Pro Flacco,* 67.

6. On the much debated question whether such an influence is conceivable at such an early date already, see E. Bickerman, review on S. Luria, *Der Antisemitismus in der alten Welt*, in *Philologische Wochenschrift* 46, 1926, col. 907; Leon, *Jews of Ancient Rome*, pp. 5, 8; Stern, *GLAJJ*, vol. 1, p. 199.

7. L. E. Lord in the previous edition of the *LCL* has "for the welfare of the state."

8. Lord, ibid., has "every respectable man."

9. Leon, *Jews of Ancient Rome*, p. 8. See also L. Herrmann, "Cicéron et les Juifs," in *Atti del I Congresso Internazionale di Studi Ciceroniani*, Roma 1961, pp. 113–117.

10. Ibid. The Optimates and the Populares were not, of course, "parties" in the modern sense but fluid groupings promoting their traditional interests.

11. II, 71.

12. This is Lord's translation; Macdonald has "the demands of their religion."

13. *Pro Flacco*, 69.

14. See most recently on *mos maiorum* B. Schröder, *Die "väterlichen Gesetze": Flavius Josephus als Vermittler von Halachah an Griechen und Römer*, Tübingen 1996.

15. Of course, one has to take into consideration that Cicero's speech is a piece of forensic rhetoric which must be used with care as a guide to his own views. But it does show what Cicero felt he could get away with and is therefore a perfect representation of Roman prejudices against the Jews.

16. Therefore, Cicero can also argue against the unwelcome behavior of the Greeks in the *contiones*: "our own public meetings *(contiones)* are often thrown into disorder by men of these nations [Greeks and other foreigners]"; *Pro Flacco*, 17.

17. See also Stern, *GLAJJ*, vol. 1, p. 194.

18. See above, Chapter 2. On his mockery of statues of gods, see Arnobius, *Adversus Nationes*, VII, 1: "Because . . . true gods neither desire nor demand them [sacrifices], and those [gods] made of bronze, baked clay, plaster, or marble, care for them much less, for they lack feeling" (trans. G. E. McCracken, *Arnobius of Sicca: The Case against the Pagans*, vol. 2, Westminster, Maryland, 1949, p. 481).

19. Except, probably, for Julian.

20. Suetonius, *Domitianus*, 12:2; above, Chapter 6.

21. Cassius Dio, *Historia Romana*, LXVII, 14:1–3; above, Chapter 6. On the question whether Christianity and not Judaism stands behind the charge of atheism here, see Stern, *GLAJJ*, vol. 2, pp. 380ff.

22. Tacitus, *Annales*, XIII, 32:2 = *GLAJJ*, vol. 2, no. 293.

23. On this trias see W. J. Watts, "Race Prejudice in the Satires of Juvenal," *Acta Classica* 19, 1976, pp. 83–104 (p. 84), following A. N. Sherwin-White, *Racial Prejudice in Imperial Rome,* Cambridge 1967, pp. 7; 17f.; 49f.; 57f.

24. *Saturae,* III, 62–66 (trans. G. G. Ramsay, *LCL*).

25. *Saturae,* XV, 9–11.

26. Ibid., 11–13.

27. Ibid., 45f.

28. Ibid., 72ff.

29. Ibid., 119ff.

30. Cf. *Saturae,* II, 520ff.

31. On Juvenal's "romanocentrism" see Watts, Race Prejudice, esp. pp. 94ff.

32. Ibid., pp. 96ff.

33. Ibid., p. 102.

34. Ibid., p. 100.

35. Ibid., p. 104.

36. Ibid.

37. Ibid.

38. Chapters 1 and 2.

39. Namely, that they do not set up statues in honor of the Caesars (V, 5:4).

40. Note that the tribute sent to the Jerusalem Temple was Cicero's starting point; see above.

41. V, 5:2: "those who are converted to their ways" *(in morem eorum);* V, 5:3: "following the Egyptians' custom" *(e more Aegyptico);* V, 5:5: "the ways of the Jews *(Iudaeorum mos)* are preposterous and mean."

42. In general, *superstitio* designates the religion of the others, in opposition to the Roman *religio;* see D. Grodzynski, "'Superstitio,'" *Revue des Études Anciennes* 76, 1974, pp. 36–60, esp. p. 59: "Au Ier siècle avant J.-C. et jusqu'au début du IIe siècle de notre ère, la superstition représente une déviation de la religion nationale."

43. Livy, X, 39:2.

44. *Thebaid,* VI, 11 (trans. J. H. Mozley, *LCL*).

45. *Institutio Oratoria,* IV, 4:5.

46. See A. Gerber and A. Greef, *Lexicon Taciteum,* vol. 2, Hildesheim 1962, pp. 1597f.

47. *Annales,* I, 28 (trans. J. Jackson, *LCL*).

48. *Historiae,* III, 58.

49. Ibid., II, 78 (trans. C. H. Moore, *LCL*). See also *Annales,* XII, 59, where Statilius Taurus is accused, at the instigation of Agrippina, of *magicas superstitiones.*

50. Ibid., IV, 54.

51. *Agricola*, 11.

52. *Annales*, XIV, 30 (trans. J. Jackson, *LCL*).

53. *Historiae*, IV, 61.

54. *Germania*, 45.

55. See M. Hutton and E. H. Warmington, p. 194, n. 1 (next note).

56. *Germania*, 39 (trans. M. Hutton and E. H. Warmington, *LCL*).

57. *Historiae*, I, 11 (trans. C. H. Moore, *LCL*).

58. *Dedita superstitionibus gens*, literally "the nation which devotes itself to superstitions." J. Jackson *(LCL)* translates quite excessively: "this most superstitious of nations."

59. *Historiae*, IV, 81 (trans. J. Jackson).

60. *Geographica*, XVI, 2:37; see above, Chapters 1 and 5.

61. Ibid.: "which is their custom to abstain even to-day."

62. *Institutio Oratoria*, III, 7:21 = *GLAJJ*, vol. 1, no. 230.

63. *Historiae*, II, 4 (trans. C. H. Moore, *LCL*).

64. See also ibid., V, 12: *pervicacissimus quisque illuc perfugerat*, translated by Moore as "the most desperate rebels had taken refuge here."

65. Pace Gerber and Greef, *Lexicon Taciteum*, vol. 2, p. 1598: "hartnäckiger aberglaube, religiöser fanatismus."

66. *Historiae*, V, 8:2 (trans. C. H. Moore, *LCL*).

67. See P. Cornelius Tacitus, *Die Historien*, Kommentar von Heinz Heubner, Band V, Fünftes Buch, by H. Heubner and F. Fauth, Heidelberg 1982, p. 117.

68. Heubner and Fauth, *Historien*, p. 120.

69. This may well refer "to the war between King Alexander and the Pharisees that began in 92 B.C. . . .; or to the struggle for the throne that followed on the death of Alexander's widow, Salome, in 70 B.C." (C. H. Moore, ad loc., *LCL*, p. 189, n. 7).

70. *Historiae*, V, 8:3 (trans. C. H. Moore, *LCL*).

71. Ibid., V, 13:1. Moore translates "held unlawful by a people which, *though* (my italics) prone to superstition, is opposed to all propitiatory rites," giving the sentence a quite different meaning. The German translation by W. Boetticher, *Sämtliche erhaltene Werke des Cornelius Tacitus*, Wien 1935, p. 350, has correctly "das dem Aberglauben ergebene, heiligem Brauche abgeneigte Volk"; see also D. Grodzynski, Superstitio, p. 49, n. 4: "La nation juive adonnée à la superstition et ennemie des pratiques religieuses."

72. C. H. Moore, ad loc., *LCL*, pp. 196f., n. 3.

73. This has been noticed also by Heubner and Fauth, *Historien*, p. 149.

74. Livy, I, 31, 6, uses almost the same language about King Tullus, who, when Rome was afflicted with a pestilence and finally he himself was struck with

the illness, "suddenly became a prey to all sorts of superstitions great and small" *(omnibus magnis parvisque superstitionibus obnoxius)*. However, there could be no greater difference between Livy's and Tacitus' use of *superstitio* and *religio*, because Livy immediately continues: "and filled even the minds of the people with religious scruples *(religionibus)*," hence regarding *superstitio* and *religiones* as synonymous; trans. B. O. Foster, *LCL*.

75. Tacitus, *Annales*, XV, 44:3 (trans. J. Jackson). For the further development of the motif of Christian superstition see Pliny, *Epistulae ad Traianum*, X, 96: the "depraved and excessive superstition" *(superstitio prava immodica);* this "contagious superstition" *(superstitionis istius contagio);* and Suetonius, Nero, XVI, 2: "the Christians, a class of men given to a new and mischievous superstition" *(genus hominum superstitionis novae ac maleficae)*.

76. Ibid., XV, 44:4.

77. See above, Chapter 1.

78. Stern, *GLAJJ*, vol. 2, p. 93.

79. Ibid., p. 66; Jackson, *Annales, LCL,* ad loc., p. 284f., n. 2.

80. This use of language *(religio* instead of *superstitio)* obviously goes back to some later (Christian) coloring.

81. *Fragmenta Historiarum,* 2 = Sulpicius Severus, *Chronica,* II, 30:7 (*LCL,* trans. C. H. Moore).

82. See above, Chapter 6.

83. See above.

84. *Annales,* XI, 15 (trans. J. Jackson).

85. Jackson, ad loc., *LCL,* p. 272, n. 1.

86. *GLAJJ,* vol. 2, p. 11.

87. Yavetz, Judeophobia, pp. 1, 19.

88. Therefore it is just the wrong solution to translate "Judenhass" as "Judeophobia" as Z. Yavetz does in his recent article, desperately looking for "an English equivalent to the German term *Judenhass.*" In the manuscript of his article, which I saw before publication, Yavetz always uses the term "hatred of Jews," even in the title. This has been changed mysteriously in the printed version to "Judeophobia" without any further explanation. Yavetz obviously was convinced that he finally had found the English equivalent to the German "Judenhass." Since according to all English dictionaries *phobia* means "fear," "horror," or "aversion," as in *agoraphobia* ("fear of open space"), *claustrophobia* ("fear of enclosed space"), or *Anglophobia,* the neologism "Judeophobia" clearly denotes "fear/horror of," "aversion to Jews," including both fear and dislike. Hence, ironically enough, the term "Judeophobia," although not translating the more narrowly defined "Judenhass" (one may argue that the German term "Judenhass"

also contains the element of "fear," but this is true for the phenomenon only and not for the word), does convey very graphically the Roman attitude toward the Jews.

89. The other one is Plutarch, the priest of Delphi, "the only resident of Greece proper among the Greek and Latin authors of the Roman imperial period who expressed views on the Jews and their religion" (Stern, *GLAJJ*, vol. 1, p. 545). His remark on the Jews honoring the ass comes very close to Tacitus; see above, Chapter 2.

ANTI-SEMITISM

1. W. Marr (1818–1904)) wrote in 1862 his notorious *Der Judenspiegel* (which saw five editions during the same year) and in 1879 his *Der Sieg des Judenthums über das Germanenthum* (12 editions during the same year). In 1879 he also founded the "Antisemiten-Liga" (League of Anti-Semites) which seems to have introduced the term "anti-Semites."

2. *Toward a Definition of Antisemitism,* Berkeley, Los Angeles, and Oxford 1990, pp. 311–352. For a useful survey of the whole topic see N. R. M. de Lange, C. Thoma, et al., art. "Antisemitismus," in *TRE*, vol. 3, Berlin and New York 1978, pp. 113–168.

3. Langmuir, ibid., p. 328.

4. Ibid., p. 329.

5. Ibid., p. 328.

6. Ibid., p. 330.

7. Ibid., p. 331.

8. Ibid., p. 328.

9. Ibid., p. 334.

10. Ibid., p. 336.

11. Ibid., p. 338.

12. Ibid., p. 349.

13. Ibid., p. 334.

14. Ibid., p. 341.

15. Ibid., p. 351.

16. At least the assertions about witches may well have been influenced by those about Jews.

17. See also *Toward a Definition,* p. 17: "Though I think that chimerical hostility has also been directed at some other groups and their members, I am convinced that Jews in Europe have suffered in ways beyond description because of the completely irrational way in which many non-Jews—whether Christians,

Nazis, or others—tried to defend themselves from doubts about themselves by attributing unreal characteristics to 'Jews.'" This certainly being the case, the question remains whether it is only the *degree* of suffering which distinguishes Jews from "blacks" and "witches."

18. Ibid., p. 61.

19. Ibid., pp. 61f.

20. Ibid., p. 6.

21. Ibid., pp. 6f.

22. Ibid., p. 7. This argument has been developed more fully in the chapter "From Anti-Judaism to Antisemitism" in his book *History, Religion, and Anti-semitism,* London and New York 1990, pp. 275–305.

23. Ibid.

24. Ibid., pp. 5f.

25. This is part of his definition; see above.

26. Bickerman, Ritualmord und Eselskult, pp. 228ff. See also above, Chapter 2.

27. Cassius Dio, *Historia Romana,* XXXVII, 30:3; cf. the parallels in Bickerman, Ritualmord und Eselskult, p. 229.

28. The famous *tragoediae Thyestae;* see Bickerman, Ritualmord und Eselskult, pp. 231ff.

29. "'Anti-Semitism' in Antiquity: the Problem of Definition," in *History and Hate: The Dimensions of Anti-Semitism,* ed. D. Berger, Philadelphia, New York, and Jerusalem 1986, pp. 43–47.

30. Ibid., p. 45.

31. Ibid., p. 46.

32. Ibid.

33. Ibid., p. 46.

34. Ibid., pp. 46f.

35. For my view of the Hadrianic persecution see my *Bar Kokhba-Aufstand,* pp. 194–235 ("Die Hadrianische Verfolgung").

36. See above, Chapter 2.

37. Chapter 2.

38. See above, Chapter 3.

39. Diodorus Siculus, *Bibliotheca Historica,* XXXIV–XXXV, 1:1 *(to genos ardēn anelein tōn Ioudaiōn)* and 1:5 *(ardēn anelein to ethnos)* = *GLAJJ,* vol. 1, no. 63.

40. Eissfeldt, *Einleitung,* p. 629: sometime between the fourth and the second centuries B.C.E. Bickerman, *Four Strange Books of the Bible,* New York 1967, pp. 207ff.: second or third century B.C.E.

41. Esther 3:8f. Sevenster, *Roots,* p. 107, when quoting this passage, includes the addition "who keep themselves apart," which I cannot find in the Hebrew text. He needs it because of his theory of Jewish "separation" as the reason for pagan anti-Semitism (see below).

42. Eissfeldt, *Einleitung,* p. 630, suggests the end of the Persian rule, that is, about the middle of the fourth century B.C.E.

43. Eissfeldt, ibid., p. 733; Bickerman, *Four Strange Books,* pp. 227ff.

44. From *antiparagein*—"shift in order to meet attacks"; "lead an army against, advance to meet an enemy" (Liddell-Scott, s.v.); *antiparagogē* means "flank march, machinations," in plural "hostility" (Liddell-Scott, s.v.). See the military use in 1 Macc. 13:20, and V. Ryssel, in E. Kautzsch, ed., *Die Apokryphen und Pseudepigraphen des Alten Testaments,* Tübingen 1900, p. 203, n. a.

45. Greek text problematic; see Ryssel, ibid., p. 203, n. b.

46. Greek Esther 3:13d–e or 13:4f. (addition to Esther).

47. Ibid. 3:13f–g or 13:6f. (trans. *The HarperCollins Study Bible.* New Revised Standard Version, ed. W. A. Meeks, 1989).

48. *Antiquitates,* XI, 212f. (trans. R. Marcus).

49. My italics.

50. *Roots,* p. 89.

51. Gager, *Origins,* p. 31; Yavetz, Judeophobia, p. 5.

52. Gager, *Origins,* p. 31.

53. *Roots,* p. 108.

54. Cf. Yavetz, Judeophobia, p. 13: "I . . . would like to suggest that, though Jews were in many respects barbarians like all the others, they were in some respects a little more so." This "little more so" he sees in (1) that only the Jews could never be regarded as "noble savages," (2) that only the Jews were proselytizers, and (3) that *Judaeus* "never merely described someone whose origins were in Judea, but also someone faithful to the Jewish religion" (ibid., p. 17)—and this is the reason why Titus avoided the title "Judaicus." (2) and (3) are obviously related, and I would emphasize (2) in the sense in which I have dealt with proselytism in Chapter 6: if the Jews attracted "pagans" without actively proselytizing, this particular "little more so" becomes even more dangerous. This result is in striking contrast to the Nietzschean theory pulled on the Jews by Y. A. Dauge, *Le Barbare: Recherches sur la conception romaine de la barbarie et de la civilisation,* Bruxelles 1981 (Collection Latomus, vol. 176), p. 476: "Les Juifs offraient donc à l'observateur romain l'exemple même de ce qu'il estimait être l'aliénation majeure: l'incapacité d'échapper à la négativité totale. Expression typologique du *dérèglement de la volonté de puissance.*"

55. Above, Chapter 11.

Bibliography

Abel, E. L., "Were the Jews Banished from Rome in 19 A.D.?" *REJ* 127, 1968, pp. 338–386.

Abernetty, G., *De Plutarchi qui fertur de Superstitione Libello*, Diss. Phil., Königsberg 1911.

Adams, J. N., *The Latin Sexual Vocabulary*, Baltimore 1982.

Aldred, C., *Akhenaten, King of Egypt*, London 1988.

Amusin, I. D., "Ad P. Lond. 1912," *Journal of Juristic Papyrology* 9–10, 1955–56, pp. 169–209.

Arnim, H. von, ed., *Stoicorum Veterum Fragmenta*, vol. 3: *Chrysippi Fragmenta Moralia*, Leipzig and Berlin 1923.

Assmann, J., *Monotheismus und Kosmotheismus. Ägyptische Formen eines "Denkens des Einen" und ihre europäische Rezeptionsgeschichte*, Sitzungsberichte der Heidelberger Adademie der Wissenschaften, Philosophisch-historische Klasse, Jahrgang 1993, Bericht 2, Heidelberg 1993.

——— *Moses the Egyptian: The Image of Egypt in Western Monotheism. An Essay in Mnemohistory* (in press).

Aziza, C., "L'utilisation polémique du récit de l'Exode chez les écrivains alexandrins (IVème siècle av. J.-C.–Ier siècle ap. J.-C.)," in *ANRW*, II, 20.1, Berlin and New York 1987, pp. 41–65.

Barker, E., *The Politics of Aristotle*, Oxford 1946.

Barraclough, R., "Philo's Politics. Roman Rule and Hellenistic Judaism," in *ANRW*, 21.1, Berlin and New York 1984, pp. 417–553.

Bell, H. I., *Jews and Christians in Egypt*, London and Oxford 1924.

——— "Bibliography: Graeco-Roman Egypt," *Journal of Egyptian Archaeology* 11, 1925, pp. 84–106.

——— "Anti-Semitism in Alexandria," *JRS* 31, 1941, pp. 1–18.

Bergmann, W., and Hoffmann, C., "Kalkül oder 'Massenwahn'? Eine soziologische Interpretation der antijüdischen Unruhen in Alexandria 38 n. Chr.," in *Antisemitismus und jüdische Geschichte. Studien zu Ehren von Herbert A. Strauss*, ed. R. Erb and M. Schmidt, Berlin 1987, pp. 15–46.

Bernays, J., *Theophrastos' Schrift ueber Frömmigkeit*, Breslau 1866.

———— "Die Gottesfürchtigen bei Juvenal," in *Commentationes philologae in honorem Theodori Mommseni,* Berlin 1877, pp. 563–569 = *Gesammelte Abhandlungen von Jacob Bernays,* vol. II, ed. H. K. Usener, Berlin 1885, pp. 71–80.

Betz, H. D., *Plutarch's Theological Writings and Early Christian Literature,* Leiden 1975.

Bi(c)kerman(n), E., review of S. Luria, *Der Antisemitismus in der alten Welt,* in *Philologische Wochenschrift* 46, 1926, cols. 903–910.

———— "Ritualmord und Eselskult. Ein Beitrag zur Geschichte antiker Publizistik," in id., *Studies in Jewish and Christian History,* vol. 2, Leiden 1980, pp. 225–255 (first published in *MGWJ* 71, 1927).

———— Review of Stephan Lösch, *Epistula Claudiana,* Rottenburg a. N. 1930, in *Deutsche Literaturzeitung* 52, 3. Folge 2, 1931, cols. 320–322.

———— *Der Gott der Makkabäer,* Berlin 1937 (*The God of the Maccabees,* Leiden 1979).

———— "The Historical Foundation of Postbiblical Judaism," in L. Finkelstein, ed., *The Jews: Their History, Culture, and Religion,* New York 1949, pp. 70–114.

———— *Four Strange Books of the Bible,* New York 1967.

Bluck, R. S., *Plato's Phaedo,* London 1955.

Blumenkranz, B., "Tacite antisémite ou xénophobe? (A propos de deux livres récents)," *REJ* 111, 1951–52, pp. 187–191.

Bochart, S., *Hierozoicon,* Frankfurt a.M. 1675.

Boetticher, W., *Sämtliche erhaltene Werke des Cornelius Tacitus,* Wien 1935.

Bostock, D., *Plato's Phaedo,* Oxford 1986.

Bosworth, A. B., *From Arrian to Alexander: Studies in Historical Interpretation,* Oxford 1988.

Botermann, H., "Griechisch-Jüdische Epigraphik: Zur Datierung der Aphrodisias-Inschriften," *ZPE* 98, 1993, pp. 184–194.

Bousset, H., and Gressmann, W., *Die Religion des Judentums im späthellenistischen Zeitalter,* Tübingen 1926.

Bovie, S. P., *The Satires and Epistles of Horace,* Chicago and London 1959.

Bowersock, G., "Old and New in the History of Judaea," *JRS* 65, 1975, pp. 180–185.

Braund, S. H., *Roman Verse Satire,* Greece and Rome. New Surveys in the Classics, no. 23, Oxford 1992.

Bresciani, E., and Kamil, M., "Le lettere aramaiche di Hermopoli," *Atti della Accademia Nazionale dei Lincei,* Classe di Scienze Morali, Memorie, Ser. VIII, 12, 1966, pp. 357–428.

Bringmann, K., *Hellenistische Reform und Religionsverfolgung in Judäa,* Göttingen 1983.

Bücheler, F., *Petronii Satirarum Reliquiae,* Berlin 1862.

Büchner, K., *Horaz. Die Satiren,* Bologna 1970.

Burger, R., *The Phaedo: A Platonic Labyrinth,* New Haven and London 1984.

Cameron, A., "Rutilius Namatianus, St. Augustine, and the Date of the *De Reditu,*" *JRS* 57, 1967, pp. 31–39.

Castritius, H., "Die Haltung Roms gegenüber den Juden in der ausgehenden Republik und der Prinzipatszeit," in T. Klein et al., eds., *Judentum und Antisemitismus von der Antike bis zur Gegenwart,* Düsseldorf 1984, pp. 15–40.

Cohen, S., "'Anti-Semitism' in Antiquity: the Problem of Definition," in *History and Hate: The Dimensions of Anti-Semitism,* ed. D. Berger, Philadelphia, New York, and Jerusalem 1986, pp. 43–47.

———— *Diasporas in Antiquity,* Atlanta, Ga., 1993.

Cohn, L., Heinemann, I., Adler, M., and Theiler, W., eds., *Philo von Alexandria. Die Werke in deutscher Übersetzung,* vol. 7, Berlin 1964.

Courtney, E., *A Commentary on the Satires of Juvenal,* London 1980.

Cowley, A., *Aramaic Papyri of the Fifth Century B.C.,* Oxford 1923.

Cumont, F., "Les Mystères de Sabazius et le Judaïsme," *CRAI,* 1906, pp. 63–79.

———— "A propos de Sabazius et du Judaïsme," *Musée Belge* 14, 1910, pp. 55–60.

Dauge, Y. A., *Le Barbare: Recherches sur la conception romaine de la barbarie et de la civilisation,* Bruxelles 1981 (Collection Latomus, vol. 176).

Davis, S., *Race-Relations in Ancient Egypt,* New York 1952.

de' Dominicis, M. A., "Di alcuni testi occidentali delle 'Sententiae' riflettenti la prassi postclassica," in *Studi in Onore di Vincenzo Arangio-Ruiz,* vol. 4, Naples 1953, pp. 507–542.

de Lange, N. R. M., Thoma, C., et al., art. "Antisemitismus," in *TRE,* vol. 3, Berlin and New York 1978, pp. 113–168.

———— "The Origins of Anti-Semitism: Ancient Evidence and Modern Interpretations" in S. L. Gilman and S. T. Katz, eds., *Anti-Semitism in Times of Crisis,* New York and London 1991, pp. 21–37.

de Liagre Böhl, F. M. T., *Opera Minora,* Groningen and Djakarta 1953.

De Sanctis, G., "Claudio e i giudei d'Alessandria," *Rivista di Filologia e di Istruzione Classica* 52, N.S. 2, 1924, pp. 473–513.

———— "I Giudei e le fazioni dei Iudi," *Rivista di Filologia e di Istruzione Classica* 53, N.S. 3, 1925, pp. 245–246.

Dover, K. J., *Greek Homosexuality,* Cambridge, Mass., 1978.

Drijvers, H. J. W., *The Book of the Laws of Countries,* Assen 1965.

———— *Bardaiṣan of Edessa,* Assen 1966.

Driver, G. R., *Aramaic Documents of the Fifth Century B.C.,* Oxford 1957.

Duff, J. D., ed., *D. Iunii Iuvenalis Saturae XIV. Fourteen Satires of Juvenal*, Cambridge 1898 (rpt. 1970).

Eissfeldt, O., *Einleitung in das Alte Testament*, Tübingen ³1964.

Errington, R. M., "Die Juden im Zeitalter des Hellenismus," in T. Klein et al., eds., *Judentum und Antisemitismus von der Antike bis zur Gegenwart*, Düsseldorf 1984, pp. 1–13.

Feldman, L. H., *Josephus and Modern Scholarship (1937–1980)*, Berlin and New York 1984.

———— "The Omnipresence of the God-Fearers," *BAR* 12.5, 1986, pp. 58–69.

———— "Pro-Jewish Intimations in Tacitus' Account of Jewish Origins," *REJ* 150, 1991, pp. 331–360.

———— *Jew and Gentile in the Ancient World*, Princeton, N.J., 1993.

Flusser, D., "'Alilot ha-dam' neged ha-yehudim le-'or ha-hashkafot shel ha-tequfah ha-hellenistit," in *Sefer Yohanan Lewy. Mehqarim be-Hellenismus yehudi*, ed. M. Schwabe and J. Gutman, Jerusalem 1949, pp. 104–124.

Fraser, P. M., *Ptolemaic Alexandria*, Oxford 1972, pp. 54ff.

Friedlaender, J., *M. Valerii Martialis Epigrammaton Libri*, vol. 1, Leipzig 1886.

———— *Darstellungen aus der Sittengeschichte Roms*, vol. 3, Leipzig ¹⁰1923.

Funkenstein, A., "Anti-Jewish Propaganda: Pagan, Christian and Modern," *Jerusalem Quarterly* 19, 1981, pp. 56–75.

———— *Perceptions of Jewish History*, Berkeley, Los Angeles, and Oxford 1993.

Gabba, E., "The Growth of anti-Judaism or the Greek Attitude towards Jews," in *The Cambridge History of Judaism*, ed. W. D. Davies and L. Finkelstein, vol. 2, *The Hellenistic Age*, Cambridge etc. 1989, pp. 614–656.

Gager, J. G., *Moses in Greco-Roman Paganism*, Nashville and New York 1972.

———— *The Origins of Anti-Semitism*, New York and Oxford 1983.

Galling, K., *Studien zur Geschichte Israels im persischen Zeitalter*, Tübingen 1964.

Garzetti, A., *From Tiberius to the Antonines: A History of the Roman Empire AD 14–192*, London 1974.

Geiger, J., "The Earliest Reference to Jews in Latin Literature," *JSJ* 15, 1984, pp. 145–147.

Gerber, A., and Greef, A., *Lexicon Taciteum*, vol. 2, Hildesheim 1962.

Gilman, S. L., and Katz, S. T., eds., *Anti-Semitism in Times of Crisis*, New York and London 1991.

Gilula, D., "Did Marial have a Jewish Slave?" *Classical Quarterly* N.S. 37, 1987, pp. 532–533.

Giovannini, A., "Les origines de l'antijudaïsme dans le monde grec," *Cahiers du Centre G. Glotz* 6, 1995, pp. 41–60.

Goodman, M., "Nerva, the *Fiscus Judaicus* and Jewish Identity," *JRS* 79, 1989, pp. 40–44.

———— "Jewish Proselytizing in the First Century," in J. Lieu, J. North, and T. Rajak, eds., *The Jews among Pagans and Christians in the Roman Empire*, London and New York 1992, pp. 53–78.

———— *Mission and Conversion: Proselytizing in the Religious History of the Roman Empire*, Oxford 1994.

Goldenberg, R., "The Jewish Sabbath in the Roman World up to the Time of Constantine the Great," in *ANRW*, II, 19.1, pp. 414–447.

Goudriaan, K., "Ethnical Strategies in Graeco-Roman Egypt," in *Ethnicity in Hellenistic Egypt*, ed. P. Bilde et al., Aarhus 1992, pp. 74–99.

Gow, A. S. F., and Page, D. L., eds., *The Greek Anthology: Hellenistic Epigrams*, vol. 1, Cambridge 1965.

Grelot, P., "Études sur le 'papyrus pascale' d'Éléphantine," *VT* 4, 1954, pp. 349–84.

Griffiths, J. G., *Plutarch, De Iside et Osiride*, [Cardiff] 1970.

Grintz, Y. M., art. "Solomon, Wisdom of," in *EJ*, vol. 15, Jerusalem 1971, col. 120.

Groag, E., art. "Corvinus (5)," in *PW*, IV, 1901, col. 1662.

Grodzynski, D., "'Superstitio,'" *Revue des Études Anciennes* 76, 1974, pp. 36–60.

Gudemann, A., art. "Lysimachos (20)," in *PW*, XXVII, 1928, cols. 32–39.

Habicht, C., "Hellenismus und Judentum in der Zeit des Judas Makkabäus," in *Jahrbuch der Heidelberger Akademie der Wissenschaften für das Jahr 1974*, Heidelberg 1975, pp. 97–110.

Hackforth, R., *Plato's Phaedo*, Cambridge 1955.

Halévy, J., "Le Calembour dans la judéophobie alexandrine," *Revue Semitique* 11, 1903, pp. 263–268.

Heinemann, I., "Ursprung und Wesen des Antisemitismus im Altertum," in *Festgabe zum Zehnjährigen Bestehen der Akademie für die Wissenschaft des Judentums 1919–1929*, Berlin 1929, pp. 76–91.

———— art. "Antisemitismus," in *PW*, Suppl. V, 1931, cols. 3–43.

Hengel, M., *Judentum und Hellenismus*, Tübingen ²1973 (*Judaism and Hellenism*, Philadelphia 1981).

Herrmann, L., "Cicéron et les Juifs," in *Atti del I Congresso Internazionale di Studi Ciceroniani*, Rome 1961, pp. 113–117.

Heubner, H., and Fauth, F., *P. Cornelius Tacitus. Die Historien*, Kommentar von Heinz Heubner, Band V, Fünftes Buch, by H. Heubner and F. Fauth, Heidelberg 1982.

Hoffmann, C., *Juden und Judentum im Werk Deutscher Althistoriker des 19. und 20. Jahrhunderts*, Leiden etc. 1988.

Hohl, E., et al., *Historia Augusta. Römische Herrschergestalten,* vol. 1, Zürich and München 1976.

Hopfner, T., *Plutarch über Isis und Osiris,* vol. 2, Prag 1941.

Horst, P. W. van der, *Chaeremon: Egyptian Priest and Stoic Philosopher,* Leiden 1984 (²1987).

———— "The Altar of the 'Unknown God' in Athens (Acts 17:23) and the Cult of 'Unknown Gods' in the Hellenistic and Roman Periods," in *ANRW,* II, 18.2, Berlin and New York 1989, pp. 1426–1456.

Housman, A. F., "Praefanda," *Hermes* 66, 1931, pp. 402–412.

Isaac, J., *Jésus et Israël,* Paris 1948 (*Jesus and Israel,* New York 1971).

———— *Genèse de l'Antisémitisme,* Paris 1956.

Izaac, H. J., *Martial. Épigrammes,* vol. 1, Paris 1961.

Jacob, B., "Antisemitismus: I. Im Altertum," in *EJ,* vol. 2, Berlin 1928, cols. 957–972.

Jacoby, A., "Der angebliche Eselskult der Juden und Christen," *ARW* 25, 1927, pp. 265–282.

Jacoby, F., *Die Fragmente der griechischen Historiker,* vol. 3a (Kommentar), Leiden 1954; vol. 3c, Leiden 1958.

Jaeger W., *Diokles von Karystos,* Berlin 1938.

———— "Greeks and Jews: The First Greek Records of Jewish Religion and Civilization," *JR* 18, 1938, pp. 127–143 = id., *Scripta Minora,* vol. 2, Rome 1960, pp. 169–183.

Johnson, S. E., "The Present State of Sabazios Research," in *ANRW,* II, 17.3, Berlin and New York 1984, pp. 1583–1613.

Kasher, A., *The Jews in Hellenistic and Roman Egypt: The Struggle for Equal Rights,* Tübingen 1985.

Kautzsch, E., ed., *Die Apokryphen und Pseudepigraphen des Alten Testaments,* Tübingen 1900.

Kay, N. M., *Martial Book XI: A Commentary,* London 1985.

Kees, H., art. "Seth," in *PW* IV², 1923, cols. 1896–1922.

Kiessling, A., and Heinze, R., *Q. Horatius Flaccus. Satiren,* Berlin 1957.

Kißel, W., *Aules Persius Flaccus. Satiren,* Heidelberg 1990.

Kraeling, E. G., *The Brooklyn Museum Aramaic Papyri: New Documents of the Fifth Century B.C. from the Jewish Colony at Elephantine,* New Haven 1953.

Kraus, W., art. "Ovidius Naso," in *PW,* XVIII, 1942, cols. 1910–1986.

Lane, E. N., "Sabazius and the Jews in Valerius Maximus: A Re-examination," *JRS* 69, 1979, pp. 35–38.

Langmuir, G. I., *Toward a Definition of Antisemitism,* Berkeley, Los Angeles, and Oxford 1990.

———— *History, Religion, and Antisemitism,* London and New York 1990.

Laqueur, R., art. "Manethon (1)," in *PW*, XXVII, 1928, cols. 1060–1101.

Lausberg, M., *Untersuchungen zu Senecas Fragmenten,* Berlin 1970.

Lee, G., *Tibullus: Elegies,* Liverpool ²1982.

Leon, H. J., *The Jews of Ancient Rome,* Philadelphia 1960.

Levy, E., "Rehabilitierung einiger Paulussentenzen," *Studia et Documenta Historiae et Iuris* 31, 1965, pp. 7–9.

Lévy, J., "Tacite et l'origine du peuple juif," *Latomus* 5, 1946, pp. 331–340.

Le[v]wy, Johanan (Hans), "Divre Tacitus ꜥal qadmoniut ha-yehudim," *Zion* 8, 1942/43, pp. 1–34 and 61–84.

———— "Tequfat ha-bayyit ha-sheni le-'or ha-sifrut ha-yewwanit we-ha-romit," in *Sefer Yoḥanan Lewy. Meḥqarim be-Hellenismus yehudi,* ed. M. Schwabe and J. Gutman, Jerusalem 1949, pp. 1–12.

———— *Chaldaean Oracles and Theurgy,* Cairo 1956.

———— *Studies in Jewish Hellenism,* Jerusalem 1960 (in Hebrew).

———— "Die Epoche des Zweiten Tempels im Lichte der griechischen und römischen Literatur. Ursachen und Aspekte der Judenfeindschaft in der Antike," trans. into German by M. Brocke, in *Freiburger Rundbrief* 24, 1972, pp. 20–26.

Lewy, Heinrich, "Philologisches aus dem Talmud," *Philologus* 84, 1929, pp. 377–398.

Linder, A., *The Jews in Roman Imperial Legislation,* Detroit, Mich., and Jerusalem 1987.

Littmann, R., "Anti-Semitism in the Greco-Roman Pagan World," in Y. Bauer et al., eds., *Remembering for the Future: Working Papers and Addenda,* vol. 1: *Jews and Christians during and after the Holocaust,* Oxford 1989, pp. 825–835.

Long, G., *The Discourses of Epictetus,* London 1890.

Lüderitz, G., "What is the Politeuma?" in J. W. van Henten and P. W. van der Horst, eds., *Studies in Early Jewish Epigraphy,* Leiden, New York, and Köln 1994, pp. 183–225.

Luria (Lur'e), S., *Antisemitizm v drevnem mire (Der Antisemitismus in der alten Welt),* Petersburg and Moscow 1923.

Mackail, J. W., *The Aeneid of Virgil,* London 1885 (Oxford 1930).

MacLennan, R. S., and Kraabel, T., "The God-Fearers—a Literary and Theological Invention," *BAR* 12.5, 1986, pp. 46–53.

Marcus, R., "Antisemitism in the Hellenistic-Roman World," in K. S. Pinson, ed., *Essays on Antisemitism,* New York ²1946, pp. 61–78.

Marquart, J., "Chronologische Untersuchungen," *Philologus,* Suppl. 7, Leipzig 1899, pp. 637–720 (also issued separately).

Marr, W., *Der Judenspiegel,* Hamburg 1862.

——— *Der Sieg des Judenthums über das Germanenthum vom nicht confessionellen Standpunkt aus betrachtet,* Bern 1879.

Mastandrea, P., *Un Neoplatonico Latino: Cornelio Labeone,* Leiden 1979.

Mattingly, H., and Sydenham, E. A., *The Roman Imperial Coinage,* vol. 2, London 1926.

Mattingly, H., *Coins of the Roman Empire in the British Museum,* vol. 3, London 1936.

McCracken, G. E., *Arnobius of Sicca: The Case against the Pagans,* vol. 2, Westminster, Md., 1949.

Mélèze Modrzejewski, J., "Sur l'antisémitisme païen," in M. Olender, ed., *Pour Léon Poliakov. Le racisme: Mythes et sciences,* Brussels 1981, pp. 411–439.

——— *The Jews of Egypt: From Ramses II to Emperor Hadrian,* Philadelphia and Jerusalem 1995.

Meyer, E., *Aegyptische Chronologie,* Berlin 1904.

——— *Der Papyrusfund von Elephantine,* Leipzig 1912.

——— *Ursprung und Anfänge des Christentums,* vol. 2: *Die Entwicklung des Judentums und Jesus von Nazaret,* Stuttgart and Berlin 1921 (^{5}1925).

——— *Geschichte des Altertums,* vol. 2.1, *Die Zeit der ägyptischen Großmacht,* Stuttgart and Berlin ^{2}1928.

Meyer, R., art. "*peritemnō,*" in *ThWNT,* vol. 6, Stuttgart 1959, pp. 72–83.

Michael, J. H., "The Jewish Sabbath in the Latin Classical Writers," *AJSL* 40, 1923–24, pp. 117–124.

Millar, F., *A Study of Cassius Dio,* Oxford 1964.

——— "Epictetus and the Imperial Court," *JRS* 55, 1965, pp. 141–148.

Mittwoch, E., "Der Wiederaufbau des jüdischen Tempels in Elephantine—ein Kompromiß zwischen Juden und Samaritanern," in *Judaica. Festschrift zu Hermann Cohens Siebzigstem Geburtstage,* Berlin 1912, pp. 227–233.

Moehring, H., "The Persecution of the Jews and the Adherents of the Isis Cult at Rome A.D. 19," *NT* 3, 1959, pp. 293–304.

Moellering, H. A., *Plutarch on Superstition,* Boston ^{2}1963.

Mommsen, Theodor, *Römische Geschichte,* vol. 3, Berlin ^{9}1904; vol. 5, Berlin ^{5}1904.

Moore, J. M. *Aristotle and Xenophon on Democracy and Oligarchy,* London 1975.

Münschel, K., *Senecas Werke,* Leipzig 1922.

Murgatroyd, P., *Tibullus I: A Commentary on the First Book of the Elegies of Albius Tibullus,* Pietermaritzburg 1980.

Musurillo, H. A., ed., *The Acts of the Pagan Martyrs. Acta Alexandrinorum*, Oxford 1954.

Nilsson, M. P., *Geschichte der griechischen Religion*, vol. 2, München ²1961.

Nock, A. D., "Oracles Théologiques," *Revue des Études Anciennes* 30, 1928, p. 280–290.

Nolland, J., "Proselytism or Politics in Horace Satires I, 4, 138–143?" *Vigiliae Christianae* 33, 1979, pp. 347–355.

———— "Uncircumcised Proselytes?" *JSJ* 12, 1981, pp. 173–194.

Norden, E., *Agnostos Theos*, Leipzig and Berlin 1923.

Oliver, J. H., *Greek Constitutions of Early Roman Emperors from Inscriptions and Papyri*, Philadelphia 1989 (Memoirs of the American Philosophical Society, vol. 178).

Oppelt, I., art. "Esel," in *RAC*, 6, Stuttgart 1966, cols. 592–594.

Pappenheim, E., *Erläuterungen zu des Sextus Empiricus Pyrrhoneïschen Grundzügen*, Leipzig 1881.

Phillips, C. R., "The Sociology of Religious Knowledge in the Roman Empire to A.D. 284," *ANRW*, II, 16.3, 1986, pp. 2677–2773.

Pötscher, W., ed., *Porphyrios Pros Markellan*, Leiden 1969.

Poliakov, Léon, *Histoire de l'antisémitisme*, vol 1: *Du Christ aux Juifs de cour*, Paris 1955 (*The History of Anti-Semitism*, vol 1: *From Roman Times to the Court Jews*, New York 1965; London 1974).

Porten, B., "The Jews in Egypt," in *The Cambridge History of Judaism*, ed. W. D. Davies and L. Finkelstein, vol. 1, *Introduction: The Persian Period*, Cambridge etc. 1984, pp. 372–400.

———— *Archives from Elephantine: The Life of an Ancient Jewish Military Colony*, Berkeley and Los Angeles 1986.

Porten, B., and Greenfield, J. C., *Jews of Elephantine and Arameans of Syene*, Jerusalem 1984 (in Hebrew).

Porten, B., and Yardeni, A., *Textbook of Aramaic Documents from Ancient Egypt*, newly copied, ed., and trans. into Hebrew and English, vol. 1: *Letters*, Jerusalem 1986; vol. 2, *Contracts*, [Jerusalem] 1989.

Radin, M., *The Jews among the Greeks and Romans*, Philadelphia 1915.

———— review of H. I. Bell, *Jews and Christians in Egypt*, *Classical Philology*, 20, 1925, pp. 368–375.

Raspe, L., *Die ägyptischen Exodustraditionen und die Entstehung des antiken Antisemitismus*, unpublished M.A. thesis, FU Berlin, Berlin 1994.

Redford, D. B., "The Hyksos Invasion in History and Tradition," *Orientalia* 39, 1970, pp. 1–51.

———— *Akhenaten, the Heretic King*, Princeton 1984.

———— *Pharaonic King-lists, Annals and Day-books: A Contribution to the Study of the Egyptian Sense of History,* Mississauga, Ont., 1986.

Reitzenstein, R., *Die hellenistischen Mysterienreligionen,* Leipzig and Berlin ³1927.

Rudd, N., *The Satires of Horace and Persius,* London 1973.

Ruether, R., *Faith and Fratricide: The Theological Roots of Antisemitism,* Minneapolis 1974.

Rutgers, L. V., "Roman Policy towards the Jews: Expulsions from the City of Rome during the First Century C.E.," *Classical Antiquity* 13, 1994, pp. 56–74.

Sachau, E., *Aramäische Papyrus und Ostraka aus einer jüdischen Militärkolonie zu Elephantine,* vols. 1–2, Leipzig 1911.

Ste. Croix, G. E. M. de, *The Class Struggle in the Ancient Greek World from the Archaic Age to the Arab Conquests,* London 1981.

Sayce, A. H., and Cowley, A. E., *Aramaic Papyri Discovered at Assuan,* London 1906.

Schäfer, P., *Der Bar Kokhba-Aufstand,* Tübingen 1981.

———— "Hadrian's Policy in Judaea and the Bar Kokhba Revolt: a Reassessment," in *A Tribute to Geza Vermes: Essays on Jewish and Christian Literature and History,* ed. P. R. Davies and R. T. White, Sheffield 1990, pp. 281–303.

———— *The History of the Jews in Antiquity: The Jews of Palestine from Alexander the Great to the Arab Conquest,* Luxembourg 1995.

———— "Die Manetho-Fragmente bei Josephus und die Anfänge des antiken 'Antisemitismus,'" in *Aporemata,* I, in press.

Schanz, M., and Hosius, C., *Geschichte der römischen Literatur,* vol. 2, München ⁴1935.

Scheller, M., "*Sabbō* und *Sabbatōsis,*" *Glotta* 34, 1955, pp. 298–300.

Schröder, B., *Die "väterlichen Gesetze": Flavius Josephus als Vermittler von Halachah an Griechen und Römer,* Tübingen 1996.

Schürer, E., *The History of the Jewish People in the Age of Jesus Christ (175 B.C.–A.D. 135),* rev. and ed. G. Vermes et al., vols. 1–3, Edinburgh 1973–1987.

Schwabe, M., art. "Cornelius Tacitus (395)," in *PW,* VII, 1900, cols. 1566–1590.

Schwartz, D., *Agrippa I: The Last King of Judaea,* Tübingen 1990.

Schwartz, E., art. "Chaeremon (7)," in *PW,* III, 1899, cols. 2025–2027.

———— review of H. I. Bell, *Jews and Christians in Egypt,* in *Deutsche Literaturzeitung für Kritik der internationalen Wissenschaft* 45, N.F. 1, 1924, cols. 2093–2101.

Scott, R. T., *Religion and Philosophy in the Histories of Tacitus,* Rome 1968.

Segré, A., "Antisemitism in Hellenistic Alexandria," *JSS* 8, 1946, pp. 127–136.

Sevenster, J. N., *The Roots of Pagan Anti-Semitism in the Ancient World*, Leiden 1975.

Sherwin-White, A. N., *Racial Prejudice in Imperial Rome*, Cambridge 1967.

———— "Philo and Avillius Flaccus: a Conundrum," *Latomus* 31, 1972, pp. 820–828.

Simon, M., *Verus Israel*, Oxford 1986 (Paris 1948, ²1964).

———— "Jupiter-Yahvé. Sur un essai de théologie pagano-juive," *Numen* 23, 1976, pp. 40–66 = id., *Scripta Varia*, vol. 2, pp. 622–648.

———— *Le christianisme antique et son contexte religieux: Scripta Varia*, vols. 1–2, Tübingen 1981.

Simonsen, D., "Kleinigkeiten," in *Judaica. Festschrift zu Hermann Cohens Siebzigstem Geburtstage*, Berlin 1912, pp. 297–301.

Smallwood, E. M., "The Legislation of Hadrian and Antoninus Pius against Circumcision," *Latomus* 18, 1959, pp. 334–347.

———— *The Jews under Roman Rule: From Pompey to Diocletian*, Leiden 1976.

Smith, M., "De Superstitione (Moralia 164E-171F)," in H. D. Betz, ed., *Plutarch's Theological Writings and Early Christian Literature*, Leiden 1975, pp. 1–35.

Solin, H., "Juden und Syrer im westlichen Teil der römischen Welt," in *ANRW*, II, 29.2, Berlin and New York 1983, pp. 587–789.

Sperling, A. G., *Apion der Grammatiker und sein Verhältnis zum Judentum. Ein Beitrag zu einer Einleitung in die Schriften des Josephos*, Dresden 1886 (Programm des Gymnasiums zum heiligen Kreuz in Dresden, erste Abteilung, pp. III-XXII).

Spoerri, W., art. "Hecataios von Abdera," in *RAC*, XIV, Stuttgart 1988, cols. 278–286.

Staehelin, F., *Der Antisemitismus des Altertums in seiner Entstehung und Entwicklung*, Winterthur 1905.

Stella, L. A., *Cinque poeti dell' antologia palatina*, Bologna 1949.

Sterling, G. E., *Historiography and Self-Definition: Josephos, Luke-Acts and Apologetic Historiography*, Leiden, New York, and Köln 1992.

Stern, M., "Nevu'ah miṣrit-yewanit we-ha-masoret ᶜal gerush ha-yehudim mi-miṣrayim be-historiyah shel Chaeremon," *Zion* 28, 1962/63, pp. 223–227.

———— *Greek and Latin Authors on Jews and Judaism*, ed. with introductions, translations, and commentary by M. Stern, vols. 1–3, Jerusalem 1974–1984.

Stricker, B. H., "Asinarii," *Oudheidkundige mededelingen uit het Rijksmuseum van Oudheden te Leiden* 46, 1965, pp. 52–75.

Tcherikover, V., *Hellenistic Civilization and the Jews*, Philadelphia 1959 (New York 1979).

Tcherikover, V., Fuks, A., and Stern, M., eds., *Corpus Papyrorum Judaicarum*, vols. 1–3, Cambridge, Mass., 1957–1964.

Theodor, J., and Albeck, C., *Bereshit Rabba*, Jerusalem ²1965.

Thompson, L. A., "Domitian and the Jewish Tax," *Historia* 31, 1982, pp. 329–342.

Trebilco, P. R., *Jewish Communities in Asia Minor*, Cambridge 1991.

Tuland, C. G., "Hanani-Hananiah," *JBL* 77, 1958, pp. 157–161.

Turcan, R., *Sénèque et les religions orientales*, Bruxelles 1967.

Veltri, G., *Eine Tora für den König Talmai. Untersuchungen zum Übersetzungsverständnis in der jüdisch-hellenistischen und rabbinischen Literatur*, Tübingen 1994.

Versnel, H. S., "Some Reflections on the Relationship Magic-Religion," *Numen* 37, 1991, pp. 177–197.

Villeneuve, F., *Horace. Satires*, Paris 1958.

Vincent, A., *La Religion des Judéo-Araméens d'Éléphantine*, Paris 1937.

Vollmer, F., art. "Iunius (Iuvenalis)," in *PW*, XIX, 1918, cols. 1041–1050.

Wardy, B., "Jewish Religion in Pagan Literature during the Late Republic and Early Empire," in *ANRW*, II, 19.1, Berlin and New York 1979, pp. 613–635.

Watts, W. J., "Race Prejudice in the Satires of Juvenal," *Acta Classica* 19, 1976, pp. 83–104.

Weill, R., *La Fin du Moyen Empire Égyptien*, vols. 1–2, Paris 1918.

Wellman, M., "Aegyptisches," *Hermes* 31, 1896, pp. 221–253.

Wickert, L., *Theodor Mommsen. Eine Biographie*, vols. 1–4, Frankfurt a. Main 1959–1980.

Wilcken, U., *Chrestomatie*, in L. Mitteis and U. Wilcken, *Grundzüge und Chrestomatie der Papyruskunde*, Erster Band, Zweite Hälfte, Leipzig and Berlin 1912.

Will, E., and Orrieux, C., *"Prosélytism Juif"? Histoire d'une erreur*, Paris 1992.

Williams, M. H., "The Expulsion of the Jews from Rome in A.D. 19," *Latomus* 48, 1989, pp. 765–784.

Willrich, H., "Die Entstehung des Antisemitismus," *Deutschlands Erneuerung* 5, 1921, pp. 472–483.

————— "Zum Brief des Kaisers Claudius an die Alexandriner," *Hermes* 60, 1925, pp. 482–488.

Wissowa, G., "Die Varronischen *Di Certi* und *Incerti*," *Hermes* 56, 1921, pp. 113–130.

Wolff, E., "Das geschichtliche Verstehen in Tacitus Germania," *Hermes* 69, 1934, pp. 121–166.

Yavetz, Z., "Judeophobia in Classical Antiquity: A Different Approach," *JJS* 44, 1993, pp. 1–22.

Yoyotte, J., "L'Égypte ancienne et les origines de l'antijudaïsme," *RHR* 163, 1963, pp. 133–143 = *Bulletin de la Société Ernest Renan,* N.S. 11, 1962, pp. 13–23.

Zacher, K., "Antisemitismus und Philosemitismus im klassischen Alterthum," *Preußische Jahrbücher* 94, 1898, pp. 1–24.

Ziegler, K., *Plutarchos von Chaironeia,* Stuttgart 1949.

Index

Adonai, 43. *See also* God

Adonis, 53

Adora, 56

Aelia Capitolina, 103

Aemilius Rectus, 138

Agatharchides of Cnidus, 83, 84, 88, 89, 188, 193

Agrippa I, 79, 135, 136, 139, 141, 143, 145, 153, 154, 155, 156, 158

Agrippa II, 79, 153

Akhenaten. *See* Amenophis IV

alazoneia. *See* Arrogance

Alexander the Great, 136, 146

Alexandria, 6, 28, 29, 30, 31, 33, 55, 61, 64, 83, 84, 86, 97, 135, 205, 207; riots of, 9–10, 20–21, 206, 265n73; citizenship of, 39, 136, 137, 140, 146, 147, 149, 156, 157, 160. *See also* Civic rights; politeia

Amarna, 165, 166, 220n28, 275n18

Amenophis III, 275n17

Amenophis IV, 18, 30, 163, 165, 166, 167, 275n17

amixia, 172, 209

Ammon, 31, 32, 43, 62

Amyrtaeus of Saïs, 122, 124

anoia, 83–84, 89, 193

anthrōpophagia, 62, 203, 204

Antiochus III, 67

Antiochus IV Epiphanes, 5, 10, 58, 59, 60, 62, 65, 66, 67, 68, 76, 82, 83, 93, 177, 189, 194, 207, 233n138, 236n182

Antiochus VII Sidetes, 22, 58, 59, 68, 176, 207

Antoninus Pius, 103, 104, 117, 118

Apion, 1, 23, 27, 28–29, 30, 31, 39, 55, 56, 58, 59, 60, 61, 62, 63, 64, 65, 69, 72, 86, 87, 89, 97, 137, 146, 160, 176, 193, 194, 204, 205, 206, 207

Apis, 31, 32, 166, 168

Apollo, 56

Apollonius Molon, 21–22, 23, 27, 33, 36, 39, 41, 47, 58, 60, 65, 182, 193

Apollo of Clarus, 52, 55

Aristeas: letter of, 164, 231n106, 262n3, 275n9

Aristobulus I, 96, 97

Aristotle, 35, 170

Arrogance, 34, 44, 49, 95, 172, 174, 185

Arsames: satrap, 122, 123, 124, 127, 128, 129, 131, 132

Artaxerxes I, 123, 127, 134

Artaxerxes II, 122, 124

Artaxerxes III Ochus, 166, 168, 234n157

Asclepius, 71, 72

asōmatos, 42, 47. *See also* God

Ass: pack-ass, 55–56; statue in Jewish Temple, 23, 31, 55, 59, 62, 67, 74; wild, 57, 74; -worship, 55–62, 64, 73, 160, 168, 176, 177, 179, 194

Astrology, 187

Atheism, 21, 23, 36, 41, 47, 114, 115, 116, 183, 193, 194. *See also* Impiety, motif of

Atonement. *See* Day of Atonement

Atun-Re, 165

Auaris, 18, 57, 167

Augustine, 36, 38, 50, 86, 111

Augustus, 81, 90, 136, 146, 148, 154

Aulus Plautius, 183

Avillius Flaccus, 136, 137, 138, 139, 140, 141, 142, 143, 144, 156, 158

Ba'al Shamem, 36. *See also* God

Babylonia, 127

Bacchus, 53, 54

Bagohi, 123, 129, 130, 131, 132, 133

Bar Kokhba revolt, 103, 104, 252n82

Bocchoris, 27, 31

Cadmus, 15, 94

caeli numen, 41, 79, 80, 194. *See also* Heaven; God

Caesar, 136

Caligula. *See* Gaius Caligula

Lydus. *See* Johannes Lydus
Lysimachus, 23, 27–28, 32, 33, 64, 89, 167, 175

Maccabees: battles, 60, 83, 177; Jonathan, 68;
  Judas, 178; period, 56, 68, 69, 81, 95, 176, 178,
  179, 189, 233n138, 238n18; revolt, 5, 10, 56,
  88; Simon, 51, 68
Macrinus, 104
Macrobius, 52, 53, 81
maiestas, 114, 116
Manasseh, 121, 262n3
Manetho, 9, 17, 19–21, 22, 23, 27, 28, 30, 33, 36,
  39, 41, 47, 57, 58, 163, 164, 165, 166, 167, 168,
  172, 175, 178, 193, 208, 216n24, 220n31,
  221n32, 225n19, 274n7, 275n17, 279n50
Marcus Aurelius, 103
Marisa, 56
Martial, 90, 99, 100–102, 183
Marr, Wilhelm, 197
Meleager, 92
Memphis, 122
Menelaus, 67
Merneptah, 163
metuentes. *See* Godfearers
misanthrōpia, 19, 21, 22, 23, 27, 28, 29, 30, 32,
  35, 36, 45, 58, 59, 64, 65, 66, 80, 98, 168, 170,
  173–177, 179, 185, 186, 191, 193, 206, 207,
  208, 209, 210, 220n22, 221n38, 276n24,
  278n31. *See also* Hostility; Xenophobia
misogynia, 174
misoinia, 174
misoxenia. *See* Xenophobia
Mnaseas of Patara, 55, 56, 58, 59, 64
Monotheism, 9, 35, 48, 166. *See also* God
mos maiorum, 182, 185, 186. *See also*
  Customs
Moses, 15, 16, 17, 19–21, 23, 24, 25, 26, 27, 28,
  29, 31, 32, 36, 40, 42, 44, 50, 58, 59, 61, 64, 67,
  74, 80, 89, 188, 220n22, 220n31, 228n59,
  230n95, 238n9; his Egyptian name, 30

Naevius, 96
Naevius Macro, 136, 138, 153, 271n127
Naphaina, 122, 123, 128, 129
Nehemiah, 125
Neoplatonism, 46, 47, 49, 53, 71, 99
Neopythagorism, 53
Nepherites I, 124
Nero, 30, 77, 138, 190
Nerva, 104, 114, 259n60

nomima, 45; customs, 68; misoxena, 67;
  outlandish laws, 22, 23, 58; patria, 37, 44, 76,
  77; unutterable law, 62, 63
nous. *See* Reason
nubes. *See* Clouds
Numenius of Apamea, 42, 194

onolatreia. *See* Ass-worship
Optimates, 181
Oracle of Clarus, 52, 53
Origen, 42, 95, 103
Osarseph, 18–21, 23, 36, 57, 58, 165, 167,
  220n31
Osiris, 57, 168, 176
Ovid, 85, 86

Papaeus, 43
Passover, 124, 125, 127, 164, 203; Letter, 123,
  124–125, 127, 128, 129, 134; sacrifice, 126
Pater Liber, 52, 54. *See also* Dionysus
Paul: jurist, 118
pax Romana, 152
Pericles, 170
Persius, 90, 91, 99
Pestilence, 15, 23. *See also* Leprosy
Petronius, 77–78, 79, 80, 81, 90, 98, 99, 116, 183,
  193, 194
Philo, 136, 137, 138–145, 148, 149, 151, 156,
  158, 159, 160, 175
phoros. *See* Tribute
Photius, 15
Phritibautes, 30
Pig, 240n54; dislike of, 53, 71, 72, 75; -god,
  77–81, 99; sacrifice of, 58, 66–68, 81, 82, 193,
  207, 237n5, 238n14. *See also* Pork
Plague, 32, 74, 75, 88. *See also* Leprosy
Plato, 47, 170, 173, 228n59
Pliny the Elder, 88, 194
Plutarch, 53, 57, 61, 69, 72, 74, 77, 78, 88, 89, 91,
  172, 188
Plutarch of Athens, 71, 72
polis, 147, 150, 156, 157
politeia, 137, 140, 144, 146; isopoliteia, 146, 147,
  149; politeuma, 147, 152, 156, 157, 158,
  269n88, 272n138. *See also* Alexandria, citizen-
  ship of
Pompeius Trogus, 26–27, 28, 33, 89, 194
Pompey, 45, 88, 89, 245n53
Pomponia Graecina, 183, 191, 192
Pontius Pilatus, 190